..ry of

FAMILY OF FAITH
LIBRARY

Contemporary Science—Book 3

MILTON LESSER
Formerly Chairman
Department of Biological Sciences
Abraham Lincoln High School
New York City

CONSTANTINE CONSTANT
Teacher of Earth Science
Forest Hills High School
New York City

JULES J. WEISLER
Assistant Principal
Supervision of Science
Robert A. Van Wyck Junior High School 217
New York City

General Editor
SAUL L. GEFFNER
Formerly Chairman
Department of Physical Sciences
Forest Hills High School
New York City

Family of Faith Library

CONTEMPORARY SCIENCE
BOOK 3

Dedicated to serving

AMSCO

our nation's youth

When ordering this book, please specify:
either **R 192 P** or CONTEMPORARY SCIENCE—BOOK 3

AMSCO SCHOOL PUBLICATIONS, INC.
315 Hudson Street
New York, N.Y. 10013

The publisher is indebted to the following suppliers of photographs: The Bettmann Archive: page 493; Paul Levesque: 490 (top); Lick Observatory: 424; NASA: 427; United Press International Photo: 490 (bottom; two photos); U.S. Fish and Wildlife Service: 492; U.S. Geological Survey: 275, 276, 442. Cover photograph by Grant Heilman.

ISBN 0-87720-008-4

Copyright © 1978 by
AMSCO SCHOOL PUBLICATIONS, INC.

No part of this book may be reproduced in any form without written permission from the publisher.

Printed in the United States of America

PREFACE

Contemporary Science—Books 1, 2, and *3*—presents a modern, comprehensive general science course. Content from the areas of life science, physical science, and earth science, carefully integrated, emphasizes fundamental principles and current problems. Among these problems are the environment, conservation, and energy. Depending on local needs, the three books may be used for a three-year science sequence, or individual books may be used for single-year courses.

Organization of the Series

Each book in the series has the same structure of units and chapters. A general overview of content opens each unit. Then, each chapter in the unit sets forth learning objectives for the student. A laboratory experience follows these objectives and stresses the role of experimentation in the development of scientific ideas. The laboratory experience opens the door, and leads to an introduction to the essential facts, principles, and concepts within the chapter. Every chapter closes with a summary; a glimpse of what is to come in the next chapter; and review questions to test recall and reasoning.

Scientific models are employed, where pertinent, to enable students to relate abstract ideas to more easily understood situations.

Outstanding Features of These Books

1. *Laboratory Experiences.* Every chapter introduces a laboratory exercise that is closely integrated with one or more major ideas in the chapter. These exercises are well within the range of comprehension and manipulative ability of most students above the elementary grades. Much of the laboratory work can be carried out either at home or in classrooms, and requires simple equipment. If the teacher so desires, the laboratory experiences can readily be converted to classroom demonstrations. In addition to simple, clear instructions, each laboratory exercise includes questions that direct observation and evoke the independent formulation of conclusions. These same conclusions become focal points in the development of the text content, and ap-

pear in the text where pertinent. Where feasible, a portion of the laboratory exercise is open-ended—the student is encouraged to investigate further.

2. *Language Level.* The language level is kept as simple as possible. Although many terms are introduced, they are carefully defined.

Some technical terms recur from book to book. The first time such a term is encountered in a book, the term is defined (or redefined or reexplained, if necessary). Thus, each book is independent of the others and may be used without reference to the others.

3. *Illustrations.* All three books are profusely illustrated with drawings, photographs, and cartoons. All illustrations assist the learning and retention of scientific principles. Each illustration is keyed to the text to make the illustration readily available to the reader.

4. *Questions.* The end-of-chapter questions are numerous and varied. They include short-answer types such as multiple-choice, modified true-false, and matching, as well as thought questions requiring longer answers. Where applicable, simple numerical problems are also given, but only after sample exercises and solutions have been discussed.

5. *Appendix.* A useful appendix appears in each book. The appendix contains metric conversion tables and a periodic table of the elements modified to suit the intermediate level. Books 2 and 3 also provide an explanation of significant figures and rules for their use. This section can be particularly valuable for the ambitious, abler student.

6. *Answer Keys.* Answers to the end-of-chapter questions are contained in an answer key, available to teachers. Included in this key are lists of materials and equipment for the laboratory experiences as well as notes regarding experimental techniques and teaching emphases. Answers to the questions posed in the laboratory experience sections are also included.

7. *Multiple Uses.* The books lend themselves to a variety of uses, depending on the local situation.

a. *As Basic Texts.* Selected content in life science, physical science, and earth science is presented in each book in adequate depth for the needs of students at the intermediate level. Thus, the books can be used in any spiral, integrated type of general science sequence. Alternatively, since each book can stand alone, these books may be used in any order. In either case, they provide a solid foundation for later study in each major science.

b. *As Alternate Texts.* The content of these books relates readily to other modern general science texts. Consequently, the content may be used to provide the student with an alternate approach or a second view. Such a procedure may help the underachiever and at the same time stimulate the more able pupils.

c. *As a Sourcebook for Experiments.* Although it is recommended that a laboratory experience introduce each topic, the laboratory work can be fitted in wherever it suits the teacher's unit plan. In addition to the opening laboratory experience associated with each chapter, other experiments are described as integral parts of the text. These experiments provide the teacher with an extensive source of ideas and materials for illustrating principles.

d. *For Pretesting.* The inclusive end-of-chapter questions are suitable as a pretest for a chapter. The results of such testing will indicate how much of the chapter should be taught and with what emphasis the chapter should be taught.

e. *For Adapting to Individual Needs.* Since students in general can independently carry out most of the work set forth in this book, the teacher can assign specific sections to ambitious students, to students who have been absent, or to students who need more repetition and drill before they can consolidate their learning. To the small number of students for whom the study of general science is terminal, these books contain sufficient material to provide a broad, unified understanding and appreciation of the earth, its inhabitants, its composition and features, the forces that act on it, and its place in the universe.

f. *For Evaluation.* The learning objectives set the instructional goals of each chapter. Students can also use the questions at the end of each chapter as self-testing devices. The coverage of the questions is sufficiently broad to enable the teacher to use them to measure student progress, chapter by chapter. The questions can also serve as homework for students or for drill work in class.

The topics and laboratory experiences presented in *Contemporary Science— Book 3* have been selected to match the comprehension and maturity levels usual for the school grade. Accordingly, the major topics from the areas of life science, physical science, and earth science include: nonliving matter, forces in our environment, living things, and environments—past, present, and future.

In Chapter 1, the first discussion involving quantities is presented, as a transition, in both customary and metric units. Thereafter, metric units are used exclusively. Later chapters emphasize problems associated with renewable and nonrenewable resources, mining and metallurgical wastes, and conservation. The final chapter presents specific steps each individual can take in doing his or her part toward maintaining a viable environment.

CONTENTS

ix

UNIT I
The Nonliving Matter
of the Environment

Overview

Planet Earth, with its soil, its atmosphere, its water, and its energy from the sun, is the only environment in which the living things we know can survive. Before any living things appeared, our planet consisted of various substances in uncombined form (*elements*) and in combined form (*compounds*). Some of these substances were liquids, some were solids, and others were gases. Thus, when the first living things did appear, their environment consisted only of these lifeless elements and compounds, plus energy.

Eventually, green plants developed in the ocean, spread there, and then spread over the land. Using energy from sunlight, the plants converted some of the substances present in the soil, air, and water of their environment into food for themselves. These plants, in turn, became food for other organisms. As a result, all organisms have come to contain in their bodies many of the same elements present in their environment. Among these elements are carbon (C), oxygen (O), hydrogen (H), nitrogen (N), sulfur (S), and phosphorus (P).

When humans first appeared on earth, they required certain elements for their life activities, as did all other organisms. Humans obtained these elements in the same way all other organisms did—from the immediate environment.

As humans progressed and developed civilizations, they began to seek elements and other substances for purposes beyond basic life activities. In time, as their knowledge of chemistry grew, people learned how to obtain these substances from the earth—from its surface and from its depths.

In this unit, we will study chemistry in some detail in order to understand better the elements and compounds that make up our environment, and to see how we are able to extract substances useful to ourselves from that environment.

CHAPTER 1
WHAT IS THE STRUCTURE
OF ELEMENTS AND COMPOUNDS?

When you have completed this chapter, you should be able to:

1. *Distinguish* between (*a*) elements and compounds (*b*) atoms and molecules (*c*) electrons, protons, and neutrons (*d*) atomic weight and atomic number (*e*) ions and isotopes.
2. *Discuss* the evidence for the electrical nature of matter.
3. *State* the contributions of the following scientists to our ideas about the composition of matter: Crookes, Thomson, Rutherford, and Bohr.
4. *Construct* diagrams of atoms after consulting the Periodic Table.
5. *Relate* orbits of electrons to energy levels of electrons.
6. *Describe*, with examples, how atoms unite to form molecules.
7. *Explain* why the forming and breaking of bonds is important to living things.

In the laboratory experience that follows, you will discover some important properties of matter.

Laboratory Experience

WHAT ARE SOME IMPORTANT PROPERTIES OF MATTER?

A. Briskly rub a glass rod with a piece of silk cloth for about 1 minute. Bring the rod close to (but not touching) a pith ball, suspended from a stand by a piece of string, as shown in Fig. 1–1.
    1. What do you observe?
B. Briskly rub a rubber rod with a piece of fur for about 1 minute. Bring one end of the rod close to the suspended pith ball.
    2. What do you observe?
C. Briskly rub a glass rod with a piece of silk cloth. Suspend the rod from a stand by a piece of string.

    Briskly rub another glass rod with a piece of silk cloth. Bring the rod close to the suspended rod.
    3. What do you observe?

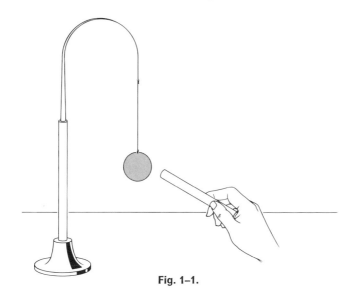

Fig. 1–1.

D. Briskly rub a rubber rod with a piece of fur, and suspend the rod from a stand by a piece of string.

Briskly rub another rubber rod with the piece of fur. Bring one end of the rod close to one end of the suspended rod.
4. What do you observe?

E. Repeat part C, but this time bring a rubber rod that has been rubbed with the piece of fur close to the suspended glass rod.
5. What do you observe?

F. Repeat part D, but this time bring a glass rod that has been rubbed with the piece of silk cloth close to the suspended rubber rod.
6. What do you observe?
7. Summarize all the observations you made when
   a. you rubbed two different rods and then brought them close together.
   b. you rubbed two similar rods and then brought them together.
8. How do you explain these observations?

Introduction

As you know, all matter in the world is composed of elements, either in pure form or in combinations called compounds. Two or more elements can unite chemically with one another to form new substances—compounds.

In 1803, *John Dalton*, an English chemist, formulated his atomic theory, which states that matter consists of extremely small particles called *atoms*. According to this theory, atoms of the same element are alike in all respects, whereas atoms of different elements are different. In chemical changes, atoms unite to form *molecules*—the smallest units of a compound.

The manner in which atoms join to form molecules, or elements combine to form compounds, is essential to an understanding of the matter in our environment. To understand this process, we must consider the inside of the atom itself.

SUBATOMIC PARTICLES

Until the latter part of the nineteenth century, most people believed that atoms were the smallest particles of matter. At that time, however, certain experiments led scientists to suspect the presence of particles even smaller than the atom. Before the close of the nineteenth century, scientists discovered that every atom is composed of at least two kinds of smaller, subatomic particles. Each of these particles, moreover, carries a different electric charge.

Electrons and Protons

In 1870, *Sir William Crookes*, a British scientist, observed that gases under low pressure conduct electricity. He used a glass tube containing a very small quantity of gas. Metal electrodes were sealed into each end (Fig. 1–2). When a high voltage was established between the electrodes, Crookes saw a green glow in the walls of the tube. To account for this observation, he suggested that something comes from the electrodes, travels in a straight line, and strikes the glass walls of the tube.

Numerous experiments with low-pressure gas tubes during the next ten years established that negatively charged particles called *electrons* are emitted from the negative electrode (also called the *cathode*). In

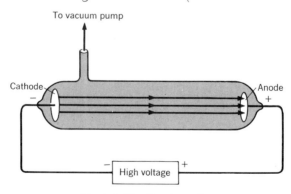

Fig. 1–2. The Crookes tube.

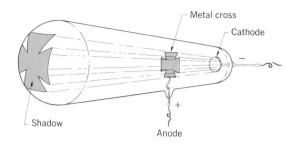

Fig. 1–3. Cathode rays travel in straight lines.

one such experiment, a metal cross was inserted in a gas tube, as shown in Fig. 1–3. The green glow appeared as before, except in the region of the shadow cast by the cross. Apparently, the metal stopped the flow of electrons. Other experiments showed that positively charged particles, called *protons*, are emitted from the positive electrode (also called the *anode*). From experiments of this kind, it became clear that matter is electrical in nature.

The discovery of electrons helps to explain *static electricity*. This type of electricity does not flow in a wire as does electric current (*current electricity*). Rather, static electricity seems to be concentrated or stored on the surface of a substance.

Many years ago, it was observed that certain nonmagnetic objects attract and repel one another after being rubbed briskly. You made these observations in your laboratory experience. When the rods were rubbed, the two glass rods repelled each other (Fig. 1–4), and the

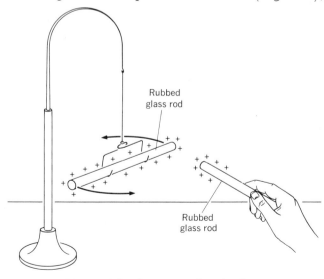

Fig. 1–4. Like charges repel each other.

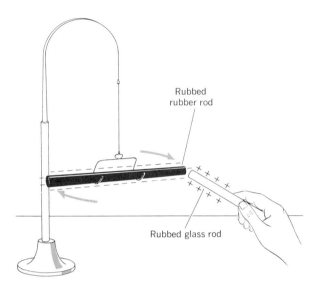

Fig. 1–5. Unlike charges attract each other.

two rubber rods repelled each other, but the glass rod and the rubber rod attracted each other (Fig. 1–5). Each of these observations can be explained in terms of electrical charges. According to the *law of electrical attraction and repulsion*, opposite electric charges attract each other, whereas like electric charges repel each other.

When rubber is rubbed with fur, electrons are transferred from the fur to the rubber. As a result, the rubber, having gained electrons, becomes negatively charged, while the fur, having lost electrons, becomes positively charged. On the other hand, glass rubbed with silk gives up electrons and becomes positively charged, while the silk becomes negatively charged. When the positively charged glass rod is brought near the negatively charged rubber rod, the unlike charges attract each other. The repulsions you observe when two rubber rods or two glass rods are brought near each other are the result of the repelling forces between like electrical charges.

Today, the law of electrical attraction and repulsion helps us understand the behavior of the glass and rubber rods. However, the reasons for the presence of positive and negative electrical charges did not become clear until a satisfactory theory, or "model," of the atom had been developed.

Models of Atoms

Before the close of the nineteenth century, *J. J. Thomson*, a British physicist, suggested that the interior of an atom might be like a "plum pudding." He pictured the atom as a positively charged sphere with negatively charged electrons spaced all through the sphere, just as raisins or plums might be found in a pudding (Fig. 1–6). As more was learned about the atom, however, Thomson's model could not satisfactorily explain many of the properties of the atom. A new model seemed necessary.

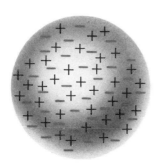

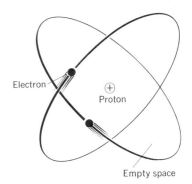

Fig. 1–6. The Thomson model.   Fig. 1–7. The Bohr model.

In 1911, *Ernest Rutherford*, a native of New Zealand, suggested another model of the atom, based on experiments he performed. In this model, the positive charges of the atom, the protons, are concentrated in a small region inside the atom, called the *nucleus*. The negatively charged particles, the electrons, are located outside the nucleus. The number of electrons outside the nucleus is equal to the number of protons inside the nucleus.

Other experiments have shown that the positive electrical charge of a proton is equal in strength to the negative charge of an electron. This accounts for the observation that atoms are electrically neutral. The weight or mass of a proton, however, is about 1837 times greater than the weight of the electron.

Following Rutherford, the Danish scientist *Niels Bohr* suggested that an atom consists of electrons revolving around the central nucleus. Bohr believed that the electrons revolve around the nucleus in orbits very much like the orbits in which planets revolve around the sun (Fig. 1–7). Bohr also suggested that the negatively charged electrons are held in orbit by the attraction of the positive charge of the nucleus. Unlike Thomson's model of the atom, the Bohr model contains large amounts of empty space between the electrons and the nucleus.

Although the Bohr model of the atom may not be perfect, it does provide a basis for a simple understanding of atomic structure. Today, scientists employ a new model of the atom, discussed in more advanced courses. In our study, however, we will use the Bohr model of the atom.

Neutrons

In the early twentieth century, the British chemist *F. W. Aston*, while trying to determine the weight of atoms of the gaseous element neon, discovered two different types of neon atoms. Although each type of neon atom has a slightly different weight, he found that the number of protons and electrons in these neon atoms remains the same. Atoms of the same element that differ slightly in weight are known as *isotopes*. Aston could not satisfactorily account for the presence of isotopes.

In 1932, *James Chadwick*, an English scientist, found another particle present in atoms besides protons and electrons. The new particles, called *neutrons*, helped to solve the mystery of isotopes.

Neutrons, like protons, are found in the nucleus of atoms. The weight of a neutron is approximately the same as that of a proton. Unlike the proton or the electron, however, the neutron has no electrical charge—it is neutral.

It is the presence of neutrons in atomic nuclei that explains the existence of isotopes of many elements. Thus, neon atoms all have the same number of protons and electrons, but some neon atoms have more neutrons than others (Fig. 1–8). Consequently, some neon atoms are heavier than others. This knowledge makes it possible to account for the slight differences in the weights of neon atoms, first noted by Aston.

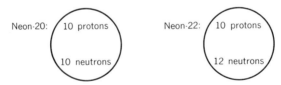

Fig. 1–8. Neon isotopes.

Summary: Electrons, Protons, Neutrons

A summary of the characteristics of the three fundamental particles of atoms is found in Table 1–1. These characteristics are based on the Bohr model of the atom.

Other Subatomic Particles

Scientists conducting nuclear research have found many particles in addition to electrons, protons, and neutrons. These other particles include *neutrinos, muons, mesons,* and *hyperons.* The properties of these particles and their relationship to the three fundamental particles found in atoms are a matter of great interest to scientists today. It may be that all

Table 1–1. Fundamental Atomic Particles

Particle	Charge	Location	Number	Weight
Electron	Negative	Around the nucleus	The same in all atoms of the same element Equal to the number of protons in the same atom	Approximately $\dfrac{1}{1837}$ the weight of a proton
Proton	Positive	In the nucleus of the atom	The same in all atoms of the same element Equal to the number of electrons in the same atom	Approximately equal to the weight of a neutron
Neutron	Neutral	In the nucleus of the atom	May vary in atoms of the same element	Approximately equal to the weight of a proton

these particles are composed of some still smaller fundamental building block. Theories about the nature of such particles are discussed in more advanced courses.

ATOMIC WEIGHTS

Chemists, going back to Dalton himself, were interested in the weights of atoms of different elements that combined to form compounds. Since atoms were too small to be weighed, it was decided to determine the weights of combining elements by using some given weight as a standard. For example, suppose you weigh 65 kilograms (143 pounds), and we assign 16 units as the relative weight. Another individual, weighing 98 kilograms (216 pounds), would then have a relative weight of $\dfrac{98 \text{ kg}}{65 \text{ kg}} \times 16 = 24$, or $\dfrac{216 \text{ lbs}}{143 \text{ lbs}} \times 16 = 24$ (rounded off), or 24 weight units. Originally, hydrogen was chosen as the standard, but later oxygen was used and was assigned a relative weight of 16. On this scale, hydrogen had a weight of 1, which was called the *relative atomic weight*, or simply *atomic weight*.

In 1961, chemists agreed to accept the element carbon-12 as the standard for all atomic weights. Carbon-12 (the most common form of carbon) was assigned an atomic weight of exactly 12.

Table 1–2 gives a partial listing of atomic weights. Note that the atomic weights are not whole numbers. This results from the presence of varying percentages of different isotopes in most elements. Thus, carbon contains about 99% carbon-12 and about 1% carbon-13, for a weighted average of 12.01115. In Table 1–2, the atomic weights (except for chlorine and copper) are rounded off to whole numbers. For a complete listing of atomic weights, see the Periodic Table, pages 500–501.

Table 1–2. Rounded-Off Atomic Weights

Element	Symbol	Atomic Weight (carbon-12 = 12)	Atomic Weight (rounded off)
Hydrogen	H	1.00797	1
Helium	He	4.0026	4
Lithium	Li	6.939	7
Carbon	C	12.01115	12
Nitrogen	N	14.0067	14
Oxygen	O	15.9994	16
Fluorine	F	18.9984	19
Sodium	Na	22.9898	23
Magnesium	Mg	24.312	24
Aluminum	Al	26.9815	27
Phosphorus	P	30.9738	31
Sulfur	S	32.064	32
Chlorine	Cl	35.453	35.5
Potassium	K	39.102	39
Calcium	Ca	40.08	40
Copper	Cu	63.54	63.5

With the discovery of subatomic particles, atomic weight was redefined. Atomic weight is now defined as the total weight of the protons and neutrons in an atom. (Recall that the weight of an electron is only about 1/1837 the weight of either a proton or a neutron.) Both a proton and a neutron are assigned a weight of 1 on the atomic weight scale. Thus, an atom of hydrogen (containing 1 proton) has an atomic weight of 1. Similarly, the weight of helium is 4 (2 protons + 2 neutrons); the weight of nitrogen is 14 (7 protons + 7 neutrons); the weight of oxygen is 16 (8 protons + 8 neutrons).

Since the weight of a proton or a neutron is assigned a value of 1, atomic weight is equal to the total number of protons and neutrons in an atom. The number of protons and neutrons is also called the *mass number*; the atomic weight is also called *atomic mass*.

ATOMIC NUMBERS

According to the Bohr model, each atom of a particular element contains a specific number of electrons and protons. No two elements are alike in this respect. Present knowledge indicates that the number of protons or electrons in the known elements may vary from 1 to 105. The specific number of either protons or electrons in an atom is known as the *atomic number* of the element.

THE PERIODIC TABLE

By 1860, chemists had discovered about 63 different elements. In the late 1860s, *Dmitri Mendeleev*, a Russian scientist, arranged these elements according to the weight of their atoms, from the lightest atom to the heaviest. In doing so, he noted that every seventh atom had certain similar properties. Because of this regular repetition, or *periodicity*, Mendeleev arranged the elements into a table of seven columns, called a *periodic table*. Table 1-3, page 12, shows only a small part of Mendeleev's table. Mendeleev's classification of the elements was later used by other chemists as the basis of the modern Periodic Table.

In 1912, *Henry Moseley*, a British chemist, experimentally determined the atomic numbers of many elements. He then modified Mendeleev's periodic table by arranging the elements in order of their atomic numbers. This arrangement differed from the Mendeleev table, which arranged the elements according to their atomic weights. In the complete Mendeleev table (not shown in Table 1-3), there are three instances where lighter elements (because of their periodic characteristics) follow heavier elements: argon—potassium, cobalt—nickel, and tellurium—iodine. The Mendeleev table could not account for this. Discovery of atomic numbers, however, solved this problem. In each of these cases, the lighter element has a larger atomic number than the heavier element (which contains more neutrons).

Moseley's arrangement is the Periodic Table of the Elements that we use today. It is based upon the idea that the properties of the elements repeat themselves when they are arranged according to increasing atomic number. In the modern Periodic Tables (pages 500–501), an atom of hydrogen, which has one proton and one electron, is the element with atomic number 1. Helium, with two protons and two electrons, has atomic number 2. Further along in the Periodic Table, we find that an atom of oxygen, containing 8 protons and 8 electrons, has the atomic number 8. Thus, by referring to the Periodic Table, we can

Table 1–3. Mendeleev's Arrangement of Some of the Elements

I	II	III	IV	V	VI	VII
atomic weight: 7 Lithium Li	atomic weight: 9 Beryllium Be	atomic weight: 11 Boron B	atomic weight: 12 Carbon C	atomic weight: 14 Nitrogen N	atomic weight: 16 Oxygen O	atomic weight: 19 Fluorine F
atomic weight: 23 Sodium Na	atomic weight: 24 Magnesium Mg	atomic weight: 27 Aluminum Al	atomic weight: 28 Silicon Si	atomic weight: 31 Phosphorus P	atomic weight: 32 Sulfur S	atomic weight: 35.5 Chlorine Cl

find the atomic number of any element. This tells us the number of protons or electrons present in the atom.

The modern Periodic Table, like the Mendeleev table, consists of horizontal rows, called *periods*, and vertical columns, called *groups* or *families*. In Chapter 2, we will return to a study of the relationships in the Periodic Table.

STRUCTURE OF THE ATOM

According to Bohr, electrons in atoms follow paths called orbits, or *shells*. Each shell contains a specific maximum number of electrons. This number of electrons generally depends upon the distance of the shell from the nucleus. The total number of electrons in all the shells equals the atomic number.

Electrons in a particular orbit have a certain amount of energy that allows them to move in that orbit. The energy associated with a given orbit is referred to as an *energy level*. If energy is added to an atom—for example, if the atom is heated—an electron moves outward to an orbit more distant from the nucleus. The atom is then said to be unstable, excited, or at a higher energy level than ordinarily. When the electron returns to its original energy level, the added energy is liberated. We see this energy sometimes as colored light. Thus, when sodium metal is heated in a flame, the electrons in the sodium atoms enter higher energy levels. When the electrons return to the original energy level, they emit energy and color the flame yellow.

Identifying Electron Shells

The energy levels, or shells, of electrons are identified by letters, as shown in Fig. 1–9. The shell closest to the nucleus is known as the K-shell, or K-energy level. The K-shell can hold a maximum of 2 electrons. The next shell is the L-shell, which can hold no more than 8 electrons. The M-shell also holds a maximum of 8 electrons (with some exceptions, as we shall see). As the atomic numbers of the elements increase, each shell is generally filled to capacity before the next shell is started.

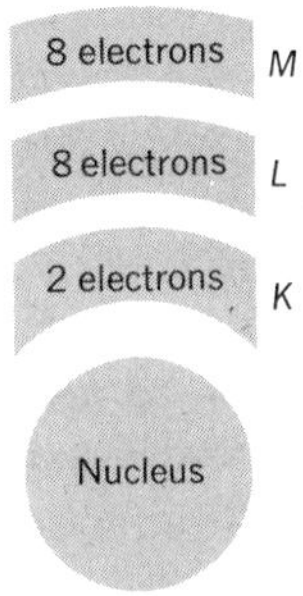

Fig. 1–9. Energy levels.

Table 1–4, page 14, lists the first 21 elements in order of increasing atomic numbers. In the first 20 elements, notice that each shell is filled in turn. Thus, the L-shell of lithium contains 1 electron, the L-shell of beryllium contains 2 electrons, and so on, until neon, where the L-shell is completely filled with 8 electrons.

We have included scandium in the table (atomic number 21) because this is the first element that does not follow the rule for the orderly filling of shells. It would seem logical that, since calcium has 8 electrons in its M-shell and 2 electrons in its N-shell, scandium should have 8 electrons in its M-shell and 3 electrons in its N-shell. But, as Table 1–4 reveals, scandium does not follow the rule. Since this situation cannot be explained by means of the Bohr model of the atom, in this book we shall be concerned chiefly with elements of atomic numbers 1 to 20.

Constructing Atomic Diagrams

From the arrangement of electrons in their shells, it is possible to construct diagrams of the atoms of different elements. Such atomic diagrams are *not* pictures of actual atoms; they are only models that help us to understand the properties of atoms.

In order to construct a diagram for an atom, we need to know three things: (1) the symbol for the element, (2) its atomic number, and (3) its atomic weight. All of this information is recorded in the Periodic Table.

Table 1–4. Electron Arrangements

Element	Symbol	Atomic Number	Number of Electrons in Shells			
			K	L	M	N
Hydrogen	H	1	1			
Helium	He	2	2			
Lithium	Li	3	2	1		
Beryllium	Be	4	2	2		
Boron	B	5	2	3		
Carbon	C	6	2	4		
Nitrogen	N	7	2	5		
Oxygen	O	8	2	6		
Fluorine	F	9	2	7		
Neon	Ne	10	2	8		
Sodium	Na	11	2	8	1	
Magnesium	Mg	12	2	8	2	
Aluminum	Al	13	2	8	3	
Silicon	Si	14	2	8	4	
Phosphorus	P	15	2	8	5	
Sulfur	S	16	2	8	6	
Chlorine	Cl	17	2	8	7	
Argon	Ar	18	2	8	8	
Potassium	K	19	2	8	8	1
Calcium	Ca	20	2	8	8	2
Scandium	Sc	21	2	8	9	2

Turn now to the Periodic Table on pages 500–501. Each element is represented by a box of the table. The box shows the chemical symbol for the element. The number above the symbol is the atomic number of the element, and the number below the symbol is the atomic weight. With this information, we can draw the diagram of any atom. (The box contains other useful data.)

Take the element sodium as an example. The Periodic Table shows:

$$
\begin{array}{c}
11 \\
Na \\
22.9898
\end{array}
$$

According to the number above the symbol, the atomic number of sodium is 11. According to the number below the symbol, its rounded-off atomic weight is 23. However, for convenience in notation, chemists generally write this information as $^{23}_{11}Na$ (the atomic weight above the atomic number). *Remember that the larger number is always the atomic weight.*

The atomic number indicates the number of protons or electrons that an atom contains. Therefore, we know that the sodium atom contains 11 protons and 11 electrons. The atomic weight of an atom is equal to the combined number of protons and neutrons in the nucleus. Therefore, we can find the number of neutrons in a sodium atom by subtracting the atomic number (number of protons) from the atomic weight (number of protons plus neutrons). In the case of sodium, since the atomic weight is 23 and the number of protons is 11, the number of neutrons is $23 - 11 = 12$.

In drawing the atom, protons are abbreviated by the letter p, neutrons by the letter n, and electrons by the letter e with a superscript minus sign, e^-. (The minus sign reminds us that an electron has a negative charge.) Keep in mind that each electron shell can hold only a specific maximum number of electrons. If necessary, we can refer to Table 1–4, or to the Periodic Table on pages 500–501, to find the electron arrangement in a specific atom. Many students merely memorize the maximum number of electrons in each shell. Thus:

$$
\begin{array}{c}
K—L—M \\
2—8—8
\end{array}
$$

Now we are ready to draw a diagram of the sodium atom (Fig. 1–10). These are the steps to follow:

Step 1. Collect the necessary information:
number of protons $= 11\ p$
number of neutrons $= 12\ n$
number of electrons $= 11\ e^-$

Fig. 1–10. An atomic diagram of sodium.

Step 2. Draw a circle to represent the nucleus of the sodium atom, showing the number of protons and neutrons.

Step 3. Indicate the electrons in their shells around the nucleus, filling each shell to capacity as we move away from the nucleus.

THE FORMATION OF COMPOUNDS

Of the 88 elements found on earth, only a few occur in uncombined form. Among these are gold and neon. Most elements, because of their tendency to react with one another, occur in natural compounds. When elements combine, the individual elements lose their own physical and chemical properties. The compound that forms has an entirely new set of properties.

You are probably familiar with a number of natural compounds. Sodium reacts with chlorine to form sodium chloride ($NaCl$), or table salt; hydrogen reacts with oxygen to form water (H_2O); carbon reacts with oxygen to form carbon dioxide (CO_2). These are only a few examples of compounds. More than a million different compounds can be formed from the 88 elements. Our atomic diagrams can help us to see why elements react as they do and how molecules of compounds are formed.

Electrons and Chemical Reactions

In nature, things tend to become more stable. Thus, a stone rolls downhill unaided, but it does not roll uphill. The stone at the bottom of the hill is more stable than the same stone on top of the hill.

Chemists have observed that certain elements are more stable—that is, less reactive—than others. These stable elements are the ones whose outermost shells are filled to capacity. These elements are called the *noble gases.* Table 1–4, page 14, shows that helium has 2 electrons in its outermost shell (K-shell); neon has 8 electrons in its outermost shell (L-shell); and argon has 8 electrons in its outermost shell (M-shell). In each of these cases, the outermost shell is filled to capacity. Thus, among the first 20 elements, helium, neon, and argon are all noble gases.

When the outermost electron shell of an atom is filled, then, the atom is stable. In general, it will not combine with other atoms. If the outermost shell is not filled to capacity, on the other hand, the atom is unstable. It has a tendency to react with other atoms.

Nature, as we know, favors changes making for greater stability. Therefore, we might expect that elements, when they react, would tend to acquire electron arrangements that fill their outermost shells. This, in fact, is the case. When elements combine to form compounds, the outermost shell of the atoms of the elements usually becomes complete. In effect, these elements attain the electron structure of the noble gas nearest them in the Periodic Table.

Formation of a Molecule From Two Atoms

Let us take as an example the sodium atom, which contains only 1 electron in its M-shell (Fig. 1–10, page 15). The sodium atom would be far more stable if its outermost shell were complete. This could happen in one of two ways. The sodium atom might give up its single electron in the M-shell, thus leaving the L-shell as the outermost filled shell. On the other hand, the sodium atom might gain 7 additional electrons, thus completing its M-shell. In the former case, it would come to resemble neon; in the latter case it would resemble argon (Table 1–4, page 14). Experiments have shown that less energy is required for a sodium atom to lose 1 electron than to gain 7 electrons. Therefore, when the sodium atom combines with another atom, the sodium atom loses the electron from its M-shell, acquiring the structure of neon.

The chlorine atom contains 7 electrons in its M-shell (Table 1–4, page 14). This atom could become more stable either by accepting 1 electron in its outer shell or by giving away 7 electrons. Again, experiments show that it is easier for a chlorine atom to gain 1 electron than to lose 7 electrons.

If 1 atom of sodium and 1 atom of chlorine are sufficiently close to each other, they may combine (Fig. 1–11). In this process, the single electron of the M-shell of the sodium atom is transferred to the M-shell of the chlorine atom. When this occurs, the sodium atom is left with an outer L-shell containing 8 electrons. At the same time, the chlorine atom now has 8 electrons in its M-shell. Each atom now has a completely filled outermost shell of electrons. As a result of the transfer of 1 electron, the two unstable atoms have united to form one molecule of sodium chloride, which is stable.

Note that the tendency of one element to combine with another element depends to some extent on the number of electrons in the outermost shell that can be transferred. This number of electrons, which represents the combining tendency of the atoms of an element, is known as the *valence number*, or simply *valence*. Valence number will be studied further in the next chapter.

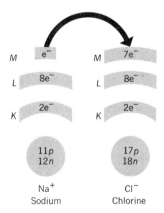

Fig. 1–11. An atom of sodium combines with an atom of chlorine.

Formation of a Molecule From Three Atoms

Often, more than two atoms are required for the formation of a stable compound. This is the case, for example, when atoms of calcium and chlorine unite. The calcium atom contains 2 electrons in its N-shell. These electrons must be lost for the atom to become stable. For a chlorine atom to become stable, only 1 electron is required. When a second chlorine atom is present, also requiring 1 electron, all 3 atoms achieve stability by the transfer of electrons. Any sample of calcium metal or chlorine gas contains large numbers of atoms. Consequently, when calcium and chlorine react, 1 atom of calcium combines with 2 atoms of chlorine to form calcium chloride (Fig. 1–12).

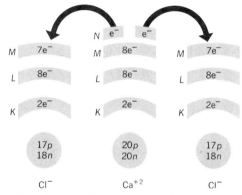

Fig. 1–12. One atom of calcium reacts with two atoms of chlorine.

Similarly, two sodium atoms and one oxygen atom combine to form sodium oxide (Fig. 1–13).

The chemical formula for sodium chloride is NaCl, meaning that 1 atom of sodium (Na) is combined with 1 atom of chlorine (Cl). The formula for calcium chloride is $CaCl_2$, meaning that 1 atom of Ca is combined with 2 atoms of Cl. The formula for sodium oxide is Na_2O, meaning that 2 atoms of Na are combined with 1 atom of O.

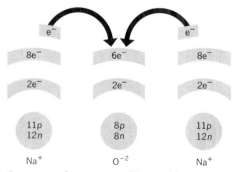

Fig. 1–13. One atom of oxygen combines with two atoms of sodium.

Noble Gases

Recall that an element having a completed outermost shell is called a noble gas. In addition to helium, neon, and argon, the noble gases include krypton, xenon, and radon.

From their electron structures, we can predict that these elements should not react with other elements. An element that does not react with other elements is said to be *inert*. Under ordinary conditions, this prediction is accurate. Recently, however, scientists have discovered that xenon and krypton do react and combine with active nonmetallic elements such as fluorine and oxygen. This discovery provides further evidence that the Bohr model of the atom is faulty; noble gas compounds can be explained only on the basis of a more advanced model.

CHEMICAL BONDS

Understanding how atoms combine helps us to understand the attractive forces, or *bonds*, that hold different atoms together in a molecule.

Bonds Formed by Transfer of Electrons

We know that a sodium atom combines with a chlorine atom by transferring one of its electrons to the chlorine atom. After this transfer, the sodium atom remains with 11 protons but only 10 electrons. As a result, the sodium atom now carries a positive electric charge. The chlorine atom, after accepting the electron from the sodium atom, has 18 electrons and only 17 protons. It now has an excess of 1 electron and thus carries a negative charge (Fig. 1–14).

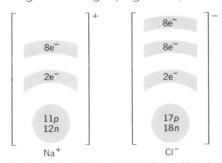

Fig. 1–14. Ionic bonding in sodium chloride.

Atoms that become electrically charged after donating or receiving electrons are called *ions*. Since the sodium and chlorine ions are oppositely charged, they attract each other. Thus, they are held together, or bonded, by electrical forces resulting from their opposite charges. This type of bonding is known as *ionic bonding*, or *electro-valent bonding*.

Bonds Formed by Sharing Electrons

When some atoms form molecules, the atoms do not donate or receive electrons. Instead, these atoms share their electrons.

A molecule of hydrogen gas consists of 2 atoms of hydrogen. That is, its formula is H_2 and not H. Each hydrogen atom has 1 electron in the K-shell. However, by sharing a pair of electrons, each nucleus "feels" the presence of 2 electrons (Fig. 1–15). Two electrons in the K-shell is the stable arrangement found in helium. In this case, however, the 2 electrons are shared—not transferred as in ionic bonding. The bonding between the 2 H atoms in H_2 is known as *covalent bonding*.

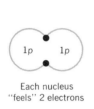

Each nucleus
"feels" 2 electrons

**Fig. 1–15. Covalent
bonding in hydrogen gas.**

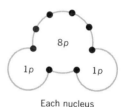

Each nucleus
"feels" 2 electrons

**Fig. 1–16. Covalent
bonding in water.**

Covalent bonding also occurs between the atoms of hydrogen and oxygen in a molecule of water (Fig. 1–16). Note that each hydrogen atom has only 1 electron in its K-shell. To complete this shell, each of the hydrogen atoms requires an additional electron. The oxygen atom requires 2 electrons to complete its L-shell. When hydrogen and oxygen atoms combine to form a water molecule, neither atom gains or loses electrons. Rather, the oxygen and hydrogen atoms share their electrons, making it possible for the K-shells of the hydrogen atoms and the L-shell of the oxygen atom to be filled to capacity. As with the H_2 molecule, the nucleus of each atom "feels" a completed outer shell.

Breaking Bonds

Molecules are formed from atoms when the atoms react. The atoms in molecules are held together by bonds. To decompose molecules, it is necessary to break bonds that have already been established. The breaking of some types of bonds uses up energy. The breaking of other types of bonds releases energy.

We find many instances of both the making and breaking of bonds in the reactions that take place within living things. For example, when living things grow, the new living material (protoplasm) is formed from nutrients present in the body. To produce this new material, new molecules must be made by forming new chemical bonds. This process requires energy.

When starch—a large, complex molecule—is digested, its complex bonds are first broken down. Then new bonds are formed to make glucose, a simpler compound than starch. This process also requires energy.

When glucose, in turn, is oxidized (combined with oxygen), more bonds are broken, and other bonds are formed. As a result, two new compounds are produced—carbon dioxide and water. This process releases energy.

As a result of the formation of compounds during oxidation, the energy that living things need is released. When we say that glucose (sugar) is an energy food, we really mean that the bonds in glucose have chemical energy stored in them. When oxidation takes place, the stored energy is released.

Looking Back

The basic unit of an element is an atom. According to the Bohr model, the atom has protons and neutrons, contained in a nucleus, and electrons moving in orbits around the nucleus. Together, the weights of the protons and neutrons in an atom equal the atomic weight of an element. The number of either protons or electrons in an atom equals the atomic number of an element.

Noble gases (inert elements) do not ordinarily form bonds with other elements because noble gases are exceptionally stable. Most elements tend to react with others, forming compounds. The basic unit of a compound is a molecule. Each molecule is composed of a combination of atoms held together by attractive forces, or bonds. The bonds are formed by the transfer or sharing of electrons between atoms. Energy is involved when bonds are established or broken. In forming molecules, atoms attain the stable structure of noble gases.

Looking Ahead

Different elements have different tendencies to react. Why do elements react as they do? The chemical reactivity of elements is discussed in the next chapter.

Multiple-Choice Questions

*Write the letter preceding the word or expression that best completes the
statement or answers the question.*

1. The tiny, negatively charged particles first described by Crookes are
   called
   a. neutrinos   b. protons   c. electrons   d. neutrons
2. The attraction of a rubbed comb for paper gives evidence that
   a. matter is electrical in nature   c. matter contains protons
   b. matter is magnetic   d. matter is electrically neutral
3. When two similarly charged objects are brought close together they
   a. attract each other   c. stick to each other
   b. have no effect on each other   d. repel each other
4. An object becomes positively charged when it
   a. has an excess of electrons
   b. has a deficiency of electrons
   c. has an equal number of protons and neutrons
   d. has an equal number of protons and electrons
5. The "plum pudding" model of the atom was proposed by
   a. Rutherford   b. Democritus   c. Thomson   d. Bohr
6. The central portion of an atom is called the
   a. nucleus   b. shell   c. electron   d. ring
7. In an atom, the number of electrons is
   a. equal to the number of neutrons
   b. greater than the number of protons
   c. less than the number of protons
   d. equal to the number of protons
8. Atoms of the same element which differ slightly in weight are called
   a. neutrons   b. ions   c. isotopes   d. positrons
9. The differences in weights of atoms of the same element are attributed
   to different numbers of
   a. protons   b. neutrons   c. electrons   d. positrons
10. Of the following, the particle generally not found in the nucleus of an
    atom is
    a. a hyperon   b. a meson   c. an electron   d. a muon
11. An atomic particle with a weight of approximately 1/1837 of a proton is
    a. a hyperon   b. a neutron   c. a muon   d. an electron
12. The atomic number of an element indicates
    a. the number of protons plus electrons
    b. the number of protons plus neutrons
    c. the number of protons or electrons
    d. the number of neutrons only
13. The scientist who arranged the elements in the Periodic Table according
    to their atomic numbers is
    a. Moseley   b. Mendeleev   c. Rutherford   d. Bohr
14. The atomic weight of an atom is equal to the weight of the
    a. protons   b. protons and neutrons   c. neutrons   d. electrons

15. At present, the element used as a standard for atomic weights is
    a. hydrogen   b. neon   c. oxygen   d. carbon
16. The electron shell closest to the nucleus of an atom is called the
    a. A-shell   b. K-shell   c. M-shell   d. L-shell
17. The maximum number of electrons found in the K-shell of any atom is
    a. 1   b. 2   c. 8   d. 18
18. In the atom $_{11}^{23}$Na, the number of protons is
    a. 11   b. 12   c. 23   d. 34
19. Of the following, the element that has an outermost shell that is complete is
    a. sodium   b. neon   c. chlorine   d. oxygen
20. To achieve stability when it combines with chlorine, a sodium atom will
    a. accept 1 electron   c. donate 1 electron
    b. accept 7 electrons   d. donate 7 electrons
21. An element that has fewer than 2 electrons in its K-shell is
    a. neon   b. hydrogen   c. oxygen   d. fluorine

Modified True-False Questions

In some of the following statements, the italicized term makes the statement incorrect. For each incorrect statement, write the term that must be substituted for the italicized term to make the statement correct. For each correct statement, write the word "true."

1. An element that does not react with other elements is said to be *bonded*.
2. Electrically charged atoms are called *ions*.
3. Atoms of elements, held together by opposite electrical charges, are bonded by *covalent bonds*.
4. When elements are held together by a covalent bond, the electrons in the outermost shell are *shared*.
5. A molecule of hydrogen gas is held together by *an ionic bond*.
6. Atoms of different elements unite during chemical changes to produce new *elements*.
7. Glass, when rubbed with silk, becomes *negatively* charged.
8. The positive charges of atoms are found inside the *nucleus*.
9. The Bohr model of the atom suggests that the atom is mostly composed of *empty space*.
10. The proton is thought to be heavier than *a neutron*.
11. An atom containing 13 protons contains 13 *electrons*.
12. The element $_{13}^{27}$Al contains 14 *protons*.
13. A maximum of 8 electrons will fit in the *K-shell*.
14. An electron, when supplied with *energy*, moves farther away from the nucleus.
15. When the outermost shell of an atom becomes complete, the element is said to be *unstable*.
16. Carbon, with an atomic number of 6, contains 4 electrons in the *L-shell*.
17. The combining tendency of an element is called the *atomic number*.

18. When bonds are formed between atoms, *mixtures* result.
19. When food is digested, energy is used in breaking bonds between *molecules.*
20. The growth of living things requires *energy* obtained from bonds in food substances.

Matching Questions

Write the letter of the item in column B which is most closely related to the item in column A.

Column A	Column B
1. charged atom	a. Moseley
2. discovered conduction of electricity through gases	b. atomic number
	c. valence number
3. arranged Periodic Table by using atomic numbers	d. proton
	e. fluorine
4. particle of relatively negligible weight	f. Rutherford
	g. neutron
5. combining tendency of atoms	h. helium
6. energy of an electron in a particular orbit	i. electron
	j. Bohr
7. inert element	k. ion
8. shared electrons	l. covalence
9. believed that electrons travel in orbits around the nucleus	m. Crookes
	n. isotopes
10. atoms with same atomic number but different atomic weights	o. energy level

Thought Questions

1. Describe the differences between the terms in each of the following pairs:
   a. proton and neutron   c. ionic bond and covalent bond
   b. ion and isotope   d. atomic number and atomic weight
2. Explain how rubbing rubber with fur causes the rubber to become negatively charged.
3. Construct atomic diagrams for each of the following elements:

   a. $^{16}_{8}O$ b. $^{39}_{19}K$ c. $^{19}_{9}F$ d. $^{40}_{20}Ca$ e. $^{20}_{10}Ne$

4. Explain how calcium $\left(^{40}_{20}Ca\right)$ and fluorine $\left(^{19}_{9}F\right)$ become stable when they form calcium fluoride.
5. Complete the table.

Particle	Mass	Electric Charge	Location
Proton			
Electron			
Neutron			

CHAPTER 2
WHY DO ELEMENTS
REACT AS THEY DO?

When you have completed this chapter, you should be able to:

1. *Distinguish* between metals, nonmetals, and metalloids.
2. *Define* valence number and radical.
3. *Relate* the number of electrons in the shells of metals, nonmetals, and metalloids to their position in the Periodic Table and to their tendency to react.
4. *List* the factors that affect the reactivities of elements.
5. *Discuss*, with examples, why some elements have two or more valence numbers.
6. *Describe* the reactivity series of metals.

In the laboratory experience that follows, you will test the reactivities of some familiar metals.

Laboratory Experience

Note: The units of measurement used in this laboratory experience and in the rest of this book are given in the metric system, which is used in most countries. For convenient conversion tables, refer to the Appendix.

HOW CAN WE COMPARE THE REACTIVITIES OF SOME METALS?

A. Place three test tubes in a rack. Place a sample of the metallic element magnesium (Mg) in the first tube, about the same quantity of zinc (Zn) in the second, and about the same quantity of iron (Fe) in the third.

Add about 10 cubic centimeters of dilute hydrochloric acid (HCl) to each test tube. Observe the test tubes carefully to determine how

25

rapidly each metal reacts with the acid. The more reactive the metal, the more gas bubbles are formed.

1. List the three metals in their order of reactivity, listing the most reactive metal first.

B. Another way of determining whether one metal is more reactive than another metal is to see whether the first metal can replace the second metal from a water solution containing a compound of the second metal. You can tell when a metal has been replaced because the replaced metal appears on the surface of the first metal.

Copy the following table into your notebook.

Test Tube	Solution of Metallic Compound	Solid Metal	Reaction	More Reactive Metal	Less Reactive Metal
1	Copper (II) nitrate	Zn			
2	Iron (II) nitrate	Zn			
3	Silver nitrate	Zn			
4	Zinc nitrate	Cu			
5	Iron (II) nitrate	Cu			
6	Silver nitrate	Cu			

a. Using a grease pencil, mark the numbers 1, 2, and 3 on separate test tubes.

b. To test tube 1, add 10 cubic centimeters of dilute copper (II) nitrate solution.

c. To test tube 2, add 10 cubic centimeters of dilute iron (II) nitrate solution.

d. To test tube 3, add 10 cubic centimeters of dilute silver nitrate solution.

e. Add a small piece of mossy zinc to each of the three test tubes.

f. After 5 minutes, observe each test tube, and record your observations in the table.

C. Perform the second part of this experiment as follows.

a. Using a grease pencil, mark the numbers 4, 5, and 6 on separate test tubes.

b. To test tube 4, add 10 cubic centimeters of dilute zinc nitrate solution.

    c. To test tube 5, add 10 cubic centimeters of dilute iron (II) nitrate solution.

    d. To test tube 6, add 10 cubic centimeters of dilute silver nitrate solution.

    e. Add a small piece of copper to each of the test tubes.

    f. After 5 minutes, observe each test tube, and record your observations in the table.

2. Which is the most reactive metal in the table? Why?

3. How does copper compare with silver in reactivity?

4. According to the observations you have made in parts A, B, and C, prepare a list in which the metals copper, zinc, iron, magnesium, and silver are arranged according to their reactivity. List the most reactive metal first.

Introduction

A very important property of an element is the way in which it reacts with other elements. Some elements react more readily than do others. For example, when a sample of the element magnesium comes into contact with hydrochloric acid, as you observed in the laboratory experience, the magnesium reacts vigorously with the acid, forming the compound magnesium chloride and liberating the element hydrogen. However, when a sample of the element gold comes into contact with the same acid, no reaction takes place. In this chapter, we will consider the factors that affect the reactive properties of the elements.

In general, elements can be grouped into three classes according to their properties.

CLASSES OF ELEMENTS

When classified according to their physical and chemical properties, the elements fall into three classes—*metals, nonmetals,* and *metalloids.*

Metals

Examples of metals are sodium, nickel, copper, aluminum, and calcium. The electron arrangements of the atoms of metals show that these atoms generally have fewer than 4 electrons in their outermost shells. (See, for example, the electron arrangement of sodium in Fig. 1–10, page 15, and of calcium in Fig. 1–12, page 18.) We noted in the previous chapter that a sodium atom loses its single electron when it reacts with a chlorine atom to form sodium chloride. Also, a calcium atom loses its 2 outer electrons when it reacts with 2 chlorine atoms to form calcium chloride. Similarly, the atoms of all metallic elements tend to lose electrons when they react.

Nonmetals

Examples of nonmetals are sulfur, chlorine, oxygen, and iodine. The electron arrangements of the atoms of nonmetals show that these atoms generally have more than 4 outermost electrons. Consequently, when 2 chlorine atoms react with calcium to form calcium chloride, each chlorine atom gains a single electron. In a similar manner, all nonmetallic atoms tend to gain electrons when they react.

Metalloids

The elements of this class have some properties of metals and some of nonmetals. Examples of metalloids are carbon, silicon, boron, and arsenic. The electron arrangements of the atoms of metalloids reveal that these atoms generally have either 3, 4, or 5 outermost electrons. Experiments show that the atoms of metalloids, such as carbon or silicon, may either gain, lose, or share electrons when they react.

THE TENDENCY OF ELEMENTS TO FORM COMPOUNDS

In the formation of compounds, note that the tendency of one element to combine with another element depends to some extent on the number of electrons in the outermost shell that can be gained or lost. This number of electrons, which represents the combining tendency of the atoms of an element, has been defined as the valence number. Thus, the valence numbers of the atoms described before are: sodium = 1; chlorine = 1; calcium = 2; oxygen = 2.

The valence number often tells us with how many other atoms a particular atom can unite. For example, one sodium atom (valence number = 1) can join with only one other atom, whereas one calcium atom (valence number = 2) can join with two other atoms each having a valence number of 1.

Valence number usually is preceded by a plus or minus sign. The element that loses electrons has a positive valence number, whereas the element that gains electrons has a negative valence number. We will return to valence numbers later in this chapter.

FACTORS AFFECTING THE REACTIVITY OF ELEMENTS

The valence number, or combining tendency, of an atom depends on the number of electrons in the outermost shell of the atom. The electrons in the outermost shell that an atom can transfer (gain, lose) or share when reacting with other atoms are called *valence electrons*.

Valence Electrons and Chemical Reactivity

The reactivity and other properties of an element are related to the number of electrons (valence electrons) in the outermost shell of its atoms. The elements in period (row) 2 of the Periodic Table are lithium, beryllium, boron, carbon, nitrogen, oxygen, and fluorine. This portion of the Periodic Table, shown in Table 2–1, enables us to see this relationship at a glance.

Table 2–1. Electrons in the Outermost Shells of Metals and Nonmetals (Period 2)

| | GROUPS | | | | | | |
	I A	II A	III A	IV A	V A	VI A	VII A
Symbol	$^{7}_{3}Li$	$^{9}_{4}Be$	$^{11}_{5}B$	$^{12}_{6}C$	$^{14}_{7}N$	$^{16}_{8}O$	$^{19}_{9}F$
Electrons in outermost shell	1	2	3	4	5	6	7

decreasing metallic properties

————————————————————————————→

increasing nonmetallic properties

Notice that lithium has 1 valence electron, beryllium has 2 valence electrons, and boron has 3 valence electrons. These electrons are given away when these elements react with nonmetals. Of these three elements, lithium is the most reactive, beryllium is next in reactivity, and boron is least reactive.

We can account for this difference in reactivity by assuming that less energy is needed to transfer the single outermost (valence) electron of lithium than to transfer the 2 or 3 outermost electrons of the other two metals. (Recall that, of the three elements, lithium has the smallest positive charge and, hence, shows the least tendency to attract electrons.)

Notice that the outermost shell of an atom of nitrogen has 5 electrons; that of oxygen, 6; and that of fluorine, 7. These atoms gain electrons when the elements react with metals. Of the three elements, fluorine, having the largest positive charge, is the most reactive, oxygen is next in reactivity, and nitrogen is least reactive.

As you move toward the right across period 2 from Group I A to Group VII A, the number of outermost electrons increases by one in each successive group. The change in electron number from group to group appears to correspond with the differences in the reactivities of the elements in this period. Thus, since the tendency to lose electrons is characteristic of metals, the elements on the far left side of the Periodic Table are more metallic than are those on the far right side. In going from left to right across a given row in the Periodic Table, metallic properties decrease, and nonmetallic properties increase.

The atoms of the elements in Group IV A (the metalloids), represented by carbon in Table 2–1, page 29, have 4 electrons in their outermost electron shells. To complete their outermost shells, these elements can either gain, lose, or share 4 electrons. Therefore, these elements can act either as metals or as nonmetals. The properties of the metalloids lie between the properties of the metals and nonmetals.

Atomic Radius and Chemical Reactivity: Metals

The distance from the nucleus of an atom to its outermost electron shell is the *radius* of the atom, also called *covalent atomic radius*. This distance is a measure of the size of an atom and is represented by a sphere (see Periodic Table, pages 500–501). This distance affects the reactivity of metals and nonmetals differently.

In any group (column) of metals in the Periodic Table, the most reactive metal in the group is found near the bottom of the column, whereas the least reactive member of the group is found near the top. Thus, in Group I A, shown in Table 2–2, cesium is more reactive than lithium.

The reason for the differences in chemical reactivity within a group can be understood by studying the electron arrangements of the atoms of these metals.

Table 2–2. Common Elements in Group I A

Metal	Symbol	Electron Shells					
		K	L	M	N	O	P
Lithium	Li	2	1				
Sodium	Na	2	8	1			
Potassium	K	2	8	8	1		
Rubidium	Rb	2	8	18	8	1	
Cesium	Cs	2	8	18	18	8	1

In Table 2–2, note that the outermost shell of the less reactive metal, lithium, is much closer to the nucleus of the atom than is the outermost shell of the more reactive metal, rubidium. Fig. 2–1 shows a spherical comparison of the atomic radii of the elements in Group I A. We already know that the negatively charged electrons are held in their orbits by the attraction of the positively charged nucleus. This force of attraction decreases considerably as the distance from the nucleus increases. Therefore, electrons that are more distant from the nucleus are held less tightly and are more easily lost than are electrons closer to the nucleus. Since the more distant electrons are more easily lost, metals having distant electrons react readily with other elements and are, therefore, reactive.

Thus, since the atomic radius of the element rubidium is greater than that of lithium, the outermost electron of rubidium is more easily lost than the outermost electron of lithium. Consequently, rubidium is more reactive chemically than lithium.

Atomic Radius and Chemical Reactivity: Nonmetals

In any group of nonmetals in the Periodic Table, the most reactive nonmetal in the group is found near the top of the column, whereas the least reactive nonmetal is found near the bottom. For example, in Group VII A, shown in Table 2–3, page 32, fluorine is the most reactive nonmetal, and iodine is the least reactive.

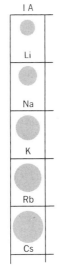

Fig. 2–1. Atomic radii:
Group I A.

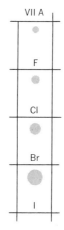

Fig. 2–2. Atomic radii:
Group VII A.

Fig. 2–2 shows that the atomic radii of the elements of Group VII A increase as we move from the top to the bottom of a group. Nonmetals combine chemically by attracting, or gaining, electrons. Since the attraction for electrons by the nucleus is greater when the atomic radius is small, the closer the outermost orbit is to the nucleus of a nonmetal,

Table 2–3. Common Elements in Group VII A

Nonmetal	Symbol	Electron Shells				
		K	L	M	N	O
Fluorine	F	2	7			
Chlorine	Cl	2	8	7		
Bromine	Br	2	8	18	7	
Iodine	I	2	8	18	18	7

the more reactive the element is. Accordingly, the elements at the top of nonmetallic groups are more reactive than those at the bottom of these groups.

Summary of Factors Determining Chemical Reactivity

Chemical reactivity is determined, to a large measure, by the number of electrons transferred between combining atoms and by the distance between these electrons and the nuclei of the atoms. The Periodic Table enables us to make useful predictions concerning reactivity. We can compare elements in the same row or elements in the same column. In the same row, elements show small differences in atomic radius. Within a row, it is the number of electrons that chiefly determines reactivity. In the same column, elements have the same number of outermost electrons, and it is the atomic radius that largely determines reactivity.

The factors determining chemical reactivity may be summarized as follows:

1. In a given row of the Periodic Table, the smaller the number of electrons transferred between reacting atoms, the more vigorous is the reaction.

2. For metals: In a given column of the Periodic Table, the most reactive element generally has the largest atomic radius.

3. For nonmetals: In a given column of the Periodic Table, the most reactive element generally has the smallest atomic radius.

VALENCE NUMBERS IN CHEMICAL REACTIONS

Valence electrons, those in the outermost electron shell, are usually the only parts of atoms that are involved in chemical reactions. The shell bearing valence electrons is called the *valence shell*. The valence shell of an atom often reveals the number of electrons (valence number) the atom may lose, gain, or share when the element reacts with other substances.

Positive and Negative Valence Numbers

As we indicated previously, the valence number of an element is expressed by a sign (+ or −) and by a number. A positive sign (+) indicates that the atom tends to lose electrons; a negative sign (−) indicates that the atom tends to gain electrons. The number indicates how many valence electrons must be gained or lost to produce a complete outermost shell. (Such a shell has the electron arrangement of a noble gas.)

In Fig. 2–3a, the valence number of aluminum is +3. The positive sign tells us that, in a chemical change, atoms of aluminum tend to lose electrons. The number 3 tells us that there are 3 electrons in the valence shell of the atom which, when lost, will leave a complete outermost shell. This is the electron arrangement of neon.

Fig. 2–3. Valence numbers.

The valence number of oxygen is −2, as shown in Fig. 2–3b. The negative sign indicates that atoms of oxygen tend to gain electrons in order to complete their outermost shells. An oxygen atom normally has 6 electrons in its valence shell. The number 2 indicates that there is room in the valence shell of the atom for 2 more electrons. A gain of 2 electrons results in a complete outermost shell of 8 electrons (the new particle now has a total of 10 electrons, or has the electron arrangement of neon).

Table 2–4 lists the valence numbers for some common metals and

Table 2–4. Valence Numbers of Common Elements

Element	Symbol	Valence Number
Lithium	Li	+1
Sodium	Na	+1
Potassium	K	+1
Calcium	Ca	+2
Magnesium	Mg	+2
Aluminum	Al	+3
Fluorine	F	−1
Chlorine	Cl	−1
Oxygen	O	−2
Sulfur	S	−2

nonmetals. Note that the valence numbers of the metals are positive (+), and the valence numbers of the nonmetals are negative (−).

From a study of the valence numbers, we can see that, when aluminum and oxygen combine to form the compound aluminum oxide, two atoms of aluminum lose 6 electrons, which three atoms of oxygen gain. In this manner, each atom attains a stable noble gas structure. It is possible to represent this compound, using symbols, as Al_2O_3—which is the formula for aluminum oxide. We shall use some simple formulas in this chapter, but will return to a more detailed study of valence numbers and formulas in the next chapter.

It is just as easy to follow the valence electrons in molecules in which valence electrons are shared rather than gained or lost. Recall the situation where two hydrogen atoms shared two electrons in H_2 (see Fig. 1–16, page 20). The metalloids tend to share electrons, usually 4. Thus, in CH_4 (methane), a carbon atom shares 4 electrons with four hydrogen atoms.

Elements With More Than One Valence Number

Many experiments with different elements have shown that, under different conditions, some elements may have more than one valence number. In different reactions, nonmetallic elements such as sulfur, phosphorus, and nitrogen may have either positive or negative valence numbers. This occurs because these nonmetals can either gain or lose (or sometimes share) electrons to complete their outermost shells. For example, in the compound Na_2S (sodium sulfide), sulfur has a valence number of −2, while in the compound SO_2 (sulfur dioxide), sulfur has a valence number of +4.

Some metallic elements such as iron, copper, and lead may also have more than one valence number. Atoms of these elements, which have atomic numbers beyond 20, have more complex electron arrangements than atoms with atomic numbers below 20. For example, the element iron (atomic number 26) may form compounds in which the valence number of iron is either +2 or +3. This means that an atom of iron can lose either two or three electrons with relatively equal ease, depending on the specific reaction. Similarly, copper (atomic number 29) may form compounds in which the valence number of copper is either +1 or +2. These examples indicate that the simple atomic model we are using does not satisfactorily explain the behavior of these atoms. Another, more advanced model, which we will not study, has been devised.

To differentiate between the compounds of metals with more than one valence number, the following general rules for naming such compounds have been established:

1. If the compound contains the metallic atom with the lower valence number, the suffix -ous is added to the name of the metal.

Example: Iron may have a valence number of +2 or +3.
Compound: FeO
Valence number of iron: +2
Name: ferr*ous* oxide

A newer system has been recently adopted for naming such compounds. The valence number of the metal in Roman numerals follows the name of the metal. Thus, ferrous oxide becomes iron (II) oxide. This notation has been used in your laboratory experience.

2. If the compound contains the metallic atom with the higher valence number, the suffix -ic is added to the name of the metal.

Example: Iron may have a valence number of +2 or +3.
Compound: Fe_2O_3
Valence number of iron: +3
Name: ferr*ic* oxide or iron (III) oxide

Table 2–5 lists some of the metals having more than one valence number and their compounds.

Table 2–5. Metals With More Than One Valence Number

Metal	Symbol	Valence Numbers	Typical Compound	Formula
Iron	Fe	+2	ferrous chloride iron (II) chloride	$FeCl_2$
		+3	ferric chloride iron (III) chloride	$FeCl_3$
Tin	Sn	+2	stannous chloride tin (II) chloride	$SnCl_2$
		+4	stannic chloride tin (IV) chloride	$SnCl_4$
Chromium	Cr	+2	chromous chloride chromium (II) chloride	$CrCl_2$
		+3	chromic chloride chromium (III) chloride	$CrCl_3$
Mercury	Hg	+1	mercurous chloride mercury (I) chloride	Hg_2Cl_2
		+2	mercuric chloride mercury (II) chloride	$HgCl_2$

Valence Numbers of Groups of Atoms

In many reactions, it appears that a group of atoms behaves as though it were but one single atom. Such groups of atoms are known as *radicals*. The atoms in most radicals are bonded together by sharing the electrons in their valence shells. It is interesting to note that radicals, like atoms of elements, have specific valence numbers.

Table 2–6 summarizes the formulas, names, and valence numbers of some common radicals. With one exception (the ammonium radical), radicals generally have a negative valence number—that is, they behave as though they were nonmetals.

Table 2–6. Radicals

Radical	Formula	Valence Number	Typical Compound	Formula
Ammonium	NH_4	+1	Ammonium chloride	NH_4Cl
Carbonate	CO_3	−2	Sodium carbonate	Na_2CO_3
Chlorate	ClO_3	−1	Sodium chlorate	$NaClO_3$
Hydroxide	OH	−1	Sodium hydroxide	$NaOH$
Nitrate	NO_3	−1	Sodium nitrate	$NaNO_3$
Sulfite	SO_3	−2	Sodium sulfite	Na_2SO_3
Sulfate	SO_4	−2	Sodium sulfate	Na_2SO_4
Phosphate	PO_4	−3	Sodium phosphate	Na_3PO_4

DIFFERENCES IN THE REACTIVITY OF METALS

So far, we have seen how a study of atomic structure can help us to determine the relative reactive properties of various elements. However, we have limited our study to elements that lie in the same row or same column of the Periodic Table. Let us now consider three metals that do not lie in the same row or column: magnesium, iron, and zinc.

As you observed in the laboratory experience, the reactions of these metals with hydrochloric acid reveal that magnesium reacts more vigorously than zinc, and zinc reacts more vigorously than iron. Since the reactivity of a metal represents the tendency of the metal to lose electrons, we know that magnesium loses electrons more readily than zinc, and zinc loses electrons more readily than iron. Since each of these metals has 2 electrons in its valence shell, the difference in reactivity is due largely to the differences in atomic radii. The atomic radius of magnesium is greater than the atomic radius of zinc, which, in turn, is greater than the atomic radius of iron (see the Periodic Table, pages 500–501).

Replacement Reactions

Experiments with solutions of compounds of magnesium, iron, and zinc reveal that the following reactions always take place when the pure metal is immersed in a compound of another metal:

(zinc) + (iron compound) → (iron) + (zinc compound)

(magnesium) + (zinc compound) → (zinc) + (magnesium compound)

In the first reaction, note that zinc (which is more reactive than iron) *replaces* iron; that is, the iron compound becomes a zinc compound. Similarly, in the second reaction, magnesium (which is more reactive than zinc) replaces zinc, and the zinc compound becomes a magnesium compound.

Other experiments, such as those in your laboratory experience with the nitrates, reveal that zinc replaces copper and silver from solutions of copper and silver compounds. Copper replaces silver from a solution of a silver compound, but copper does not replace zinc or iron from solutions of their compounds. In general, experiments reveal that the following reaction always takes place in water solution:

$$\left(\begin{array}{c} \text{more reactive} \\ \text{metal} \end{array} \right) + \left(\begin{array}{c} \text{compound of less} \\ \text{reactive metal} \end{array} \right) \rightarrow$$

$$\left(\begin{array}{c} \text{less reactive} \\ \text{metal} \end{array} \right) + \left(\begin{array}{c} \text{compound of more} \\ \text{reactive metal} \end{array} \right)$$

This type of reaction is called a *replacement reaction*. Note that the more reactive metal, in becoming a compound, loses electrons.

The Order of Reactivity of Metals

As the result of studying the preceding replacement reactions, we can arrange the metals in decreasing order of reactivity: magnesium (most reactive), zinc, iron, copper, silver (least reactive). This list is known as the *Reactivity Series of the Metals* and is shown, in part, in Table 2–7, page 38.

Note the presence of hydrogen on this list. Although hydrogen is not a metal, it has been placed on the list because it behaves as though it were a metal in certain reactions. Metals found above hydrogen will replace hydrogen in acids, while those metals below hydrogen will not replace the hydrogen in acids. Hydrogen is therefore used as a convenient reference point.

The reactivity series lists the different metals (and hydrogen) in

Table 2–7. The Reactivity Series (At 20°C)

Order of Reactivity	Metal	Symbol
Most reactive	Lithium	Li
	Potassium	K
	Barium	Ba
	Calcium	Ca
	Sodium	Na
	Magnesium	Mg
decreasing reactivity	Aluminum	Al
	Zinc	Zn
	Iron	Fe
	Tin	Sn
	Lead	Pb
	Hydrogen	H
	Copper	Cu
	Mercury	Hg
	Silver	Ag
	Platinum	Pt
Least reactive	Gold	Au

order of their decreasing tendencies to lose electrons in water solution. Since reactivity also depends upon temperature, the series is usually listed at a given temperature.

As we know, the tendency of a metal to lose electrons depends chiefly on the nuclear charge and on the atomic radius of the metal atom. The reactivity series may be used to make reasonable predictions concerning the reactivities of different metals. According to this table, for example, aluminum will replace mercury in a solution of a mercury compound. Silver will not replace tin from a solution of a tin compound. Remember, however, that these conclusions are *predictions*. To be completely sure of any reaction, it is necessary to carry out the reaction in the laboratory. From time to time, we may note exceptions from what we predict. The reasons for these exceptions will become more and more apparent as we continue to gain more knowledge in our study of chemistry.

Looking Back

Major factors that account for the reactivity of elements include valence number and atomic radius. The smaller the number of valence electrons transferred in a reaction, the greater, generally, is the reactivity of the elements involved. Metals with a larger atomic radius are generally more reactive than those with a smaller radius. Nonmetals with a smaller atomic radius are generally more reactive than those with a larger radius. Metals can be arranged in order according to their reactivity as is shown in the Reactivity Series of the Metals.

Looking Ahead

The large number of compounds in our environment is the result of the reactions of elements. Chemical formulas contain information about the elements making up the compounds. These formulas are the subject of Chapter 3.

Multiple-Choice Questions

1. When metals react chemically, they
   a. gain electrons   c. gain protons
   b. lose electrons   d. lose protons
2. When elements with four electrons in their outermost shell react chemically, they
   a. always gain 4 electrons
   b. always lose 4 electrons
   c. may lose, gain, or share 4 electrons
   d. may lose or gain 4 electrons
3. As we move from left to right across a period in the Periodic Table, metallic activity
   a. decreases   c. remains the same
   b. increases   d. increases then decreases
4. In the Periodic Table, the element that exhibits the strongest non-metallic properties is found
   a. on the upper left side   c. on the right side
   b. on the lower left side   d. in the middle
5. In the outermost electron shell of most metalloids, the number of electrons we find is
   a. 8   b. 4   c. 2   d. 6
6. In any group of metals in the Periodic Table, the most active metal in the group is found
   a. at the top
   b. in the middle
   c. at the bottom
   d. in different places depending on the group
7. Potassium is more active than sodium, and both metals are found in the same group. The atomic radius of potassium is
   a. larger than that of sodium   c. smaller than that of sodium
   b. the same as that of sodium   d. variable

8. The most active nonmetal in a group is found
   a. at the bottom
   b. at the top
   c. in the middle
   d. in different places depending on the group
9. The valence number of aluminum is +3. This means that, in a chemical reaction, aluminum may
   a. gain 5 electrons   c. give away 5 electrons
   b. gain 3 electrons   d. give away 3 electrons
10. As the size of an atom of a nonmetal decreases, electrons are
    a. lost more easily   c. attracted more easily
    b. lost with greater difficulty   d. attracted with greater difficulty
11. Of the following, the metal that exhibits more than one valence number is
    a. sodium   b. potassium   c. calcium   d. iron
12. Of the following nonmetals, the element that does not exhibit more than one valence number is
    a. chlorine   b. sulfur   c. carbon   d. nitrogen
13. In the compound FeO, iron has a valence number of
    a. −2   b. +2   c. +3   d. −3
14. The compound $FeCl_3$ is best named
    a. ferric chloride   c. iron chloride
    b. ferrous chloride   d. iron (II) chloride
15. When an iron nail is placed in a solution of copper sulfate,
    a. no reaction occurs   c. iron copper sulfate is formed
    b. iron (II) chloride is formed   d. the iron replaces the copper

Modified True-False Questions

1. Groups of atoms that behave as though they were single atoms are called *compounds.*
2. When copper is placed in a solution of zinc nitrate, *no reaction occurs.*
3. The carbonate radical is represented as $ClO_3{}^{-1}$.
4. A list of metals arranged according to their activity is called the *Periodic Table of the Elements.*
5. Metals that are higher in the activity series have *a lesser* tendency to lose electrons.
6. Elements that can behave either as metals or nonmetals in chemical reactions are called *mixtures.*
7. Metals that have fewer electrons in their valence shell require *less* energy when they react than metals with more valence electrons.
8. In nonmetals, as the distance of the valence electrons from the nucleus increases, the activity of the nonmetal *increases.*
9. The number of electrons lost, gained, or shared when an element reacts with other elements is given by the *atomic radius* of the element.
10. When a metal that can exhibit more than one valence number reacts with another element to form a compound with the higher valence number, the suffix *-ic* is added to the name of the metal.

Thought Questions

1. Give a scientific explanation for each of the following statements:
   a. Potassium is a more reactive metal than sodium.
   b. Sodium is a more reactive metal than magnesium.
   c. Fluorine is a more reactive nonmetal than chlorine.
   d. Chlorine is a more reactive nonmetal than sulfur.
   e. When zinc is placed in a solution of copper sulfate, the zinc replaces the copper.
2. The following reactions were performed to test the activity of iron, hydrogen, copper, silver, and lead. From the information given by these reactions, arrange the five elements in order of increasing activity.
   a. copper + hydrochloric acid → no reaction
   b. lead + hydrochloric acid → hydrogen + lead chloride
   c. iron + lead nitrate → lead + iron nitrate
   d. copper + silver nitrate → silver + copper nitrate
3. Explain why there is danger of an explosion when potassium metal is placed in water.
4. Give two ways of naming the compound, Fe_2O_3. Give a reason for each of the methods you used.
5. Complete the table.

Radical	Valence Number	Formula
Ammonium		
		CO_3
Chlorate		
		OH
Nitrate		
		SO_3
Sulfate		
Phosphate		

CHAPTER 3
WHAT DO CHEMICAL FORMULAS TELL US?

When you have completed this chapter, you should be able to:

1. *State* the information contained in a chemical formula.
2. *Describe* the steps involved in writing a chemical formula.
3. *Explain* the method of naming compounds.
4. *Determine* molecular weight from a chemical formula.
5. *Find* the percentage composition by weight of elements in a compound.

In the laboratory experience that follows, you will determine the percentage composition by weight of the elements in a common compound.

Laboratory Experience

HOW CAN WE FIND THE PERCENTAGE COMPOSITION BY WEIGHT OF AN ELEMENT IN A COMPOUND?

Copy the following table into your notebook.

1. Weight of beaker and test tubes	grams
2. Weight of beaker, test tubes, and manganese dioxide	grams
3. Weight of beaker, test tubes, manganese dioxide, and hydrogen peroxide	grams
4. Calculate weight of hydrogen peroxide (item 3 minus item 2)	grams
5. Weight of beaker, test tubes, and contents after the reaction	grams
6. Calculate weight of oxygen released during reaction (item 3 minus item 5)	grams

A. Place two 150-millimeter test tubes in a small beaker. Place the beaker on a balance. Record the weight of the beaker and test tubes in item 1 of the table.

B. Add 1 centimeter of manganese dioxide (MnO_2) to one of the test tubes. Weigh the beaker, test tubes, and manganese dioxide on the scale. Record the weight in item 2 of the table:

C. Add 2 centimeters of a 3% solution of hydrogen peroxide (H_2O_2) to the other test tube. Weigh the beaker, test tubes, manganese dioxide, and hydrogen peroxide on the scale. Record the weight in item 3 of the table.

D. Pour the hydrogen peroxide into the test tube containing the manganese dioxide. Place the emptied test tube back in the beaker.

E. After about 1 minute, hold a glowing splint near the mouth of the test tube containing the hydrogen peroxide and manganese dioxide.
  1. What happens to the glowing splint?
  2. What gas is at the mouth of the test tube? Explain.

F. After the bubbling has stopped, wait 1 minute and then weigh the beaker, test tubes, and contents. Record the weight in item 5 of the table.

G. From the table, determine the weight lost during the decomposition of the hydrogen peroxide. This equals the weight of the oxygen in the hydrogen peroxide.

(In this reaction, oxygen is not released from the manganese dioxide. The manganese dioxide is a *catalyst*; it merely hastens the release of the oxygen from the hydrogen peroxide.)

H. From the results of this experiment, find the percentage of oxygen in hydrogen peroxide, by weight, as follows:

$$\text{oxygen (in percent)} = \frac{\text{weight of oxygen released}}{\text{weight of hydrogen peroxide}} \times 100\%$$

  3. Suppose you were to repeat this experiment several times. Would you expect to get the same value for the percent of oxygen? Explain. (See pages 497–499 for use of significant figures.)

Introduction

The matter of our environment, whether living or nonliving, is composed of elements or compounds or both. You have already learned that when two or more elements unite chemically, they unite in definite proportions by weight and form a compound. Examples of compounds present within the living things of our environment are sugars, proteins, and vitamins. Examples of compounds present in the nonliving part of our environment are water, carbon dioxide, and table salt (sodium chloride).

The compounds characteristic of living things are generally very complex. These compounds consist of many more bonded (joined) atoms than the compounds characteristic of nonliving things. The formula for a particular compound tells us the composition, by weight, of the compound in much the same way that a recipe for a cake tells the ingredients in the cake. Now that you have studied valence numbers of elements and realize their importance in the reactivity of the elements, you will readily understand the chemical information represented in the chemical formula for a compound.

WHAT A CHEMICAL FORMULA MEANS

Each element is represented by a different chemical symbol. Each compound is represented by a different chemical formula. A formula contains the symbols of the elements present in the compound and numbers that indicate the number of atoms of each element present. We have seen some examples of formulas in the last chapter. Since a symbol of an atom represents a specific atomic weight, the formula reveals the weight composition of the compound.

The number of atoms, called *subscripts*, are written to the right of and below the symbol for each element in a formula. For example, the formula for one molecule of water is H_2O. This formula tells us that hydrogen (H) and oxygen (O) are present. It also tells us that 2 atoms of hydrogen are combined with 1 atom of oxygen (O_1 or O). This means that the weight composition of water is 2 atomic weights of hydrogen to 1 atomic weight of oxygen, or H:O = 2:16 (1:8).

Note that in the formula H_2O no subscript is shown near the symbol for oxygen. In such cases, it is understood that only one atom of the element is present. Similarly, the formula for sulfur dioxide is SO_2. This means that a molecule of sulfur dioxide contains 1 atom of sulfur and 2 atoms of oxygen.

Table 3–1 shows the formulas of some common compounds. Using a few of these simple compounds, let us review what a chemical formula tells us.

The formula for water, H_2O, indicates that a molecule of this compound is composed of 2 atoms of hydrogen and 1 atom of oxygen, a total of 3 atoms. The formula also indicates that this molecule consists of 2 atomic weights of hydrogen and 1 atomic weight of oxygen.

The formula for hydrogen peroxide, H_2O_2, indicates that a molecule of this substance is composed of 2 atoms of hydrogen and 2 atoms of

Table 3–1. Formulas of Some Common Compounds

Compound	Formula
Water	H_2O
Carbon dioxide	CO_2
Sodium chloride	NaCl
Hydrogen peroxide	H_2O_2
Sulfuric acid	H_2SO_4
Sodium hydroxide	NaOH
Alcohol (grain alcohol)	C_2H_5OH
Glucose (a sugar)	$C_6H_{12}O_6$

oxygen, a total of 4 atoms. The formula, H_2O_2, also reveals that the molecule is composed of 2 atomic weights of hydrogen and 2 atomic weights of oxygen.

The formula for sodium hydroxide, NaOH, indicates the presence of 1 atom (1 atomic weight) of sodium, 1 atom (1 atomic weight) of oxygen, and 1 atom (1 atomic weight) of hydrogen in a molecule of sodium hydroxide.

We shall return to the use of atomic weights in formulas later in this chapter.

HOW TO WRITE CHEMICAL FORMULAS

Recall that the number of atoms of each element in a compound is determined by the valence numbers, or the combining tendencies, of the atoms. Let us use this knowledge to write the formulas for a few compounds.

Let us start with the formula for the compound formed when aluminum and oxygen unite. This compound is called aluminum oxide.

Each aluminum atom must lose 3 electrons to combine chemically, whereas each oxygen atom must gain 2 electrons (Fig. 3–1, page 46). In order to form complete outermost (valence) shells for both atoms, 2 atoms of aluminum must combine with 3 atoms of oxygen. The 2 atoms of aluminum give up 6 electrons, which are accepted by the outermost shells of 3 atoms of oxygen. (Each atom attains the stable electron arrangement of neon.)

Thus, we see that the electron arrangement of the valence shells of the combining elements determines how many atoms of each are necessary for the atoms to combine to form one molecule of a compound. This knowledge enables us to write the formula for aluminum oxide as Al_2O_3.

Using electron arrangements for working out formulas is slow and cumbersome. If we know the valence number of each element, working

out correct formulas is quicker and easier. Table 2–4 on page 33 shows
that aluminum has a valence number of +3, whereas oxygen has a
valence number of −2. The +3 valence number indicates that aluminum loses 3 electrons when it combines chemically. The −2 valence
number of oxygen indicates that the oxygen atom gains 2 electrons
when it combines chemically.

To write the chemical formula for the compound formed by two
elements having different valence numbers, such as aluminum oxide,
proceed as follows:

1. Write the symbols for the elements present in the compound listing
   the element with the positive valence number first.

$$Al \qquad O$$

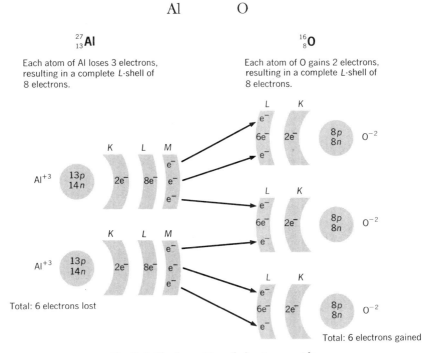

Fig. 3–1. The formation of aluminum oxide.

2. Above and to the right of each chemical symbol, place the valence
   number of the element. (This is called a *superscript*.)

$$Al^{+3} \qquad O^{-2}$$

3. To determine the correct subscripts for the formula, "crisscross" the
   valence numbers, but drop the sign.

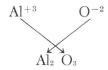

4. The final formula for aluminum oxide is:

$$Al_2O_3$$

To write the chemical formulas for compounds formed by two elements having the same valence numbers, follow the preceding four steps. However, if the valence numbers of both elements are 1, the subscript 1 need not be written in the final step. It is understood to be present.

Example: Write the formula for potassium chloride.

1. Write the symbols: K   Cl

2. Insert the valence numbers: $K^{+1}Cl^{-1}$

3. Crisscross the valence numbers
   and drop the signs: K_1Cl_1

4. Omit the subscript 1:   KCl

If the valence numbers of the elements are greater than 1 but still equal, the subscript 1 is also understood.

Example: Write the formula for magnesium oxide.

1. Write the symbols: Mg   O

2. Insert the valence numbers: $Mg^{+2}O^{-2}$

3. Crisscross the valence numbers
   and drop the signs: Mg_2O_2

4. Omit the equal subscripts: MgO

(In some cases, such as H_2O_2, it is necessary to retain the equal subscripts so that the structure of the compound may be better understood. In H_2O_2—and in other peroxides—the valence number of oxygen is -1.)

To write the chemical formula for a compound that contains a radical, follow the preceding four steps. However, treat the formula of the radical as if it were an element. Table 2–6 (page 36) gives the formulas and valence numbers of common radicals.

Example: Write the formula for calcium nitrate.

1. Write the symbols: Ca NO_3

2. Insert the valence numbers: $Ca^{+2}NO_3^{-1}$

3. Crisscross the valence numbers
and drop the signs: $Ca_1(NO_3)_2$
Note: If more than one unit of the radical is required, place parentheses around the radical before writing the subscript.

4. Omit the subscript 1: $Ca(NO_3)_2$

Table 3–2 gives several more examples.

Table 3–2. Using Valence Numbers to Write Formulas

Compound	Symbols and Valence Numbers	Formula
Sodium phosphate	$Na^{+1}\ PO_4^{-3}$	Na_3PO_4
Zinc nitrate	$Zn^{+2}\ NO_3^{-1}$	$Zn(NO_3)_2$
Aluminum sulfide	$Al^{+3}\ S^{-2}$	Al_2S_3
Ammonium nitrate	$NH_4^{+1}\ NO_3^{-1}$	NH_4NO_3
Aluminum hydroxide	$Al^{+3}\ OH^{-1}$	$Al(OH)_3$

NAMING COMPOUNDS

In Chapter 2, we indicated some general rules for naming the metallic elements in compounds of metals (see page 35). The nonmetallic elements in compounds are named as follows:

1. For compounds that contain only two elements, name the metal first, and then add the suffix -ide to the nonmetal.

Examples: NaCl   sodium chlor*ide*
CaO   calcium ox*ide*
K₂S   potassium sulf*ide*

2. For compounds containing three elements, such as a metal combined with a radical that behaves as a nonmetal, write the symbol of the metal first and the formula of the radical last. With the exception of hydroxides, compounds of more than two elements often have last names ending in the suffix -ite or -ate. Both suffixes indicate the presence of oxygen in the compound. The suffix -ite indicates a compound that generally has one fewer oxygen atom than the corresponding -ate compound.

Examples: NaNO₃   sodium nitr*ate*
NaNO₂   sodium nitr*ite*
Ca(OH)₂   calcium hydrox*ide*

3. For compounds containing two radicals, one of which acts as a metal and the other as a nonmetal, write the formulas for both radicals, placing the one that has the positive valence number first. Then follow the same procedure as in rule 2.

Examples: $(NH_4)_2SO_4$ ammonium sulf*ate*
          NH_4OH ammonium hydrox*ide*

4. Use the prefixes *mono-*, *di-*, and *tri-* to represent 1, 2, and 3 atoms of an element.

Examples: CO   carbon *mono*xide
          CO_2 carbon *di*oxide
          P_2O_3 *di*phosphorus *tri*oxide

HOW FORMULAS ARE USEFUL

You are now aware what chemical formulas reveal about compounds. Since formulas contain information about the weights and proportions of the elements in a compound, formulas are invaluable to chemists who try either to separate elements from compounds or to put elements together to form new substances.

Finding Molecular Weights

The sum of all the atomic weights in a molecule is called the *molecular weight*. Let us suppose we want to find the molecular weight of a compound. The formula for a compound tells us the elements in the compound and how many atoms of each element are present. We can consult a table of atomic weights or the Periodic Table for the atomic weight of each element. We will need to round off the atomic weights that are not whole numbers. With this information, we can readily calculate the molecular weight.

To calculate the molecular weight of a compound, such as water, first determine the number of atoms of each element present in the compound. Then consult the Periodic Table for the atomic weight of each element. For example, there are 2 hydrogen atoms and 1 oxygen atom present in one molecule of H_2O. The table shows that the atomic weight of hydrogen is 1, and that the atomic weight of oxygen is 16. Multiply the number of atoms of each element by the atomic weight of the element. Thus, 2 atoms of hydrogen have a total atomic weight of 2. One atom of oxygen has an atomic weight of 16. Adding the total atomic weights of the elements gives the molecular weight of the compound. Thus, the molecular weight of H_2O is $2 + 16$, or 18.

Table 3–3, page 50, provides examples for finding the molecular weights of more complex compounds.

Table 3–3. Determining Molecular Weights

Find the molecular weight of $CaCO_3$.

Element	Number of Atoms		Atomic Weight		Total Atomic Weight of Element
Ca	1	×	40	=	40
C	1	×	12	=	12
O	3	×	16	=	48
			molecular weight	=	100

Find the molecular weight of $(NH_4)_3PO_4$.

Element	Number of Atoms		Atomic Weight		Total Atomic Weight of Element
N	3	×	14	=	42
H	12	×	1	=	12
P	1	×	31	=	31
O	4	×	16	=	64
			molecular weight	=	149

Finding Percentage Composition by Weight

Knowledge of the molecular weight of a compound is especially valuable to the chemist who is concerned with extracting elements from compounds. For example, a chemist might be interested in knowing how many kilograms of a useful metal can be extracted from some given weight of a compound containing the metal combined with other elements. This information could be determined by carrying out time-consuming reactions and keeping careful records, as you did in your laboratory experience. By experimental means, you determined the *percentage composition* of a metal in a particular compound.

Percentage composition can be calculated directly, and much more rapidly, from the molecular weight of a compound. For example, to find out how many kilograms of copper can be obtained from 100 kilograms of copper (II) carbonate, you could follow these steps:

1. Use the formula $CuCO_3$ to determine the molecular weight of copper (II) carbonate.

Element	Number of Atoms		Atomic Weight		Total Atomic Weight of Element
Cu	1	×	63.5	=	63.5
C	1	×	12	=	12
O	3	×	16	=	48
			molecular weight	=	123.5

2. Determine the percentage composition of copper in copper (II) carbonate according to the following equation:

$$\% \text{ composition} = \frac{\text{total atomic weight of element}}{\text{molecular weight of compound}} \times 100$$

$$\% \text{ composition of Cu} = \frac{63.5}{123.5} \times 100 = 51.4\% = 51\%$$

Using this information, the chemist knows that approximately 51% of any amount of pure copper (II) carbonate is copper. Accordingly, we know that every 100 kilograms of copper (II) carbonate contains $100 \times \frac{51}{100} = 51$ kilograms of copper.

As another example, let us find the percentage composition by weight of each element in pure $CaCO_3$. First, determine the molecular weight of $CaCO_3$.

Element	Number of Atoms		Atomic Weight		Total Atomic Weight of Element
Ca	1	×	40	=	40
C	1	×	12	=	12
O	3	×	16	=	48
			molecular weight =		100

Then, find the percentage composition of each element from the formula

$$\% \text{ composition} = \frac{\text{total atomic weight of element}}{\text{molecular weight of compound}} \times 100$$

$$\% \text{ composition of Ca} = \frac{40}{100} \times 100 = 40\%$$

$$\% \text{ composition of C} = \frac{12}{100} \times 100 = 12\%$$

$$\% \text{ composition of O} = \frac{48}{100} \times 100 = 48\%$$

As a check, note that total = $\overline{100\%}$

Looking Back

Chemical formulas consist of symbols of elements with a subscript next to each element. The subscript indicates the number of atomic weights of the element. (If the subscript is 1, it is omitted.) A complete formula—symbols and subscripts—reveals the composition of a compound.

With the aid of formulas and the Periodic Table, we can calculate the molecular weight of a compound and the percentage composition by weight of each element in the compound.

Looking Ahead

Several different types of chemical reactions can take place when different elements or different compounds come into close contact. These types of reactions are described in the next chapter.

Multiple-Choice Questions

1. A chemical compound is represented by a
   a. symbol   b. equation   c. formula   d. none of these
2. To indicate the number of atoms of an element in a compound, we use
   a. a subscript to the right of the symbol
   b. a superscript to the right of the symbol
   c. a subscript to the left of the symbol
   d. a superscript to the left of the symbol
3. In the formula $(NH_4)_2SO_4$, the number of atoms of sulfur present is
   a. 1   b. 2   c. 4   d. 8
4. When using the "crisscross" method for writing formulas, the valence number of the nonmetal
   a. precedes the symbol for the metal
   b. follows the symbol for the metal
   c. follows the symbol for the nonmetal
   d. neither precedes nor follows the symbol for the metal
5. In writing a formula when the valence numbers of both the metal and nonmetal in a compound are 1,
   a. no number is written
   b. the numeral 1 is written after the metal only
   c. the numeral 1 is written after the nonmetal only
   d. the numeral 1 is written after the metal and nonmetal
6. When writing a chemical formula, the element with a positive valence number
   a. is written last   c. is written first
   b. needs no subscript   d. is placed in parentheses

7. The formula for the compound formed when Al^{+3} combines with S^{-2} is
   a. Al_3S_2 b. AlS c. AlS_3 d. Al_2S_3
8. The compound whose formula is ZnS is named
   a. zinc sulfate   b. zinc sulfite   c. zinc sulfide   d. zinc and sulfur
9. The compound whose formula is $Ca(OH)_2$ is named
   a. calcium oxygen hydride   c. carbon hydrogen oxide
   b. calcium hydroxide   d. calcium oxide
10. The compound, CO_2, is best named
    a. carbon oxide   c. carbon monoxide
    b. carbon dioxide   d. carbon trioxide
11. Chemical formulas give no information about the
    a. elements in the compound
    b. molecular weight of the compound
    c. chemical properties of the compound
    d. percentage composition of elements in the compound
12. The total number of atoms present in one molecule of $(NH_4)_2CO_3$ is
    a. 9   b. 10   c. 12   d. 14
13. The total atomic weight of an element in a compound is 12. The molecular weight of the compound is 100. The percentage composition of the element in the compound is
    a. 12%   b. 88%   c. 0.12%   d. 1.2%
14. The formula H_2O_2 represents the compound
    a. water   c. hydrogen monoxide
    b. hydrogen peroxide   d. hydrogen dioxide

Modified True-False Questions

1. The number of atoms of each element in a compound is determined by the *atomic weight* of the elements.
2. The valence number of an element in a given compound is *fixed*.
3. A negative valence number indicates that an element *donates* electrons when it combines.
4. To determine the correct subscripts for the elements in a compound, we "*crisscross*" the valence numbers.
5. In writing a chemical formula, if a radical is to be taken more than once, we separate the radical from the subscript by using *a comma*.
6. In general, compounds composed of more than two elements have last names ending in *-ide*.
7. In naming a compound, the element with a positive valence number is named *last*.
8. The weight of one molecule of a substance is known as the *atomic weight*.
9. The relative proportion by weight of an element in a compound can be found by determining the *percentage composition*.
10. To find the percentage composition, we must first determine the *molecular weight* of the compound.

Thought Questions

1. Complete the table by writing the formulas for the compounds formed by each combination of elements.

	O^{-2}	Cl^{-1}	S^{-2}	I^{-1}	N^{-3}
Na^{+1}					
Ca^{+2}					
Mg^{+2}					
Zn^{+2}					
Al^{+3}					

2. Name the compounds represented by the following formulas:
   a. $AlCl_3$ b. Na_2O c. $(NH_4)_2SO_4$ d. $Ca(NO_3)_2$ e. KOH
3. Write chemical formulas for each of the following pairs. Then write the name of the compound formed when the elements or radicals combine.
   a. Na^{+1}, PO_4^{-3} c. Al^{+3}, CO_3^{-2} e. K^{+1}, ClO_3^{-1}
   b. Ca^{+2}, SO_4^{-2} d. Zn^{+2}, NO_3^{-1}
4. Find the molecular weight of each of the following compounds:
   a. Na_2O b. $(NH_4)_2CO_3$ c. $Zn(NO_3)_2$
5. a. Find the percentage composition of iron in Fe_2O_3.
   b. How many kilograms of iron can be obtained from 100 kilograms of this compound?
   c. How many kilograms of iron can be obtained from one metric ton of the compound?

CHAPTER 4

WHAT ARE SOME TYPES
OF CHEMICAL REACTIONS?

When you have completed this chapter, you should be able to:

1. *Explain* and illustrate the law of conservation of matter.
2. *Relate* the law of conservation of matter to chemical equations.
3. *State* the rules for writing a chemical equation.
4. *Distinguish* between (*a*) direct combination and decomposition (*b*) single and double replacement reactions.

In the laboratory experience that follows, you will test the law of conservation of matter as it applies to one type of chemical reaction.

Laboratory Experience

DOES MATTER DISAPPEAR IN A CHEMICAL REACTION?

CAUTION: Silver nitrate will stain your clothes and skin. Be careful not to spill the solid or the solution.

A. Cover the pan of a balance with a small piece of clean paper (filter paper will do). Weigh out about 0.5 gram of silver nitrate ($AgNO_3$).

Transfer the silver nitrate to a 100-millimeter test tube half-filled with distilled water. Gently shake the test tube until all of the silver nitrate dissolves.

B. Weigh out 1 gram of sodium chloride ($NaCl$) as in part A.

Transfer the sodium chloride to a 250-cubic-centimeter Erlenmeyer flask. Add 25 cubic centimeters of water to the flask, and shake the flask until the salt dissolves.

C. Carefully lower the test tube containing the silver nitrate solution into the Erlenmeyer flask, as shown in Fig. 4–1, page 56. The solutions should not mix with each other. Stopper the flask.

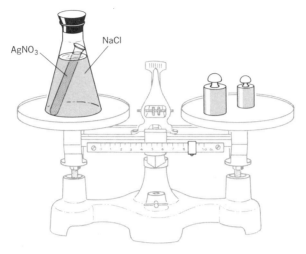

Fig. 4–1.

   1. Describe the appearance of the solutions.
D. Place the apparatus prepared in part C on the balance and weigh it.
   2. What is the weight of the Erlenmeyer flask and its contents?
E. Carefully tip the Erlenmeyer flask until all of the silver nitrate solution runs out of the test tube and mixes with the salt solution in the flask.
   3. What do you observe?
   4. How do you account for what you see?
F. Reweigh the Erlenmeyer flask and its contents on the balance.
   5. What is the weight of the Erlenmeyer flask?
   6. How does this weight compare with the weight obtained in part D?
   7. From the data obtained in this experiment, what can you conclude about the weight of the products of a reaction (that is, the new substances that are formed) compared to the weight of the reactants (that is, the substances you started with)?
   8. If you repeated this experiment using different quantities of silver nitrate, sodium chloride, and water, how would the results be affected?

Introduction

All the matter in the earth consists of elements and compounds. Some elements and compounds have been part of the earth since the earth came into existence. Others were formed as a result of natural chemical reactions that took place afterward. After humans appeared on earth, they began to use natural elements and compounds to make tools, weapons, and other objects and, in the process, developed the science of chemistry. Since then, we have learned much about why elements and compounds react. As a result, we have been able to create many substances that do not exist naturally. Among such substances are steel, nylon, plastics, and synthetic rubber. We can better understand how such substances are made by learning more about chemical reactions.

MATTER MAY CHANGE BUT CANNOT BE DESTROYED

When a photographer puts a flash bulb into his camera and takes a picture, it is apparent that the bulb undergoes a chemical change. We see the flash of light; the bulb feels hot to the touch; the flash bulb looks different. The unused bulb had a metallic filament inside a clear glass bulb, but now the filament is gone, and the bulb is blackened and cloudy.

If we weigh a flash bulb before and after it is used, however, we find that the weight is unchanged (Fig. 4–2, page 58). This would seem to indicate that no matter was used up or destroyed by the chemical change. The laboratory experience, in which solutions of silver nitrate and sodium chloride reacted with each other, also indicated that matter was changed but not consumed.

The study of most types of chemical reactions leads to this observation: Although matter may change its form, or state, matter cannot be created or destroyed. This statement, called the *law of conservation of matter*, was first suggested by the French chemist, *Antoine Lavoisier*, in the eighteenth century. Lavoisier heated mercury (II) oxide for several days in a sealed glass vessel. Although the compound changed color, indicating a chemical change, the sealed tube showed no change in weight. We can more readily understand this law by studying some chemical equations that represent various reactions.

CHEMICAL EQUATIONS

Just as a chemical formula is used to represent a compound, a *chemical equation* is used to represent a chemical reaction. An equation shows the reacting substances (*reactants*) as well as the substances produced (*products*) as a result of the reaction. We write equations to describe reactions that occur in the laboratory or in nature.

The reaction that takes place when a solution of silver nitrate is added to a sodium chloride solution, as you did in your laboratory experience, can be represented by the following word equation:

sodium chloride + silver nitrate → silver chloride + sodium nitrate

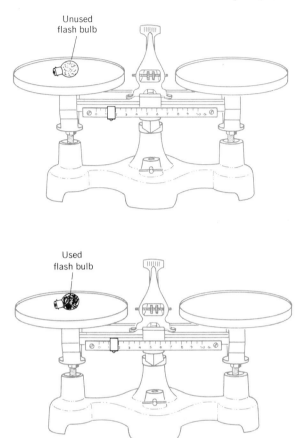

Fig. 4–2. Conservation of matter when a flash bulb burns.

We can also use symbols and formulas in an equation for the same reaction:

$$NaCl\ (aq) + AgNO_3\ (aq) \rightarrow AgCl\ (s) + NaNO_3\ (aq)$$

The plus sign indicates that one substance is added to the other. The horizontal arrow means "yields" or "forms." The term (aq) represents the word *aqueous* and tells us that we are dealing with water solutions. The term (s) represents the word *solid* and tells us that silver chloride does not dissolve appreciably in water. Thus, it *precipitates* (separates) from the solution as a solid. In the laboratory experience, the milky white substance that formed in the flask (silver chloride) is an example of a precipitate.

The term (g), when used in an equation, stands for the word *gas* and represents a gaseous reactant or product in a reaction. This is shown in the following equation in which oxygen gas is released:

$$\text{potassium chlorate} \xrightarrow{\triangle} \text{potassium chloride} + \text{oxygen}$$

$$2 \text{ KClO}_3 \ (s) \quad \xrightarrow{\triangle} \quad 2 \text{ KCl} \ (s) \quad + 3 \text{ O}_2 \ (g)$$

The meaning of the numbers in front of the formulas will be discussed later. The small triangle ("delta" symbol) above the horizontal arrow indicates that heat is used to start the reaction.

CHEMICAL EQUATIONS AND
THE LAW OF CONSERVATION OF MATTER

We recall that, when silver nitrate and sodium chloride solutions are mixed, a chemical reaction occurs that produces new substances. However, when we weighed the substances before and after the reaction, we found that no weight change had occurred. Similar results have been obtained from a study of many other reactions. Such results indicate that, during a chemical reaction, atoms are neither created nor destroyed —that is, atoms are conserved.

Thus, in a reaction, if we begin with 10 atoms of sodium and 10 of chlorine, we end up with 10 atoms of sodium and 10 of chlorine. These atoms, however, may be rearranged and joined (bonded) to other atoms, forming new molecules different from those present at the beginning of the reaction.

Let us now use the chemical equation

$$\text{NaCl} \ (aq) + \text{AgNO}_3 \ (aq) \rightarrow \text{AgCl} \ (s) + \text{NaNO}_3 \ (aq)$$

to illustrate the law of conservation of matter. Stated in another way, the law tells us that the total weight of the reactants in a chemical change equals the total weight of the products. Therefore, let us calculate the molecular weights of the reactants and then calculate the molecular weights of the products.

As we already know, the molecular weight of a compound is found by adding the atomic weights of the atoms in the compound. We find these atomic weights by consulting the Periodic Table (pages 500–501).

In this case, the molecular weight of the silver nitrate (AgNO_3) is determined by adding together the atomic weights of one atom of silver (108), one atom of nitrogen (14), and three atoms of oxygen ($3 \times 16 = 48$). Thus, the molecular weight of AgNO_3 is found to be $108 + 14 + 48 = 170$. The molecular weights of each of the other compounds in the equation are found in a similar manner. To simplify the calculations, we use 35 as the atomic weight of chlorine.

$$\text{molecular weight of NaCl} = 23 + 35 = 58$$

molecular weight of $AgCl = 108 + 35 = 143$

molecular weight of $NaNO_3 = 23 + 14 + (3 \times 16) = 85$

Let us indicate the molecular weight of each substance in the chemical equation and then deti rmine the total molecular weights of the reactants and the products:

	Reactants				Products		
	sodium chloride (*aq*)	+	silver nitrate (*aq*)	→	silver chloride (*aq*)	+	sodium nitrate (*aq*)
molecular weights:	58		170		143		85
total molecular weight:		228				228	

Notice that the total weight of the reactants is, in fact, equal to the total weight of the products. This can only be possible if the numbers of atoms of each of the elements are the same on both sides of the equation. Since the law of conservation of matter governs all chemical reactions, we will use the relation

$$\left(\begin{array}{c} \text{total molecular weight} \\ \text{of reactants} \end{array} \right) = \left(\begin{array}{c} \text{total molecular weight} \\ \text{of products} \end{array} \right)$$

to write the chemical equation for any reaction.

Writing Equations for Chemical Reactions

The following rules will help us write chemical equations for most reactions:

1. We must know the proper reactants and products. This may require performing the experiment in the laboratory.

2. Write the word equation. That is, write the names of the reactants on the left side of the horizontal arrow, and those of the products on the right side of the arrow. Be sure to include the state: (g), (l), (s), or (aq). For example, if we know that aluminum metal, when heated, reacts with oxygen gas to form aluminum oxide, we would write the reaction as follows:

$$\text{aluminum } (s) + \text{oxygen } (g) \xrightarrow{\triangle} \text{aluminum oxide } (s)$$

3. Write the symbols and formulas for the products and the reactants

under each substance. Keep in mind that the formulas for compounds are determined by crisscrossing the valence numbers of the elements in them (see pages 46–47). For example, the formula for aluminum oxide is found by writing $Al^{+3}O^{-2}$ which, when the valence numbers are crisscrossed, gives Al_2O_3.

In the case of gaseous elements, it has been found that one molecule of some gases may consist of more than one atom. For example, each molecule of oxygen, hydrogen, and nitrogen consists of 2 atoms. Accordingly, a molecule of oxygen is represented as O_2, of hydrogen as H_2, and of nitrogen as N_2. Now, we can write proper symbols and formulas under the word equation thus:

$$\text{aluminum } (s) + \text{oxygen } (g) \xrightarrow{\triangle} \text{aluminum oxide } (s)$$

$$Al\ (s) \quad + \quad O_2\ (g) \quad \xrightarrow{\triangle} \quad Al_2O_3\ (s)$$

(In the discussions that follow, we are omitting the states of the reactants and products in reactions that are familiar to you.)

4. Examining the equation reveals that there is 1 atom of aluminum on the left side of the equation and 2 atoms of aluminum on the right. Also, there are 2 atoms of oxygen on the left side, and 3 atoms of oxygen on the right. Remember that each atom represents a specific weight—the relative atomic weight. It appears as though matter has been created. According to the law of conservation of matter, this is impossible.

To satisfy the law of conservation of matter, and to write an equation that is correct, we must now *balance the equation*. When this is done, the same number of atoms of each element will appear on both sides of the equation.

Balancing a Chemical Equation

To balance an equation, use the following steps as a guide:

1. *Balance the nonmetallic elements.* In the equation

$$Al + O_2 \xrightarrow{\triangle} Al_2O_3$$

there are 2 atoms of oxygen on the left side of the arrow and 3 atoms of oxygen on the right side. To balance the atoms of oxygen, we must multiply the number of oxygen atoms on each side of the arrow by numbers that will make the numbers of oxygen atoms on both sides equal. If we multiply the oxygen on the left side of the equation by 3 and the oxygen on the right side of the equation by 2, this results in 6 atoms of oxygen on each side. (Note: Mathematically, it is also possible to multiply the oxygen on the left by $1\frac{1}{2}$, resulting in 3 atoms of oxygen on each side of the equation.)

These multipliers are called *coefficients*. Each coefficient refers only to the atoms in a particular molecule. Place each coefficient in front of the molecule that is being multiplied. In this case, write the number 3 in front of the O_2 and the number 2 in front of the Al_2O_3. The equation now becomes

$$Al + 3\,O_2 \xrightarrow{\triangle} 2\,Al_2O_3$$

When no coefficient is shown, it is understood that the coefficient is 1.

Coefficients must never be placed within the formula of a compound, because doing so would change the composition of the compound itself. Thus, we write

$$2\,Al_2\,O_3 \text{ and } not\ Al_2\,2\,O_3.$$

2. *Balance the metallic elements.* Note that the left side of the equation now shows 1 atom of aluminum, whereas the right side now shows 2 Al_2, or 4 atoms of aluminum. Balance the metallic atoms by multiplying the aluminum on the left side by the coefficient 4, thus:

$$4\,Al + 3\,O_2 \xrightarrow{\triangle} 2\,Al_2O_3$$

3. *Check the numbers of atoms on both sides of the equation.* Count the number of atoms of each element on each side of the arrow. Begin with the first reactant on the left side of the arrow. The 4 Al means 4 atoms (4 atomic weights) of aluminum. Notice that now there are also 4 atoms of aluminum on the right side of the arrow, since 2 Al_2 equals 4 atoms. Go on to the next reactant on the left side of the arrow. Note that there are 6 atoms (6 atomic weights) of oxygen or 3 molecules of O_2 reacting with aluminum. Since 2 is the coefficient of the Al_2O_3 on the right side of the arrow, 6 atoms of oxygen are also present on this side. Checking this equation shows that it is now correctly balanced because atoms have been conserved.

4. *Never alter the subscripts within a formula to balance an equation.* Altering the subscripts changes the formula which, in effect, changes the composition of the substance. Thus, if we wrote the formula for aluminum oxide as AlO_2, the equation would not require coefficients to be balanced. But according to the valence numbers, the correct formula for aluminum oxide is Al_2O_3.

5. *Confirm the conservation of matter.* Before the equation was balanced, we noted that the weights of the reactants were not equal to the weights of the products.

	Reactants	Products
Unbalanced equation:	Al + O_2	$\rightarrow Al_2O_3$
Atomic weights:	$(1 \times 27) + (2 \times 16)$	$= 1 \times 102$
Molecular weights:	27 + 32	$= 102$
Total molecular weights:	59	$\neq 102$

Now that the equation is balanced, we can see that this condition has been corrected.

	Reactants	Products
Balanced equation:	$4\,Al$ + $3\,O_2$	$\rightarrow 2\,Al_2O_3$
Atomic weights:	$(4 \times 27) + (6 \times 16)$	$= 2 \times 102$
Molecular weights:	108 + 96	$= 204$
Total molecular weights:	204	$= 204$

Balancing Another Chemical Equation

Write and balance the chemical equation for the combination of hydrogen and oxygen to form water.

$$\text{hydrogen} + \text{oxygen} \rightarrow \text{water}$$
$$H_2 + O_2 \rightarrow H_2O$$

1. Balance the nonmetallic elements.

$$H_2 + O_2 \rightarrow 2\,H_2O$$

Both sides of the equation now contain 2 atoms of oxygen.

2. Balance the metallic elements.

$$2\,H_2 + O_2 \rightarrow 2\,H_2O$$

Both sides of the equation now contain 4 atoms of hydrogen.

3. Check the number of atoms of each element on both sides of the equation.

$$2\,H_2 + O_2 \rightarrow 2\,H_2O$$

Number of atoms	Left side	Right side
Hydrogen	4	4
Oxygen	2	2

Note that the total molecular weight on the left side of the equation is

$$(4 \times 1) + (2 \times 16) = 4 + 32 = 36$$

and the total molecular weight on the right side is

$$(4 \times 1) + (2 \times 16) = 4 + 32 = 36$$

We see that, in a balanced equation, the total molecular weights of the reactants equal the total molecular weights of the products. Although the substances in the reaction may have changed their form, the total amount of matter present is still the same.

TYPES OF CHEMICAL REACTIONS

In general, there are four types of chemical reactions: *direct combination, decomposition, single replacement,* and *double replacement.*

Direct Combination (Synthesis)

A reaction in which two or more elements form a compound is called a direct combination reaction, or *synthesis* (Fig. 4–3).

Fig. 4–3. Synthesis.

Examples of direct combination reactions that have already been mentioned are:

$$2 H_2 (g) \quad + \quad O_2 (g) \quad \longrightarrow \quad 2 H_2O (l)$$
hydrogen   oxygen   water

(*Note:* The (*l*) after H_2O indicates the liquid state.)

$$4 Al (s) \quad + \quad 3 O_2 (g) \quad \longrightarrow \quad 2 Al_2O_3 (s)$$
aluminum   oxygen   aluminum
                                          oxide

$$Ca (s) \quad + \quad Cl_2 (g) \quad \longrightarrow \quad CaCl_2 (s)$$
calcium   chlorine   calcium
                                          chloride

Notice that, in each of these reactions, a compound is formed from elements. Such a reaction may be represented by the following general equation:

$$A + B \rightarrow AB$$

A and B are elements, and AB is a compound.

Decomposition (Analysis)

A reaction in which a compound is broken down into two or more elements is called a decomposition reaction or *analysis* (Fig. 4–4). Such reactions are generally the opposite of synthesis reactions.

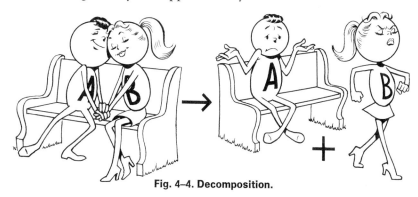

Fig. 4–4. Decomposition.

Examples of decomposition reactions are:

$$2\,HgO\,(s) \longrightarrow 2\,Hg\,(l) \quad + \quad O_2\,(g)$$
mercuric oxide — mercury — oxygen

$$2\,H_2O\,(l) \longrightarrow 2\,H_2\,(g) \quad + \quad O_2\,(g)$$
water — hydrogen — oxygen

$$2\,KClO_3\,(s) \longrightarrow 2\,KCl\,(s) \quad + \quad 3\,O_2\,(g)$$
potassium chlorate — potassium chloride — oxygen

(In the last example, we have a more complicated type of decomposition—a complex compound breaking down into simpler substances.)

Following is the general equation for a decomposition reaction:

$$AB \rightarrow A + B$$

Note that the compound AB breaks down to form elements, A and B. (In the last example above, compound ABC breaks down to form compound AB and element C: ABC → AB + C.)

Single Replacement

In Chapter 2, we noted that an element in a compound can be replaced by another element (see page 37). A reaction in which one element reacts with one compound to form another element and another compound is called a single replacement reaction (Fig. 4–5).

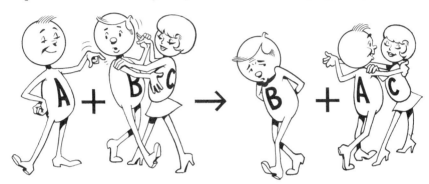

Fig. 4–5. Single replacement.

Examples of single replacement reactions that have been mentioned earlier are:

$$Zn\,(s) + Cu(NO_3)_2\,(aq) \longrightarrow Cu\,(s) + Zn(NO_3)_2\,(aq)$$
zinc   copper (II)   copper   zinc nitrate
nitrate

$$Cu\,(s) + 2\,AgNO_3\,(aq) \longrightarrow 2\,Ag\,(s) + Cu(NO_3)_2\,(aq)$$
copper   silver   silver   copper (II)
nitrate   nitrate

$$Mg\,(s) + 2\,HCl\,(aq) \longrightarrow H_2\,(g) + MgCl_2\,(aq)$$
magnesium   hydrochloric   hydrogen   magnesium
acid   chloride

As our study of the reactivity series of the metals showed, single replacement reactions occur when a free metal is more reactive than a metal combined in a compound (see pages 37–38).

In the examples cited, one metal replaced another in its compound. More reactive nonmetals may also replace less reactive nonmetals in compounds.

$$Cl_2\,(g) + 2KBr\,(aq) \rightarrow Br_2\,(aq) + 2KCl\,(aq)$$

Following is the general equation for a single replacement reaction:

$$A + BC \longrightarrow B + AC$$
element₁   compound₁   element₂   compound₂

Observe that the elements A and B have merely changed places, so that

B is now uncombined and A has combined with C to form the new compound AC.

Double Replacement

A reaction in which the metals present in two compounds change places to form two new compounds is called a double replacement reaction (Fig. 4–6). The chemical reaction between solutions of sodium chloride and silver nitrate is an example of a double replacement reaction:

$$AgNO_3 \ (aq) + NaCl \ (aq) \rightarrow AgCl \ (s) + NaNO_3 \ (aq)$$

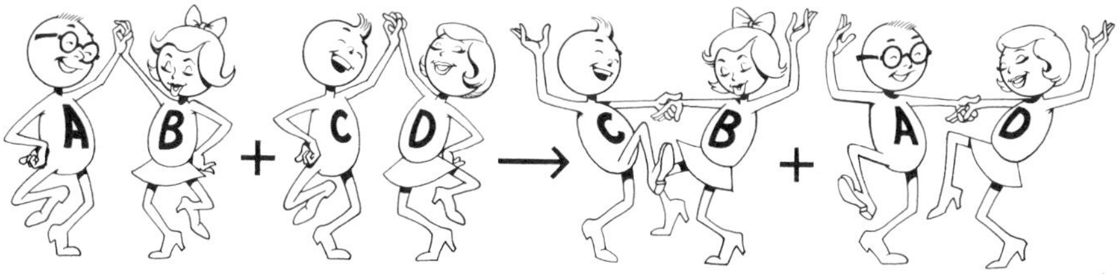

Fig. 4–6. Double replacement.

Note that the elements silver and sodium have exchanged places to form the new compounds, silver chloride and sodium nitrate. Other examples of double replacement reactions are:

$$\underset{\substack{\text{sodium} \\ \text{hydroxide}}}{NaOH \ (aq)} + \underset{\substack{\text{hydrochloric} \\ \text{acid}}}{HCl \ (aq)} \longrightarrow \underset{\substack{\text{sodium} \\ \text{chloride}}}{NaCl \ (aq)} + \underset{\text{water}}{H_2O \ (l)}$$

$$\underset{\substack{\text{barium} \\ \text{nitrate}}}{Ba(NO_3)_2 \ (aq)} + \underset{\substack{\text{sodium} \\ \text{sulfate}}}{Na_2SO_4 \ (aq)} \longrightarrow \underset{\substack{\text{barium} \\ \text{sulfate}}}{BaSO_4 \ (s)} + \underset{\substack{\text{sodium} \\ \text{nitrate}}}{2 \ NaNO_3 \ (aq)}$$

The general equation that represents this type of reaction is

$$AB + CD \rightarrow CB + AD$$

In this case, the elements A and C exchange places to form the new compounds AD and CB.

Looking Back

The law of conservation of matter is readily observable in correctly balanced chemical equations. The study of an equation can reveal whether the type of reaction that has taken place is a direct combination, a decomposition, or a replacement reaction.

Looking Ahead

Upon being mixed, some substances react and form new matter. Other substances on mixing, however, may form either solutions or suspensions. Solutions are the subject of Chapter 5, and suspensions are the subject of Chapter 6.

Multiple-Choice Questions

1. The law of conservation of matter was first suggested by
   a. Dalton   b. Lavoisier   c. Democritus   d. Rutherford
2. Of the following, the one used to represent a chemical reaction is
   a. an atom   b. a formula   c. an equation   d. a symbol
3. A chemical equation describes
   a. only the reactants
   b. only the products
   c. neither the reactants nor the products
   d. both the reactants and the products
4. Of the following, a chemical equation does *not* tell us
   a. the rate of the reaction
   b. the formulas for the reactants
   c. when heat is used in the reaction
   d. when a gas is formed
5. We can represent a water solution in a chemical equation by the symbol
   a. (s) b. (g) c. (aq) d. (Δ)
6. In a chemical equation, a small triangle found above the horizontal arrow tells us that
   a. a gas is produced   c. a liquid is formed
   b. a precipitate is produced   d. heat is used
7. In a chemical reaction,
   a. atoms may be rearranged   c. atoms may be created
   b. atoms may be destroyed   d. all atoms become molecules
8. In a chemical reaction, the total weight of the reactants
   a. is greater than the total weight of the products
   b. is equal to the total weight of the products
   c. is less than the total weight of the products
   d. cannot be determined
9. To satisfy the law of conservation of matter, an equation
   a. must first be written in words
   b. should show the atomic weights of the reactants and products
   c. must be balanced
   d. must indicate the physical state of each of the reactants and products
10. To balance an equation, we use
    a. exponents   b. subscripts   c. superscripts   d. coefficients
11. The number of atoms of oxygen present in $2 \text{ Al}(NO_3)_3$ is
    a. 6   b. 8   c. 9   d. 18

12. In a synthesis reaction,
    a. two metals change places
    b. two or more elements form a single compound
    c. a compound is broken down
    d. heat energy is not released
13. When iron is placed into copper sulfate solution,
    a. no reaction occurs   c. sulfur is released
    b. copper is released   d. copper becomes coated with iron

Modified True-False Questions

1. In a synthesis reaction, the substance produced is usually *simpler* than the reactants.
2. In the reaction, AB → A + B, AB represents *an element.*
3. In a single replacement reaction, one *nonmetal* may replace another.
4. A single replacement reaction takes place when a free metal is *more* reactive than a metal combined in a compound.
5. In the reaction

$$AgNO_3 \, (aq) + NaCl \, (aq) \rightarrow AgCl \, (s) + NaNO_3 \, (aq)$$

AgCl (s) is *soluble.*
6. In a reaction, atoms are always *conserved.*
7. In a chemical reaction, the total weight of the reactants is *greater than* the total weight of the products.
8. In a chemical equation, the reactants are written on the *right* side of the horizontal arrow.
9. The term 3 Al_2O_3 represents 3 *atoms* of aluminum oxide.
10. When a chemical equation is balanced, the total numbers of atoms of each element on both sides of the equation are *equal.*

Matching Questions

Column A	Column B
1. decomposition reaction	a. A + B → AB
2. single replacement reaction	b. AB → A + B
3. synthesis reaction	c. A + BC → B + AC
4. double replacement reaction	d. AB + CD → AD + CB
	e. A + BC → C + AB

Thought Questions

1. Explain the differences between each of the following pairs:
    a. formula and equation
    b. synthesis and decomposition reactions
    c. single replacement and double replacement reactions
    d. the terms (s) and (g) written in a chemical equation
    e. subscript and coefficient

2. Identify the type of chemical reaction shown in each of the following:
   a. $AgNO_3 (aq) + NaCl (aq) \rightarrow AgCl (s) + NaNO_3 (aq)$
   b. $Zn (s) + 2 HCl (aq) \rightarrow H_2 (g) + ZnCl_2 (aq)$
   c. $2 HgO (s) \rightarrow 2 Hg (l) + O_2 (g)$
   d. $2 H_2 (g) + O_2 (g) \rightarrow 2 H_2O (l)$
   e. $Fe (s) + CuSO_4 (aq) \rightarrow Cu (s) + FeSO_4 (aq)$

3. Complete each of the following word equations:
   a. barium nitrate + sodium sulfate $\rightarrow$
   b. magnesium + hydrochloric acid $\rightarrow$
   c. zinc + copper nitrate $\rightarrow$
   d. magnesium + oxygen $\rightarrow$
   e. sodium hydroxide + hydrochloric acid $\rightarrow$

4. Prove mathematically that each of the following equations satisfies the law of conservation of matter:
   a. $Cu + 2 AgNO_3 \rightarrow 2 Ag + Cu(NO_3)_2$
   b. $2 KClO_3 \rightarrow 2 KCl + 3 O_2$

5. Balance each of the following equations:
   a. $H_2O_2 (l) \rightarrow H_2 (g) + O_2 (g)$
   b. $Al (s) + HCl (aq) \rightarrow H_2 (g) + AlCl_3 (aq)$
   c. $BaCl_2 (aq) + Na_3PO_4 (aq) \rightarrow Ba_3(PO_4)_2 (s) + NaCl (aq)$
   d. $Fe (s) + O_2 (g) \rightarrow Fe_2O_3 (s)$
   e. $Mg (s) + HCl (aq) \rightarrow H_2 (g) + MgCl_2 (aq)$

CHAPTER 5
WHAT ARE THE CHARACTERISTICS OF SOLUTIONS?

When you have completed this chapter, you should be able to:

1. *Define* mixture, solution, solvent, distillation, and evaporation.
2. *State* the characteristics of a solution.
3. *Discuss* (*a*) the factors that determine the quantity of a solute that can dissolve (*b*) the factors that determine the rate of dissolving of the solute.
4. *Distinguish* between (*a*) dilute and concentrated solutions (*b*) saturated and unsaturated solutions.
5. *Predict* the solubility of a substance with the aid of a solubility curve.
6. *Explain* why some kinds of matter undergo spontaneous changes such as dissolving.
7. *Describe* some common methods of separating the components of a solution.
8. *Appreciate* the problems involved in removing polluting solutes from solutions.

In the laboratory experience that follows, you will investigate some of the factors involved in increasing the rate of dissolving.

Laboratory Experience

WHAT CONDITIONS INCREASE THE RATE OF DISSOLVING?

CAUTION: Be careful not to spill a solution of potassium permanganate; it may stain your clothes permanently.

A. Using a spatula or a spoon, place a very tiny crystal of potassium permanganate ($KMnO_4$) in a 150-millimeter test tube containing 5 cubic centimeters of water. Stopper the tube, and shake carefully. Hold it up to the light.

    1. What happens to the crystal?
    2. What is the color of the mixture of potassium permanganate and water?
    3. How does the color of the mixture compare with the color of the crystal?

B. Using a glass rod, place a drop of the potassium permanganate solution on a clean microscope slide. Examine the drop with a magnifying glass.
    4. Do you see any crystals? Explain.
    5. What do you conclude regarding the size of solid particles in this mixture?

C. Divide the contents of the test tube into two *equal* parts. Compare the colors of the two parts.
    6. What do the colors of the two parts of the mixture suggest to you?
    7. State the characteristics of a mixture of potassium permanganate and water.
    8. What is such a mixture called?

D. Copy the following table into your notebook. Then weigh out four samples of copper (II) sulfate crystals. Each sample should weigh about 2 grams.

Beaker	Treatment of Copper Sulfate	Starting Time	Ending Time	Time Necessary to Dissolve Completely
1	None			
2	Ground			
3	Ground and stirred			
4	Ground, stirred, heated			

Grind *three* of the samples with a mortar and pestle. Keep all the samples separate.

Number four 250-cubic-centimeter beakers from 1 through 4 with a grease pencil. Place the unground crystals in beaker 1. Place the ground crystals in beakers 2, 3, and 4. In the following experiment, use the table to record the length of time it takes each sample to dissolve. (Use the second hand of a wristwatch to measure the time.)

    Beaker 1: Add 100 cubic centimeters of water. Allow the mixture to stand undisturbed.

Beaker 2: Add 100 cubic centimeters of water. Allow the mixture to stand undisturbed.

Beaker 3: Add 100 cubic centimeters of water. Stir the mixture with a glass rod.

Beaker 4: Add 100 cubic centimeters of water. Heat the mixture over an alcohol lamp, stirring the mixture as it heats.

9. Comparing beakers 1 and 2, how does grinding the crystals affect the rate at which the copper (II) sulfate dissolves?
10. Comparing beakers 2 and 3, how does stirring affect the rate at which the copper (II) sulfate dissolves?
11. Comparing beakers 3 and 4, how does heating affect the rate at which the copper (II) sulfate dissolves?
12. In order to dissolve a lump of sugar as fast as possible, what procedure would you follow?

Introduction

We know that compounds are composed of elements chemically combined in definite proportions by weight. In the compound iron (II) sulfide, for example, the ratio by weight of iron to sulfur is 56 : 32. If we try to form this compound by combining any other ratio of iron to sulfur, some iron or sulfur will remain uncombined. For example, in Fig. 5–1, page 74, a mixture of 9 grams of iron and 4 grams of sulfur is heated. After heating, a magnet removes 2 grams of uncombined iron. Thus, iron combines with sulfur in the ratio of 7 grams to 4 grams, or 56 : 32.

We recall that, when a compound forms, each element loses its own characteristics and adopts the new properties of the compound. Thus, iron is magnetic and sulfur is yellow; however, the compound iron (II) sulfide is nonmagnetic and black.

Unlike compounds, which have a definite composition, mixtures have a variable composition. Using iron filings and powdered sulfur, we can make mixtures of these elements in any proportion whatever, merely by varying the amounts of the two elements. If we divide the mixture into equal smaller portions, each portion will not necessarily have the same proportion of iron to sulfur. In any such mixture, we can distinguish between the iron and the sulfur by simple means, such as color or the magnetic property of iron.

When we mix table salt (a solid) and water (a liquid), the salt seems to disappear in the water. We say that the salt *dissolves* in the water. The mixture that results when one substance dissolves in another is called a *solution*.

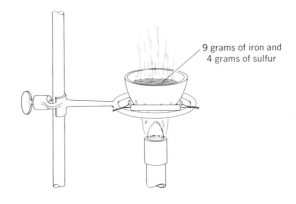

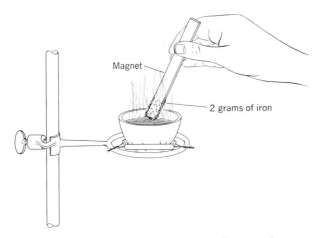

Fig. 5–1. Iron combines with sulfur in the ratio of 7 : 4.

MIXTURES AND SOLUTIONS

A solution is a combination quite different from a mixture of two solids, such as iron and sulfur, in which any equal portions of the mixture may have different amounts of iron and sulfur. Equal portions of a salt-water mixture have the same quantities of solid and liquid, and the mixture is said to be *uniform* or *homogeneous*. Thus, a solution is a mixture in which one ingredient dissolves in another to form a uniform system.

In a solution, the substance that is dissolved is called the *solute*, and the substance that dissolves it is called the *solvent*. Thus, in a solution of salt in water, the salt is the solute, and the water is the solvent. Similarly, when copper (II) sulfate is dissolved in water, the copper (II) sulfate is the solute, and the water is the solvent.

In all of the solutions discussed so far, water has been used as the solvent. Water dissolves so many substances that it is often referred to as the *universal solvent*. Water, however, is not the only useful solvent. Many substances can be dissolved in alcohol, and the resulting solutions are known as *tinctures*. Thus, iodine crystals are dissolved in alcohol to form tincture of iodine.

In some solutions, it is not always clear which substance is the solvent and which is the solute, as in the case of an alcohol-water mixture. Usually, however, it is not necessary to make this distinction.

CHARACTERISTICS OF SOLUTIONS

If we blow chalk dust into a beaker of air and shine a bright light through the dust, we see some of the particles of dust floating in the air (Fig. 5–2a). This is because we can see very tiny particles, such as dust, when the particles reflect light. When we shine a light through a solution, however, we see no such particles (Fig. 5–2b).

When we examine a test tube containing a solution of salt and water, the solution appears to be clear and transparent. Even with a powerful microscope, we cannot see particles of the solute. Evidence of this kind indicates that the particles making up a solution are extremely small.

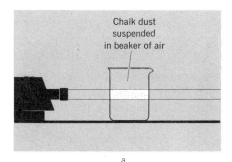

Chalk dust
suspended
in beaker of air

a.

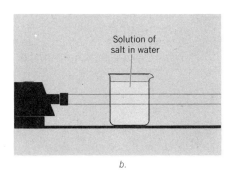

Solution of
salt in water

b.

Fig. 5–2. Light passes through a solution.

When we examine a colored solution, such as weak tincture of iodine, we see that the amber or brown color is uniform throughout. Solutions of copper (II) sulfate are blue. Solutions of potassium permanganate, as we observed in the laboratory, are purple. Solid copper (II) sulfate and solid potassium permanganate have the same color as the solutions, but the solids appear darker. This similarity in color indicates that, although the particles of a solution are very small in size, the particles are still present in the solution and still retain physical properties such as color.

Let us summarize the characteristics of solutions.

1. The particles of solute in a solution are very small (molecular) in size and are not visible.

2. The particles of solute do not settle to the bottom of the container.

3. If a solute is colored, the solution generally takes on the color of the solute. If the solution is weak, that is, if there is relatively little solute in it, the color of the solution may be lighter than the color of the solute.

4. A solution is homogeneous. Every drop of the solution contains the same amount of solute as any other drop of the same solution.

5. A solution is transparent. Light readily passes through a solution, enabling us to see through the solution.

TYPES OF SOLUTES AND SOLVENTS

Although solutions containing a solid in a liquid are very common, solutions involving other physical states of matter also exist. Table 5–1 gives examples of solutions containing other types of solutes and solvents.

Table 5–1. Types of Solutes and Solvents

Solvent	Solute	Example
Solid	Solid Liquid Gas	Solder (tin in lead) Dental fillings (mercury in silver) Hydrogen in palladium metal
Liquid	Solid Liquid Gas	Seawater (salt in water) Rubbing alcohol (alcohol in water) Carbonated beverages (carbon dioxide in water)
Gas	Solid Liquid Gas	Dust in air Fog (water droplets in air) Air (oxygen in nitrogen and other gases)

FACTORS AFFECTING THE RATE OF DISSOLVING

Some solutes, when mixed with a solvent, dissolve slowly. Others dissolve rapidly. Factors that determine the rate at which substances dissolve include *temperature, size of solute particles,* and *movement of solute and solvent.*

Effect of Temperature

As you have probably observed, temperature affects the rate at which a solid dissolves in a liquid. Sugar, for example, dissolves much more quickly in hot tea than in iced tea.

Why does an increase in temperature generally increase the rate of dissolving? According to the *kinetic-molecular theory,* molecules are in constant motion. When a substance is heated, its molecules move faster. Thus, heating causes solvent molecules to move farther apart and to move more rapidly. Consequently, the solute particles come in contact with solvent molecules more often. As a result, we find that heating a mixture of a solute and a solvent generally increases the rate of dissolving.

Effect of Particle Size

If you add 5 grams of granulated (ground) sugar to a cup of tea, the sugar dissolves more rapidly than if you add a 5-gram lump of sugar. This shows that a mass of small particles dissolves more rapidly than the same mass in the form of a single large lump. The rate of dissolving is greater because the many small particles have a greater surface area than does the single large lump. Thus, more molecules of the solute are exposed to the solvent.

Effect of Stirring

The stirring of solute in a solvent tends to bring the solute particles into contact with all particles of the solvent. As a result, every part of the solvent dissolves some of the solute, increasing the rate of dissolving. This explains why we stir a cup of tea after adding sugar to it.

Since heating, grinding, and stirring increase the rate of dissolving, using all of these methods together provides the quickest means for preparing a solution of a solid in a liquid (Fig. 5–3, page 78). As you discovered in the laboratory, to dissolve copper sulfate crystals in water quickly, it is necessary to (1) grind the crystals to a fine powder, (2) heat the water, and (3) stir the mixture constantly as you add the powdered crystals to the heated water.

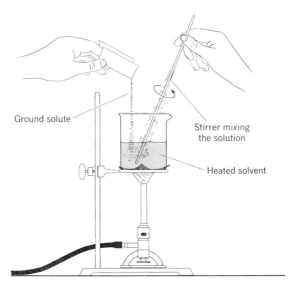

Ground solute

Stirrer mixing
the solution

Heated solvent

Fig. 5–3. The quickest way to prepare a solution.

TYPES OF SOLUTIONS

When we prepare a solution we may use little or much of a solute, relative to the amount of solvent. Thus, we can make solutions of different strengths.

Dilute and Concentrated Solutions

Some people prefer to dissolve one teaspoonful of sugar in their tea. Others prefer two or more teaspoonfuls. In general, solutions vary in the amount of solute that dissolves in the solvent. The amount of solute in a given quantity of solvent determines the *concentration*, or strength, of the solution. A solution that contains relatively little solute in a given amount of solvent is generally said to be *dilute*, or weak. A solution that contains a relatively large amount of solute in a given amount of solvent is generally said to be *concentrated*, or strong.

Expressing the concentration of a solution using the terms concentrated or dilute is only an approximate measure of the strength of the solution. Chemists generally tend to express the concentration of a solution in more precise terms, such as percentage. For example, a 10% solution is twice as concentrated as a 5% solution. For the purposes of this book, however, we need not be concerned with these precise terms.

Unsaturated and Saturated Solutions

All solutions may be considered as either unsaturated or saturated. An *unsaturated solution* is one in which the solvent can dissolve more solute at the same temperature. As we continue to add more solute to such a solution, a point is reached where no more solute can dissolve. Any additional solute that is now added to the solution settles to the bottom of the container. Such a solution, in which the solvent has dissolved as much solute as it can hold at a given temperature, is called a *saturated solution*.

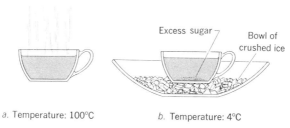

a. Temperature: 100°C   *b.* Temperature: 4°C

Fig. 5–4. Unsaturated and saturated solutions.

The effect of different temperatures on the ability of a solution to hold solute may be illustrated with a cup of tea. In Fig. 5–4a, the hot tea readily dissolves 3 teaspoonfuls of sugar and can dissolve even more sugar. The resulting solution is therefore unsaturated. But when the same cup of tea (containing three teaspoonfuls of dissolved sugar) is cooled, some sugar crystallizes out of the solution and settles to the bottom of the cup (Fig. 5–4b). The cold tea cannot hold three teaspoonfuls of sugar; only part of the sugar remains dissolved in cold tea. Since the excess sugar settles to the bottom of the cup, we know that this cold solution of tea and sugar is now a saturated solution.

SOLUBILITY CURVES AND HOW THEY ARE USED

Figure 5–4 shows the effect of varying the temperature of a sample of tea on the quantity of sugar that can dissolve—that is, on the *solubility* of the sugar. By carefully noting how much solute dissolves at different temperatures, chemists prepare graphs called *solubility curves*.

Solubility curves for several solid solutes in water are shown in Fig. 5–5, page 80. For each solute, the solubility curve shows how much solute dissolves in 100 cubic centimeters of the solvent (water) at different temperatures. Thus, each curve reveals the amount of solute to use in order to prepare a saturated solution at a particular temperature.

For example, to determine how much solute is needed to prepare a

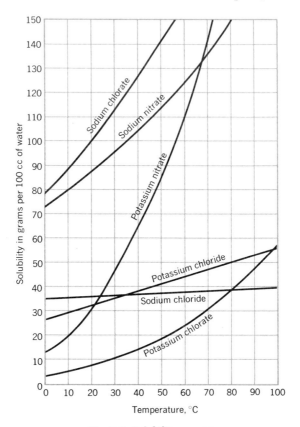

Fig. 5–5. Solubility curves.

saturated solution of potassium chloride at a temperature of 80°C, proceed as follows:

1. Move across the horizontal axis of the graph until you find the 80°C line.

2. Move upward along this line to the point where the curve for potassium chloride crosses this line.

3. From this point, extend a horizontal line to the vertical axis.

4. Read the value on the vertical axis.

Note that the horizontal line crosses the vertical axis at the number 50. This means that 50 grams of potassium chloride will dissolve in 100 cubic centimeters of water at 80°C. The resulting solution will be saturated because the solubility curve gives the maximum quantity of solute the solvent can hold.

Similarly, to determine the amount of potassium nitrate needed to saturate 100 cubic centimeters of water at 70°C, first find the 70°C line on the horizontal axis. Then, move upward along this line to the point where the curve for potassium nitrate crosses this line. From this point, extend a horizontal line to reach the vertical axis. Note that this line crosses the vertical axis at the number 140. This means that 140 grams of potassium nitrate will dissolve in 100 cubic centimeters of water at 70°C to form a saturated solution.

FACTORS AFFECTING THE QUANTITY OF SOLUTE THAT CAN DISSOLVE

We have discussed the factors that determine the *rate* of dissolving: temperature, particle size, and stirring. Now we will concern ourselves with the factors that determine the *quantity* of solute that can dissolve in a given quantity of solvent.

Effect of Temperature

When the temperature of a liquid solvent is increased, the solvent is able to dissolve more solid solute than at the lower temperature. Thus, when the temperature of water is increased by several degrees, the water can hold more solute at the new temperature than before. In other words, the quantity of solute required to saturate the water increases as the temperature rises. If the temperature is lowered, the quantity of solute required to saturate the water decreases.

For example, at a temperature of 50°C, a saturated solution of potassium nitrate (KNO_3) can be prepared by adding 85 grams of KNO_3 to 100 cubic centimeters of water. When the temperature of the water is increased to 60°C, 110 grams of potassium nitrate can be dissolved in the same volume of water. When the solution is cooled back to 50°C and is stirred, the excess 25 grams of KNO_3 crystallizes out of the solution and settles to the bottom of the container.

Although an increase in temperature usually increases the quantity of solid that can dissolve in water, there are some exceptions. Sodium chloride (table salt) is almost equally soluble in cold or hot water. Calcium sulfate, on the other hand, is more soluble in cold water than in hot water.

Increases in temperature affect the dissolving of gases in liquids in a manner opposite to the dissolving of most solids in liquids. Ordinary tap water has some air dissolved in it. When the water is warmed, bubbles of air gather and rise to the surface (Fig. 5–6, page 82). The increase in temperature decreases the ability of the water to dissolve the air. Thus, heating the solution causes the air to bubble out of the solution.

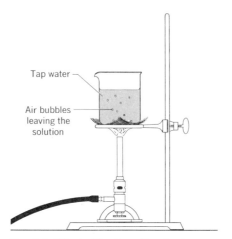

Fig. 5–6. Effect of heat on dissolved gases.

Effect of Pressure

An increase or decrease in pressure has little effect on the solubility of solid solutes in liquid solvents. This is because solids and liquids are virtually incompressible.

Gases, however, can be compressed. This means that differences in pressure markedly affect the solubility of gases in liquids. When the pressure of a gas is increased, the solubility of the gas also increases. When the pressure of a gas decreases, the gas becomes less soluble and leaves the solution.

You see this effect when you open a bottle of soda water. When bottled and capped, the soda is under greater pressure than normal atmospheric pressure. Under this condition, more carbon dioxide gas dissolves in water and remains dissolved. When the bottle cap is removed, the pressure inside the bottle is reduced, and you can see bubbles of carbon dioxide gas leave the solution and come to the surface of the liquid.

WHY THINGS CHANGE

Why do substances dissolve? The reason can best be understood by first considering the answer to a broader question: "Why do things change?" To answer this question, we need to develop a model—something we understand. Then we will use the model to help explain why substances dissolve.

Spontaneous Changes

We notice that many things in our environment change. Some change slowly; others change rapidly. When iron rusts, the iron changes slowly. When a match burns, the match changes rapidly.

Once iron starts rusting, the iron continues to rust until all the iron has been changed to rust (largely iron oxide). Once we light a match, the match continues to burn until it is consumed. Once we light a candle, the candle continues to burn unaided. In all these cases, the changes are *exothermic*—they give off heat. Moreover, each change, once begun, continues without outside help. Changes that continue unaided—that is, without outside help—are said to be *spontaneous*.

Stability and Potential Energy

Why are exothermic changes spontaneous? That is, why do changes in which heat is released proceed unaided?

To try to answer this question, we will use a rock rolling downhill —a readily understood situation—as our model. We observe that the rock, given a push, rolls downhill without further help. We can account for this observation by saying that the rock at the bottom of the hill is more stable than the same rock on top of the hill. Nature seems to want to make things more stable; thus, nature encourages the rock to roll downhill.

It seems reasonable that, as an object is raised to a greater height, its capacity for doing work increases. Thus, when a pile driver is dropped from a great height, it does more work than when the same pile driver is dropped from a lesser height. As we raise the height of a body above ground, we say that the *potential energy* of the body, or its ability to do work, increases. On the other hand, as the object is lowered, its height above ground decreases, and its potential energy decreases.

Thus, the potential energy of the rock at the bottom of a hill is less than its potential energy when on top of the hill. Considering the model of a rock rolling downhill, we conclude that nature apparently favors those changes making for greater stability or for decreased potential energy.

Potential Energy and Heat

Consider a burning candle. According to the kinetic-molecular theory, the particles or molecules in matter are constantly moving. In solids, such as the wax of the candle, the moving molecules constantly brush against one another. In gases, such as oxygen, the moving molecules (although much farther apart) also strike one another from time to time. Since some quantity of heat is always associated with these molecular contacts, we can say that all matter contains some quantity of heat.

Why does the burning of the candle represent an exothermic change?

That is, why does the burning candle give off heat? By making reasonable assumptions, based on our observation of the burning candle, let us attempt to answer this question.

First, remember that burning uses up oxygen. Let us assume that a certain quantity of heat is present in the candle wax and in the oxygen—heat derived from the motions of the molecules. It is reasonable to assume that a certain quantity of heat is also present in the products of the burning candle, products such as carbon dioxide and water (this heat is also derived from the motions of the molecules). Finally, we will learn later that energy cannot be created or destroyed. This means that the total amount of energy in a system (a burning candle is an example of a chemical system) remains unchanged.

Scientists have estimated that the heat (energy) contained in the candle wax and the heat in the oxygen are greater than the heat contained in the products of burning. Therefore, in order for the total amount of energy to remain unchanged, a quantity of heat must be given off. This amount of heat represents the difference between the heat contained in the candle wax and oxygen and the heat contained in the products of burning. Thus, burning is an exothermic change.

Now let us consider why an exothermic change proceeds spontaneously (unaided). The heat energy contained in matter is also called *chemical energy*, which is a type of potential energy. If our previous assumptions are correct, the total potential energy in the candle wax and in the oxygen consumed during burning (the starting substances) is greater than the potential energy contained in the products of burning. In other words: As the candle burns, its potential energy decreases.

Remember that, as the rock rolls downhill unaided, it goes from a position of greater potential energy (on top of the hill) to a position of lesser potential energy (on the bottom of the hill). The potential energy decreases during this spontaneous change. When burning takes place, the potential energy involved in the change also decreases. Since a rock rolls downhill spontaneously—a change that nature favors—then burning should also take place spontaneously (Fig. 5–7). This explains, according to our model, why exothermic changes such as burning are spontaneous.

Endothermic Changes

Endothermic changes absorb energy. Let us use our previous reasoning and try to predict whether or not endothermic changes will be spontaneous.

Since we have reasoned that exothermic changes result in decreased potential energy, it is logical to assume that endothermic changes

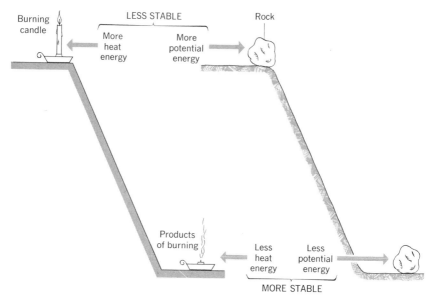

Fig. 5–7. Changes involving decreasing potential energy.

result in increased potential energy. Since increasing the potential energy makes things less stable than before, we can predict that endothermic changes will not proceed unaided.

Another way of testing the prediction is to consider again our model of the rock rolling downhill. Will the rock, lying at the bottom of the hill, move back to the top without help? Since an endothermic change can be compared to the rock moving up the hill, it seems unlikely that an endothermic change would proceed unaided.

Endothermic Changes and Stability

We know that water, on standing, evaporates to form water vapor. This means that evaporation takes place spontaneously. Is this an endothermic change?

According to the kinetic-molecular theory, heat energy is required to change the molecules of a liquid into the faster-moving molecules of a gas. As a result, the gas possesses more heat, or more potential energy, than the liquid. Therefore, according to our previous reasoning, the gas possesses less stability than the liquid. Thus, the change is endothermic.

We have noted previously that nature seems to want things to become more stable. Thus (we reasoned), endothermic changes do not take place spontaneously. But nature permits evaporation to proceed spontaneously. It would appear that nature, under one set of conditions, favors changes that make for greater stability; on the other hand, under another set of conditions, nature appears to favor changes that make for lesser stability. Does this make sense?

Randomness

To explain this seeming contradiction in our reasoning, we must discard—or revise—our model. Up to now, we have assumed that nature always favors an increase in stability. Is there another law of nature that we have overlooked? It seems probable that the tendency for a change to proceed spontaneously in the direction of greater stability is only one of the factors that governs the tendency of things to change. However, our model of the rock rolling downhill does not account for any other factors.

When a bottle of perfume is opened, perfume molecules spread out in all directions. This would seem to imply that nature favors those changes that form products that are more spread out, or more randomly arranged. Scientists recognize that nature, in addition to favoring changes towards greater stability, also favors those changes towards greater *randomness*. This tendency explains why even a small amount of a gas spontaneously fills an entire room.

Let us now return to our problem. From an energy viewpoint, more stable liquid water evaporates to form less stable water vapor (a change that nature does *not* favor). From a randomness viewpoint, the less randomly arranged particles in liquid water evaporate to form more randomly arranged particles of water vapor (a change that nature *does* favor).

We can now explain why evaporation, an endothermic change, can take place spontaneously. Despite the fact that water vapor is more unstable than liquid water, the molecules in water vapor are more randomly arranged (more spread out) than the molecules of liquid water. This tendency towards randomness predominates; therefore, liquid water is observed to evaporate spontaneously.

Thus, there are two factors, or natural drives, that govern the tendency of matter to undergo change:

1. The tendency to form products that are more stable (possess less potential energy) than the original matter.

2. The tendency to form products that are more randomly arranged than the original matter.

WHY SUBSTANCES DISSOLVE

The act of dissolving represents a change in matter that may occur unaided (spontaneously). In the preceding section, we learned that such changes take place from the competition between two drives that nature favors:

1. Spontaneous changes form products that possess less energy (are more stable) than the starting substances. Remember the example of the rock rolling downhill.

2. Spontaneous changes form products that possess more randomness (are more spread out) than the starting substances. Remember the example of the aroma from the bottle of perfume.

When a solid dissolves in a liquid, the arrangement of the particles in the solution becomes more random than the arrangement of particles in the solid. The attractive forces (bonds) in solids are much stronger than the attractive forces in liquids. This means that the particles in a solid have less freedom of movement. The particles in a liquid are more weakly bonded. They have greater freedom of movement and' are therefore more randomly arranged.

Thus, when a solid dissolves in a liquid, the randomness change is always in the direction that nature favors (drive 2). Does this mean that the same quantities of different solids will dissolve in a given amount of water? From the differences among solubility curves (Fig. 5–5), we know this is not so. Why?

Careful measurements reveal that, on dissolving in water, solids either give off heat or absorb heat. The solution becomes warmer or colder. For example, solid sodium hydroxide dissolves spontaneously in water, giving off considerable heat. We interpret this change by saying that the products of the change possess less heat energy than the starting substances. Note that the energy change and the randomness change are both in the direction that nature favors. This explains why solid sodium hydroxide dissolves in water without outside help.

On the other hand, when silver nitrate dissolves in water, the solution becomes cold. Heat has been absorbed, suggesting that the products of the change possess more heat energy than the starting substances. The products are also less stable than the starting substances, a direction of change that nature does *not* favor. Yet, silver nitrate dissolves spontaneously. Recall that the randomness change (drive 2) is in the direction that nature favors. Apparently, the randomness drive is stronger and overcomes the energy drive. Dissolving takes place spontaneously.

Why do all solids not dissolve equally as well in water, despite the fact that the randomness drive is in the direction that nature favors? Solids, on dissolving in water, liberate different amounts of energy. In some cases, energy may even be absorbed. It is the magnitude (size) and the direction of this energy factor that determine how much solid will dissolve.

This discussion of solubility is restricted to the factors that make substances dissolve more or less readily in water. Do not confuse the factors that make things dissolve with the *rate* of dissolving, which depends on factors such as temperature, particle size, and stirring.

HOW COMPONENTS OF A SOLUTION
CAN BE SEPARATED

The components of many solutions can be separated by a variety of special methods. Among these methods are *evaporation, distillation, fractional distillation,* and *chromatography.*

Evaporation

When a solvent evaporates from a solution, the solute is left behind. When a drop of salt solution is placed in a teaspoon and heated, the water of the solution evaporates and tiny, white salt crystals remain in the spoon. This method is used when the purpose of the separation is to recover only the solute from the solution. Although evaporation always occurs, the rate of evaporation of the liquid is usually increased by heating the solution in an open container.

Distillation

One of the methods used to separate and recover both the solute and the solvent of a liquid solution is known as distillation. In this process, the solution is heated in a distilling flask. As the liquid evaporates, the vapor is collected and then cooled. The solid remains behind. Fig. 5–8 shows a laboratory apparatus for this process.

For example, to separate the components of a solution of potassium permanganate dissolved in water, the solution is placed in a flask as shown in the figure. As the solution is heated, the water evaporates. As the water evaporates, the vapor enters the inner condenser tube. This tube is cooled by a constant flow of cold water in the outer tube. As the water vapor in the inner tube is cooled by the flowing water in the outer tube, the vapor condenses to a liquid. The liquid water drains into the collecting beaker. The collected water is clear and free of all solid substances that had been dissolved in it. This water, called *distilled water,* is chemically pure. The solute (potassium permanganate) remains in the flask. By this means, the components of the solution can be separated and both the solute and solvent can be recovered.

The demand for fresh water has increased enormously. The Federal government is spending huge sums of money to develop methods of removing salt from seawater (*desalinization*), to provide an almost

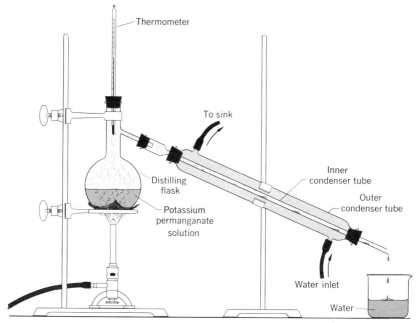

Fig. 5–8. A laboratory apparatus for distillation.

unlimited source of fresh water. Distillation of seawater is impractical for such large-scale usage, and therefore other desalinization techniques are being studied.

Fractional Distillation

The separation of the components of liquid mixtures can be accomplished by a process known as fractional distillation. This process is used commercially to separate the components of petroleum, or crude oil, which is a liquid mixture of hydrocarbons—compounds of hydrogen and carbon. Gasoline, kerosene, and lubricating oils are examples of such mixtures of hydrocarbons.

In this process, the crude oil is heated and piped into a fractionating tower (Fig. 5–9, page 90). The gasoline portion, or fraction, boils off before any of the other components in the oil because the hydrocarbons in gasoline have a low boiling point. After all of the gasoline has been evaporated, it is collected from the top of the fractionating tower. The temperature of the crude oil is then raised, and the kerosene fraction boils off. The kerosene vapors condense and are then collected from a level of the tower lower than that of the gasoline level. The temperature of the crude oil is then raised again, and the process is repeated for the collection of fuel oils, lubricating oils, and other heavy substances.

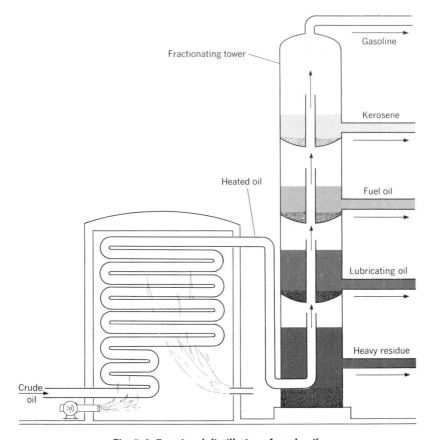

Fig. 5–9. Fractional distillation of crude oil.

The yield of gasoline is increased considerably by a process called "cracking," which does not involve fractional distillation. In cracking, large oil molecules present in petroleum are split into smaller molecules that make good motor fuel.

Chromatography

To separate a mixture of solutes from a small quantity of solution, the process of chromatography is used. *Paper chromatography* is based upon the ability of some solutes to stick to the molecules on the surface of a piece of porous paper. The process by which solute molecules stick to a solid surface is called *adsorption*. Since some molecules of solute are adsorbed on paper more readily than others, a mixture of solutes can be separated by this method.

A simple method for chromatography of liquid solutions is shown

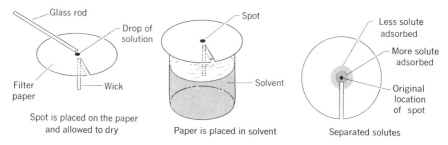

Fig. 5–10. Paper chromatography.

in Fig. 5–10. A drop of the solution containing one or more solutes is placed at the center of the filter paper and allowed to dry. The filter paper is cut and folded so that a part of it extends downward into a solvent, behaving as a wick. When a solvent, such as water or alcohol, wets the paper, the solvent and solutes in it travel upward in the paper. The solute that tends to be less strongly adsorbed on the paper moves outward from the center faster than the others and is thus separated from them. For example, when a drop of blue ink is allowed to dry on a piece of filter paper, and water is used as the traveling solvent, bands of different colors appear at different distances from the center of the paper. Each band is a solute of different color that was used in preparing the ink.

DISSOLVED POLLUTANTS

Many wastes of civilization are pollutants that usually dissolve in air or water. For example, sulfur dioxide, an exhaust from the burning of fuels, dissolves in air and pollutes it. Phosphate salts, nitrate salts, detergents, and other chemicals pollute fresh and salt water. Distillation and chromatography can purify air and water on a small scale in the laboratory. However, on a large scale, the same pollutants are very difficult and expensive to remove from the atmosphere, rivers, and ocean. The task is so great that we have no practical method for purifying air and water at the present time. Consequently, we have no choice now but to keep conditions from getting worse and to do everything we can to prevent increased pollution of our air and water.

Looking Back

Solutions, like other mixtures, have variable compositions. However, unlike some mixtures, solutions are homogeneous, transparent, and have particles of molecular size. Solutions of solid solutes in liquids usually form more readily when the solute particles are very small, are heated, and are stirred. Solutions of gaseous solutes in liquids usually form more readily when cooled and subjected to high pressure.

Matter undergoes change spontaneously if (1) the products of the change are more stable than the starting materials, and (2) if the products are more randomly arranged than the original matter.

Looking Ahead

Suspensions, like solutions, are mixtures. However, the characteristics of suspensions differ from those of solutions, as described in the next chapter.

Multiple-Choice Questions

1. When salt dissolves in water, equal portions of this mixture contain the same quantities of solid and liquid. Such a mixture is said to be
   a. unstable   b. a tincture   c. uniform   d. a suspension
2. In a solution, the dissolved substance is called
   a. solute   b. solvent   c. tincture   d. suspension
3. The liquid referred to as the "universal solvent" is
   a. benzene   b. oil   c. alcohol   d. water
4. When held up to light, solutions appear
   a. cloudy and opaque   c. clear and translucent
   b. clear and transparent   d. cloudy and transparent
5. A beam of light can be used to see
   a. water molecules   c. the particles of a sodium chloride solution
   b. dust in the air   d. the particles of a copper sulfate solution
6. The particles in a solution
   a. can be seen with a microscope
   b. settle to the bottom of the container
   c. are molecular in size
   d. are large
7. When purple-colored potassium permanganate is dissolved in water, the solution formed
   a. becomes purple   c. becomes blue
   b. remains clear   d. changes from purple to clear
8. An example of a solution that is affected by changes in pressure is
   a. sodium chloride in water   c. alcohol in water
   b. mercury in silver   d. carbon dioxide in water
9. Weak solutions are said to be
   a. concentrated   b. dilute   c. saturated   d. supersaturated
10. A solution to which more solute can be added at the same temperature is said to be
    a. saturated   b. unsaturated   c. supersaturated   d. unstable

11. In general, when a hot saturated solution cools,
    a. the solution becomes unsaturated
    b. the solution becomes dilute
    c. the solution becomes concentrated
    d. excess solute settles to the bottom of the container
12. In general, when the temperature of a liquid is raised, its ability to dissolve a solid solute
    a. decreases
    b. increases
    c. increases then decreases
    d. decreases then increases
13. When a solution of carbon dioxide in water is heated,
    a. no change is observed
    b. more carbon dioxide can dissolve
    c. carbon dioxide bubbles disappear
    d. carbon dioxide leaves the solution
14. An increase in pressure on a sodium chloride solution
    a. has no effect
    b. causes more solute to dissolve
    c. causes less solute to dissolve
    d. produces a saturated solution
15. When the pressure on a gas increases, the solubility of the gas in a liquid
    a. decreases
    b. increases
    c. increases then decreases
    d. remains the same
16. The best method to use to recover both the solute and solvent of a liquid solution is
    a. evaporation   b. chromatography   c. distillation   d. filtration
17. Distilled water
    a. contains microscopic solute particles
    b. is chemically pure
    c. contains suspended particles
    d. is obtained by using chromatography
18. Fractional distillation can be used to obtain
    a. water   b. crude oil   c. petroleum   d. kerosene
19. The process of chromatography is based on the principle of
    a. adsorption   b. absorption   c. filtration   d. desalinization
20. Silver nitrate absorbs energy as it dissolves spontaneously. The silver nitrate dissolves because
    a. the randomness drive is greater than the stability drive
    b. the stability drive is greater than the randomness drive
    c. only the stability drive is at work
    d. only the randomness drive is at work
21. Changes that continue unaided are said to be
    a. consistent   b. spontaneous   c. reversible   d. models
22. When an object is raised to a greater height, it experiences an increase in
    a. kinetic energy   b. stability   c. potential energy   d. heat
23. A rock is most stable when it is
    a. at the top of a hill
    b. in the middle of a hill
    c. rolling downhill
    d. at the bottom of a hill

Modified True-False Questions

1. Mixtures in which one ingredient dissolves in another to form a uniform system are known as *suspensions*.
2. The substance in which a second substance dissolves is called the *solute*.
3. Solutions in which alcohol is the solvent are called *tinctures*.
4. Since each drop of a solution contains the same amount of solute, the solution is said to be *transparent*.
5. In a solution, the amount of solute in a given amount of solvent determines the *saturation* of the solution.
6. Solutions that contain little solute are said to be *concentrated*.
7. A solution that holds as much solute as it can hold at a given temperature is said to be *saturated*.
8. Graphs showing the amount of solute that dissolves in a given amount of solvent at a given temperature are called *solubility curves*.
9. A chemical reaction, in which energy is released, is called *an endothermic* reaction.
10. The particles in solids are *more* randomly arranged than the particles in gases.

Thought Questions

1. Tell the difference between the terms in each of the following pairs:
   a. solute and solvent   d. evaporation and distillation
   b. concentrated and dilute   e. mixture and solution
   c. saturated and unsaturated
2. Why does the application of heat increase the solubility of some substances while lessening the solubility of other substances?
3. Give a scientific explanation for each of the following:
   a. Hot tea can hold more sugar than iced tea.
   b. As water is warmed, bubbles of air in the water gather and rise to the surface of the water.
   c. As the pressure on a sodium chloride solution is increased, the solution is not affected.
   d. As a soda bottle cap is removed, a gas bubbles to the surface of the soda.
   e. Ground copper sulfate dissolves faster than a large crystal of copper sulfate.
4. Describe the steps that you would perform to prepare a copper sulfate solution in the fastest possible way.
5. Refer to the solubility curves (Fig. 5–5, page 80). For each of the following situations, tell the number of grams of solute that will dissolve in 100 cc of water.
   a. potassium chlorate at 30°C   d. sodium chloride at 50°C
   b. potassium nitrate at 60°C   e. sodium nitrate at 10°C
   c. sodium chloride at 100°C
6. Describe how you might use laboratory methods to remove sea salt and phosphates from a sample of polluted water.

CHAPTER 6
WHAT ARE THE CHARACTERISTICS OF SUSPENSIONS?

When you have completed this chapter, you should be able to:

1. *Distinguish* between (*a*) suspension and solution (*b*) colloid and emulsion.
2. *List,* with examples, the different types of suspensions.
3. *Discuss* the value of detergents.
4. *Explain* the methods used to separate the components of suspensions.
5. *Describe* how water supplies are treated to remove pollutants.

In the laboratory experience that follows, you will use some procedures to separate parts of a suspension.

Laboratory Experience

HOW CAN WE SEPARATE THE PARTS OF A SUSPENSION?

A. Into each of three 150-millimeter test tubes pour 10 cubic centimeters of water. Add a pinch of clay to one test tube, a pinch of sand to the second test tube, and a pinch of powdered chalk to the third. Stopper the tubes, and place them in a rack.
B. Carefully examine the solid particles in each test tube with a magnifying glass.
   1. Which of the substances has the largest particles?
   2. Which substance has the smallest particles?
C. Shake each test tube vigorously for a few seconds, and then return it to the rack. Note how long it takes for most of the solid matter in each test tube to settle to the bottom of the tube.
   3. Which substance settles fastest?
   4. Which substance settles slowest?
   5. Which substance fails to settle completely?
   6. What is the relation between the size of the particles and the

      rate at which the particles settle to the bottom of the test tubes?

D. Pour 10 cubic centimeters of water into each of three 150-millimeter test tubes. Add a pinch of clay to each tube. Place the test tubes in a rack.

E. Take one of the test tubes and shake it thoroughly. Pour the contents of the test tube onto a sheet of filter paper properly set up in a funnel (Fig. 6–1). Collect in a beaker the liquid that passes through the funnel. When a liquid stops dripping from the end of the funnel, carefully observe both the filter paper and the liquid in the beaker.

    7. What has happened to the solid substance that was in the test tube?

    8. Describe the appearance of the *filtrate* (the liquid that has passed through the filter paper).

F. Add a pinch of alum and a little ammonium hydroxide to the second test tube. Shake both the second and third test tubes vigorously for a few seconds, and then return them to the rack. Observe both test tubes for about 5 minutes. Record how long it takes for any solid substances to settle to the bottom of the test tubes.

    9. How does the addition of alum and ammonium hydroxide to the test tube affect the length of time it takes for the solid substance to settle?

    10. What is the purpose of the third test tube?

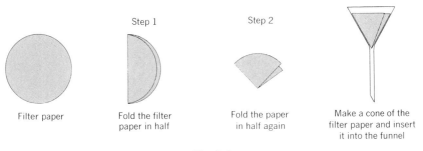

                Step 1   Step 2   Step 3

Filter paper   Fold the filter   Fold the paper   Make a cone of the
                paper in half   in half again   filter paper and insert
                                              it into the funnel

Fig. 6–1.

Introduction

    As we have learned, a solution is a clear, homogeneous (uniform) mixture. Because the particles of solute are molecular in size, they are not visible. The solute particles are evenly distributed throughout the solvent.

Other types of mixtures can be prepared in which the particles remain visible and give the mixture a cloudy appearance. In some of these mixtures, the particles are larger than molecules and are not evenly distributed throughout the liquid.

SUSPENSIONS

A *heterogeneous* (nonuniform) mixture of solid particles in a liquid is known as a *suspension*. The mixture is heterogeneous because equal quantities contain different amounts of suspended material. Some common examples of suspensions are milk of magnesia, calamine lotion, and any medicine that requires shaking before using. Large-scale suspensions are formed when mud is stirred up from the bottom of a lake, river, or reservoir, and when soil particles (sediment) are washed into a body of water by rainstorms or by human activities. In recent years, many bodies of clear, fresh water have become cloudy and unattractive owing to the pollutants that are suspended in them.

The laboratory experience allows us to observe some of the characteristics of suspensions. We observe that each mixture (suspension) is cloudy in appearance. However, the sand quickly settles out of the suspension and falls to the bottom of the tube. Some of the clay in the clay–water suspension also settles to the bottom of the tube. In this suspension, however, more time is required for the separation of the clay from the water. Since the particles of clay are smaller and lighter (less dense) than those of sand, the clay settles out of the suspension more slowly. If some particles of clay are small enough, they may remain suspended in the water indefinitely. Finally, we observe that nearly all the particles of chalk dust remain in suspension. Because the chalk dust particles are smaller than those of clay or sand, most of the chalk dust will remain in suspension (Fig. 6–2).

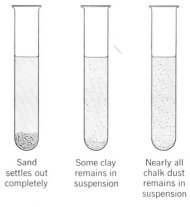

Sand settles out completely   Some clay remains in suspension   Nearly all chalk dust remains in suspension

Fig. 6–2. Behavior of solids in liquids.

The sizes of the particles in suspensions and in solutions can be compared by passing a beam of light through each mixture. In a solution, the particles of the solute are molecular in size and do not interfere with the beam of light. The beam, therefore, passes through the solution unaffected. This effect was observed in Fig. 5–2b (page 75). In a suspension, however, the solid particles vary in size but are larger than molecules. The light beam becomes visible in a suspension because particles that are just slightly larger than molecules reflect light to our eyes. This type of light reflection is known as the *Tyndall effect.* The particles of chalk dust suspended in water reflect the light beam in the same manner as the particles of chalk dust suspended in air in Fig. 5–2a (page 75). The Tyndall effect can be used to determine whether a liquid mixture is a solution or a suspension in which the particles are very tiny.

The Tyndall effect can be used also to detect certain types of suspensions called *colloidal suspensions.* These include suspensions in liquids of particles so small that they do not generally settle on standing. Colloidal suspensions are discussed more fully later in this chapter.

Table 6–1 compares suspensions with solutions.

Table 6–1. Comparison of Suspensions and Solutions

Suspensions	Solutions
Are cloudy	Are clear
Contain particles that generally settle out on standing; they do not dissolve	Contain particles that do not settle out on standing; they dissolve
Contain particles that vary in size but are larger than molecules	Contain particles that are molecular in size
May reflect light	Permit light to pass through
Are heterogeneous mixtures	Are homogeneous mixtures

TYPES OF SUSPENSIONS

The components of a suspension, like those of a solution, may consist of gases, liquids, or solids. Some common examples of suspensions follow.

Suspensions of Solids in Liquids

Earlier in this chapter, we mentioned that milk of magnesia and disturbed mud in bodies of water are examples of suspensions. Milk of magnesia consists of magnesium hydroxide, which is a white powder, thoroughly mixed with water. Mud consists of small soil particles suspended in water.

Suspensions of Solids in Gases

When chalk dust floats in air, and a light beam is sent through it, the dust particles reflect the light. This means that the dust particles and the light beam both become visible. Chalk dust in air is an example of a suspension in which very tiny solid particles are scattered, or dispersed, in a gas.

Smoke from volcanic eruptions usually contains very tiny particles of ash. Smoke from burning fuels and factory exhausts often contains tiny particles of carbon (soot) and of ash. The particles in smoke often remain suspended in air for long periods of time and contribute to air pollution.

Suspensions of Liquids in Liquids

Although butter appears to be a solid, it is really a suspension of water in liquid butterfat. Other familiar examples of liquid-in-liquid suspensions are salad dressings that are mixtures of an oil and vinegar.

Suspensions of Liquids in Gases

We often see suspensions of a liquid in a gas. For example, when someone takes a hot shower, the room fills with steam. The steam is composed of small droplets of water dispersed in air. Clouds and fog, if the water droplets are large enough, are other examples of this type of suspension, as are hair, deodorant, and insecticide sprays produced by pressurized (aerosol) cans.

Suspensions of Gases in Solids

Floating soap and artificial sponges are examples of this type of suspension. In these cases, air is blown into a liquid mass which hardens and entraps the bubbles.

Suspensions of Gases in Liquids

Whipped cream is an example of a suspension of a gas in a liquid. When cream is whipped (stirred rapidly) tiny bubbles of air become suspended in the cream.

Suspensions of Gases in Gases

The particles in gases are molecular in size. This means that such particles tend to mix uniformly with one another. Thus, suspensions of a gas in a gas do not exist. Mixtures of gases in gases are considered to be solutions rather than suspensions. Clear air is a solution of oxygen, carbon dioxide, and other gases in nitrogen.

TEMPORARY SUSPENSIONS

Many suspensions of solids in liquids and of liquids in liquids are temporary; that is, the suspended particles settle when the mixture comes to rest after having been stirred or shaken. For example, when oil and water are poured into the same container, two distinct layers form. The oil and water are said to be *immiscible*. The oil, because it is less dense than the water, floats above the water. When this mixture is vigorously shaken, the oil breaks up into tiny droplets which are distributed throughout the water. After a few moments, the droplets form larger drops, which rise to the surface, and the oil again separates from the water. Such separation of oil from water also occurs when oil tankers, ships, and offshore oil wells "spill" oil into a body of water and thereby pollute the water.

PERMANENT SUSPENSIONS

A permanent suspension is called an *emulsion*. In making emulsions, certain chemicals, called *emulsifying agents*, are added to liquid-in-liquid or solid-in-liquid suspensions. These chemicals cause the suspension to become permanent; that is, the components of the emulsion do not separate out on standing. For example, a mixture of salad oil and vinegar separates rather quickly after being shaken. When egg yolk is added to this mixture, and it is then beaten or mixed in a blender, a permanent emulsion called mayonnaise is produced. The egg yolk acts as an emulsifying agent; it prevents the droplets of oil from separating from the vinegar.

Soap and synthetic detergents (soaplike materials) are other examples of emulsifying agents. When added to water and brought into contact with dirt, these agents form an emulsion composed of the dirt or grease, the emulsifying agent, and water. The dirt is trapped in the emulsion, which can then be rinsed away easily. Fig. 6–3 shows how soap is used in preparing an emulsion.

COLLOIDAL SUSPENSIONS

We know that a colloidal suspension (or, simply, a *colloid*) is a suspension of one substance in another that shows the Tyndall effect (see page 98). The basic difference between solutions, suspensions, and colloids is the size of the particles in them. Solutions contain tiny, molecular particles. Suspensions contain relatively large, or coarse, particles. Colloids contain particles of a size intermediate between those of solutions and suspensions. Colloids are generally clear in appearance.

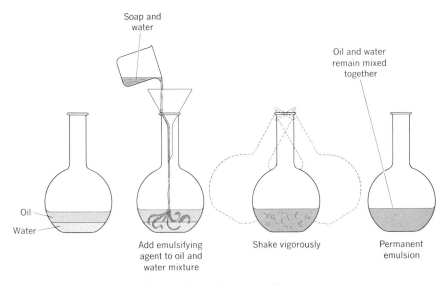

Fig. 6–3. Preparing an emulsion.

Because of the small size of the particles in them, colloids have certain distinctive properties:

1. *Colloidal particles have a large surface area.* If a large rock were ground into particles of colloidal size (a powder consisting of very tiny particles), the total surface area of the powder particles would be enormous compared to the surface area of the original rock. This large surface area permits suspended colloidal particles to come in contact with, attract, and hold (or adsorb) other kinds of matter.

2. *Colloidal particles usually have an electrical charge.* Because of their large surface area, colloidal particles in a suspension adsorb charged particles when such particles are also present in the suspension. As a result, the colloidal particles themselves acquire a positive or negative electrical charge, depending on the substance in which they are suspended. When a wire from the positive side of a battery and another from the negative side are placed in a colloid, positively charged colloidal particles migrate toward the negative wire, and negatively charged colloidal particles migrate toward the positive wire.

3. *Colloidal particles reflect light.* Colloids reflect a beam of light that is sent through them—the Tyndall effect.

4. *Colloidal particles exhibit Brownian motion.* When a colloid is observed through the high power of a microscope, the particles look like pinpoints of light that zigzag rapidly (Fig. 6–4, page 102). This move-

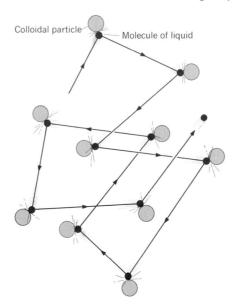

Fig. 6–4. Brownian motion.

ment, known as *Brownian motion*, is thought to be caused by collisions between the larger, slower colloidal particles and the smaller, more rapidly moving molecules of the liquid. These collisions keep the particles bouncing around, preventing them from settling to the bottom of the container.

Colloids are extremely important systems. They are, perhaps, as important as life itself because the contents of cells, which make up our bodies, are colloidal systems. Much still remains to be discovered in this most important area of science.

SEPARATING THE COMPONENTS OF SUSPENSIONS

Since the particles in a suspension are larger than molecules, the effect of gravity on such particles may be used to separate the component parts of a suspension. Among such methods of separating the suspended material are *sedimentation, filtration, centrifugation,* and *coagulation.*

Sedimentation

The settling of solid particles, such as clay or sand, from suspensions is known as sedimentation. The rate at which sedimentation occurs depends upon the size and density of the suspended solid particles. We know that the particles of sand in a sand-water mixture settle much faster than the particles of clay in a clay-water mixture. This occurs because particles of sand are much larger and denser than those of clay. The earth's gravity affects larger, denser particles more than smaller, less dense particles because gravity exerts more force on particles with greater mass.

When a mixture of gravel, sand, clay, and water is shaken in a container and then allowed to settle, the results give evidence that the sedimentation rate is determined by the size and weight of the suspended particles (Fig. 6–5). The gravel (the largest and heaviest particle) is found at the bottom of the container. The sand (the next largest particle) is found immediately above the gravel. The clay (the smallest and lightest particle) is found at the top of the sediment because clay settles at the slowest rate.

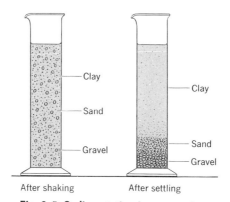

After shaking   After settling

Fig. 6–5. Sedimentation in suspensions.

Filtration

The components of a suspension of solids in liquids can be separated by passing the suspension through a porous solid, if the openings in the solid are smaller than the suspended particles. Filter paper and cheesecloth are typical porous solids that may be used to separate suspended particles from a liquid. This process is called filtration. We observe filtration when a cook prepares spaghetti. After the spaghetti is cooked, the suspension of spaghetti in water is poured through a strainer. The water passes through the strainer, but the spaghetti remains behind.

In the laboratory, filtration is normally used as a means of separating the liquid from the solid in a suspension. You used this method in your laboratory experience (Part E). The water that passes through the filter is called the *filtrate*.

Dissolved solid particles in a solution cannot be removed by filtration because the dissolved particles are of molecular size—much smaller than the pore openings of any ordinary filter.

Centrifugation

Particles settle out of a suspension because of the attractive force of gravity. When a force stronger than gravity acts on a suspension, the rate of sedimentation is increased. To understand this process, recall the feeling you have on a spinning ride at an amusement park. When the spinning ride is rapid, you are thrown outward by a force created by the spinning. In the laboratory, a machine that can produce such a force is called a *centrifuge* (Fig. 6–6). The process is called centrifugation.

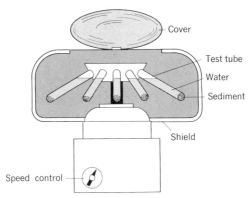

Fig. 6–6. A centrifuge.

When a clay-water suspension is placed in a test tube in a centrifuge and spun, the sediment moves to the farthest end of the tube. The water, free of solid particles, is clear, and stays above the solid. When the centrifuge stops spinning, most of the clear water can be poured off, or *decanted*, and is thus separated from the clay.

Coagulation

Another method of hastening the sedimentation of suspensions is known as coagulation. You carried out this process in the laboratory experience by adding alum and ammonium hydroxide to a suspension. These compounds react and form a jellylike mass to which the suspended particles adhere. Since the particles and jelly are heavy, the mass settles rapidly.

REMOVING POLLUTANTS FROM WATER SUPPLIES

Supplying pure water for drinking purposes is perhaps one of our most important problems. Some of the water we use is obtained through wells from underground water sources. The remainder of our water supply is obtained by collecting water in reservoirs from direct rainfall, and from runoff of rain and melted snow. Water runoff often carries into reservoirs certain undesirable materials such as fertilizers, sewage, chemical wastes from industrial plants, distasteful dissolved gases, and suspended material. Under natural conditions, even without the products of human activity, runoff often carries into reservoirs dissolved soil minerals and bacteria. Before the water from a reservoir reaches the home, the water is usually purified by several of the following processes:

1. *Sedimentation.* In a reservoir, large suspended particles, such as sand, settle to the bottom. Small suspended particles, such as clay, still remain in the water and must be removed by other means.

2. *Coagulation.* The addition of chemicals such as alum and lime produces a jellylike mass to which small suspended particles adhere. This causes many of the tiny suspended particles to settle to the bottom of the reservoir.

3. *Filtration.* The remaining water is filtered through beds of gravel and sand. Filtration removes more of the suspended particles, but some suspended material and bacteria may still remain in the filtrate.

4. *Aeration.* In this process, the water is sprayed high into the air. As this occurs, gases and other substances which give water an unpleasant odor and taste are oxidized. The spraying causes some air to dissolve in the water, thereby improving the taste of the water. Since the ultraviolet rays of the sun kill many bacteria, the aeration of water is generally carried out on sunny days.

5. *Chlorination.* To destroy the bacteria still remaining after aeration, chlorine is added in the proportion of about 4 kilograms of chlorine to about one million kilograms of water. In this proportion, chlorine destroys the bacteria but is relatively harmless to people.

Looking Back

Suspensions, like solutions, are mixtures of variable composition. However, unlike solutions, suspensions are heterogeneous, cloudy, and contain particles of varying sizes. The characteristics of a suspension depend on the size of the particles suspended in it. Coarse particles settle rapidly. Very fine particles remain suspended. Emulsifying agents keep some types of coarse particles suspended indefinitely.

The sizes of colloidal particles are intermediate between molecules and suspended particles. Living systems are colloidal in nature.

Suspended particles are often pollutants in water supplies. Before water is used, it must be treated to remove the pollutants.

Looking Ahead

Particles that are either suspended or dissolved in water change the properties of the water. In Chapter 7, we will study how dissolved particles affect these properties.

Multiple-Choice Questions

1. A type of mixture that always has a cloudy appearance is
   a. a solution   b. a tincture   c. a suspension   d. a colloid
2. Of the following, the one that is *not* an example of a suspension is
   a. sugar water   b. milk   c. milk of magnesia   d. sand in water
3. When sand is shaken in water and allowed to stand,
   a. the sand dissolves   c. the sand remains suspended
   b. the sand settles to the bottom   d. the sand evaporates
4. When clay and sand are mixed with water and allowed to stand,
   a. the sand dissolves, but the clay settles to the bottom
   b. the clay dissolves, but the sand settles to the bottom
   c. both the clay and sand settle to the bottom, but the clay settles faster
   d. both the clay and sand settle to the bottom, but the sand settles faster
5. In a suspension, the solid particles
   a. are molecular in size
   b. are larger than molecules
   c. are smaller than molecules
   d. are sometimes larger and sometimes smaller than molecules
6. The Tyndall effect can best be used to identify
   a. a colloid   b. a suspension   c. a solution   d. an emulsion
7. Of the following, the one that is an example of a suspension is
   a. oil in water   c. dust in air
   b. salt in water   d. sugar in water
8. Of the following, the type of suspension that does *not* exist is
   a. solid in a liquid   c. solid in a gas
   b. liquid in a gas   d. gas in a gas
9. Of the following, the method that is *not* used to separate the parts of a suspension is
   a. sedimentation   c. chromatography
   b. filtration   d. coagulation
10. The speed at which sedimentation occurs depends upon the
    a. nature of the solid particles
    b. size of the particles
    c. pressure on the particles
    d. temperature of the surroundings

11. The process in which a suspension is poured through a porous solid is called
    a. filtration
    c. coagulation
    b. centrifugation
    d. sedimentation
12. The clear liquid that remains after suspended particles are removed by a filter is called the
    a. solution   b. centrifugate   c. sediment   d. filtrate
13. The sedimentation rate of a suspension is increased when the suspension is spun in a centrifuge because
    a. the mass of the particles increases
    b. the velocity of the particles increases
    c. the mass of the particles decreases
    d. the force on the particles increases
14. The process of separating a suspension in which a jellylike mass results is called
    a. sedimentation   b. distillation   c. coagulation   d. filtration
15. In the purification of drinking water, large suspended particles are generally removed by
    a. aeration   b. sedimentation   c. chlorination   d. filtration
16. To remove unpleasant odors and tastes from drinking water, the water is subjected to
    a. chlorination   b. coagulation   c. aeration   d. filtration
17. The process used to destroy bacteria in water involves the use of the element
    a. chlorine   b. bromine   c. iodine   d. sulfur
18. A substance which can be used to prepare an emulsion of oil and vinegar is
    a. egg white   b. alcohol   c. mayonnaise   d. egg yolk
19. The particles of colloids are
    a. molecular in size
    b. larger than those of a solution
    c. larger than those of a suspension
    d. intermediate between the particles of a solution and those of a suspension
20. Colloidal particles
    a. have a small surface area
    c. do not reflect light
    b. have an electric charge
    d. settle out on standing
21. Positively charged colloid particles
    a. migrate toward a negative pole
    b. migrate toward a positive pole
    c. do not move
    d. migrate toward both a negative and a positive pole
22. Brownian motion describes the movement of
    a. atoms
    c. colloidal particles
    b. particles in a suspension
    d. coagulated particles
23. The particles of a solution
    a. absorb all light
    c. reflect light
    b. do not affect light
    d. are opaque to light

Modified True-False Questions

1. A suspension is *a homogeneous* mixture.
2. The reflection of light by the particles in a suspension is called the *colloidal effect*.
3. The settling of solid particles from suspensions is known as *sedimentation*.
4. Cheesecloth can be used to separate suspended solid particles from a liquid in the process of *centrifugation*.
5. A device that produces a force that is used to separate the components of a suspension is *a centrifuge*.
6. A chemical used with ammonium hydroxide or lime to coagulate suspended particles is *chlorine*.
7. The formation of a jellylike mass takes place in the process of *aeration*.
8. The zigzagging motion of the particles in a colloid suspension is called *atomic motion*.

Matching Questions

(Answers may be used more than once.)

Column A

1. always a clear mixture
2. exhibits Tyndall effect
3. two liquids that mix temporarily
4. particles are molecular in size
5. exhibits Brownian motion
6. mixture of a gas in a gas
7. permanent mixture of two immiscible liquids
8. particles have an electric charge
9. no components may be separated by filtration

Column B

a. solution
b. suspension
c. emulsion
d. colloid

Thought Questions

1. Define each of the following terms:
   a. suspension
   b. emulsion
   c. colloid
   d. emulsifying agent
   e. Brownian motion
2. State the processes that are used to purify drinking water.
3. Describe how you could determine whether an unknown mixture is a colloid.
4. Describe how a soap or a detergent is useful in cleaning a grease-covered pan.
5. A suspension of gravel, sand, and clay in water is shaken together and is allowed to settle. Explain why the gravel is always found at the bottom and the clay is always found at the top.

CHAPTER 7

HOW DO DISSOLVED PARTICLES AFFECT THE PROPERTIES OF WATER?

When you have completed this chapter, you should be able to:

1. *State* the physical properties of pure water.
2. *Contrast* the effects of different solutes on the boiling and freezing points of water.
3. *Account* for the physical properties of water and the effects of solutes on these properties, according to the kinetic-molecular theory.
4. *Relate* the ionization theory to electrolytes, nonelectrolytes, and the conductivity of solutions.
5. *Distinguish* between acids, bases, and salts according to the ionization theory.
6. *Define* heat of fusion and heat of vaporization.

In the laboratory experience that follows, you will determine the boiling point of pure water and the boiling point of some solutions.

Laboratory Experience

HOW DO DISSOLVED PARTICLES AFFECT THE BOILING TEMPERATURES OF SOLUTIONS?

A. Pour 50 cubic centimeters of distilled (pure) water into a small beaker. Place the beaker on a piece of iron gauze on a tripod. Insert a thermometer in the water, as shown in Fig. 7–1, page 110.

B. Add several glass beads to the water. Place a Bunsen burner under the beaker, and heat the water until it begins to boil. As the liquid begins to boil, the glass beads will begin to bounce on the bottom of the beaker. As they bounce, they burst the large bubbles of steam in the water. This enables the water to boil safely.

    1. What happens to the temperature of the water as heat is applied?

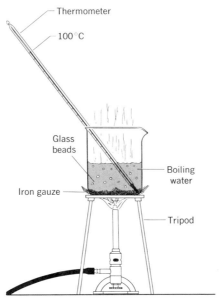

Fig. 7–1.

2. How long did it take for the water to boil after heat was applied?

C. Allow the water to boil until only a quarter of the original quantity remains in the beaker. In the meanwhile, copy the following table into your notebook. Then record in the table the temperature of the water at 1-minute intervals, for 3 minutes. Turn off the burner.

Time (minutes)	Boiling Temperature of Distilled Water	Boiling Temperature of Water + 5 Grams of NaCl	Boiling Temperature of Water + 10 Grams of NaCl
1			
2			
3			

3. What happens to the temperature of the water after it begins to boil and you continue to heat it?

4. What is the temperature at which distilled water boils?

D. Weigh out 5 grams of sodium chloride (NaCl). Dissolve the sodium chloride in a beaker containing 50 cubic centimeters of distilled water. Add several beads to the beaker, insert the thermometer, and heat the water until it boils.

5. How long did it take for the solution to boil after heat was applied?

E. Allow the water to boil until only a quarter of the original quantity remains in the beaker. Then record in the table the temperature of the water at 1-minute intervals, for 3 minutes. Turn off the burner.

6. What is the temperature at which the salt solution boils?

7. How does the boiling temperature of distilled water compare with the boiling temperature of an equal quantity of distilled water to which salt has been added?

F. Repeat the experiment in parts D and E. This time, however, add 10 grams of sodium chloride to the same quantity of distilled water. Record in the table the temperature of the water at 1-minute intervals, for 3 minutes.

8. How long did it take for the water to boil after heat was applied?

9. What is the temperature at which the salt solution boils?

10. What effect does adding 10 grams of sodium chloride to distilled water have on the boiling temperature of the water?

Introduction

When two or more solid substances are mixed, the mixture often has the properties of the individual solids. Thus, when sugar crystals are mixed with sand grains, we can still distinguish the sugar and sand particles. However, when a solid solute is mixed with a liquid solvent, forming a solution, the properties of the solution become different from those of the pure solvent. As we shall see, the boiling temperature, the freezing temperature, and the *conductivity* (ability to carry an electric current) of a solution all differ from those of the pure solvent.

BOILING TEMPERATURE

The temperature at which a liquid begins to boil at sea level is known as the *boiling temperature*, or *boiling point*, of that liquid. The boiling temperature of a liquid is one of its characteristic properties.

The Boiling Point of Water

In the laboratory, we found the boiling temperature of distilled water. We observed that when the temperature of the water reaches approximately 100° Celsius, the water begins to boil. At the boiling point, however, the temperature of the water remains the same even though we continue to heat the liquid. The change of temperature with time in heating a sample of water until it boils is shown by the graph in Fig. 7–2.

The behavior of water as it becomes warmer and then boils can be explained by means of the kinetic-molecular theory. According to this theory, when heat energy is supplied to water, the water molecules move faster. As still more heat is supplied, the molecules increase their speed, and the attractive forces between the water molecules decrease—until the boiling temperature is reached. At this point, any additional heat energy that is supplied causes the water molecules to move fast enough to separate from one another in the liquid and to break away from the surface of the water, forming a gas—water vapor. This is an example of a change of *state*; the water changes from the liquid state to the gaseous state. The amount of heat needed to change 1 gram

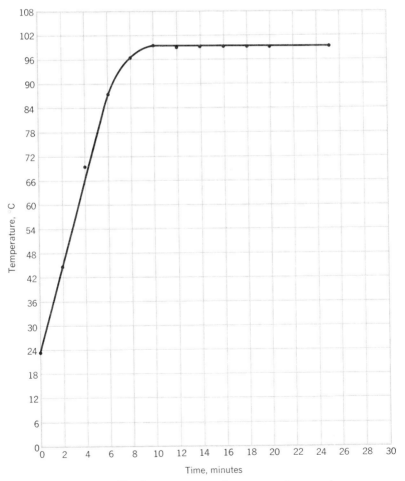

Fig. 7–2. Heating pure water: time-temperature graph.

of a liquid to a gas at its boiling temperature is called the *heat of vaporization*. (This change is also called a *phase change*.)

When water boils and heat energy continues to be supplied to the boiling water, the extra energy is used up as the liquid water changes into water vapor. As a result, the temperature of the water does not increase during boiling, but remains the same as long as any liquid water remains. Note the flat portion of the curve in Fig. 7–2.

Effect of Solutes on the Boiling Point of Water

In the laboratory experience, you dissolved 5 grams of sodium chloride (NaCl) in a 50-cubic-centimeter sample of distilled water. When the temperature of the solution reached approximately 101°C, the solution began to boil. It appears, therefore, that adding the solute (5 grams of NaCl) raises the boiling temperature of water. When you dissolved 10 grams of sodium chloride in a 50-cubic-centimeter sample of distilled water, the boiling temperature of the solution was about 103°C. Adding more solute raised the boiling point still further. Fig. 7–3, page 114, shows these results in the form of graphs.

As you study the two curves that represent the boiling points of the salt solutions, keep in mind that the boiling points differ because there are different amounts of sodium chloride present and dispersed among molecules of water. Again, the kinetic-molecular theory helps us understand what is happening. As heat is supplied to a mixture of water and sodium chloride, the water molecules move more rapidly than they did before they were heated. However, the molecules of water no longer have the complete freedom of motion they had before the sodium chloride was added. This occurs because the solute particles (NaCl) collide with the solvent molecules (H_2O) and interfere with their motion. This means that more heat energy must be supplied to boil the solution than was required to boil the water alone.

When you cook spaghetti or vegetables, you may add salt to the water in which you cook them. In doing so, you try to improve the taste of the food. Now you know that by adding salt, you are also raising the boiling point of the water above 100°C.

FREEZING TEMPERATURE

The temperature at which a liquid begins to solidify (becomes solid) is known as the *freezing temperature*, or *freezing point*. It is also the same temperature at which the solid melts to re-form the liquid (the melting point). Like the boiling point, the freezing point is a characteristic property of a substance. The freezing point of water is the temperature at which water changes to ice at sea level.

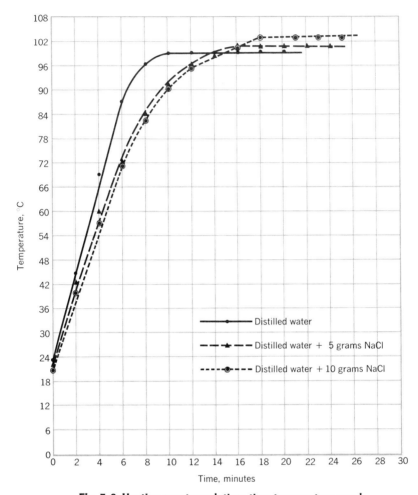

Fig. 7–3. Heating a water solution: time-temperature graph.

The Freezing Point of Water

To determine the freezing point of pure water, we pour 10 cubic centimeters of distilled water into a small beaker and place a thermometer in the water. Then we place this beaker in a larger beaker that contains cracked dry ice (Fig. 7–4).

CAUTION: Be very careful. Dry ice can cause severe burns. Do not handle dry ice with your bare hands.

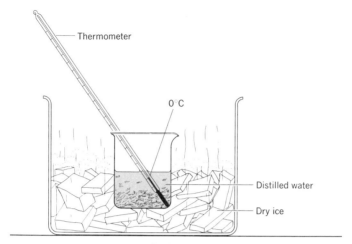

Fig. 7–4. Determining the freezing temperature of water.

In a few minutes, the thermometer shows a drop in the temperature of the water. As the temperature of the water continues to decrease and reaches 0°C, particles of ice form in the water. As more of the water continues to form ice, the temperature remains the same. This temperature is the freezing point of water, which is 0° Celsius. The change of temperature with time in a sample of water until it freezes is shown by the graph in Fig. 7–5.

Here, too, the kinetic-molecular theory helps us understand why the temperature of the water remains constant as it freezes. We know that molecules of the water in the liquid state are in constant motion. As heat energy is removed from the liquid, the water molecules slow down and attract one another more strongly. As more heat is removed,

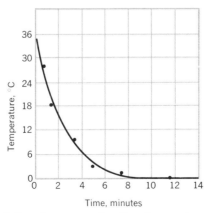

Fig. 7–5. Freezing pure water: time-temperature graph.

these processes continue until the attractive forces between the water molecules are sufficiently great to change the water from a liquid to a solid. During freezing, as long as any liquid water remains, the temperature remains constant because continued withdrawal of heat energy results only in changing more of the liquid to solid.

The amount of heat that must be removed to change 1 gram of a liquid to a solid, at its freezing point, is known as the *heat of fusion*. Similarly, the heat of fusion is the quantity of heat required to melt 1 gram of solid at its melting point.

Effect of Solutes on the Freezing Point of Water

The freezing point of a liquid, as well as its boiling point, changes on the addition of a solute. When we add a solute to water and attempt to freeze this solution, we find that the freezing point of the water is lower than 0°C. The more solute we add, the further the freezing point is lowered. This occurs because the molecules of the solute prevent the molecules of water from coming together to form ice.

The fact that solutes lower the freezing temperature of water is put to use in many ways. For example, when a sufficient amount of salt is used, the freezing point of water can be lowered to about −2°C. If the temperature of an area, such as a sidewalk or highway, is −2°C or higher, any ice present will begin to melt, reducing the hazard to pedestrians and to cars (Fig. 7–6).

Most automobile owners use antifreeze in their car radiators in the

Fig. 7–6. Salt lowers the freezing temperature of water.

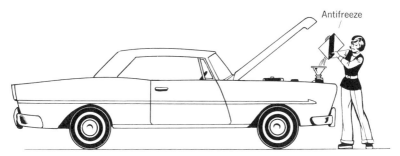

Fig. 7–7. Protecting car radiators from freezing.

winter (Fig. 7–7). Permanent antifreeze mixtures generally contain *ethylene glycol*. When this substance is dissolved in water, the freezing point of the mixture is reduced to a temperature below 0°C. As more ethylene glycol is added, the freezing point is lowered still further. Thus, the water in the radiator does not freeze even though the outside temperature may be far below freezing. Freezing would cause the water to expand and possibly crack the engine block.

CONDUCTIVITY

Solid substances such as graphite (carbon), silver, and copper are excellent conductors of electricity. Is the property of electrical conductivity restricted to solids only? To determine whether or not liquids conduct electricity, we employ a *conductivity apparatus*. This consists of two graphite electrodes and an electric light bulb connected through a switch to a source of electric current, such as a dry cell battery (Fig. 7–8).

When a piece of metal is placed across the two dry graphite electrodes, and the conductivity apparatus is properly connected to a

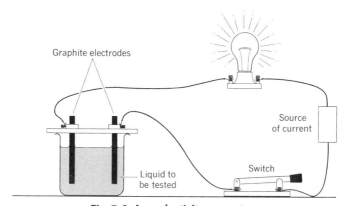

Fig. 7–8. A conductivity apparatus.

source of electricity, the bulb lights. This shows that the metal is a conductor of electricity.

If the two electrodes are now placed in a sample of sugar or in a sample of salt, the bulb does not light. Other solid compounds, such as potassium nitrate or camphor, behave in the same manner. Compounds that do not conduct electricity are called *nonelectrolytes*.

When the sugar is dissolved in water, and the solution is tested for conductivity, we find that the sugar solution is also a nonelectrolyte. However, when the salt is dissolved in water, and the solution is tested for conductivity, we find that this solution does conduct electricity. (Melted salt also conducts electricity.) Compounds that conduct electricity are called *electrolytes*.

Electrolytes and Nonelectrolytes

The ability of compounds to conduct electricity varies considerably. Chemists recognize three classes of compounds:

1. Strong electrolytes—good conductors
2. Weak electrolytes—poor conductors
3. Nonelectrolytes—nonconductors

We distinguish strong electrolytes from weak electrolytes by the effect they have on the brightness of the bulb in the conductivity apparatus. Strong electrolytes cause the bulb to glow brightly; weak electrolytes cause the bulb to glow dimly; nonelectrolytes produce no glow at all. Chemists also employ more sensitive electrical measuring equipment to study conductivity. Such equipment may reveal that certain nonelectrolytes, such as water, are, in reality, weak electrolytes.

In Table 7–1, we have summarized the results of a conductivity experiment involving compounds that are solids (s), compounds that are liquids (l), and aqueous solutions of compounds (aq). Aqueous solutions, you will recall, are solutions in which water is the solvent.

The table reveals that substances conducting electricity are:

1. Aqueous solutions of *acids*, such as hydrochloric acid.
2. Aqueous solutions of *bases*, such as sodium hydroxide.
3. Aqueous solutions of *salts*, such as sodium chloride.

(We will study acids, bases, and salts in the next chapter.) These same compounds, in the absence of water, do not conduct electricity. In addition, a number of pure liquids, such as alcohol and benzene, do not conduct electricity. Although water appears in the column for nonelectrolytes, water is a weak electrolyte, as more sensitive equipment reveals. Let us see how we can explain these observations.

Table 7–1. Conductivity of Some Compounds

Strong Electrolytes (bulb glows brightly)	Weak Electrolytes (bulb glows dimly)	Nonelectrolytes (bulb does not light)
Sulfuric acid (aq) Hydrochloric acid (aq) Sodium hydroxide (aq) Calcium hydroxide (aq) Copper (II) sulfate (aq) Sodium chloride (aq) Sodium nitrate (aq)	Acetic acid (aq) Carbonic acid (aq) Ammonium hydroxide (aq)	Alcohol (l) Benzene (l) Concentrated acetic acid (l) Concentrated sulfuric acid (l) Distilled water (l) Glycerine (l) Sodium chloride (s) Sodium hydroxide (s) Sugar (aq) Turpentine (l)

Ionization

In 1887, *Svante Arrhenius,* a Swedish scientist, attempted to explain the conductivity of electrolytes. He proposed the *theory of electrolytic dissociation.* This theory states that, when certain compounds are dissolved in water, some change in the compound occurs that results in the formation of charged particles. This means that the compound has become an electrolyte.

The Arrhenius theory is very limited in scope because it is based upon the concept that the atom is the smallest particle of matter. Since we now know that atoms consist of electrons, protons, and neutrons, we have modified the views of Arrhenius and are better able to explain the nature of the conductivity process. These ideas may be summarized as follows:

1. Only mobile (moving) charged particles can conduct electricity. The mobile electrons in metals and in some nonmetals permit these solids to behave as conductors. *Ions* are electrically charged atoms or radicals. Compounds made up of ions will also conduct electricity if the ions are free to move.

2. A salt, such as sodium chloride, consists of positively charged sodium ions attracted to negatively charged chloride ions. Because of their opposite charges, these ions are bound together. In the solid form, therefore, these ions cannot move, and the solid compound is a nonelectrolyte. In the presence of water (or some other solvent), however, the attractive forces between these ions are weakened, and the ions become free to move. (Melting also weakens these forces.)

A word equation to show this change is

$$\text{sodium chloride} \xrightarrow{\text{water}} \text{sodium ions} + \text{chloride ions}$$
$$\qquad\quad (solid) \qquad\qquad\qquad (aqueous) \qquad\quad (aqueous)$$

Expressed with symbols, this equation is

$$\text{Na}^+\text{Cl}^- \ (s) \xrightarrow{\text{H}_2\text{O}} \text{Na}^+ \ (aq) + \text{Cl}^- \ (aq)$$

To show the effect of water, chemists generally write Na^+ (*aqueous*) or Na^+ (*aq*), indicating that the free ions are bound to water molecules.

3. A base, such as sodium hydroxide, consists of positively charged sodium ions and negatively charged hydroxide ions bound together. The addition of water produces the same effect as is produced when water is added to sodium chloride. As happens with the salt, freely moving ions are formed. The formation of freely moving ions from ions that are bound together—as in salts and bases—is called *dissociation*.

A word equation to show this change is

$$\text{sodium hydroxide} \xrightarrow{\text{water}} \text{sodium ions} + \text{chloride ions}$$
$$\qquad\quad (solid) \qquad\qquad\qquad (aqueous) \qquad\quad (aqueous)$$

Expressed with symbols, this equation is

$$\text{Na}^+\text{OH}^- \ (s) \xrightarrow{\text{H}_2\text{O}} \text{Na}^+ \ (aq) + \text{OH}^- \ (aq)$$

4. An acid, such as hydrochloric acid, consists of molecules of gaseous hydrogen chloride. These molecules, in turn, consist of atoms of hydrogen covalently bonded to atoms of chlorine (see page 20). The molecules react with water to form freely moving charged particles, as shown in the equation that follows:

$$\text{HCl} \ (g) \xrightarrow{\text{H}_2\text{O}} \text{H}^+ \ (aq) + \text{Cl}^- \ (aq)$$

The formation of freely moving ions from the reaction between molecules, such as HCl and H_2O, is called *ionization*.

5. Certain other covalently bonded molecules, such as sugar or alcohol, do not react with water to produce ions. Hence, they cannot conduct electricity, either in pure form or in water solution.

6. Ions are electrically charged atoms or groups of atoms (radicals).

Ions carry a charge that is generally equal to the valence number of the atom or the radical.

For our purposes, we will use the terms dissociation and ionization interchangeably. It is the freely moving ions, or *mobile ions*, in a solution that carry an electric current. This is why solid salt, which contains bound ions, cannot conduct. A salt solution, or melted salt, permits the ions to become mobile; then, conductivity can take place.

Other examples of ions formed when certain substances are dissolved in water are shown in the following equations:

$$Na_2SO_4 \ (s) \longrightarrow 2\,Na^+ \ (aq) + SO_4^{-2} \ (aq)$$
sodium sulfate

$$HBr \ (g) \longrightarrow H^+ \ (aq) + Br^- \ (aq)$$
hydrogen bromide

$$H_2SO_4 \ (l) \longrightarrow 2\,H^+ \ (aq) + SO_4^{-2} \ (aq)$$
hydrogen sulfate (sulfuric acid)

$$KOH \ (s) \longrightarrow K^+ \ (aq) + OH^- \ (aq)$$
potassium hydroxide

$$KCl \ (s) \longrightarrow K^+ \ (aq) + Cl^- \ (aq)$$
potassium chloride

Explaining Electrical Conductivity

As you know, the term *electricity* means a flow of electrons. The electric plug of a lamp or appliance has two electrical terminals, or prongs, with wire running from each prong. When the plug is inserted into an electrical outlet, the two prongs permit electrons to flow from their source, pass through one wire into the electrical appliance, and then return to the source through the other wire.

Electrons can flow from one point to another only under the following condition (Fig. 7–9, page 122):

1. The point *from* which electrons flow (electrode A) must have more electrons present than the point *to* which they flow (electrode B).

or

2. The point *to* which electrons flow (electrode B) must have fewer electrons present than the point *from* which they flow (electrode A).

We say that, at electrode A, the electrons are in *excess*; at electrode B, the electrons are in *deficiency*.

The terminal or prong (in the plug) having the excess of electrons

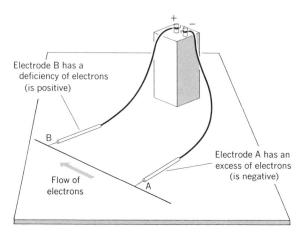

Electrode B has a
deficiency of electrons
(is positive)

B

Flow of
electrons

A

Electrode A has an
excess of electrons
(is negative)

Fig. 7–9. Electrons flow from — to +.

is labeled the *negative terminal*. The terminal having a deficiency of
electrons (which means an excess of protons) is labeled the *positive
terminal*.

When the electrodes of the conductivity apparatus (Fig. 7–10) are
placed in an electrolyte, and the apparatus is properly connected, the
ions in the solution are attracted to the electrode that has a charge
opposite to their own. Thus, in a hydrochloric acid solution, the positive
hydrogen ions are attracted to the negative electrode, also called the
cathode; here they lose their charge and become hydrogen gas. The
negative chloride ions are attracted to the positive electrode, also called
the *anode*; here they lose their charge and become chlorine gas. Thus,
the moving ions permit the electrons to flow through the solution from

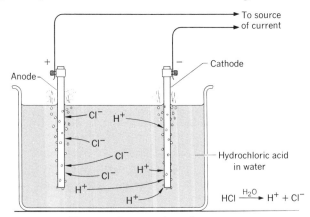

To source
of current

Anode

Cathode

Hydrochloric acid
in water

$HCl \xrightarrow{H_2O} H^+ + Cl^-$

Fig. 7–10. Ions conduct electricity.

one electrode to the other. Thus, conduction occurs through the solution, resulting in chemical changes at each electrode.

As we have noted before, certain substances, such as vinegar, are weak electrolytes. In such cases, only a small number of ions are formed because weak electrolytes ionize only slightly. Most of the acetic acid molecules in vinegar do not react with water, and few ions are formed. Since only a small number of mobile ions are present, vinegar is a poor conductor of electricity.

Nonelectrolytes, such as sugar, do not conduct electricity because the sugar is a covalently bonded molecule; that is, the electrons in sugar molecules are shared electrons that are not free to move. Hence, ions are not present. Furthermore, since sugar molecules do not react with water, ionization does not occur in a sugar solution. In the absence of ions, electrons (or an electric current) cannot be transferred across the solution from one electrode to the other.

THE EFFECT OF IONS ON THE BOILING POINTS AND FREEZING POINTS OF WATER SOLUTIONS

A comparison of the effects of electrolytes and nonelectrolytes on the boiling point and freezing point of water indicates that electrolytes have a greater effect than do nonelectrolytes on these properties of water. Both of these properties are affected when solute particles interfere with the motion of water molecules as the temperature changes. The extent of interference depends upon the number of solute particles present.

When one million molecules of a nonelectrolyte such as sugar are dissolved in water, the molecules do not ionize. The solution still contains one million dissolved sugar particles. The presence of these particles changes the boiling point to some extent. On the other hand, when one million particles of an electrolyte such as sodium chloride (NaCl) are dissolved in water, two million ions are formed. This occurs because each particle of sodium chloride forms two ions (one sodium ion and one chloride ion). The two million ions change the boiling and freezing points more than do the one million molecules of sugar.

Thus, electrolytes in solution form more solute particles than do nonelectrolytes of the same concentration or strength. Therefore, electrolytes have a greater effect on boiling and freezing points. Increasing the concentration of particles means increasing the numbers of particles in a given space. Thus, increasing the concentrations of electrolytes or nonelectrolytes also increases the effects on the boiling and freezing points.

Looking Back

Dissolved particles—particles of electrolytes (ions) and particles of nonelectrolytes—raise the boiling temperature and lower the freezing temperature of water. Particles of electrolytes have a more marked effect than particles of nonelectrolytes. Because the ions of electrolytes are mobile, electrolytes conduct electricity.

Looking Ahead

As a result of ionization, some aqueous solutions of electrolytes give an acid reaction; some give a basic reaction; and some are neither acidic nor basic. Why this occurs is explained in Chapter 8.

Multiple-Choice Questions

1. When the boiling temperature of a liquid is reached, the temperature of the liquid
   a. continues to increase   c. begins to decrease
   b. remains the same   d. decreases a little and then increases again
2. Generally, the boiling temperature of water at sea level is
   a. 0°C   b. 32°C   c. 100°C   d. 212°C
3. When heat is supplied to water, molecular motion
   a. increases then decreases   c. decreases
   b. increases   d. remains the same
4. When water boils and heat energy continues to be applied, the extra energy
   a. increases the water temperature
   b. decreases the water temperature
   c. is not used
   d. changes water to water vapor
5. When sodium chloride is added to water, the boiling temperature of water
   a. decreases   b. increases   c. stays the same   d. none of these
6. The freezing point and the melting point of a substance
   a. may be the same   c. are the same
   b. may be different   d. are different
7. Water freezes at sea level at a temperature of
   a. 32°C   b. 0°C   c. 100°C   d. 212°C
8. As heat energy is removed from water, water molecules
   a. speed up and attract one another
   b. slow down and repel one another
   c. slow down and attract one another
   d. speed up and repel one another

9. When salt is added to water, the freezing point of water is
   a. less than 0°C
   b. 0°C
   c. more than 0°C
   d. more than 100°C
10. Distilled water
    a. boils at 50°C
    b. freezes at 32°C
    c. does not conduct an electric current appreciably
    d. contains dissolved minerals
11. Solid sodium chloride
    a. does not conduct electricity
    b. is a good conductor of electricity
    c. is a poor conductor of electricity
    d. is an electrolyte
12. Of the following, an example of an electrolyte is
    a. dilute hydrochloric acid
    b. sugar solution
    c. alcohol
    d. distilled water
13. Benzene is an example of
    a. a weak electrolyte
    b. a nonelectrolyte
    c. a strong electrolyte
    d. an ionic compound
14. In terms of conducting electricity, a weak electrolyte is a
    a. nonconductor   b. good conductor   c. poor conductor
15. Sodium chloride is composed of
    a. positive sodium and positive chloride ions
    b. negative sodium and negative chloride ions
    c. negative sodium and positive chloride ions
    d. positive sodium and negative chloride ions
16. In the presence of water, the attractive forces between ions
    a. are weakened   b. are made stronger   c. remain unchanged
17. The sodium ion in water can be represented as
    a. Na^+ b. $Na^-\ (aq)$ c. Na^- d. $Na^+\ (aq)$
18. In water solution, bases release
    a. hydrogen ions
    b. chloride ions
    c. hydroxide ions
    d. sulfide ions
19. In water solution, acids release
    a. hydrogen ions
    b. chloride ions
    c. hydroxide ions
    d. sulfide ions
20. In an electrolyte, the electric current is carried by
    a. electrons   b. ions   c. atoms   d. molecules
21. In a hydrochloric acid solution,
    a. hydrogen ions migrate to the negative terminal
    b. chloride ions migrate to the negative terminal
    c. the ions are not mobile
    d. no ions are formed
22. In weak electrolytes,
    a. no ions are formed
    b. few ions are formed
    c. many ions are formed
23. Nonelectrolytes do not conduct an electric current because
    a. no molecules are formed
    b. no ions are formed
    c. no atoms are formed

Modified True-False Questions

1. The amount of heat needed to change a liquid to a gas at its boiling point is called the *heat of fusion.*
2. When salt is added to water, the boiling point of the water *increases.*
3. The temperature at which a liquid becomes a solid is known as the *boiling temperature.*
4. The amount of heat loss needed to change 1 gram of a liquid to a solid at its freezing point is known as the *heat of fusion.*
5. In order to lower the freezing point of water in car radiators, automobile owners use *antifreeze.*
6. Liquid solutions that can conduct an electric current are called *electrodes.*
7. Antifreeze is generally composed of a substance called *isopropyl alcohol.*
8. The theory of electrolytic dissociation was proposed by *Svante Arrhenius.*
9. Electrically charged atoms are called *electrons.*
10. The formation of freely moving ions from ions that are bound together is called *mobility.*
11. As heat is supplied to water, the attractive forces between the water molecules *increase.*
12. The behavior of water molecules during boiling or freezing can be explained by the *chemical theory.*
13. When water begins to freeze, its temperature *remains the same.*

Thought Questions

1. Compare the two terms in each pair:
   a. boiling temperature and freezing temperature
   b. heat of vaporization and heat of fusion
   c. electrolyte and nonelectrolyte
2. Write an equation to show the formation of ions for each of the following substances:
   a. NH_4OH b. HNO_3 c. K_2SO_4 d. $Ca(OH)_2$ e. HI
3. Give a scientific explanation for each of the following:
   a. The addition of solutes increases the boiling temperature of water.
   b. The addition of solutes lowers the freezing temperature of water.
4. Explain why distilled water cannot conduct an electric current, but a sodium chloride solution can conduct a current.
5. Why do some melted solids conduct electricity, while other melted solids do not?

CHAPTER 8

HOW DO ACIDS, BASES, AND SALTS DIFFER?

When you have completed this chapter, you should be able to:

1. *Classify* some common substances as acids, bases, or salts, and state their formulas.
2. *Describe* how to test for acids, bases, and salts.
3. *Discuss* the general methods of preparing each of the following substances: acids, bases, salts.
4. *Compare* the properties of an acid, a base, and a salt.
5. *State* the uses of some common acids, bases, and salts.
6. *Distinguish* between neutralization and hydrolysis.

In the laboratory experience that follows, you will discover the properties of some acids and bases.

Laboratory Experience

WHAT ARE THE PROPERTIES OF ACIDS AND BASES?

CAUTION: Strong acids and strong bases can cause serious burns. Do not spill any on your skin or clothing. If you do, rinse with water.

A. Place a strip of red litmus paper and a strip of blue litmus paper in each of four dishes. Using a clean glass rod, place a drop of dilute hydrochloric acid on each strip of litmus paper in the first dish. Rinse the glass rod thoroughly in running water.
   1. Describe what happens on each piece of litmus paper.
B. Repeat the procedure in part A, this time using dilute sulfuric acid and the second dish. Again rinse the glass rod thoroughly after using it.

2. Describe what happens on each piece of litmus paper in the second dish.

C. Repeat the procedure in part A, this time using acetic acid and the third dish. Again rinse the glass rod thoroughly after using it.

3. Describe what happens on each piece of litmus paper in the third dish.

D. Repeat the procedure in part A, this time using tap water and the fourth dish.

4. Describe what happens to each piece of litmus paper in the fourth dish.

5. What is the purpose of using tap water in the last part of this experiment?

6. What kind of litmus paper can be used as a test for acids? Explain.

E. Place four 150-millimeter test tubes in a rack. Place a small piece of mossy zinc in each of the test tubes. To the first test tube, add 10 cubic centimeters of dilute hydrochloric acid. To the second test tube, add 10 cubic centimeters of dilute sulfuric acid. To the third test tube, add 10 cubic centimeters of dilute acetic acid. To the fourth test tube, add 10 cubic centimeters of water.

7. Describe what you observe in each of the test tubes.

8. Hold a burning splint to the mouth of each test tube. Describe what happens.

9. Explain your observation.

10. What substance is present in all the acids you used?

F. As you did in part A, place a strip of red litmus paper and a strip of blue litmus paper into each of four dishes. Using a clean glass rod, place a drop of dilute sodium hydroxide on the strip of red litmus paper in one of the dishes. Place a drop of dilute sodium hydroxide on the strip of blue litmus paper in the same dish. Rinse the glass rod thoroughly in running water.

Repeat the procedure, using a solution of calcium hydroxide in the second dish, dilute ammonium hydroxide in the third dish, and tap water in the fourth dish.

11. In each case, describe what happens to the litmus paper in the dishes.

12. What kind of litmus paper can be used as a test for bases? Explain.

13. If you have an unknown liquid that does not respond to the litmus test, should you conclude that the liquid is water? Explain.

Introduction

In everyday life we deal with many compounds that chemists classify as acids, bases, and salts. Many of these compounds are present in the body, in food, and in medicines. A few of these compounds are air and water pollutants.

ACIDS

An acid most of us ingest daily is citric acid, which is present in orange juice and grapefruit juice. These juices, and others, also contain ascorbic acid, a substance more commonly known as vitamin C. Salads are often flavored with vinegar, which contains dilute acetic acid. Boric acid is a substance that is sometimes used to wash the eyes.

Among important acids used in oil refining, drug manufacturing, fertilizer production, and other industries are hydrochloric acid, sulfuric acid, and nitric acid. These acids, called mineral acids, are also found in any chemical laboratory. They are called mineral acids because they can be prepared from naturally occurring compounds called minerals. Mineral acids are generally stronger than household acids. They should be handled with great care because they can burn skin and clothing.

Testing for Acids

Many dyes change color in the presence of an acid. Such dyes show, or indicate, when an acid is present and, hence, are called *indicators*. *Litmus* is an example of a vegetable dye. Litmus, which is blue, can be prepared in the laboratory. When blue litmus is exposed to an acid, the litmus turns red. This is the test for an acid.

For convenience in use, filter paper is dipped into a litmus solution, and the paper is allowed to dry. When a sample of an acid is placed on *blue litmus paper*, the color changes to *red*. When acid is placed on red litmus paper, the color does not change. (Red litmus paper has been previously treated with acid. Adding more acid does not change the red color.)

How Acids Are Prepared

In general, acids may be prepared by two methods: (1) certain gases, related to the acids, are dissolved in water; (2) certain compounds (salts), related to the acids, are allowed to react with sulfuric acid. These compounds are combinations of a metal and a nonmetal.

1. *Preparing acids from gases.* To prepare sulfurous acid (H_2SO_3) in the laboratory, powdered sulfur, held in a deflagrating spoon (a long-handled iron spoon) is burned in air, forming sulfur dioxide gas (SO_2). The sulfur dioxide is then dissolved in water to form sulfurous acid (Fig. 8–1). The reactions take place according to the following equations:

$$S\ (s) \quad + \quad O_2\ (g) \quad \longrightarrow \quad SO_2\ (g)$$
sulfur   oxygen   sulfur
                                                                  dioxide

$$SO_2\ (g) \quad + \quad H_2O\ (l) \quad \longrightarrow \quad H_2SO_3\ (aq)$$
sulfur   water   sulfurous
dioxide   acid

Note that *sulfur dioxide* gas produces *sulfurous acid.* When sulfurous acid is tested with blue litmus paper, the litmus turns red, indicating the presence of an acid.

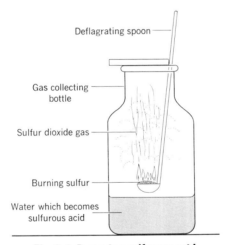

Fig. 8–1. Preparing sulfurous acid.

The second equation should help you understand why air polluted with sulfur dioxide is harmful. When sulfur dioxide is inhaled, it dissolves in the moisture present in the breathing passages and around the eyes and forms sulfurous acid. The acid then irritates the membranes of the eyes, nose, throat, and lungs.

When carbon dioxide gas dissolves in water, carbonic acid is formed according to the following equation:

$$CO_2\ (g) \quad + \quad H_2O\ (l) \quad \longrightarrow \quad H_2CO_3\ (aq)$$
carbon   water   carbonic
dioxide   acid

Note that *carbon dioxide* gas produces *carbonic acid*. When carbonic acid (soda water) is tested with blue litmus paper, the litmus turns red, indicating the presence of an acid.

2. *Preparing acids from salts.* Hydrochloric acid can be prepared from table salt (a compound of a metal and a nonmetal) by heating a mixture of sodium chloride and sulfuric acid. The reaction is:

$$2\,NaCl\,(s) \quad + \quad H_2SO_4\,(aq) \longrightarrow 2\,HCl\,(g) \quad + \quad Na_2SO_4\,(aq)$$

| sodium chloride | sulfuric acid | hydrochloric acid | sodium sulfate |

Nitric acid can be prepared similarly by heating sodium nitrate (a salt) with sulfuric acid:

$$2\,NaNO_3\,(s) \quad + \quad H_2SO_4\,(aq) \longrightarrow 2\,HNO_3\,(aq) \quad + \quad Na_2SO_4\,(aq)$$

| sodium nitrate | sulfuric acid | nitric acid | sodium sulfate |

In the preceding two equations, notice that *hydrochloric acid* (HCl) is made from *chloride* (Cl) salts, and that *nitric acid* (HNO_3) is made from *nitrate* (NO_3) salts.

Properties of Acids

The water solutions of acids have the following properties:

1. *Acids taste sour.* Citric acid is responsible for the sour taste of lemons, limes, grapefruit, and oranges. Acetic acid is responsible for the sour taste of vinegar. Because of the risk involved, it is generally unwise to taste any unknown substances. However, chemists have found that a sour taste is a charactertistic of all acids.

2. *Acids turn litmus red.* As we have noted before, acids turn blue litmus red. You have observed this effect in your laboratory experience.

3. *Acids contain combined hydrogen.* In the laboratory, you observed that when a sample of zinc, a fairly reactive metal, is dropped into a test tube containing an acid such as hydrochloric acid, a reaction occurs. The bubbling in the tube indicates that a gas is released. When you inserted a burning splint into the test tube, the gas burst into flame and may have produced a small popping sound (Fig. 8–2, page 132). This is a characteristic test for hydrogen gas. In general, when certain acids react with reactive metals, hydrogen gas is released. The following equations are some typical examples of these reactions:

| $Zn\ (s)$ | $+$ | $2\,HCl\ (aq)$ | $\longrightarrow$ | $H_2\ (g)$ | $+$ | $ZnCl_2\ (aq)$ |
| zinc | | hydrochloric acid | | hydrogen | | zinc chloride |

| $Zn\ (s)$ | $+$ | $H_2SO_4\ (aq)$ | $\longrightarrow$ | $H_2\ (g)$ | $+$ | $ZnSO_4\ (aq)$ |
| zinc | | sulfuric acid | | hydrogen | | zinc sulfate |

| $Mg\ (s)$ | $+$ | $2\,HCl\ (aq)$ | $\longrightarrow$ | $H_2\ (g)$ | $+$ | $MgCl_2\ (aq)$ |
| magnesium | | hydrochloric acid | | hydrogen | | magnesium chloride |

| $Fe\ (s)$ | $+$ | $H_2SO_4\ (aq)$ | $\longrightarrow$ | $H_2\ (g)$ | $+$ | $FeSO_4\ (aq)$ |
| iron | | sulfuric acid | | hydrogen | | iron (II) sulfate |

From a study of many such reactions, chemists have concluded that an element common to all acids is hydrogen.

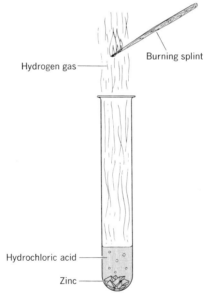

Fig. 8–2. Acids react with some metals to form hydrogen.

4. *Acids release hydrogen ions in water solutions.* When an acid is dissolved in water, the acid ionizes, releasing both positively charged hydrogen ions and negatively charged ions of a nonmetal or nonmetallic radical. Thus, when hydrochloric acid is dissolved in water, the acid ionizes, forming hydrogen ions and chloride ions, as shown in the following equation:

HCl (aq)	$\longrightarrow$	H$^+$ (aq)	$+$	Cl$^-$ (aq)
hydrochloric acid		hydrogen ion		chloride ion

Other examples of the ionization of acids in water are:

H$_2$SO$_4$ (aq)	$\longrightarrow$	2 H$^+$ (aq)	$+$	SO$_4{}^{-2}$ (aq)
sulfuric acid		hydrogen ion		sulfate ion

HNO$_3$ (aq)	$\longrightarrow$	H$^+$ (aq)	$+$	NO$_3{}^-$ (aq)
nitric acid		hydrogen ion		nitrate ion

HC$_2$H$_3$O$_2$ (aq)	$\underset{\longleftarrow}{\longrightarrow}$	H$^+$ (aq)	$+$	C$_2$H$_3$O$_2{}^-$ (aq)
acetic acid		hydrogen ion		acetate ion

H$_3$PO$_4$ (aq)	$\longrightarrow$	3 H$^+$ (aq)	$+$	PO$_4{}^{-3}$ (aq)
phosphoric acid		hydrogen ion		phosphate ion

(Note the use of a double arrow in the ionization of acetic acid. In Chapter 7, we found that acetic acid is a *weak* electrolyte. The smaller arrow pointing to the right indicates that the change to the right (ionization) is relatively small. This means that, in a solution of acetic acid, we have a large number of acetic acid molecules with a few hydrogen ions and a few acetate ions.)

From a knowledge of the properties of acids, we can define acids as substances that release hydrogen ions in solution. It is these H$^+$ (aq) ions that are responsible for the properties of acids. The properties of acids, such as hydrochloric acid, are summarized in Fig. 8–3. (The

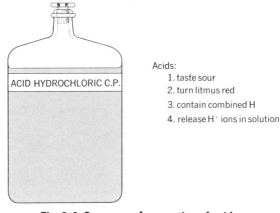

Acids:
1. taste sour
2. turn litmus red
3. contain combined H
4. release H$^+$ ions in solution

ACID HYDROCHLORIC C.P.

Fig. 8–3. Summary of properties of acids.

designation C.P. refers to the purity of the acid and means *chemically pure*.)

Uses of Acids

Sulfuric acid is the chemical most widely used in industry. One use of sulfuric acid is in producing other acids, such as hydrochloric and nitric acids, because the boiling point of sulfuric acid is higher than that of other acids. This allows the acid being produced to be distilled and collected separately from the starting materials.

Sulfuric acid is also used to remove the surface oxide layers on metals (a process called *pickling*) before the metals are coated with materials that prevent rusting. For example, before iron is coated with chromium (in chromium plating), the iron is dipped into dilute sulfuric acid to remove the iron oxide normally present on the surface of the iron.

Another important use of sulfuric acid is in the storage cell. In a lead storage cell (Fig. 8–4), dilute sulfuric acid serves as the electrolyte through which ions move between one electrode composed of lead and another electrode composed of lead dioxide. The lead electrode acts as the cathode; the lead dioxide acts as the anode. Several such cells connected together make up the type of storage battery used in automobiles.

Nitric acid, another important industrial acid, is used in the manufacture of fertilizers, plastics, photographic film, and dyes. Nitric acid is also used in the preparation of such explosives as dynamite and TNT.

Hydrochloric acid, like sulfuric acid, is used to clean metals; it is

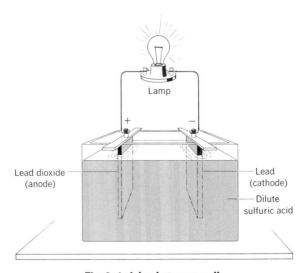

Fig. 8–4. A lead storage cell.

also used to clean brick and tile. Hydrochloric acid is used in the manufacture of sugar and glue. Hydrochloric acid is also produced in small quantities in the stomach, where the acid aids digestion.

BASES

Bases (*hydroxides*) are found in many kitchens because bases dissolve grease and are generally good cleaning agents. A base commonly used for cleaning is ammonia water, or ammonium hydroxide (NH_4OH). Other examples of bases are milk of magnesia (magnesium hydroxide), which is used as an antacid remedy, and lye (sodium hydroxide), which is used in clearing stuffed kitchen and bathroom drains. Commercially, sodium hydroxide is used to make soap and to refine petroleum.

Testing for Bases

Most indicators used in testing for acids are also used in testing for bases. These indicators have one color in the presence of an acid but change to another color in the presence of a base. For example, whereas a sample of an acid changes blue litmus paper to red, a sample of a base changes *red litmus paper* (which has been treated with an acid) back to *blue*. When a base is placed on blue litmus paper, the color does not change.

Another common indicator used to detect the presence of a base is the compound *phenolphthalein*. This compound is a white powder which forms a colorless solution in water or alcohol. When mixed with a base, phenolphthalein solution turns pink. (When mixed with an acid, this indicator solution remains colorless.)

How Bases Are Prepared

In general, bases may be prepared by two methods: (1) by the reaction of water and very reactive metals that are related to the bases; (2) by the reaction of water and certain oxides that are related to the bases.

1. *Preparing bases from water and metals.* When sodium metal is placed in water, sodium hydroxide is formed, and hydrogen gas is released (Fig. 8–5). Since the formula for water can be written as HOH instead of H_2O, the reaction may be represented as follows:

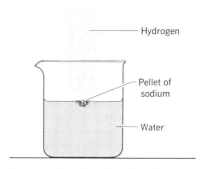

Fig. 8–5. Reaction of sodium in water.

$$2\,\mathrm{Na}\ (s) + 2\,\mathrm{HOH}\ (l) \longrightarrow 2\,\mathrm{NaOH}\ (aq) + \mathrm{H_2}\ (g)$$
sodium   water   sodium   hydrogen
                                                  hydroxide

Similar reactions occur with the metals potassium and calcium:

$$2\,\mathrm{K}\ (s) + 2\,\mathrm{HOH}\ (l) \longrightarrow 2\,\mathrm{KOH}\ (aq) + \mathrm{H_2}\ (g)$$
potassium   water   potassium   hydrogen
                                                hydroxide

$$\mathrm{Ca}\ (s) + 2\,\mathrm{HOH}\ (l) \longrightarrow \mathrm{Ca(OH)_2}\ (aq) + \mathrm{H_2}\ (g)$$
calcium   water   calcium   hydrogen
                                                hydroxide

In the preceding three equations, note that *sodium* forms *sodium hydroxide*; *potassium* forms *potassium hydroxide*; *calcium* forms *calcium hydroxide*.

CAUTION: Care must be exercised in performing these reactions, since the metals react very vigorously with water. Only very small quantities of metal should be used.

---

2. *Preparing bases from water and oxides.* When calcium oxide is mixed with water, calcium hydroxide is formed:

$$\mathrm{CaO}\ (s) \quad + \quad \mathrm{HOH}\ (l) \longrightarrow \mathrm{Ca(OH)_2}\ (aq)$$
calcium   water   calcium
oxide   hydroxide

Note that *calcium oxide* forms *calcium hydroxide*. Since considerable heat is released in this reaction, suitable precautions must be taken.

Properties of Bases

The water solutions of bases have the following properties:

1. *Bases taste bitter.* A bitter taste is characteristic of all bases. It is the presence of a base that gives unflavored milk of magnesia its bitter taste.

2. *Bases feel slippery.* If you rub a drop or two of household ammonia between your fingers, you experience the slippery feeling of a base. Wet soap is also slippery because of the presence of a base.

3. *Bases turn litmus blue.* As you noted in the laboratory experience, bases change red litmus paper to blue. All bases have the same effect on litmus.

4. *Bases release hydroxide ions in water solution.* When dissolved in water, bases ionize, releasing positively charged metal ions (or metallic radical ions) and negatively charged hydroxide ions. For example, when sodium hydroxide is dissolved in water, the sodium hydroxide ionizes as follows:

$$\text{NaOH } (s) \quad \xrightarrow{\text{H}_2\text{O}} \quad \text{Na}^+ (aq) \quad + \quad \text{OH}^- (aq)$$

sodium   sodium   hydroxide
hydroxide   ion   ion

Other bases ionize as follows:

$$\text{KOH } (s) \quad \xrightarrow{\text{H}_2\text{O}} \quad \text{K}^+ (aq) \quad + \quad \text{OH}^- (aq)$$

potassium   potassium   hydroxide
hydroxide   ion   ion

$$\text{NH}_4\text{OH } (aq) \quad \underset{\longleftarrow}{\overset{\longrightarrow}{}} \quad \text{NH}_4^+ (aq) \quad + \quad \text{OH}^- (aq)$$

ammonium   ammonium   hydroxide
hydroxide   ion   ion

(Note the use of a double arrow in the ionization of the weak base ammonium hydroxide. Recall the ionization of weak acetic acid.)

From a knowledge of the properties of bases, we can define bases as substances that release hydroxide (also called *hydroxyl*) ions in solution. It is these OH^- (aq) ions that are responsible for the properties of bases. The properties of bases, such as sodium hydroxide, are summarized in Fig. 8–6, page 138. (DIL. means dilute.)

Uses of Bases

Ammonium hydroxide, frequently called ammonia, is used in the preparation of important related compounds, such as nitric acid and ammonium chloride. As we mentioned before, ammonia is also used as a cleaning agent.

Sodium hydroxide is used in the manufacture of soap, rayon, and paper. Strong solutions of this base are very *caustic;* that is, they are extremely harmful to the skin.

Calcium hydroxide, commonly known as *slaked lime,* is used in the preparation of plaster and mortar. Water solutions of calcium hydroxide,

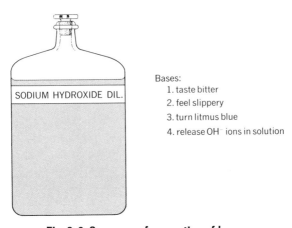

Fig. 8–6. Summary of properties of bases.

called *limewater*, can be used in the laboratory as a test for the presence of carbon dioxide.

SALTS

Many chemical compounds may be classified as salts. The salt most familiar to all of us is table salt—sodium chloride. Baking soda is another salt—sodium bicarbonate. Magnesium sulfate, also called Epsom salts, is a salt used as a laxative.

How Salts Are Prepared

In general, salts are ionic compounds that are composed of tightly bonded metallic ions and nonmetallic ions. For example, sodium chloride is composed of metallic sodium ions and nonmetallic chloride ions. (Some salts are composed of metallic radical ions and nonmetallic radical ions. For example, ammonium nitrate is composed of ammonium ions and nitrate ions.)

In general, salts may be prepared by three methods: (1) the reaction of acids and bases; (2) direct combination; (3) the reaction of a metal oxide with an acid.

1. *Preparing salts from acids and bases.* When an acid and a base react, they counteract, or *neutralize*, each other. Such a reaction, known as a *neutralization reaction*, results in the formation of water and a salt.

For example, when sodium hydroxide and hydrochloric acid react, water and the salt sodium chloride are formed. First, the hydrochloric acid ionizes, releasing hydrogen ions and chloride ions. At the same time, the sodium hydroxide ionizes, releasing sodium ions and hydroxide ions.

$$HCl \rightarrow H^+ (aq) + Cl^- (aq)$$
$$NaOH \rightarrow Na^+ (aq) + OH^- (aq)$$

Then, since these four ions are mobile in the solution, hydrogen ions meet hydroxide ions and unite to form water. At the same time, sodium ions and chloride ions remain as aqueous salt.

$$H^+ (aq) + Cl^- (aq) + Na^+ (aq) + OH^- (aq) \rightarrow HOH (l) + NaCl (aq)$$

Other examples of neutralization reactions are:

$$HNO_3 (aq) + NaOH (aq) \rightarrow HOH (l) + NaNO_3 (aq)$$

nitric acid   sodium hydroxide   water   sodium nitrate

$$HCl (aq) + KOH (aq) \rightarrow HOH (l) + KCl (aq)$$

hydrochloric acid   potassium hydroxide   water   potassium chloride

$$H_2SO_4 (aq) + 2 NH_4OH (aq) \rightarrow 2 HOH (l) + (NH_4)_2SO_4 (aq)$$

sulfuric acid   ammonium hydroxide   water   ammonium sulfate

A study of many neutralization reactions reveals that neutralization reactions may be generalized as follows:

$$\text{an acid} + \text{a base} \rightarrow \text{water} + \text{a salt}$$

2. *Preparing salts by direct combination.* When a metal reacts with a nonmetal, a salt is generally formed. For example, when the metal magnesium is burned in the nonmetal chlorine, the salt magnesium chloride is formed:

$$Mg (s) + Cl_2 (g) \longrightarrow MgCl_2 (s)$$

metal   nonmetal   salt

3. *Preparing salts from a metal oxide and an acid.* When a metal oxide reacts with an acid, a salt is formed. For example, when calcium oxide reacts with nitric acid, the salt calcium nitrate is formed:

metal oxide   acid   salt
$$CaO (s) + 2 HNO_3 (aq) \longrightarrow Ca(NO_3)_2 (aq) + HOH (l)$$
calcium oxide   nitric acid   calcium nitrate   water

Properties of Salts

Salts are ionic compounds that have the following properties:

1. *Salts taste salty.* The salty taste of ocean water is due to the presence of such salts as sodium chloride and magnesium bromide. Chemical analysis reveals that seawater contains many salts. Table 8–1 lists these salts and their approximate percentage in seawater.

Table 8–1. Percentage of Salts in Seawater

Salt	Formula	Percentage
Sodium chloride	$NaCl$	2.72
Magnesium chloride	$MgCl_2$	0.38
Magnesium sulfate	$MgSO_4$	0.17
Calcium sulfate	$CaSO_4$	0.13
Potassium chloride	KCl	0.09
Calcium carbonate	$CaCO_3$	0.01
Magnesium bromide	$MgBr_2$	0.01

2. *Salts dissociate in water.* We have already indicated that salts consist of tightly bonded ions. When a salt is dissolved in water, these bonds are weakened, and the ions become mobile. This accounts for the fact that salt solutions are generally electrolytes (see Chapter 7, pages 118–119).

In water, for example, sodium chloride ionizes, or dissociates, according to the following equation:

$$NaCl\ (s) \xrightarrow{\ H_2O\ } Na^+\ (aq) \quad + \quad Cl^-\ (aq)$$

sodium	sodium	chloride
chloride	ion	ion

Other examples of the ionization of salt solutions are as follows:

$$K_2SO_4\ (s) \xrightarrow{\ H_2O\ } 2\,K^+\ (aq) \quad + \quad SO_4{}^{-2}\ (aq)$$

potassium	potassium	sulfate
sulfate	ion	ion

$$NaNO_3\ (s) \xrightarrow{\ H_2O\ } Na^+\ (aq) \quad + \quad NO_3{}^-\ (aq)$$

sodium	sodium	nitrate
nitrate	ion	ion

$$CaSO_4\ (s) \xrightarrow{\ H_2O\ } Ca^{+2}\ (aq) \quad + \quad SO_4{}^{-2}\ (aq)$$

calcium	calcium	sulfate
sulfate	ion	ion

$$KCl\ (s) \xrightarrow{\ H_2O\ } K^+\ (aq) \quad + \quad Cl^-\ (aq)$$

potassium ⟶ potassium ⟶ chloride
chloride   ion   ion

$$MgBr_2\ (s) \xrightarrow{\ H_2O\ } Mg^{+2}\ (aq) \quad + \quad 2\,Br^-\ (aq)$$

magnesium ⟶ magnesium ⟶ bromide
bromide   ion   ion

3. *Salts may react with water.* When solutions of salts are tested with litmus paper, we find that some salts change blue litmus to red, indicating the presence of an acid. Other water solutions of salts cause red litmus to become blue, indicating the presence of a base. Still other salt solutions have no effect on litmus. To understand this situation, let us examine what occurs when a salt such as sodium carbonate dissolves in water.

When sodium carbonate dissolves in water, the salt liberates sodium ions and carbonate ions. At the same time, the water itself ionizes slightly to form hydrogen and hydroxide ions (remember that water is a weak electrolyte):

$$Na_2CO_3\ (s) \xrightarrow{\ H_2O\ } 2\,Na^+\ (aq) \quad + \quad CO_3^{-2}\ (aq)$$

sodium ⟶ sodium ⟶ carbonate
carbonate   ion   ion

$$HOH\ (l) \longrightarrow H^+\ (aq) + OH^-\ (aq)$$

Thus, the following particles may be present in a solution of sodium carbonate: water molecules, sodium ions, carbonate ions, hydrogen ions, and hydroxide ions. The ions of opposite charge attract one another and combine to form sodium hydroxide and carbonic acid:

$$2\,Na^+\ (aq) + CO_3^{-2}\ (aq) +$$
$$2\,H^+\ (aq) + 2\,OH^-\ (aq) \rightarrow 2\,NaOH\ (aq) + H_2CO_3\ (aq)$$

The reaction of a salt and water to form an acid and a base is called a *hydrolysis reaction*. The following general equation may be applied to all hydrolysis reactions:

$$a\ salt + water \rightarrow an\ acid + a\ base$$

Since acids and bases react to form water and salt (we learned this in our study of neutralization reactions), hydrolysis reactions are the reverse of neutralization reactions.

When sodium carbonate is dissolved in water, carbonic acid and sodium hydroxide are formed. Carbonic acid, H_2CO_3, is the acid that is present in soda water and is a weak electrolyte. Since carbonic acid decomposes on standing to form CO_2 gas and H_2O, it is also called a weak acid. From conductivity experiments, we know that sodium hydroxide, NaOH, is a strong electrolyte, or a strong base. When a solution of sodium carbonate is tested with blue litmus paper and red litmus paper, the red litmus becomes blue, indicating that the solution is basic. This is further proof that, in this case, the base formed during hydrolysis is stronger than the acid. Thus, the equation for this hydrolysis reaction may be written as

$$Na_2CO_3\ (aq) + 2\ HOH\ (l) \rightarrow \underset{\substack{\text{weak} \\ \text{acid}}}{H_2CO_3\ (aq)} + \underset{\substack{\text{strong} \\ \text{base}}}{2\ NaOH\ (aq)}$$

The salt of a strong acid and a weak base, on hydrolysis, yields an acid that is stronger than the base. Consequently, the effect of such a solution on litmus is that of an acid. For example, a water solution of ammonium chloride results in the formation of a weak base, ammonium hydroxide, and a strong acid, hydrochloric acid:

$$NH_4Cl\ (aq) + HOH\ (l) \rightarrow \underset{\substack{\text{weak} \\ \text{base}}}{NH_4OH\ (aq)} + \underset{\substack{\text{strong} \\ \text{acid}}}{HCl\ (aq)}$$

Thus, when a solution of ammonium chloride is tested with blue litmus and red litmus, the blue litmus turns red, indicating that the solution is acidic.

The salt of a strong acid and a strong base (or weak acid and weak base) does not hydrolyze appreciably. The effect of such a solution on litmus paper is neither that of an acid nor that of a base. For example, when sodium chloride is dissolved in water, and the solution is tested with blue litmus and red litmus, neither color changes, indicating that the solution is neither acidic nor basic. Such a solution is said to be *neutral*.

The properties of salts, such as sodium chloride, are summarized in Fig. 8–7.

Uses of Salts

Table 8–2 lists the uses of some common salts.

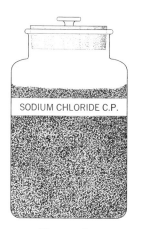

Salts:
1. taste salty
2. dissociate in water
3. may react with water

Fig. 8–7. Summary of properties of salts.

Table 8–2. The Uses of Some Salts

Salt	Formula	Use
Ammonium chloride	NH_4Cl	In soldering; as electrolyte in dry cells
Sodium bicarbonate	$NaHCO_3$	In baking powder; in manufacture of glass
Sodium chloride	$NaCl$	For seasoning and preserving food; essential in life processes
Calcium chloride	$CaCl_2$	As a drying agent to absorb moisture; in freezing mixtures
Silver bromide	$AgBr$	In making photographic film
Potassium nitrate	KNO_3	In manufacture of explosives; as a fertilizer
Sodium nitrate	$NaNO_3$	As a fertilizer; source of nitric acid

Looking Back

Acids, bases, and salts differ in taste, in their effect on litmus, and in the ions they release when dissolved in water. Acids taste sour. When dissolved in water, they release hydrogen ions and turn litmus red. Bases taste bitter. When dissolved in water, they release hydroxide ions and turn litmus blue. Salts taste salty. They react with water, forming an acid and a base, and change the color of litmus according to the strengths of the acid and the base formed. If both the acid and the base are equally strong, a salt solution has no effect on litmus.

Looking Ahead

The chemical principles we have learned are used in many chemical processes. In the next chapter, we will study the processes used in extracting useful metals from compounds found in the earth. We will also learn how these processes contribute to spoiling·our environment.

Multiple-Choice Questions

1. A common substance that contains acetic acid is
   a. vinegar   b. ammonia water   c. salad oil   d. soap
2. Of the following, the property that most closely relates to acids is
   a. bitter taste   c. sour taste
   b. contains the hydroxide radical   d. salty taste
3. The sour taste of lemons and limes is due to a substance called
   a. acetic acid   c. hydrochloric acid
   b. citric acid   d. carbonic acid
4. A dye commonly used to test the acidity of a substance is
   a. gentian violet   b. litmus   c. Congo red   d. methylene blue
5. An element common to all acids is
   a. chlorine   b. nitrogen   c. oxygen   d. hydrogen
6. When magnesium and hydrochloric acid react, they produce
   a. oxygen and magnesium chloride
   b. chlorine and magnesium oxide
   c. hydrogen and magnesium chloride
   d. hydrogen and magnesium oxide
7. When an acid is dissolved in water, it usually forms
   a. hydrogen ions   c. no ions
   b. hydroxide ions   d. chlorine ions
8. An acid used to prepare other acids because of its higher boiling point is
   a. HCl   b. H_2SO_4 c. HNO_3 d. H_2CO_3
9. The acid used in the storage battery is
   a. nitric acid   c. tartaric acid
   b. hydrochloric acid   d. sulfuric acid
10. The acid used in the preparation of dynamite is
    a. H_3PO_4 b. H_2SO_3 c. HNO_3 d. HCl
11. When water solutions of an acid and a base are mixed,
    a. no reaction occurs
    b. a new acid and a new base are formed
    c. a salt and water are formed
    d. an acid and a salt are formed
12. Milk of magnesia is an example of
    a. a base   b. an acid   c. a salt   d. a solution

13. When a water solution of a base is placed on red and blue litmus paper,
    a. no change is observed
    b. the red litmus becomes blue
    c. the blue litmus becomes red
    d. the red litmus becomes blue and the blue litmus becomes red
14. When bases ionize, they release
    a. hydrogen ions   c. chloride ions
    b. sodium ions   d. hydroxide ions
15. A base used in the manufacture of soap is
    a. $Ca(OH)_2$ b. NaOH   c. NH_4OH d. $Zn(OH)_2$
16. A base used to prepare plaster and mortar is
    a. $Mg(OH)_2$ b. NaOH   c. $Ca(OH)_2$ d. KOH
17. A base can be prepared by the reaction between
    a. an active nonmetal with water   c. a sulfide with water
    b. a gas with water   d. an active metal with water
18. In general, salts
    a. are ionic compounds   c. contain hydroxide ions
    b. contain hydrogen ions   d. turn blue litmus red
19. When dissolved in water, salts
    a. are nonelectrolytes   c. are electrolytes
    b. have a bitter taste   d. release hydrogen ions
20. When a solution of table salt is tested with litmus paper, we find that
    the salt solution
    a. is basic
    b. is acidic
    c. is sometimes basic and sometimes acidic
    d. does not affect the paper
21. In water solution, ammonium chloride produces
    a. a strong base   c. a weak acid
    b. a strong acid   d. a neutral solution
22. When a strong acid and a strong base are mixed together and tested with
    litmus paper,
    a. no change occurs
    b. the red litmus becomes blue
    c. the blue litmus becomes red
    d. both the red and blue litmus change color
23. Of the following, the salt that is used to make photographic film is
    a. NaCl   b. $Ca(NO_3)_2$ c. K_2SO_4 d. AgBr
24. A salt used as the electrolyte in dry cells is
    a. ammonium carbonate   c. silver nitrate
    b. ammonium chloride   d. sodium sulfate

Modified True-False Questions

1. Fruit juices, such as orange juice, contain *boric acid.*
2. Dyes used to determine whether a substance is an acid or a base are
   called *detectors.*

3. Substances that release hydrogen ions in solution are known as *acids*.
4. The preparation of hydrochloric acid can be accomplished by heating a mixture of sodium chloride and *sodium hydroxide*.
5. A water solution of calcium hydroxide is commonly called *litmus*.
6. Sodium bicarbonate is commonly used in *soldering*.
7. Chemical analysis of seawater reveals that it contains many *salts*.
8. When sodium chloride is dissolved in water, sodium and chloride *atoms* are formed.
9. The reaction between a salt and water to form an acid and a base is called a *neutralization* reaction.
10. A salt can be prepared by reacting a metal oxide with *an acid*.

Matching Questions

Column A
1. a strong base
2. tests for carbon dioxide
3. tests for acids
4. tests for bases
5. common acid in the stomach
6. property of bases
7. property of acids
8. magnesium sulfate
9. a weak acid
10. opposite of hydrolysis

Column B
a. red litmus paper
b. acetic acid
c. slippery to the touch
d. Epsom salts
e. sodium hydroxide
f. hydrochloric acid
g. limewater
h. blue litmus paper
i. neutralization
j. sour taste
k. ammonium hydroxide

Thought Questions

1. Complete the table.

Substance	Formula	Use
Sodium bicarbonate		
	H_2SO_4	
		Preparation of soap
Sodium nitrate		
Silver bromide		
	NH_4OH	
Calcium hydroxide		

2. Write an equation to show how each of the following ionizes in water:
   a. HNO_3 b. $Ca(OH)_2$ c. $MgCl_2$ d. H_3PO_4 e. KNO_3
3. Complete each of the following neutralization reactions:
   a. $KOH + H_2SO_4 \rightarrow$
   b. $HCl + Ba(OH)_2 \rightarrow$
   c. $NH_4OH + HCl \rightarrow$
4. Complete each of the following hydrolysis reactions:
   a. $(NH_4)_2SO_4 + HOH \rightarrow$
   b. $NaHCO_3 + HOH \rightarrow$
   c. $Zn(NO_3)_2 + HOH \rightarrow$
5. Compare each of the following pairs of terms:
   a. acid and base   b. hydrolysis and neutralization
6. Assume that you are given three liquids: an acid, a base, and distilled water. Explain what steps you would take to determine which is the acid, which is the base, and which is the distilled water.

CHAPTER 9
HOW ARE METALS EXTRACTED FROM ORES?

When you have completed this chapter, you should be able to:

1. *Define* metallurgy, mineral, ore, reduction reaction, roasting.
2. *Distinguish* between oxide, sulfide, and carbonate ores.
3. *Discuss* the general methods for extracting metals from oxide ores, sulfide ores, and carbonate ores.
4. *Describe* the production of iron and steel, including its effects on the environment.
5. *Relate* the causes of the corrosion of metals to methods of preventing corrosion.

In the laboratory experience that follows, you will extract a metal from an ore.

Laboratory Experience

HOW IS A METAL SEPARATED FROM ITS COMPOUND?

A. Place a small quantity of copper (II) carbonate in a clean crucible. Place the crucible on a wire gauze mounted on a ring stand, as shown in Fig. 9–1.

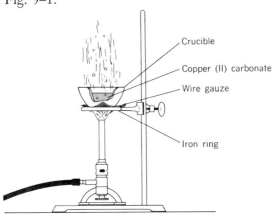

Crucible

Copper (II) carbonate

Wire gauze

Iron ring

Fig. 9–1.

B. Heat the crucible over the hot flame of a Bunsen burner for about 10 minutes. *Carefully* examine the crucible.
    1. What changes in the copper (II) carbonate do you observe?
    2. How do you account for your observations?
C. *Allow the crucible to cool.* Weigh out 5 grams of powdered charcoal on a balance. (Charcoal consists mainly of the element carbon.) Add the charcoal to the crucible. Using a glass rod, stir the substances in the crucible together.
D. Heat the crucible over the strong flame of the Bunsen burner for about 10 minutes. *Allow the crucible to cool.* Using crucible tongs, carefully pour the substance from the crucible into a beaker of water.
    3. What happens to the mixture of the copper compound and charcoal after heating?
    4. Why is the mixture poured into water?
    5. What is the color of the substance close to the surface of the water?
    6. What is this substance?
E. Carefully pour the water out of the beaker, taking care not to lose the solid at the bottom of the beaker.
    7. From its appearance, what is the solid at the bottom of the beaker? Explain.
    8. Write the equation for the reaction that took place in part B of this experiment.
    9. Write the equation for the reaction that took place in part D of this experiment.

Introduction

All the metals we use were once part of the rocks in the earth. Metals occur naturally in rocks, as free elements or combined with other elements in compounds. Only those metals that are not very reactive are usually found free in nature. Examples of such metals are gold, silver, copper, and platinum. Occasionally, even these metals are found combined with other elements. Metals that are reactive are generally found combined in compounds in the rocks of the earth. Such compounds are known as *minerals*. When a mineral contains a quantity of metal sufficient to be extracted profitably, the mineral is said to be an *ore*.

TYPES OF ORES

The metals we use are generally obtained from three types of ores. These ores are compounds of metallic oxides, sulfides, and carbonates.

The oxide ores are sources of metals such as iron, aluminum, copper, and zinc. Some common oxide ores are *hematite* (iron oxide), *magnetite* (magnetic iron oxide), *taconite* (low-grade magnetic iron oxide), *bauxite* (aluminum oxide), *cuprite* (copper (I) oxide), and zincite (zinc oxide).

The sulfide ores are sources of metals such as copper, zinc, lead, and mercury. Some common sulfide ores are *iron pyrite* (iron sulfide), *chalcocite* (copper (I) sulfide), *sphalerite* (zinc sulfide), *galena* (lead sulfide), and *cinnabar* (mercury (II) sulfide).

The carbonate ores are sources of metals such as iron and zinc. Some common carbonate ores are *siderite* (iron carbonate) and *smithsonite* (zinc carbonate).

Table 9–1 summarizes the important ores from which we obtain metals.

Table 9–1. Important Ores

Type of Ore	Chemical Formula	Name of Ore	Metal Present
Oxide	Fe_2O_3	Hematite	Iron
	Fe_3O_4	Magnetite	Iron
	Fe_3O_4	Taconite	Iron
	Al_2O_3	Bauxite	Aluminum
	Cu_2O	Cuprite	Copper
	ZnO	Zincite	Zinc
Sulfide	FeS_2	Iron pyrite	Iron
	Cu_2S	Chalcocite	Copper
	ZnS	Zinc blende	Zinc
	PbS	Galena	Lead
	HgS	Cinnabar	Mercury
Carbonate	$FeCO_3$	Siderite	Iron
	$ZnCO_3$	Smithsonite	Zinc

(Note that magnetite and taconite have the same formula, Fe_3O_4. Taconite, however, is a low-grade magnetic iron oxide. It yields less iron that does magnetite.)

Extracting Metals From Ores

Ores are useless to us until metals are extracted from them. The process that deals with the extraction of metals from their ores is known as *metallurgy*. The methods used to extract a specific metal depend on the composition of the ore, the kinds and quantities of impurities present in the ore, and the use to which the metal will be put.

Prior to the actual separation of the metal from the ore, it is economical to remove some of the impurities first. This process is called *ore concentration*. If the use of the metal will require a high degree of purity, such as is necessary when copper is used for electrical purposes, many processes are used. Each operation serves to further increase the purity of the metal.

Generally, the composition of the ore determines the chemical process to be used in extracting the metal.

Extracting Metals From Oxide Ores

If a useful metal is found in an oxide ore, it is relatively easy to extract the metal because the process involves only a single step.

Consider the ore cuprite, which is an oxide of copper (Cu_2O). According to the reactivity series of metals (see page 38), zinc is more reactive than copper. Therefore, with the aid of heat, zinc can replace the copper from copper (I) oxide in a single replacement reaction:

$$Cu_2O\ (s)\ +\ Zn\ (s)\ \xrightarrow{\triangle}\ 2\ Cu\ (s)\ +\ ZnO\ (s)$$
$$\text{copper (I) oxide} \qquad \text{zinc} \qquad \qquad \text{copper} \qquad \text{zinc oxide}$$

This replacement reaction can be considered in another way: The zinc removes the oxygen from the oxide, unites with the oxygen, and forms zinc oxide. The type of reaction in which oxygen is removed from a compound is known as *reduction reaction*. In this case, we say that the copper in the compound was *reduced* to free copper by using zinc. Substances, such as zinc, that can reduce oxides are called *reducing agents*.

When ores are reduced commercially, the least expensive reducing agents are selected. Carbon (coke or powdered charcoal) is a commonly used commercial reducing agent (Fig. 9–2). Other commercial reducing

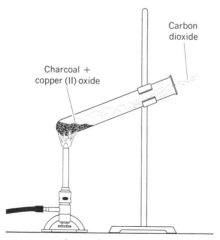

Carbon
dioxide

Charcoal +
copper (II) oxide

Fig. 9–2. Charcoal as a reducing agent.

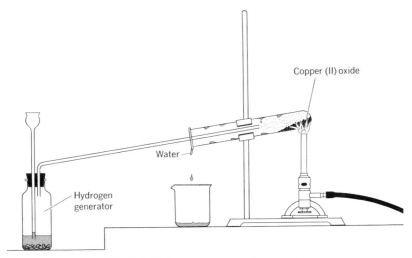

Fig. 9–3. Hydrogen as a reducing agent.

agents include hydrogen gas (Fig. 9–3) and carbon monoxide gas. The following reactions show how these reducing agents can be used to extract copper from copper (II) oxide. Note that all the reactions require heat.

$$2\,CuO\,(s) \; + \; C\,(s) \; \xrightarrow{\triangle} \; 2\,Cu\,(s) \; + \; CO_2\,(g)$$
copper (II)   coke   copper   carbon
oxide   dioxide

$$CuO\,(s) \; + \; H_2\,(g) \; \xrightarrow{\triangle} \; Cu\,(s) \; + \; H_2O\,(g)$$
copper (II)   hydrogen   copper   water
oxide

$$CuO\,(s) \; + \; CO\,(g) \; \xrightarrow{\triangle} \; Cu\,(s) \; + \; CO_2\,(g)$$
copper (II)   carbon   copper   carbon
oxide   monoxide   dioxide

Other examples of the reduction of metallic oxides are as follows:

$$2\,ZnO\,(s) \; + \; C\,(s) \; \xrightarrow{\triangle} \; 2\,Zn\,(s) \; + \; CO_2\,(g)$$
zinc oxide   charcoal   zinc   carbon
dioxide

$$2\,Fe_2O_3\,(s) \; + \; 3\,C\,(s) \; \xrightarrow{\triangle} \; 4\,Fe\,(s) \; + \; 3\,CO_2\,(g)$$
iron (III)   charcoal   iron   carbon
oxide   dioxide

$$\text{PbO }(s) \quad + \quad \text{H}_2 \,(g) \quad \xrightarrow{\triangle} \quad \text{Pb }(l) \quad + \quad \text{H}_2\text{O }(g)$$

lead (II) oxide   hydrogen   lead   water

(In the last reaction, the temperature is sufficiently high to melt the lead.)

Extracting Metals From Sulfide Ores

The extraction of metals from sulfide ores is a somewhat more difficult task than the extraction from oxide ores because the sulfur in sulfide ores is not readily removed. At least two main steps are usually involved in extracting metals from sulfide ores. First, the sulfide compounds are converted to oxide compounds. Then, the oxides are reduced.

When a sulfide compound is heated strongly in the presence of oxygen (air), a chemical change takes place in which the sulfide of the metal becomes the oxide of the metal. This process, in which compounds are converted to oxides by heating them in air, is known as *roasting*.

For example, suppose we want to obtain lead from the sulfide ore galena (PbS). We would roast the lead sulfide (Fig. 9–4) as follows:

$$2\,\text{PbS }(s) \quad + \quad 3\,\text{O}_2 \,(g) \quad \xrightarrow{\triangle} \quad 2\,\text{PbO }(s) \quad + \quad 2\,\text{SO}_2 \,(g)$$

lead (II) sulfide   oxygen   lead (II) oxide   sulfur dioxide

Note that, in addition to lead oxide, sulfur dioxide gas is produced. This gas escapes from the container, leaving the lead oxide behind.

Now, the lead oxide is mixed with powdered charcoal and heated.

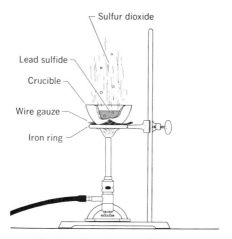

Fig. 9–4. Roasting a sulfide ore.

This reaction reduces the lead oxide and yields lead and carbon dioxide gas:

$$2\,PbO\;(s)\;+\;\underset{\text{charcoal}}{C\;(s)}\;\xrightarrow{\triangle}\;\underset{\text{lead}}{2\,Pb\;(l)}\;+\;\underset{\text{carbon dioxide}}{CO_2\;(g)}$$
lead (II) oxide   charcoal   lead   carbon dioxide

The carbon dioxide gas, like the sulfur dioxide gas formed during roasting, escapes from the container. When the lead becomes cool enough, it forms a solid.

Thus, the extraction of a metal from a sulfide ore involves (1) the roasting of the sulfide to form an oxide and (2) the reduction of the oxide to form the free metal.

The extraction of mercury (Hg) from cinnabar (HgS) follows the same procedures as does the extraction of lead from galena:

ROASTING: $2\,HgS\;(s) + 3\,O_2\;(g) \xrightarrow{\triangle} 2\,HgO\;(s) + 2\,SO_2\;(g)$

REDUCTION: $2\,HgO\;(s) + C\;(s)\;\xrightarrow{\triangle} 2\,Hg\;(l) + CO_2\;(g)$

In actual operation, however, this process requires only a single step. Since mercuric oxide is unstable, the roasting process produces the free metal directly:

$$HgS\;(s) + O_2\;(g) \xrightarrow{\triangle} Hg\;(l) + SO_2\;(g)$$

Extracting Metals From Carbonate Ores

The separation of metals from their carbonate ores is accomplished by a method similar to the one used to separate metals from sulfide ores. First, the carbonate ore is heated (roasted), causing the compound to undergo decomposition. Carbon dioxide is released to the air, and a solid oxide compound remains behind.

In your laboratory experience, you roasted a carbonate ore by heating the compound copper (II) carbonate in a crucible. The blue-green copper (II) carbonate changed to black copper (II) oxide according to the following equation:

$$\underset{\substack{\text{copper (II) carbonate}\\\text{(blue-green)}}}{CuCO_3\;(s)}\;\xrightarrow{\triangle}\;\underset{\substack{\text{copper (II) oxide}\\\text{(black)}}}{CuO\;(s)}\;+\;\underset{\text{carbon dioxide}}{CO_2\;(g)}$$

We can demonstrate that carbon dioxide is released by arranging

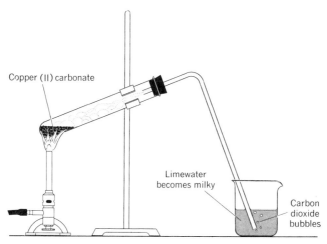

Fig. 9–5. Testing for carbon dioxide.

an apparatus as shown in Fig. 9–5 and allowing the gas that is formed to enter a container of limewater. Whenever limewater comes in contact with carbon dioxide, the limewater turns milky. This is a commonly used test for carbon dioxide.

Once an oxide has been obtained from a carbonate, any reducing agent, such as carbon, hydrogen, or carbon monoxide, can be employed to release the free metal. In your laboratory experience, you carried out such a reduction by adding charcoal to the crucible of copper (II) carbonate that had been roasted. After further heating, red-brown copper separated from the black copper oxide. The equation for the reduction of the copper oxide is:

$$2\,CuO\,(s) \quad + \quad C\,(s) \quad \xrightarrow{\triangle} \quad 2\,Cu\,(s) \quad + \quad CO_2\,(g)$$

copper (II) oxide   charcoal   copper   carbon dioxide
(black)   (red-brown)

Thus, metals are extracted from carbonate ores (1) by roasting the carbonate to decompose it to the oxide and (2) by reducing the oxide to the free metal. The following reactions illustrate other examples of the extraction of metals from carbonate ores:

Extraction of Zinc (Zn) from Zinc Carbonate (ZnCO₃)

ROASTING: $\quad ZnCO_3\,(s) \xrightarrow{\triangle} ZnO\,(s) + CO_2\,(g)$

REDUCTION: $\quad 2\,ZnO\,(s) + C\,(s) \xrightarrow{\triangle} 2\,Zn\,(s) + CO_2\,(g)$

Extraction of Lead (Pb) from Lead Carbonate (PbCO₃)

ROASTING: $PbCO_3\ (s) \xrightarrow{\triangle} PbO\ (s) + CO_2\ (g)$

REDUCTION: $2\ PbO\ (s) + C\ (s) \xrightarrow{\triangle} 2\ Pb\ (l) + CO_2\ (g)$

THE METALLURGY OF IRON

Iron, one of the most useful metals, is the fourth most abundant element in the earth's crust. Since iron is a moderately reactive metal, it is generally found combined in compounds. As we noted before, iron is found in the form of oxides in ores such as hematite (Fe_2O_3), magnetite (Fe_3O_4), and taconite (Fe_3O_4). Iron is also commonly found in the carbonate ore siderite ($FeCO_3$). Impurities, such as sand, are always found with these compounds of iron. Such impurities, which are of no immediate value to the metallurgist, are called *gangue*. Before the iron can be extracted from the ore, the gangue must be separated from the ore. Industrial chemists have designed a process in which both steps, the extraction of iron and the removal of impurities, are accomplished within one chamber called a *blast furnace*.

The Construction of a Blast Furnace

A blast furnace (Fig. 9–6) may be 30 meters high and 8 meters in diameter. The inside of the furnace is lined with special bricks that are capable of withstanding extremely high temperatures. At the top of the furnace, an opening admits a mixture of hematite (Fe_2O_3), coke (C), and limestone ($CaCO_3$). Near the bottom of the furnace is a series of pipes, called *tuyères*, through which large quantities of heated air are blown. It is this heated air which starts the reaction.

The coke burns to form carbon monoxide, which then reduces the hematite. The limestone, called a *flux*, combines with the impurities in the ore to form a *slag*, which floats on top of the iron. Waste gases escape through a pipe near the top of the furnace. Tap holes to drain the molten iron and the liquid slag are located under the air pipes, at the bottom of the furnace.

The Reactions in the Blast Furnace

Within the blast furnace, a series of reactions takes place, as follows:

1. *Oxidation of carbon.* As the coke is heated, it combines with oxygen to form carbon dioxide:

$$C\ (s) + O_2\ (g) \to CO_2\ (g)$$

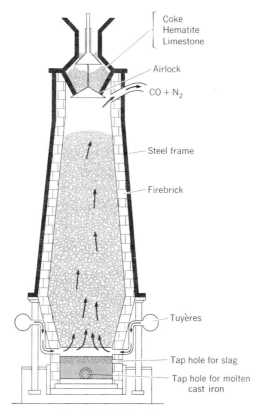

Coke
Hematite
Limestone

Airlock

$CO + N_2$

Steel frame

Firebrick

Tuyères

Tap hole for slag

Tap hole for molten
cast iron

Fig. 9–6. The blast furnace.

2. *Reduction of carbon dioxide.* As carbon dioxide is formed, it reacts with the hot coke and is reduced to form carbon monoxide gas:

$$CO_2 \, (g) + C \, (s) \rightarrow 2 \, CO \, (g)$$

3. *Reduction of hematite by carbon monoxide.* The carbon monoxide, in a series of complex reactions, reduces the hematite. The overall reaction is:

$$Fe_2O_3 \, (s) + 3 \, CO \, (g) \rightarrow 2 \, Fe \, (l) + 3 \, CO_2 \, (g)$$

The carbon dioxide formed from reaction 1 and reaction 3 is continually reduced by the coke in reaction 2 to form carbon monoxide. Thus, two reducing agents are constantly present.

4. *Formation of calcium oxide.* The limestone that is mixed with the ore and coke is roasted by the intense heat of the furnace. The limestone, on heating, decomposes to calcium oxide and carbon dioxide:

$$CaCO_3 \, (s) \rightarrow CaO \, (s) + CO_2 \, (g)$$

5. *Formation of slag.* The calcium oxide formed in reaction 4 reacts with the impurities, mainly sand (SiO_2), to form slag, which is largely calcium silicate ($CaSiO_3$):

$$CaO\ (s) \quad + \quad SiO_2\ (s) \quad \longrightarrow \quad CaSiO_3\ (l)$$

calcium   sand   calcium
oxide   silicate
(slag)

The slag, at the temperature of the furnace, is liquid. Since the slag is less dense than the molten iron, it floats on top of the iron, protecting the iron from re-oxidation. The slag is drained off from time to time. The iron is also drained from the furnace and allowed to run into rectangular forms called *pigs*, in which the iron cools and solidifies.

The iron obtained from the blast furnace is known as *pig iron.* When pig iron is melted and recooled, it is called *cast iron.* Cast iron is an impure iron that contains 3% to 5% carbon, 1% manganese, and small amounts of silicon, sulfur, and phosphorus. This type of iron is hard, extremely brittle, and cannot withstand sudden shock.

Cast iron is refined by means of a process of controlled oxidation, which eliminates the carbon and sulfur impurities in the form of the gases carbon dioxide and sulfur dioxide. The iron refined in this way is called *wrought iron.* Wrought iron is comparatively soft, *malleable* (capable of being shaped by hammering), and *ductile* (capable of being drawn out into a wire). Wrought iron can be worked into almost any shape. Since it is not brittle, it is used for bolts, nails, and chains to which great stress or shock is applied. Today, most wrought iron has been replaced by special steels.

PRODUCTION OF STEEL

Steel is prepared from cast iron and contains a fixed amount of carbon, usually between 0.2% and 2%. In addition, steel contains other elements to give it desired properties.

Steel can be prepared in several ways. Much of the steel prepared in this country is manufactured by using the *open-hearth process* (Fig.9–7) and the *oxygen top-blowing process.*

In these processes, molten cast iron is poured into special furnaces. The carbon and sulfur impurities burn in the presence of oxygen to form gaseous products which leave the furnace. Other impurities, such as phosphorus and silicon, are removed by the furnace lining to form a slag. Controlled amounts of carbon, manganese, chromium, and other elements are added to the purified molten iron. The addition of these

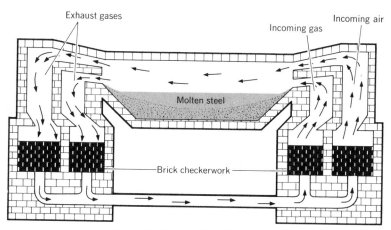

Fig. 9–7. The open-hearth furnace.

substances produces steels with different properties suitable for different uses.

Steel can be cast into molds, formed into beams, hammered into sheets, and drawn into wire. Steel represents the backbone of industrial nations. It is the primary metal used for construction of bridges, buildings, ships, armor plate, railroad tracks, and automobile bodies.

PROTECTING METALS AGAINST CORROSION

When metallic objects are exposed to air and moisture for some time, reddish-brown spots often form. These spots are generally called *rust*. The chemical analysis of rust reveals that it is composed of the compound iron (III) oxide (Fe_2O_3).

Rusting is an example of a general weathering process called *corrosion*. This process may weaken or even destroy metals. During corrosion, metals combine slowly with such chemical agents as oxygen, water, carbon dioxide, and sulfur dioxide. The new compounds formed are brittle and usually crumble. They lack the strength of the original metals.

If chemists had not developed methods to prevent the corrosion of metals, many of the metallic objects we depend upon would wear away in a relatively short time. The methods used to protect metals against corrosion involve adding a surface coating to the metal. This coating is resistant to the agents of corrosion.

Galvanizing and Tinning

Iron coated with zinc is called *galvanized iron*. Zinc is more reactive than iron and, on standing, forms a coating of zinc carbonate. This coating protects the iron underneath from corrosion.

Coating thin sheets of steel with tin is called *tinning*. This protects the metal underneath from corrosion because tin is less reactive than iron. Such "tinned" steel is used in the tin cans in which certain foods and beverages are packaged.

In both coating processes, the metal to be protected is dipped into the molten metal that serves as the protective agent. When the molten metal cools, it solidifies, forming a layer over the iron or steel. Care must be exercised so that a layer of the proper thickness is formed.

Electroplating

In the process known as *electroplating*, less reactive metals such as nickel or chromium are deposited on the surface of more reactive metals such as iron by electrical means. The less reactive metal (nickel) corrodes less rapidly than the more reactive metal (iron). Tin may also be coated on iron or steel by such processes. Since the deposited metals are more corrosion-resistant than the metals they cover, the deposited metals protect the metals beneath them from corrosion.

Coating With Nonmetallic Substances

Corrosion can also be prevented by applying coverings such as oil, grease, paint, and lacquers to metallic surfaces. By clinging to the surface of a metal, these substances keep agents of corrosion from coming in contact with the metal. This tends to preserve the metal.

EFFECTS OF MINING AND METALLURGY ON THE ENVIRONMENT

You are no doubt aware how essential metals are to our daily lives. Have you ever thought what will happen when the supply of metals, which are nonrenewable natural resources, becomes exhausted? Are you aware that in certain communities in our country (and in others) mining and metallurgical processes have destroyed the natural environment of forests, fields, and streams?

Damage by Strip Mining

Where coal and the ores of iron, copper, and other metals occur near the surface of the earth, these resources are taken from the earth by a method known as *strip mining*. In this method, topsoil and subsoil are bulldozed away until the material to be mined is exposed. After removing the coal or ore, a deep scar is left in the earth. As a result of such methods, valuable soil with its vegetation is destroyed, and the landscape is made ugly.

Damage by Metallurgy Wastes

Recall that gangue, slag, and certain waste gases are produced in extracting iron from its ores. The gangue and slag are often piled somewhere on the surface of the soil. Thus covered, the soil becomes unusable, and higher and higher piles of ugly wastes accumulate. At the same time, waste gases, which include sulfur dioxide and carbon monoxide, enter the air and pollute it. As you know, both of these gases are poisonous. When wind blows sulfur dioxide to farming areas, the sulfur dioxide often kills crop plants and harms humans and other animals.

SAVING THE ENVIRONMENT

Steps we can take to prevent the exhaustion of our supplies of mineral ores and other nonrenewable resources include:

1. Preventing the waste of minerals and fuels.

2. Developing mining practices that extract metals more efficiently.

3. Finding better ways to collect junk metals and developing cheaper ways to extract the metals from junk. In other words, we must do a better job of recycling metals and other materials.

Steps we can take to repair the damage done to the landscape and soil by strip mining include:

1. Refilling cavities left in the earth by strip mining. (Gangue and slag could be used for this purpose.)

2. Replacing topsoil that has been removed and replanting grass, trees, and other vegetation.

Steps we can take to prevent the pollution of air with the waste gases released in metallurgy include:

1. Removing gaseous exhausts of the roasting process from smokestacks before these exhausts reach the atmosphere.

2. Using waste sulfur dioxide, for example, in the manufacture of sulfuric acid.

3. Converting carbon monoxide to carbon dioxide before releasing the gas into the atmosphere.

4. Reusing carbon monoxide as a reducing agent.

Looking Back

In Unit I, we learned why elements and compounds—the matter of our environment—react as they do in different types of chemical reactions. We studied the properties of solutions, suspensions, acids, bases, and salts. At the same time, we became aware of the importance of chemistry and chemical processes in daily life.

Looking Ahead

Unit I completes our study of chemistry and its role in the environment. In Unit II, we will study the forces in our environment and the effect these forces have on us and on other matter.

Multiple-Choice Questions

1. Any rock from which metals can be extracted profitably is called
   a. a mineral   c. a sedimentary rock
   b. an ore   d. a metamorphic rock
2. An important oxide ore of iron is
   a. hematite   b. iron pyrite   c. siderite   d. bauxite
3. The process that deals with the extraction of metals from their ores is known as
   a. electroplating   c. gangue
   b. ore concentration   d. metallurgy
4. The removal of impurities from ores is accomplished through the process of
   a. roasting   c. ore concentration
   b. reduction   d. electroplating
5. Of the following, the type of reaction that can be used to obtain a metal from a compound is called
   a. synthesis   c. single replacement
   b. analysis   d. double replacement
6. The removal of oxygen from a compound can be accomplished by the process of
   a. roasting   b. electroplating   c. synthesis   d. reduction
7. Among the following, the commercially used reducing agent is usually
   a. zinc   b. carbon   c. lead   d. iron
8. Metals are extracted from sulfide ores by
   a. first roasting, then reduction   c. reduction alone
   b. first reduction, then roasting   d. roasting alone
9. An example of an ore of lead is
   a. bauxite   b. cinnabar   c. galena   d. magnetite

10. The method used to separate metals from carbonate ores is similar to that used to separate metals from
    a. oxides   b. sulfates   c. chlorides   d. sulfides
11. Impurities found in ores are known as
    a. flux   b. slag   c. gangue   d. coke
12. The reducing agent formed when carbon dioxide passes over hot coke is
    a. carbon   c. hydrogen
    b. carbon monoxide   d. calcium silicate
13. In processing iron ore, the main impurity found in the ore is
    a. $CaSiO_3$ b. Al_2O_3 c. SiO_2 d. CaO
14. When calcium oxide reacts with the impurities in iron ore,
    a. flux is formed   c. carbon dioxide is formed
    b. slag is formed   d. sand is formed
15. An impure form of iron, containing 5% carbon, is called
    a. wrought iron   b. iron ore   c. steel   d. cast iron
16. Cast iron is
    a. extremely brittle   c. relatively soft
    b. used for bridges   d. free of all impurities
17. Cast iron is refined by
    a. controlled reduction   c. electroplating
    b. controlled oxidation   d. coating processes
18. Steel is prepared from
    a. pig iron   b. wrought iron   c. cast iron   d. slag
19. Of the following, the one that is not an agent of corrosion is
    a. water   b. chromium   c. oxygen   d. sulfur dioxide
20. In the process of galvanizing, iron is coated with
    a. tin   b. lead   c. copper   d. zinc
21. Of the following, the covering that does not prevent corrosion is
    a. water   b. oil   c. grease   d. paint

Modified True-False Questions

1. Reactive metals found combined in compounds in the rocks of the earth are called *ores*.
2. Iron is separated from its ore in a large chamber called *a blast furnace*.
3. In the blast furnace, limestone is used as *a reducing agent*.
4. Liquid waste materials formed in the blast furnace are called *tuyères*.
5. Iron obtained directly from the blast furnace is called *wrought iron*.
6. When cast iron is refined to eliminate the carbon and sulfur impurities, *wrought iron* is formed.
7. Much of the steel prepared in this country is manufactured by using the *open-hearth process*.
8. An important impurity found in steel is *zinc*.
9. A general weathering process which may destroy metals is called *corrosion*.
10. A process in which inactive metals are electrically deposited on the surface of more active metals for protection is known as *rusting*.

Matching Questions

Column A	Column B
1. carbonate ore of iron	a. chalcocite
2. reducing agent	b. tuyères
3. pipes in the blast furnace	c. siderite
4. sulfide ore of lead	d. bauxite
5. gas formed as coke is heated	e. smithsonite
6. oxide ore of aluminum	f. hydrogen
7. slag	g. galena
8. corrosion product of iron	h. rust
9. sulfide ore of copper	i. calcium silicate
10. carbonate ore of zinc	j. carbon dioxide
	k. cinnabar

Thought Questions

1. Tell the difference between the terms in each of the following pairs:
   a. mineral and ore
   b. hematite and iron pyrite
   c. reduction and roasting
   d. gangue and slag
   e. cast iron and wrought iron

2. Complete and balance the following equations:

   a. $ZnO + H_2 \xrightarrow{\triangle}$ c. $CuS + O_2 \xrightarrow{\triangle}$ e. $CuCO_3 \xrightarrow{\triangle}$

   b. $Fe_2O_3 + C \xrightarrow{\triangle}$ d. $ZnS + O_2 \xrightarrow{\triangle}$

3. Using chemical equations, describe the steps we would use to obtain lead from galena (PbS).

4. Complete the table.

Ore	Formula	Metal Obtained
Zincite		
	Al_2O_3	
Magnetite		
	FeS_2	
Cinnabar		
	$FeCO_3$	

5. Discuss three methods used to protect metals from corrosion.

6. Mining and metallurgy tend to damage the environment. Indicate at least one environmental problem each process causes. State some possible measures to prevent and correct each problem.

UNIT II
Forces in Our Environment

Overview

Objects as large as a spaceship or as small as an atom are subject to the action of natural forces. A *force* is any push or pull exerted on some object. When a large enough force acts on a stationary object, the object may move. When such a force acts on a moving object, the object may slow down, stop moving, or move faster.

Examples of natural forces are gravity, magnetism, wind, and muscular activity. Gravity pulls objects toward the center of the earth. The magnetic force between like poles repels them (pushes them apart). The magnetic force between unlike poles produces an attraction between them (pulls them together). The force of wind propels sailboats (pushes the boats). The force of muscular activity enables us to push bicycle pedals, pull a sled, or do other types of work.

CHAPTER 10
WHAT ARE THE EFFECTS OF THE FORCES OF THE ENVIRONMENT?

When you have completed this chapter, you should be able to:

1. *Define* force, equilibrium, equilibrant, center of gravity.
2. *Indicate* how forces are measured and how they may be represented by diagrams.
3. *Use* diagrams and calculations to solve force problems.
4. *Distinguish* between (*a*) balanced and unbalanced forces (*b*) scalar and vector quantities (*c*) resultant and component forces.
5. *Compare* the effects of combined forces acting at an angle with forces acting in the same and opposite directions.
6. *Explain* the law of moments.
7. *Find* the center of gravity of an object.

In the laboratory experience that follows, you will explore a method of measuring the force of gravity on objects.

Laboratory Experience

HOW IS THE FORCE OF GRAVITY MEASURED?

Gravity attracts different masses with varying force called *weight*. As we change the weights loaded on a spring, the spring stretches to different lengths. We can determine the value of an unknown weight by measuring the stretch it produces.

Each of several pieces of metal—except one—is marked with a number that shows how much it weighs. In this laboratory experience, your problem is to find out the force with which gravity attracts the unmarked piece of metal.

A. Adjust the clamp as high as it will go on the ringstand, attach the pointer to one end of the spring, attach the other end of the spring to the clamp, and position the meter stick alongside the pointer (Fig. 10–1). Copy the table below into your notebook.

Pieces of Metal, in Order of Size	Weight Marked on Metal	Meter-stick Reading	Difference Between This Reading and Preceding Reading
1			0
2			
3			
4			

B. Hang the smallest piece of metal from the end of the spring. Keeping your eye level with the pointer, note the marking on the meter stick that is opposite the pointer. Record this reading in the table.

C. Hang the next largest piece of metal from the end of the spring. Again, keeping your eye level with the pointer, note the marking on the meter stick that is opposite the pointer. Record this reading in the table also.

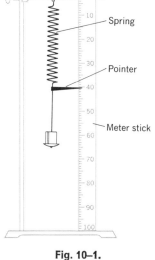

Fig. 10–1.

1. What effect do the weights have on the spring?
2. Is there a limit to the amount of weight that can be hung on a given spring beyond which the spring will be unable to return to its original shape? Explain.

D. Before proceeding further with the experiment, outline the plan you intend to follow in order to determine the force with which gravity attracts the unmarked piece of metal. Carry out your plan after your teacher has approved it, recording your results in the table.

E. Using the figures recorded in your table, prepare a graph of your results. Place the marked weights on the vertical axis and the meterstick readings on the horizontal axis.

3. What relation exists between the marked weights and the amounts they stretch the spring?
4. Based on this relation, what is the force with which gravity attracts the unmarked piece of metal? Explain.

Introduction

More than one force may act on an object at a given time. The object will not move if the forces on it are *balanced*—that is, if the forces exactly counteract each other. The book on your desk is not in motion because the downward pull of gravity on the book is counterbalanced by the equal upward push of the desk on the book. Should you pull the desk out from under the book, the book would fall because you would have upset the balance of forces. If two persons push a sled with the same force but in opposite directions, the sled will not move. However, if one person exerts less force than the other, the two forces will become unbalanced. In such a situation, the sled will begin to move in the direction in which the greater force is acting.

HOW FORCES ARE MEASURED

In our daily lives, we see that gravity is one of the major forces acting on matter all the time. Since weight is the pull, or force, exerted on a mass by gravity, the units of weight can also be used as units of force. In the metric system, the unit of force is the *newton* or the *dyne* (1 newton = 100,000 dynes).

Our laboratory experience employed a simple way of measuring the force exerted by gravity. By suspending known weights on the spring, we can determine the relation between the weight (force of gravity) and the distance the spring stretches.

A spring may be used to weigh objects or measure forces because it is *elastic*. That is, when the weight (force) is removed, the spring returns to its original shape. In all such experiments, the spring should be stretched only up to the point where it can return to its original shape. This largest stretch is called the *elastic limit* of the spring. If we exceed the elastic limit by attempting to weigh an extremely heavy object, the spring may be permanently deformed—that is, it may never return to its original shape.

The size, or amount, of a force is called the *magnitude* of the force. A device commonly used to measure the magnitude of a force is the *spring balance*, or *spring scale*, which is a convenient form of the apparatus used in our laboratory experience. The spring scale shown in Fig. 10–2 measures force in grams. The values in grams may then be converted to dynes or newtons. A mass of 1 gram weighs 980 dynes; a mass of 1 kilogram weighs 9.8 newtons.

HOW FORCES ARE REPRESENTED

When making a solution, we often need to know how much water to use. When we build a bookshelf, we want to know how much wood we need. When we push a heavy object, such as a sofa, from one part of a room to another, we may need to know how much force to use. We could ask, "What quantity of water (or of wood) do we need?" Similarly, we might ask, "What quantity of force do we need?"

Scalar Quantities

Quantities that measure the amount, or size, or magnitude of a mass are called *scalar quantities*. These quantities represent magnitude only. Thus, length, volume, and weight are examples of scalar quantities.

Vector Quantities

Forces, like masses, always have some magnitude. However, a force of any magnitude always acts in some specific direction. Quantities that express both magnitude and direction are called *vector quantities*. Thus, to describe correctly the force used when a man exerts 450 newtons (nt) of force to push a stalled car to a service station, it is not sufficient to say that the force is 450 newtons; we must say that the force is 450 newtons in a given direction (Fig. 10–3). For example, "Mr. Jones applied a force of 450 newtons in an easterly direction."

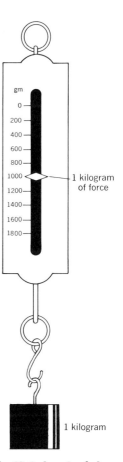

Fig. 10–2. A spring balance.

Drawing Vectors

To represent forces on a sheet of paper, *vector diagrams* are used. In such diagrams, the forces are represented by drawn arrows called *vectors*. A vector is shown as an arrow with the head pointing in the

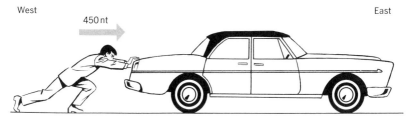

Fig. 10–3. Applying a force in a given direction.

direction of the force and the tail indicating the point at which the
force is applied. The length of the arrow represents the magnitude of
the force.

To show magnitude, we decide upon a scale, such as that found on
any map. In order to determine the distance between two points on
a map, we measure the length between the points with a ruler and then
compare this length to the map scale. Similarly, when drawing a vector,
we must first select a convenient scale. Suppose we let 1.0 cm represent
45 newtons of force. In this case, the 450-newton force applied by
Mr. Jones to his stalled car would be represented by a 10-cm line
(Fig. 10–4).

Fig. 10–4. Vector diagram of a force.

To indicate direction, it is convenient to follow the usual map con-
vention: the top of the paper is north, the bottom is south, the right
edge is east, and the left edge is west. First, we make a dot on our paper
to represent the point of application of the force. Since in this case
the force is applied in an easterly direction, we draw our line horizontally
toward the right, extend the line for 10 cm (representing 450 nt), and
then attach an arrowhead to the line pointing to the right (east). Thus,
the vector indicates three things: (1) point of application, (2) magnitude, and (3) direction.

Effect of Combinations of Forces on Objects

When two or more forces act on the same object at the same time,
the forces act together as though a single force were present. For
example, suppose two men push a large rock in the same direction,
each man exerting 225 newtons of force. If a different man could exert
450 newtons of force on the same rock (in the same direction), this
single force could replace the two 225-newton forces combined.

A single force that results from a combination of forces is called a
resultant force. Thus, the resultant force of two 225-newton forces acting
in the same direction is 450 newtons. The separate forces that produce a
resultant force are called *component forces*. Thus, the components of
the 450-newton force are the two 225-newton forces.

Whether the resultant force is greater than, less than, or equal to
the component forces depends upon the directions in which the com-

ponent forces act. Component forces may act on an object in the *same direction* (as in our example), in *opposite directions*, or *at angles to each other*.

Effect of Forces Acting in the Same Direction

When two forces act on an object in the same direction, the angle between the forces is 0°. The resultant force produced is equal to the sum of the two forces. The direction in which the resultant force acts is the same as that of the component forces.

For example, assume that two people are pulling on a rope connected to a loaded cart (Fig. 10–5a). One person pulls with a force of 270 newtons; the other person pulls in the same direction with a force of 360 newtons. The resultant force is equal to the sum of the combined forces, 270 newtons + 360 newtons, or 630 newtons, acting in the direction in which the pull is exerted.

Fig. 10–5b shows the same situation in the form of a vector diagram. In this case, the scale is 0.3 cm = 90 newtons. Thus, a line 0.9 cm in length represents the 270-newton force of the first person, and a 1.2-cm line represents the 360-newton force of the second person. The resultant force is represented by an arrow 2.1 cm in length, or 630 newtons. Since all the forces here act in the same direction, the arrowhead of the resultant force points in the same direction as that of the components.

Effect of Forces Acting in Opposite Directions

When two forces act on an object in opposite directions, the angle between the forces is 180°. The resultant force produced is equal to the difference between the two forces. The resultant force then acts

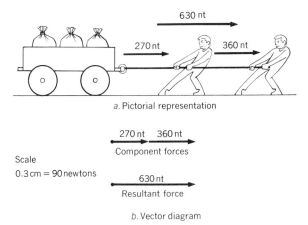

a. Pictorial representation

Scale
0.3 cm = 90 newtons

b. Vector diagram

Fig. 10–5. Forces acting in the same direction.

in the same direction as that of the *greater* component force.

For example, assume that two people are pulling on a loaded cart in opposite directions (Fig. 10–6a). The first person pulls to the east with a force of 360 newtons, while the second person pulls to the west with a force of 270 newtons. The resultant force is then equal to the difference between the two component forces, 360 newtons minus 270 newtons, or 90 newtons. The resultant force moves the cart toward the east, the direction of the greater component force.

This case can also be represented by vectors (Fig. 10–6b). We again use a scale of 0.3 cm = 90 newtons. Thus, a 1.2-cm line pointing to the east represents the 360-newton force, and a 0.9-cm line pointing to the west represents the 270-newton force. The resultant force (90 newtons) is represented by a 0.3-cm arrow whose head points to the east.

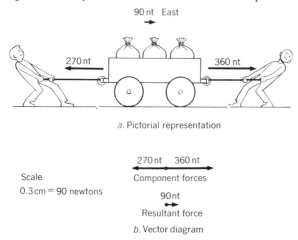

a. Pictorial representation

Scale
0.3 cm = 90 newtons

270 nt   360 nt
Component forces

90 nt
Resultant force

b. Vector diagram

Fig. 10–6. Forces acting in opposite directions.

Effect of Forces Acting at an Angle

When two forces act on an object at an angle less than 180° to each other, the magnitude and direction of the resultant force are not the same as the magnitudes and directions of the component forces. Rather, the direction of the resultant force lies somewhere between the directions of the component forces; the size of the resultant force is less than the sum of the component forces but greater than their difference.

For example, when two people pull on separate ropes attached to a cart and the angle between the ropes is 90° (Fig. 10–7a), the cart moves in a direction somewhere between the two ropes. The magnitude of the resultant force is less than 630 newtons (the sum of the components) and greater than 90 newtons (the difference between the component forces).

Using vectors to represent the component forces, we can determine the actual magnitude and direction of the resultant force. This is done by constructing a *parallelogram of force* (Fig. 10–7b).

A parallelogram is a 4-sided figure with opposite sides both equal and parallel. Using the two component vectors as two sides of a parallelogram, we can complete the other two sides simply by adding dashed lines equal to and parallel to each of the vectors. Then we draw the diagonal of the parallelogram as a solid line, placing an arrowhead at the end of it. This diagonal represents the resultant force. The arrowhead shows the direction of the resultant force, while the length of the diagonal represents the magnitude of the resultant force.

To determine the magnitude of the resultant force, measure the length of the diagonal and compare it to our scale. In our problem, the diagonal is 1.5 centimeters long. Since our scale is 0.3 centimeter = 90 newtons, the resultant force is 450 newtons.

Effect of Balanced Forces

In the three cases studied so far involving a cart pulled by two people, the cart moved in some direction because the forces acting upon

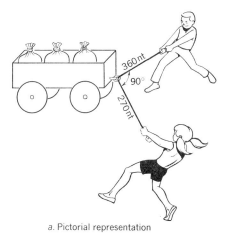

a. Pictorial representation

b. Vector diagram

Fig. 10–7. Forces acting at an angle.

it were unbalanced. An unbalanced force always produces motion. This means that the resultant force was strong enough to move the cart in some direction. If the combination of forces acting on the cart had been balanced somehow, the cart would not have moved. When a set of balanced forces acts on an object but does not move it, the object is said to be in a state of *equilibrium*.

In the first case, where two forces acted in the same direction (Fig. 10–5, page 171), the resultant force of the two component forces was 630 newtons. It is easy to see that a 630-newton force acting in the opposite direction to that of the resultant force would put the cart in a state of equilibrium. A force that balances the resultant force is called an *equilibrant* force.

In the second case, where two forces acted in opposite directions (Fig. 10–6, page 172), the resultant force was 90 newtons. Here, the equilibrant force would be 90 newtons.

In the third case, where the two forces acted at an angle to each other (Fig. 10–7, page 173), the resultant force was 450 newtons acting in a direction between the two component forces. To bring about equilibrium in this instance, the equilibrant force would have to be equal to the resultant force and would have to act in a direction exactly opposite to that of the resultant force. This equilibrant force is shown in Fig. 10–8.

EQUILIBRIUM AND CENTER OF GRAVITY

Some objects in equilibrium are easily upset when even a small unbalanced force acts on them. For example, a book set on its end on a table does not move because it is in equilibrium. When the book is tipped slightly and released, it moves, falls on its face, and stops moving. The book reaches a state of equilibrium again but in a new position. When standing on an end, the book is said to be in *unstable equilibrium*. A book lying on its face is very difficult to upset. When the book is pushed, it moves but does not tip over. In this condition, the book is said to be in *stable equilibrium*.

The tipping of the book results in its falling because the force of gravity (the weight of the book) has a chance to act as an unbalanced force. It is this force that pulls the book over to its face. This occurs because the weight of the book acts as though it were concentrated in the center of the book. When the center of weight, or *center of gravity*, of an object is high, it takes only a slight force to tip it and allow the force of gravity to act. When the center of gravity is low, it takes a much greater force to change the position of the object.

Thus, in our example, a book on end has a high center of gravity and is easy to upset; on its side, it has a low center of gravity and is

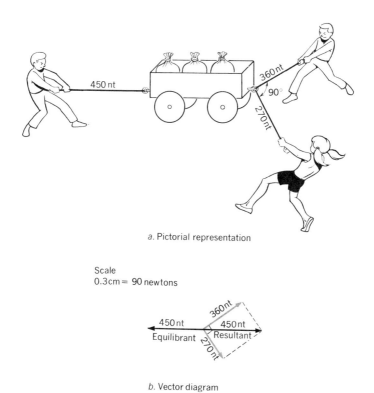

a. Pictorial representation

Scale
0.3 cm = 90 newtons

b. Vector diagram

Fig. 10–8. Equilibrant of forces acting at an angle.

difficult to upset. Similarly, a tall truck rounding a curve at high speed may overturn because its center of gravity is high. Under these conditions, the truck is in an unstable equilibrium. On the other hand, sports or racing cars, having a low center of gravity, hug the road. Such cars are less likely to overturn on sharp curves because they are in a more stable equilibrium than is a tall truck.

Since an object acts as though its weight were concentrated in its center of gravity, it is possible to balance any object on a point or pivot if the point is placed directly in line with the center of gravity of the object. Balanced in this way, the object is in a state of equilibrium. When a finger is used as a pivot under the 50-centimeter mark of a meter stick, the stick is in balance. If we try to balance the stick at any other point—the 40-centimeter mark, for example—we find that we cannot do it successfully. The reason is that the weight of the meter stick, concentrated at the midpoint of the stick, pulls one end of the stick downward and unbalances the forces acting on the stick. After determining the center of gravity of an object with either a regular or irregular shape, we can then balance the object on a point or pivot.

Finding the Center of Gravity of Regular Objects

The center of gravity of a regular object, such as a square or rectangular

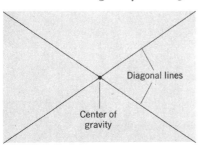

board, can be found by locating the center point of the object. We can find this point by ruling diagonal lines on the object (Fig. 10–9). The point at which the two lines cross is the center point of the object. To test this point as the location of the center of gravity of the object, we can try to balance the object at this point on a fingertip or any other suitable pivot.

Fig. 10–9. Locating the center of gravity of a regular object.

Finding the Center of Gravity of Irregular Objects

We can find the center of gravity of a flat, irregular object as follows:

1. Attach a weight, such as a plumb bob, a heavy washer, or a nut, to a string. When the weight is freely suspended on the string, it points to the center of the earth. Such a weighted string is called a *plumb line*.

2. Select any point A on the object, and drive a small nail into this point (Fig. 10–10a). Tie a string to the nail, and allow the object to swing freely. When the object comes to rest, suspend the weighted string from point A. With a pencil, draw a line from point A along the string to the other side of the object.

3. Repeat this procedure from any other point B on the object (Fig.

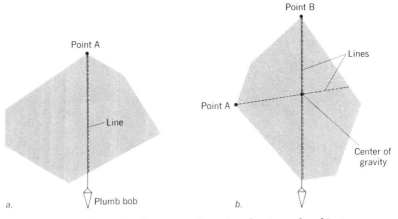

Fig. 10–10. Locating the center of gravity of an irregular object.

10–10b). When you draw the line from point B along the string, the two lines intersect, or cross, at the center of gravity.

4. Test this point as the location of the center of gravity by balancing the object at this point.

FORCES THAT CAUSE TURNING

The combinations of forces we studied earlier in this chapter dealt with forces acting together on a single point. They were applied to the point from the same direction, from opposite directions, or at an angle to each other.

In many instances, forces act together along parallel lines at different points on the same object. Such forces are called *parallel forces*. Parallel forces may act in the same or in opposite directions.

For example, suppose two people carry a load of 50 kilograms suspended halfway between them on a stick (Fig. 10–11). The 50-kilogram weight is a force acting vertically downward. Each person supports the weight with a force of 25 kilograms acting vertically upward. Here, all three forces are parallel to one another, but one acts in a direction opposite to the other two.

Whenever parallel forces acting in one direction are balanced by one or more parallel forces acting in the opposite direction, the resultant force becomes zero. In this case, the resultant force of the total upward forces (25 kilograms + 25 kilograms) and the total downward force (50 kilograms) is zero. As a result, the weight is in equilibrium and moves neither upward nor downward.

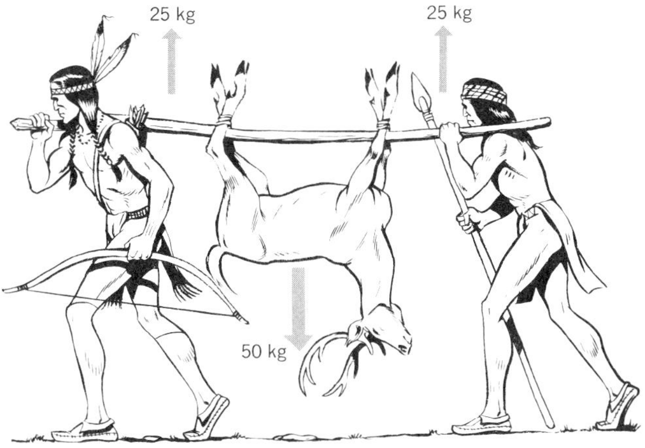

Fig. 10–11. Parallel forces.

Parallel forces may act in the same direction on an object that is balanced on a pivot, or *fulcrum*, and is free to turn, or rotate, about the fulcrum. If the parallel forces are equal, the balanced object remains balanced and does not move. Such a situation is common when two children of equal weight are placed on opposite sides of a seesaw at equal distances from the fulcrum (Fig. 10–12*a*).

If the forces on a pivoted object are unequal, the object is unbalanced and begins rotating in the direction of the larger of the two forces. The tendency of a force to produce rotation of an object is called the *moment of the force*, or *torque*. If the rotation is toward the right, the rotation is said to be *clockwise* (Fig. 10–12*b*); if in the opposite direction, it is said to be *counterclockwise* (Fig. 10–12*c*). The rotation caused by unbalanced moments of force is readily seen when two children of unequal weight are placed on a seesaw at equal distances from the fulcrum, or when two children of equal weight are placed

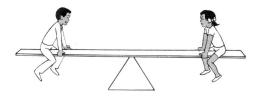

a. Parallel forces are equal

b. Unequal parallel forces (clockwise moment)

c. Unequal parallel forces (counterclockwise moment)

Fig. 10–12. Forces on a seesaw.

at unequal distances from the fulcrum. In either case, the rotation is in the direction of the greater moment of force.

Determining the Moment of Force

The moment of a force depends not only on the magnitude of the force but also on the distance of the force from the fulcrum. The moment is calculated by multiplying the force by this distance:

$$\text{moment of force} = \text{force} \times \text{distance from fulcrum}$$

$$\text{moment} = F \times D$$

For example, to find the moment of force of a 5-kilogram force acting 1 meter from a fulcrum, we substitute these values in the formula:

$$\text{moment} = F \times D$$

$$\text{moment} = 5 \text{ kilograms} \times 1 \text{ meter}$$

$$\text{moment} = 5 \text{ kilogram-meters}$$

Note that moment is expressed in kilogram-meters, a unit that includes the units of force and of distance.

Effect of Unequal Moments of Force

Let us calculate the moments when a 25-kilogram child sits on the left side of a seesaw and a 30-kilogram child sits on the right side, and the fulcrum is 2 meters from each child. The moment of force for the left side is:

$$\text{left-side moment} = F \times D$$

$$\text{left-side moment} = 25 \text{ kilograms} \times 2 \text{ meters}$$

$$\text{left-side moment} = 50 \text{ kilogram-meters}$$

The moment of force for the right side is:

$$\text{right-side moment} = F \times D$$

$$\text{right-side moment} = 30 \text{ kilograms} \times 2 \text{ meters}$$

$$\text{right-side moment} = 60 \text{ kilogram-meters}$$

In this case, the moment of force on the right side is greater, and the seesaw will rotate in a clockwise direction.

Using the same children, let us calculate the moments when the child on the left is 3 meters from the fulcrum and the one on the right is 2 meters from the fulcrum. The left-side moment is 25 kilograms × 3 meters, or 75 kilogram-meters. The right-side moment is 30 kilograms × 2 meters, or 60 kilogram-meters. Now the left-side moment is greater, and the seesaw will rotate in a counterclockwise direction.

Effect of Equal Moments of Force

When the clockwise and counterclockwise moments of force are equal, an object balanced on a fulcrum does not rotate—that is, the object is in equilibrium. This has been found to be true for a seesaw or any rod or plank in a similar situation. These facts are expressed as the *law of moments*. This law states that when a pivoted body is in equilibrium, the sum of the clockwise moments is equal to the sum of the counterclockwise moments. Expressed as a formula:

$$\text{clockwise moments} = \text{counterclockwise moments}$$

$$F_1 \times D_1 = F_2 \times D_2$$

Let us see how the law of moments operates. Suppose a 1-kilogram weight is hung on a steel rod 2 meters from a fulcrum, and a 2-kilogram weight is hung on the opposite side of the fulcrum, and 1 meter away from it (Fig. 10–13). According to the law of moments,

$$F_1 \times D_1 = F_2 \times D_2$$

Substituting,

$$1 \text{ kg} \times 2 \text{ m} = 2 \text{ kg} \times 1 \text{ m}$$

$$2 \text{ kilogram-meters} = 2 \text{ kilogram-meters}$$

The relationship expressed in the law of moments enables us to find

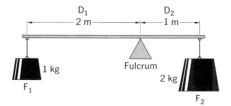

Fig. 10–13. Law of moments.

the weight of an unknown object when its distance from the fulcrum is known, if we have another known weight whose distance from the fulcrum is also known. For example, a boy on a seesaw at equilibrium weighs 60 kilograms. He is seated 1 meter from the fulcrum. A girl is seated at the other end 2 meters from the fulcrum. How much does the girl weigh?

$$\text{clockwise moments} = \text{counterclockwise moments}$$

$$F_1 \times D_1 = F_2 \times D_2$$

$$60 \text{ kilograms} \times 1 \text{ meter} = F_2 \times 2 \text{ meters}$$

$$60 \text{ kilogram-meters} = F_2 \times 2 \text{ meters}$$

$$\frac{60 \text{ kilogram-meters}}{2 \text{ meters}} = F_2$$

$$30 \text{ kilograms} = F_2$$

We know that the girl weighs 30 kilograms.

Using the same formula, we can find one unknown distance when the other three values are known. For example, how far away from a fulcrum must a 25-kilogram child sit in order to balance his father who weighs 75 kilograms and who sits 1 meter from the fulcrum?

$$F_1 \times D_1 = F_2 \times D_2$$

$$25 \text{ kilograms} \times D_1 = 75 \text{ kilograms} \times 1 \text{ meter}$$

$$D_1 = \frac{75 \text{ kilogram-meters}}{25 \text{ kilograms}}$$

$$D_1 = 3 \text{ meters}$$

Looking Back

The movement of any object in our environment is caused by unbalanced forces acting on the object at the same time. When balanced forces act on the object, the object is in equilibrium; that is, the object does not move. When parallel forces act on the same object from opposite directions, the object tends to rotate in the direction of the larger force moment.

Looking Ahead

When forces act on an object and move the object, work is done. In Chapter 11, we will learn about work and the simple machines we frequently use to help us accomplish work.

Multiple-Choice Questions

1. A push or pull exerted on an object is known as
   a. energy   b. force   c. charge   d. magnetism
2. Of the following, the example that does not create a force is
   a. magnetism   b. gravity   c. wind   d. velocity
3. When several forces act on an object, and the object does not move, the forces are said to be
   a. balanced   b. unbalanced   c. stable   d. unstable
4. A force that is exerted by gravity on the mass of an object is called
   a. density   b. volume   c. weight   d. specific gravity
5. Of the following, the one that is *not* a scalar quantity is
   a. density   b. volume   c. force   d. mass
6. When a vector is used to represent a force, the length of the vector tells us the
   a. magnitude   c. magnitude and direction
   b. direction   d. velocity
7. A single force that results from a combination of several forces is called
   a. a component   b. a vector   c. an equilibrant   d. a resultant
8. When two forces act on an object in the same direction, the resultant force is equal to the
   a. difference between the forces   c. product of the forces
   b. sum of the forces   d. ratio of the forces
9. Based on a scale of 0.6 cm = 90 nt, the number of newtons represented by a vector 3 cm long is
   a. 45   b. 180   c. 225   d. 450
10. When two forces act on an object in opposite directions, the resultant force is equal to the
    a. sum of the forces   c. difference between the forces
    b. product of the forces   d. ratio of the forces
11. When two forces, A and B, act on an object at an angle, the resultant force
    a. acts in the direction of A
    b. acts in the direction of B
    c. acts opposite to A
    d. acts in a direction between A and B
12. When balanced forces act on an object and do not move it, the object is said to be in a state of
    a. equilibrium   b. stability   c. instability   d. torque

13. An equilibrant force is
    a. of the same magnitude and direction as the resultant
    b. of different magnitude from but the same direction as the resultant
    c. of the same magnitude as but opposite direction to the resultant
    d. of different magnitude and direction from the resultant
14. A book lying flat on a table is said to be in a state of
    a. unstable equilibrium   c. equality
    b. stable equilibrium   d. rest
15. The point at which the weight of an object seems to be concentrated is known as the
    a. fulcrum   c. equilibrium point
    b. center of gravity   d. moment
16. A meterstick can usually be balanced by placing your finger at the point marked
    a. 40 centimeters   c. 80 centimeters
    b. 50 centimeters   d. 100 centimeters
17. A point around which an object can rotate is known as a
    a. stability point   b. center   c. pivot   d. center of gravity
18. If equal but opposite parallel forces act on an object, the object
    a. rotates clockwise
    b. does not rotate
    c. rotates counterclockwise
    d. rotates clockwise and counterclockwise
19. The moment of a force represents its tendency to
    a. remain stationary   c. rotate
    b. move in a straight line   d. move up and down
20. When the clockwise moment of force is greater than the counterclockwise moment of force on an object, the object
    a. rotates in a clockwise direction
    b. rotates in a counterclockwise direction
    c. does not move
    d. rotates clockwise and counterclockwise

Modified True-False Questions

1. When two forces acting on an object are unequal, the forces are said to be *unbalanced*.
2. In the metric system, the standard unit of force is the *pound*.
3. A device which can be used to measure the magnitude of a force is *a meterstick*.
4. Quantities that describe both magnitude and direction are called *scalar quantities*.
5. An arrow that is used to represent a force is known as *a vector*.
6. The forces on an object that produce a resultant force are called *component forces*.
7. To determine the exact magnitude and direction of a resultant force, we can construct *a triangle*.

8. A force that is equal to a resultant force in magnitude but is opposite in direction is called *a moment*.
9. When standing on end, a book is said to be in *unstable equilibrium*.
10. Forces acting in the same direction but at different points on an object are called *vertical forces*.

Thought Questions

1. By using vector diagrams, solve each of the following problems involving combinations of forces:
   a. Two men pull on an object in the same direction, one with a force of 180 newtons and the other with a force of 225 newtons. Find the resultant force (magnitude and direction).
   b. A man (A) pulls on an object with a force of 270 newtons. At the same time, a second man (B) pulls on the object with a force of 180 newtons in the opposite direction. Find the resultant force (magnitude and direction).
2. Two girls pull on an object using ropes fixed at the same point. One girl pulls with a force of 60 newtons (north); the second with a force of 80 newtons (east). The angle between the ropes is 90°. Find the resultant force (magnitude and direction) using the parallelogram method.
3. Explain how we can find the center of gravity of an irregular object.
4. a. Find the moment of force created when a force of 30 kilograms is exerted at a distance of 2 meters from a fulcrum.
   b. Find the moment of force created when a force of 600 kilograms is exerted at a distance of 3 meters from the fulcrum.
5. Using the law of moments, solve each of the following problems:
   a. A 50-kilogram boy is seated on a seesaw at a distance of 3 meters from the fulcrum. How far on the other side of the fulcrum must a 100-kilogram man sit to balance the seesaw?
   b. A 20-gram weight is hung 15 centimeters from a fulcrum. A second weight balances the first when it is placed at a distance of 5 centimeters on the other side of the fulcrum. How heavy is the second weight?

CHAPTER 11
WHY DO MACHINES MAKE WORK EASIER?

When you have completed this chapter, you should be able to:

1. *Define* work, newton-meter, power, watt, machine, efficiency.
2. *State* the law of machines.
3. *Distinguish* between (*a*) resistance force and effort force (*b*) ideal mechanical advantage and actual mechanical advantage.
4. *Explain* how a simple machine can be used to reduce effort or to increase speed.
5. *Use* simple formulas to calculate work, mechanical advantage, efficiency, and power.
6. *Discuss* how each of the following machines decreases effort: inclined plane, lever, pulley, wheel-and-axle, wedge, screw.

In the laboratory experience that follows, you will determine how an inclined plane and pulleys are used to decrease effort.

Laboratory Experience

WHY ARE PULLEYS AND INCLINED PLANES USED?

A. Place a 1-kilogram weight on your desk. Attach a spring scale to the weight. Lift the weight to a height of 30 centimeters above the table. Observe the reading on the spring scale.
    1. What force did you expend in order to lift the weight?

B. Assemble the rope and pulleys as shown in Fig. 11–1. The upper pulley should be at least 1 meter above the table. Attach the 1-kilogram weight to the lower pulley. Attach the spring scale to the free end of the rope. Pull straight down on the spring scale until you have raised the weight 30 centimeters above the table. Observe the reading on the spring scale.

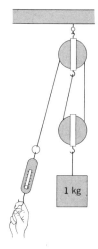

Fig. 11–1.

2. What force did you expend to lift the weight 30 centimeters?

3. What is the value of a pulley system in lifting weights?

C. Attach the small cart (Hall's carriage) to the end of the spring scale, and lift it 30 centimeters above the table. Observe the reading on the spring scale.

4. What force did you expend in order to lift the cart?

D. As shown in Fig. 11–2, set up an inclined plane so that one end of the plane is 30 centimeters above the table. Attach one end of a string to Hall's carriage, and attach the other end of the string to the spring scale. Slowly pull on the spring scale with a force that is sufficient to pull Hall's carriage to the top of the inclined plane. Pull on the scale with a steady, constant force, keeping the scale and string parallel to the inclined plane. Observe the reading on the spring scale as you pull.

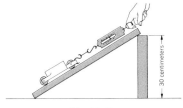

Fig. 11–2.

5. What force did you expend to lift the carriage to the top of the inclined plane?

6. What effect did the use of the inclined plane have on the amount of force you expended in order to lift the carriage 30 centimeters?

7. In terms of the force needed to lift an object, in what way are the pulley system and the inclined plane the same?

8. How would you use the inclined plane together with two pulleys to decrease the force needed to raise Hall's carriage with the kilogram weight in it to a height of 30 centimeters?

9. Use the apparatus to prove that you are right.

Introduction

Nothing in the universe moves unless energy is used. When humans first appeared on earth, they used body energy to exert the muscular force necessary to move objects in their environment. By moving objects such as stones or carrying animals they had hunted and killed, humans were able to satisfy their daily needs. As humans progressed, they used additional sources of energy in building more complex civilizations. In other words, humans have always worked. But what does work really mean?

WORK

In the scientific sense, every person, whether employed in a job or not, does work. In scientific terms, work is performed whenever any kind of matter is moved from one place to another through a particular distance. For example, when the student in Fig. 11–3 lifts her books from a desk, she performs work because the books move through a specific distance (Fig. 11–3a). However, if the books are on the floor and she jumps up and down on them, she performs no work on the books because they do not move (Fig. 11–3b). In this case, the only work she does is to move her body upward each time she jumps. Any work that we perform, whether on books or on any other type of matter, is possible because our body possesses energy, which enables us to use muscular force.

a. Work is done.   b. Work is not done.

Fig. 11–3. Work.

The forces used in building our civilization are natural forces such as those we studied in Chapter 10. Our greatest advances have come through the invention of machines that make it possible to use less force in doing work and in doing work faster. Thus, at first, in building homes, work was done in chopping down trees, shaping logs into planks, hauling the planks to building sites, and finally, fastening the planks together. Each step of this process required much labor. Many people exerted a great deal of muscular force and accomplished a great deal of work slowly. Since the invention of mechanical saws, trucks, cranes, and elevators, fewer people using less muscular force can do the same job in much less time.

Keep in mind that work is done only when an object is moved through a particular distance. Also, an object initially at rest moves only when it is acted upon by an unbalanced force. Accordingly, work involves (1) the action of a force and (2) a specific distance through which the force acts.

HOW WE COMPUTE THE AMOUNT OF WORK DONE

Since the amount of work done is determined by an unbalanced force acting on an object and the distance through which the object moves, work can be defined as follows:

Work (W) is the product of the force (F) and the distance (D) through which this force acts in moving the object. As an equation,

$$\text{work} = \text{force} \times \text{distance}$$

$$W = F \times D$$

When the force is measured in newtons and the distance is measured in meters, then the unit of work is the *newton-meter*, also called the *joule*. One newton-meter is the amount of work performed when a force of 1 newton is exerted through a distance of 1 meter. A student does 1 newton-meter of work when he or she lifts a 1-newton weight from a table to a height of 1 meter above the table.

To compute the amount of work performed in any situation, we apply the formula $W = F \times D$. Suppose a person pushes a sled with a force of 180 newtons over a distance of 3 meters. How much work has been done? Substituting in the formula,

$$W = F \times D$$

$$W = 180 \text{ newtons} \times 3 \text{ meters}$$

$$W = 540 \text{ newton-meters (or joules)}$$

We say the person has performed 540 newton-meters, or joules, of work.

HOW MACHINES HELP US DO WORK

The force exerted when a person moves an object is called the *effort force*. The force that the effort force overcomes in moving the object is called the *resistance force*. A large resistance force can be overcome with a smaller effort force by using a device called a *machine*.

A machine is an arrangement of materials that enables us to do work with less effort force (or with greater speed) than with our unaided muscles. In other words, a machine can multiply an effort force, making work easier; a machine can move some object over a given distance in a shorter time than is otherwise possible, making work quicker. When discussing work, it is usual to replace the terms effort force and resistance force with *effort* and *resistance*. We shall follow this practice for the rest of the chapter.

Reducing Effort

To lift a 250-kilogram piano to a height of 10 meters, a piano mover would need to exert a force of 2450 newtons (1 kilogram weighs 9.8 newtons). Using pulleys and a rope 50 meters long, however, the mover can lift the same piano to a height of 10 meters with a force of only 490 newtons. The same amount of work is performed with much less force. How?

To lift the piano unaided requires the expenditure of work W_1.

$$W_1 = F_1 \times D_1$$
$$W_1 = 2450 \text{ newtons} \times 10 \text{ meters} = 24,500 \text{ newton-meters}$$

Using pulleys requires the expenditure of work W_2.

$$W_2 = F_2 \times D_2$$
$$W_2 = 490 \text{ newtons} \times 50 \text{ meters} = 24,500 \text{ newton-meters}$$

The amount of work done in raising the piano to a particular height is the same whether the work is done by the piano mover's unaided muscles or by the mover, the pulleys, and the rope. However, the set of pulleys decreases the effort needed by increasing the distance over which the effort is applied.

This example shows that a simple machine makes it possible to reduce the effort necessary to move a large resistance that might otherwise be impossible to move. Note that although machines enable us to use a smaller effort for a task, *they do not reduce the total amount of work done.* The reduction in effort is always accompanied by an increase in the distance through which the effort (effort force) moves. Instead of applying a force of 2450 newtons (250 kilograms) over a distance of 10 meters, the piano mover applies a force of 490 newtons over a distance of 50 meters. This means that the mover can reduce the necessary effort by one-fifth, but the mover must increase the effort distance five times.

Increasing Speed

Suppose one person rides a bicycle, while another person walks alongside. If both people move their feet at the same pace for a given length of time, the person riding the bicycle travels farther than the one walking.

The greater speed of the rider is due to the fact that the rear wheel of a bicycle is attached to a smaller one (the axle). Both the wheel and the axle are made to turn at the same time by means of the sprocket wheel and chain. When we push on the pedals of a bicycle (Fig. 11–4), we cause the sprocket wheel to turn. If the sprocket wheel has a circumference of 50 centimeters, one turn of this wheel causes its rim to travel a circular distance of 50 centimeters. If the rear wheel has a circumference of 200 centimeters, then one turn of the rear wheel causes its rim to travel a circular distance of 200 centimeters. On some bicycles, one turn of the sprocket wheel causes the rear wheel to turn 3 times. Thus, as the 50-centimeter rim of the sprocket wheel moves through a distance of 50 centimeters, the 200-centimeter rim of the rear wheel makes 3 revolutions and moves through a distance of 200 centimeters × 3, or 600 centimeters (6 meters). Since both distances are covered during the same time interval, we can see why riding a bicycle is faster than walking.

This example shows how one type of simple machine (the wheel-and-axle) makes it possible for a given effort to move a resistance faster than would be possible without the machine. In this case, the machine serves to increase the distance per time interval (speed) rather than to decrease the force exerted.

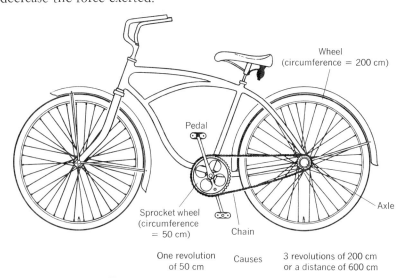

Fig. 11–4. A bicycle multiplies speed.

The Law of Machines

We have already stated that, although machines decrease effort, they do not decrease work. We cannot get more work out of a machine than we put into it. The actual work put into a machine is called the *work input*. The actual work accomplished by using a machine is called the *work output*. In an ideal machine, the work input equals the work output. This relationship, called the *law of machines*, is stated as

$$\text{work output} = \text{work input}$$

The work output is the product of the resistance and the distance through which the resistance is moved. Work input is the product of the effort and the distance through which the effort moves. Accordingly, we can express the law of machines as follows:

$$\text{resistance} \times \text{resistance distance} = \text{effort} \times \text{effort distance}$$

Using the symbols R for resistance, D_R for resistance distance, E for effort, and D_E for effort distance, the relationship may be written as

$$R \times D_R = E \times D_E$$

MECHANICAL ADVANTAGE OF MACHINES

With many machines, we use a small effort to overcome a larger resistance. In this way, machines have given us an advantage over our environment and have enabled us to change our environment in many ways. The advantage we get from machines is called *mechanical advantage*.

The mechanical advantage of a machine is the number of times that it multiplies an effort. Thus, a mechanical advantage of 3 indicates that a machine multiplies the applied force, or effort, threefold. With such a machine, an effort of 100 newtons can overcome a resistance of 300 newtons.

Ideal Mechanical Advantage

In any machine, some of the effort applied is lost (wasted) in overcoming friction. In a system of pulleys, for example, the rope rubs against the pulley wheels, and the wheels themselves create friction as they turn on their axles. Overcoming friction uses up some of the energy of motion and transforms it into heat energy. This loss of energy because of friction can never be completely overcome in a practical machine.

In theory, a machine that is completely frictionless is called an *ideal machine*. While such a machine does not exist, the concept is useful in calculating the theoretical mechanical advantage of various simple machines. The mechanical advantage of an ideal machine is called the *ideal mechanical advantage*. We find the ideal mechanical advantage (IMA) by dividing the distance the effort moves (D_E) by the distance the resistance moves (D_R):

$$\text{ideal mechanical advantage} = \frac{\text{effort distance}}{\text{resistance distance}}$$

$$IMA = \frac{D_E}{D_R}$$

The ideal mechanical advantage can also be represented as the resistance (R) divided by the effort that would ideally be used (E_{ideal}):

$$IMA = \frac{R}{E_{ideal}}$$

Actual Mechanical Advantage

Since frictionless machines do not exist, we can make use only of *actual machines*. The mechanical advantage of actual machines is called the *actual mechanical advantage* (AMA). The actual mechanical advantage of a machine is found by dividing the resistance (R) by the actual effort used (E_{actual}):

$$\text{actual mechanical advantage} = \frac{\text{resistance}}{\text{effort (actual)}}$$

$$AMA = \frac{R}{E_{actual}}$$

Calculating Mechanical Advantage

Let us return to the example of the piano mover and the piano. The mover uses a pulley system to lift the 250-kilogram piano to a height of 10 meters. The effort is 490 newtons (50 kilograms), and the length of the rope is 50 meters. In the absence of friction, we find the ideal mechanical advantage from the equation

$$IMA = \frac{D_E}{D_R}$$

Since the effort distance is 50 meters, and the resistance distance is 10 meters,

$$IMA = \frac{50 \text{ meters}}{10 \text{ meters}}$$

$$IMA = 5$$

To find the effort the mover should ideally use (the ideal effort), we use the formula

$$IMA = \frac{R}{E_{ideal}}$$

The resistance (R) is 250 kilograms, and the IMA is 5. Thus,

$$5 = \frac{250 \text{ kilograms}}{E_{ideal}}$$

$$E_{ideal} = 50 \text{ kilograms}$$

In theory, the mover should use 50 kilograms of effort to lift the 250-kilogram piano.

In reality, however, the pulley system is not frictionless, and some effort is wasted. Therefore, the actual effort used by the mover is 60 kilograms. To calculate the actual mechanical advantage, we use the equation

$$AMA = \frac{R}{E_{actual}}$$

$$AMA = \frac{250 \text{ kilograms}}{60 \text{ kilograms}}$$

$$AMA = 4.17$$

In this example, note that the IMA is 5, while the AMA is a little over 4. In the rest of this chapter, we shall be concerned mainly with the ideal mechanical advantage. Keep in mind that the ideal mechanical advantage is always somewhat greater than the actual mechanical advantage.

Efficiency of Machines

The effectiveness of a machine in reducing effort or in multiplying effort is expressed as a percentage called *efficiency*. The efficiency of a machine is calculated by dividing its actual mechanical advantage by its ideal mechanical advantage. Since the efficiency of a machine is expressed as a percent, we multiply this ratio by 100. Thus,

$$\text{efficiency} = \frac{AMA}{IMA} \times 100$$

The efficiency of any ideal machine is 100% because the AMA and IMA are equal. This means that no effort is wasted in overcoming friction. If the actual and ideal mechanical advantages were each 3, then

$$\text{efficiency} = \frac{AMA}{IMA} = \frac{3}{3} \times 100 = 1 \times 100 = 100\%$$

Since friction cannot be completely eliminated in any known machine, the actual mechanical advantage is always smaller than the ideal mechanical advantage, and the resulting efficiency is always less than 100%. In the pulley system of the piano example, we find the efficiency thus:

$$\text{efficiency} = \frac{AMA}{IMA} \times 100$$

$$\text{efficiency} = \frac{4.17}{5} \times 100$$

$$\text{efficiency} = 0.834 \times 100 = 83.4\%$$

POWER

Like the term work, the term *power* has both an everyday meaning and a scientific meaning. When we speak about power in everyday life, we generally refer to great strength or authority. The scientific meaning of power is the speed, or rate, of doing work. In other words, power (P) is the amount of work (W) performed in a given time period (T).

Expressed as an equation,

$$\text{power} = \text{work per unit of time}$$

$$\text{power} = \frac{\text{work}}{\text{time}}$$

$$P = \frac{W}{T}$$

Since work may be expressed as force (F) multipled by distance (D),

$$\text{power} = \frac{\text{force} \times \text{distance}}{\text{time}}$$

$$P = \frac{F \times D}{T}$$

In the metric system, power is expressed in *watts* or *kilowatts* (1000 watts). In this system, 1 watt = 1 newton-meter per second. In terms of the previous equation,

$$\text{watts} = \frac{\text{newtons} \times \text{meters}}{\text{seconds}}$$

Let us find the power in kilowatts of a machine that exerts a force of 5400 newtons in lifting an object to a height of 3 meters in 2 seconds.

$$P = \frac{F \times D}{T}$$

Substituting $F = 5400$ newtons, $D = 3$ meters, and $T = 2$ seconds,

$$P = \frac{5400 \text{ newtons} \times 3 \text{ meters}}{2 \text{ seconds}}$$

$$P = \frac{16,200 \text{ newton-meters}}{2 \text{ seconds}}$$

$$P = 8100 \text{ newton-meters/second} = 8100 \text{ watts} = 8.1 \text{ kilowatts}$$

TYPES OF SIMPLE MACHINES

Machines are helpful to us because they enable us to accomplish work with less effort or faster than by using our unaided muscles. Even the most complex machines used in industry are based upon six simple machines, used either individually or in combination. These simple machines are the *inclined plane*, the *lever*, the *pulley*, the *wheel-and-axle*, the *wedge*, and the *screw*.

THE INCLINED PLANE

An inclined plane, such as the one you studied in the laboratory experience, is generally used to slide an object from one level to a higher level without actually lifting the object. Examples of inclined planes include ramps and ordinary wooden planks placed with one end on the ground and the other at some higher level.

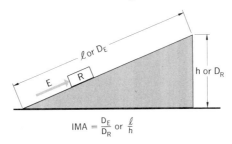

$$IMA = \frac{D_E}{D_R} \text{ or } \frac{l}{h}$$

Fig. 11–5. An inclined plane.

As shown in Fig. 11–5, the distance through which the resistance moves (D_R) is the height (h) of the inclined plane above its lowest point. The distance through which the effort moves (D_E) is the length of the inclined plane (l). Recall that the ideal mechanical advantage of a machine is found by dividing resistance distance into effort distance:

$$IMA = \frac{D_E}{D_R}$$

Accordingly, the ideal mechanical advantage of the inclined plane is found by dividing the length of the plane by the height to which the object is raised. Thus,

$$IMA \text{ (inclined plane)} = \frac{\text{length of plane}}{\text{height of plane}}$$

$$IMA = \frac{l}{h}$$

As applied to the inclined plane, the law of machines can be expressed as follows:

$$\text{work output} = \text{work input}$$

$$\text{resistance} \times \text{height of plane} = \text{effort} \times \text{length of plane}$$

$$R \times h = E \times l$$

By means of the formulas for ideal mechanical advantage and the law of machines, we can find the effort needed to push heavy objects up a frictionless inclined plane. Suppose a mover tries to push a 2450-newton piano up a 5-meter inclined plane to a height of 1 meter. What effort must be exerted, assuming no friction?

Find the ideal mechanical advantage of this inclined plane by dividing its length by its height:

$$IMA = \frac{l}{h}$$

$$IMA = \frac{5 \text{ meters}}{1 \text{ meter}}$$

$$IMA = 5$$

The mechanical advantage of a machine tells us by how much a machine multiplies effort. Therefore, we can find the effort by dividing the resistance (2450 newtons) by the mechanical advantage (5):

$$E = \frac{2450 \text{ newtons}}{5}$$

$$E = 490 \text{ newtons}$$

We can also find the ideal effort from the law of machines.

$$R \times h = E \times l$$

$$2450 \text{ newtons} \times 1 \text{ meter} = E \times 5 \text{ meters}$$

$$2450 \text{ newton-meters} = E \times 5 \text{ meters}$$

$$\frac{2450 \text{ newton-meters}}{5 \text{ meters}} = E$$

$$490 \text{ newtons} = E$$

This value of E agrees with the value found by using the IMA. Since some effort will be wasted in overcoming friction, the actual effort will be somewhat greater than 490 newtons.

THE LEVER

A lever consists of a rigid bar that can turn about a fulcrum. When effort is applied to one end of the bar, it causes the bar to rotate and move a resistance that is located at some other part of the bar. Some examples of the lever and fulcrum were considered in our discussion of moments of force in Chapter 10 (pages 178–181). Levers are perhaps the oldest of the simple machines. They were used by ancient peoples to move large objects such as boulders.

There are three kinds, or classes, of levers, depending on the locations of the effort, the fulcrum, and the resistance (Fig. 11–6).

In a *first-class lever,* the fulcrum lies somewhere between the effort and the resistance (Fig. 11–6a). In this type of lever, both the effort and the resistance act in the same direction. Examples of first-class levers are a seesaw, a balance scale, and a pair of pliers.

In a *second-class lever,* the resistance lies somewhere between the effort and the fulcrum (Fig. 11–6b). In this case, the effort and resistance act in opposite directions. The wheelbarrow and the nutcracker are examples of second-class levers.

In a *third-class lever,* the effort lies somewhere between the resistance and the fulcrum (Fig. 11–6c). Third-class levers require an effort greater than the resistance. However, they are useful because they enable us to increase the distance moved by the resistance in a short period of time. Also, some levers of this type enable us to grasp objects conveniently. Sugar tongs and the attachment of muscles in the human arm are examples of third-class levers.

The ideal mechanical advantage of levers is found by applying the formula

$$IMA = \frac{D_E}{D_R}$$

$$IMA \text{ (lever)} = \frac{\text{effort distance from fulcrum}}{\text{resistance distance from fulcrum}}$$

$$IMA = \frac{\text{length of effort arm}}{\text{length of resistance arm}} = \frac{l_E}{l_R}$$

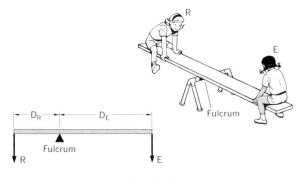

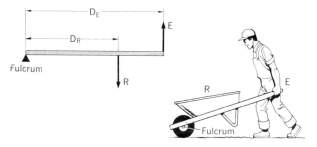

a. First-class lever

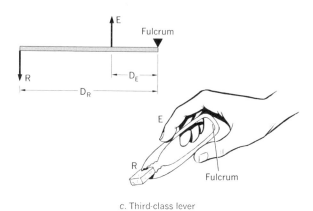

b. Second-class lever

c. Third-class lever

Fig. 11–6. Classes of levers.

Suppose the distance from the fulcrum to the effort is 5 meters, and the distance from the fulcrum to a resistance is 1 meter. Substituting these figures in the formula

$$IMA = \frac{l_E}{l_R}$$

$$IMA = \frac{5 \text{ meters}}{1 \text{ meter}}$$

$$IMA = 5$$

we find that the *IMA* of this lever is 5.

By means of the formula for ideal mechanical advantage and the law of machines, we can find the effort that should be exerted on a first-class lever to lift a 60-newton resistance that is located 1 meter from the fulcrum. The effort is to be applied at a point 2 meters from the fulcrum (Fig. 11–7). We can calculate the effort by using the formula

$$IMA = \frac{l_E}{l_R}$$

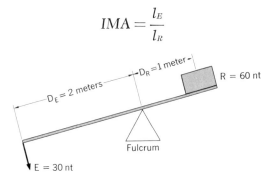

Fig. 11–7. Lever problem.

In this case, l_E is 2 meters, and l_R is 1 meter. Thus,

$$IMA = \frac{2 \text{ meters}}{1 \text{ meter}}$$

$$IMA = 2$$

Now, knowing the *IMA*, we can find the effort from the formula

$$IMA = \frac{R}{E}$$

$$2 = \frac{60 \text{ newtons}}{E}$$

$$2 \times E = 60 \text{ newtons}$$

$$E = 30 \text{ newtons}$$

The law of machines can also be applied to this problem. Substituting in the formula for the law of machines:

$$R \times D_R = E \times D_E$$

$$60 \text{ newtons} \times 1 \text{ meter} = E \times 2 \text{ meters}$$

$$60 \text{ newton-meters} = E \times 2 \text{ meters}$$

$$\frac{60 \text{ newton-meters}}{2 \text{ meters}} = E$$

$$30 \text{ newtons} = E$$

This value of E agrees with the value found by using the IMA.

PULLEYS

The simplest form of pulley, a single pulley, consists of a grooved wheel that can turn within a frame. Such a pulley can be used in two ways. When the pulley is attached to a fixed point, it is known as a *fixed pulley*. When the pulley is attached to the resistance and moves with it, it is known as a *movable pulley*. Because combinations of fixed and movable pulleys can provide large mechanical advantages, they are frequently used for moving very heavy objects.

Single Fixed Pulley

Used alone, a fixed pulley and its rope (Fig. 11–8a, page 202) provide a mechanical advantage of 1. Such a machine makes it possible to apply an effort force in a convenient direction because pulling downward is easier than pulling upward.

In this case, the resistance is supported by one length of rope. In order to raise a resistance of 500 newtons, a man must exert an effort of 500 newtons. As the weight rises 1 meter, 1 meter of rope passes through the man's hands. In effect, a single fixed pulley behaves like an equal-arm lever.

Single Movable Pulley

Although it may be awkward to use, a single movable pulley (Fig. 11–8b, page 202) provides twice the mechanical advantage of the fixed

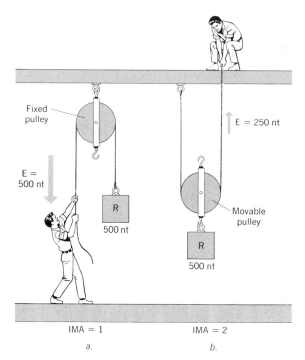

Fig. 11–8. Single pulleys.

pulley—an *IMA* of 2. In this case, one end of a rope is attached to a support, and the other end is pulled by the man. Each section of rope supports one-half the weight of the resistance. In order to raise the 500-newton resistance 1 meter, the man need use an effort of only 250 newtons. To do this, however, he must pull 2 meters of rope toward himself.

Combinations of Pulleys

In order to benefit from the good points of both the fixed pulley and the movable pulley, the two are often used together. You used a combination of a fixed pulley and a movable pulley in your laboratory experience (page 185). Several fixed and several movable pulleys may be threaded with one rope and used as a system or single unit. The mechanical advantage of any pulley system is found in one of two ways.

(1) Since the resistance is supported by several lengths of rope, counting the number of lengths tells us the ideal mechanical advantage. For example, suppose we want to find the mechanical advantage of a set of pulleys consisting of three fixed and two movable pulleys (Fig. 11–9a). The effort is directed downward. We count 5 lengths of rope

supporting the resistance. (The sixth length, along which the effort is directed, does *not* support the resistance.) The ideal mechanical advantage, therefore, is 5.

The same mechanical advantage can be obtained using two fixed and two movable pulleys (Fig. 11–9*b*), providing the effort is directed upward. In this case, five lengths support the resistance. In either case, the effort needed to lift a 500-newton resistance would be 500 newtons ÷ 5 = 100 newtons.

(2) We can also use the formula

$$IMA = \frac{D_E}{D_R}$$

In either system of pulleys shown in Fig. 11–9, we would pull 5 meters of rope in order to raise the resistance 1 meter.

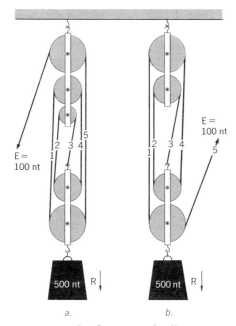

Fig. 11–9. Combinations of pulleys.

THE WHEEL-AND-AXLE

A wheel-and-axle consists of a large wheel and a smaller wheel, or axle, both firmly connected so that they turn together about the same center point (axis). The wheel-and-axle is used in such devices as an automobile steering wheel, a bicycle, a windlass, and a door knob.

When a force is applied to the wheel, the smaller axle turns through a shorter distance and can exert a force greater than that applied to the wheel. When used in this way, the wheel-and-axle multiplies effort.

Since the effort distance is determined by the radius of the wheel, and the resistance distance is determined by the radius of the axle, the ideal mechanical advantage of the wheel-and-axle is the radius of the larger wheel (R_{wheel}) divided by the radius of the axle (r_{axle}).

Thus,

$$IMA \text{ (wheel-and-axle)} = \frac{\text{radius of wheel}}{\text{radius of axle}}$$

$$IMA = \frac{R_{wheel}}{r_{axle}}$$

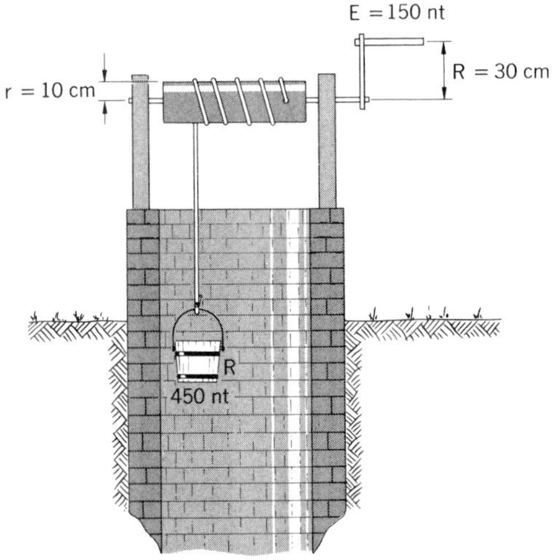

Fig. 11–10. A windlass.

Fig. 11–10 shows a windlass being used to lift a 450-newton pail of water from a well. The crank of this machine is really a rimless wheel consisting of only one spoke to which a horizontal handle has been attached. The radius (spoke) of this wheel is 30 centimeters. The axle, or drum, on which the rope is wound has a radius of 10 centimeters. To determine the ideal mechanical advantage,

$$IMA = \frac{R_{wheel}}{r_{axle}}$$

$$IMA = \frac{30 \text{ centimeters}}{10 \text{ centimeters}}$$

$$IMA = 3$$

Since the windlass has an ideal mechanical advantage of 3, we require an effort of 150 newtons to lift the 450-newton resistance.

When an effort is applied to an axle, instead of to its wheel, the rim of the wheel turns a greater circular distance than the rim of the axle. As a result, any point on the wheel rim moves more rapidly than a point on the axle. When used in this way, as in a bicycle, the wheel-and-axle becomes a means of increasing speed (see page 190).

THE WEDGE

A wedge is a modified, or double, inclined plane. In using a wedge we usually move the wedge rather than the resistance. The mechanical advantage of the wedge depends on its length and thickness. Examples of wedges are axes, knives, chisels, and carpenter's nails (Fig. 11–11).

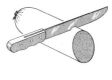

Fig. 11–11. Examples of wedges.

THE SCREW

A screw can be likened to an inclined plane that is wrapped around a cylinder. Examples are wood screws, metal screws, and the jackscrew, or jack (Fig. 11–12, page 206). The distance between two successive ridges, or threads, of a screw is called the *pitch* of the screw. When a screw is turned through one complete revolution, the screw advances a distance equal to its pitch. This is the distance through which the resistance moves. The effort E is applied to the jack through a long handle. Thus, a small effort moving through a large distance moves a large resistance through a small distance. In this manner, a jack multiplies effort.

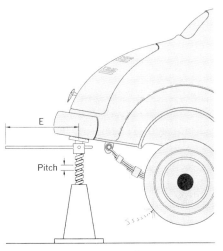

E

Pitch

Fig. 11–12. A jackscrew.

Looking Back

Machines make work easier either by reducing the effort used in moving a resistance or by increasing the speed of movement of the resistance. However, by reducing effort, machines do not reduce the total amount of work done. This is in accord with the law of machines, which states that work input equals work output.

Looking Ahead

Fluids, like solids, have weight. As a result, fluids exert force and can be used to do work. Fluids and the forces they exert are discussed in Chapter 12.

Multiple-Choice Questions

1. Work is defined as the product of
   a. force and weight   c. force and energy
   b. energy and height   d. force and distance
2. In the metric system of measurement, the unit of work is the
   a. newton   b. meter   c. watt   d. newton-meter
3. A machine
   a. can reduce our effort   c. has no effect on effort
   b. can increase our effort   d. always increases speed

4. When work is being done, a reduction in effort is generally accompanied by
   a. no change in the distance
   b. a decrease in the distance covered by the effort
   c. an increase in the distance covered by the effort
   d. a decrease in height

5. A machine that makes it possible to move a resistance faster is a
   a. wedge   b. lever   c. screw   d. wheel-and-axle

6. In an ideal machine, the work input
   a. is greater than the work output   c. is equal to the work output
   b. is less than the work output   d. never changes

7. The product of the resistance and the distance through which the resistance is moved is called the
   a. law of machines   c. work output
   b. work input   d. effort

8. When 180 newtons of effort is applied to a machine with a mechanical advantage of 3, the machine produces a force of
   a. 60 newtons   b. 90 newtons   c. 180 newtons   d. 540 newtons

9. The ideal mechanical advantage refers to a machine that
   a. cannot be built
   b. produces large amounts of friction
   c. needs no effort
   d. is easy to build

10. Actual mechanical advantage is found by dividing the resistance by the
    a. effort   b. friction   c. resistance distance   d. effort distance

11. In a frictionless machine, the IMA would be
    a. greater than the AMA   c. less than the AMA
    b. equal to the AMA   d. greater than 5

12. In a frictionless machine, the efficiency is
    a. 0%   b. 25%   c. 50%   d. 100%

13. In most machines,
    a. the AMA and IMA are equal   c. the AMA is less than the IMA
    b. the IMA is less than the AMA   d. the IMA equals zero

14. The rate of doing work is called
    a. power   b. energy   c. effort   d. mechanical advantage

15. In an inclined plane, the distance through which the resistance moves
    a. is the same as the length of the plane
    b. is greater than the length of the plane
    c. is the height of the plane
    d. is less than the height of the plane

16. The effort needed to move an object on an inclined plane is found from the formula
    a. $\dfrac{D_R}{IMA}$ b. $\dfrac{D_E}{IMA}$ c. $\dfrac{E}{AMA}$ d. $\dfrac{R}{IMA}$

17. An example of a first-class lever is a
    a. seesaw   b. wheelbarrow   c. nutcracker   d. sugar tongs

18. When the resistance in a lever lies somewhere between the effort and the fulcrum, we have a
    a. first-class lever   c. third-class lever
    b. second-class lever   d. first- or second-class lever
19. An example of a third-class lever is
    a. a wheelbarrow   b. sugar tongs   c. pliers   d. a nutcracker
20. Of the following, the simple machine that provides a mechanical advantage of 1 is a
    a. second-class lever   c. single fixed pulley
    b. single movable pulley   d. screw
21. The ideal mechanical advantage of a pulley system can be found from the formula
    a. $\dfrac{D_R}{D_E}$ b. $\dfrac{E}{R}$ c. $\dfrac{R}{D_E}$ d. $\dfrac{D_E}{D_R}$
22. A simple machine used in a steering wheel and a bicycle is a
    a. lever   b. wedge   c. pulley   d. wheel-and-axle
23. The ideal mechanical advantage of a wheel-and-axle equals
    a. the radius of the larger wheel divided by the radius of the axle
    b. the radius of the axle divided by the radius of the wheel
    c. the effort divided by the resistance
    d. the effort distance multiplied by the resistance distance

Modified True-False Questions

1. The force exerted when a person moves an object is called the *resistance force*.
2. The actual work put into a machine is called *work input*.
3. The equal nature of work input and work output of a machine is expressed in the *law of power*.
4. The effectiveness of a machine in reducing effort is expressed as a percentage called *efficiency*.
5. In the metric system, power is expressed in a unit called *a newton*.
6. One thousand watts is equal to *a milliwatt*.
7. When a pulley is attached to the resistance and moves with it, it is known as *a movable pulley*.
8. A modified double inclined plane describes a simple machine known as *a screw*.
9. An inclined plane that is wrapped around a cylinder is called *a screw*.
10. The distance between two successive ridges of a screw is called the *pitch*.

Thought Questions

1. a. Compute the work performed by a man who exerts 600 newtons of force on a sled and moves it 6 meters.
   b. If 1000 newton-meters of work is performed by a force of 50 newtons, over what distance does the object move?

2. Complete the table:

Simple Machine	Formula for IMA	Example
Lever Inclined plane Pulley Wheel-and-axle		

3. a. A 200-newton object is moved by a lever whose fulcrum is 1 meter from the object. The effort needed to move the object is exerted 2 meters on the other side of the fulcrum. What effort force is needed to move the object?

b. What is the ideal mechanical advantage of this lever?

4. Find the power developed when a force of 1000 newtons moves an object a distance of 6 meters in 2 seconds.

5. a. Find the effort necessary to move a 500-newton resistance up an inclined plane 6 meters long to a height of 1.5 meters.

b. What is the IMA of the inclined plane?

6. Find the effort needed to raise a piano that weighs 4500 newtons with a pulley system that has 4 lengths of rope supporting the piano.

7. Calculate the effort needed to raise a resistance of 600 newtons using a windlass. The radius of the wheel is 30 centimeters, while the radius of the axle is 6 centimeters.

CHAPTER 12

HOW ARE FLUIDS USED TO DO WORK?

When you have completed this chapter, you should be able to:

1. *Define* fluid, density, pressure, specific gravity.
2. *Use* simple formulas to calculate density, pressure, and specific gravity.
3. *Contrast* the characteristics of liquid pressure and air pressure.
4. *Explain,* with examples, how air pressure is used in some devices.
5. *State* Pascal's law, Boyle's law, Bernoulli's principle, and Archimedes' principle.
6. *Compare* the construction of a mercury barometer with that of an aneroid barometer, and indicate how these instruments measure air pressure.
7. *Predict* whether an object will sink or float in a fluid.

In the laboratory experience that follows, you will determine the conditions under which objects sink or float.

Laboratory Experience

WHY DO SOME OBJECTS SINK IN WATER WHILE OTHER OBJECTS FLOAT?

A. Tie a loop in one end of a piece of string. Tie the other end of the string around a small stone. Place the loop on the hook of a spring scale, and weigh the stone (Fig. 12–1).
    1. How much does the stone weigh?
B. Using a platform scale, weigh an empty catch bucket.
    2. How much does the catch bucket weigh?
C. Cover the spout of an overflow can with your finger. Fill the can with water up to the spout, remove your finger from the spout, and allow the excess water to drain into the catch bucket. Throw away the excess water, and dry the catch bucket. Place the catch bucket under the spout of the overflow can.

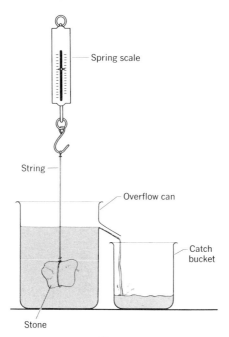

Fig. 12–1.

D. Suspend from the spring scale again the small stone you weighed in part A. Gently lower the stone into the overflow can, taking care that the stone does not touch either the sides or bottom of the can. Allow the overflow water to remain in the catch bucket.

    3. What is the weight of the stone while it is submerged in the water?

E. Using the platform scale, weigh the catch bucket partly filled with water.

    4. What is the weight of the catch bucket and water together?

F. Find the weight of the water in the catch bucket by subtracting the weight of the empty bucket found in part B from the weight found in part E.

    5. How much does the water alone weigh?

    6. What happens to the weight of the stone when it is submerged in the water?

    7. How do you account for the difference in weight?

    8. Compare the difference in weight of the stone with the weight of the water in the catch bucket. Explain your findings.

G. Empty the water from the catch bucket, and dry the bucket thoroughly. Refill the overflow can as you did in part C, and place the catch bucket under the spout of the overflow can.

H. Using a string as in part A, weigh the block of wood.
  9. How much does the wood weigh?
I. Gently lower the block of wood into the overflow can, taking care that the wood does not touch the sides of the can. Allow the wood to float on the water. Allow the overflow water to remain in the catch bucket.
J. Weigh the catch bucket partly filled with water.
  10. What is the weight of the catch bucket and water together?
K. Find the weight of the water in the catch bucket by subtracting the weight found in part B from the weight found in part J.
  11. How much does the water alone weigh?
  12. How does the weight of the displaced water compare with the weight of the block of wood?
  13. Why do certain substances float in water whereas others sink?
  14. How can you predict if a given object will sink or float in water?

Introduction

Because of gravity, a solid that rests on an object presses down on the surface of the object with a force equal to the weight of the solid. For the same reason, liquids and gases also press on surfaces with which they are in contact. The force exerted by liquids and gases is also equal to their weights. Since both gases and liquids flow, both are considered fluids.

The force exerted by liquids is used in devices such as the hydraulic brake and hydraulic lift. The force exerted by gases is used in devices such as air brakes and aerosol spray cans. The pressure of the atmosphere is due to the force of the air pressing down on us.

Pressure

The pressure exerted by any substance—solid, liquid, or gas—is the amount of force exerted by that substance on a given unit of area. For example, suppose we consider a 50-newton rectangular block of metal with the following dimensions: length—10 centimeters, width—5 centimeters, thickness—1 centimeter (Fig. 12–2a). When the block lies flat on a table, the area of the part of the table covered by the block is 50 square centimeters (the area of a rectangle is the product of the length and the width: 10 centimeters $\times$ 5 centimeters = 50 square centimeters). Since the block weighs 50 newtons, each square centimeter of the table covered by the block supports 1 newton.

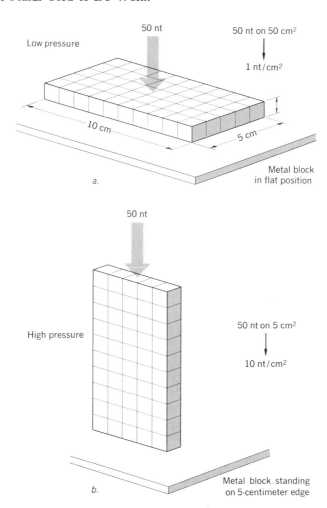

Fig. 12–2. Pressure and area.

$$\text{pressure} = \frac{50 \text{ newtons}}{50 \text{ square centimeters}} = 1 \frac{\text{newton}}{\text{square centimeter}}$$

$$= 1 \text{ newton per square centimeter}$$

Since pressure is the amount of force on a given area, we can also say that the block exerts a pressure of 1 newton on every square centimeter of the table.

If we stand the block on its 5-centimeter edge (Fig. 12–2b), it covers an area of only 5 square centimeters. Since the weight of the block is still 50 newtons, each square centimeter of table covered by the block now supports 10 newtons:

$$\text{pressure} = \frac{50 \text{ newtons}}{5 \text{ square centimeters}} = 10 \frac{\text{newtons}}{\text{square centimeter}}$$

$$= 10 \text{ newtons per square centimeter}$$

Thus, the pressure of the block in this position has increased to 10 newtons per square centimeter. Although the weight of the block of metal remains the same, the pressure it exerts has changed because its weight is now concentrated on a smaller area than before.

From this discussion, we see that pressure is equal to force divided by the area over which the force is spread. Thus,

$$\text{pressure} = \frac{\text{force}}{\text{area}}$$

When P represents pressure, F represents force, and A represents area,

$$P = \frac{F}{A}$$

In the metric system, pressure is expressed in grams per square centimeter or in newtons per square centimeter or square meter.

It is interesting to compare the pressure exerted on the ground by a woman wearing high heels with the pressure exerted by a truck. If the woman weighs 500 newtons (about 51 kilograms) and balances herself on one heel, the area of which is 5 square centimeters, then the pressure on the ground will be

$$P = \frac{F}{A}$$

$$P = \frac{500 \text{ newtons}}{5 \text{ square centimeters}}$$

$$P = 100 \text{ newtons per square centimeter}$$

If the truck weighs 50,000 newtons (about 5 tons) and has four wheels, its weight will be distributed over the four tires, each of which may have a ground contact area of about 325 square centimeters. Together, the contact area of the four tires would be 4×325 square centimeters, or 1300 square centimeters. Then, the pressure of the truck on the ground would be

$$P = \frac{F}{A}$$

$$P = \frac{50{,}000 \text{ newtons}}{1300 \text{ square centimeters}}$$

$$P = 38.5 \text{ newtons/square centimeter}$$

A 500-newton woman can exert almost three times the pressure of a 50,000-newton truck!

DENSITY

We have defined pressure as the force exerted by a substance on a given surface area. This pressure may vary from one substance to another. Thus, a block of lead exerts more pressure than would the same block made of wood; a given volume of mercury exerts more pressure than does the same volume of water. The pressures are different because the substances differ in *density*.

The density of a substance is the mass (amount of matter) of the substance contained in a given volume of the substance. This relationship can be expressed as

$$\text{density} = \frac{\text{mass}}{\text{volume}}$$

When we use D to represent density, m to represent mass, and V to represent volume, the formula for density is

$$D = \frac{m}{V}$$

In the metric system, density is measured in grams per cubic centimeter.

On earth, the weight and mass of an object are about the same. Thus, to find the density of a substance, we must know its mass (weight) and the volume it occupies. For example, suppose that a mass of 15 grams of a substance has a volume of 10 cubic centimeters. To find the density of this substance, we substitute $m = 15$ grams and $V = 10$ cubic centimeters into the formula

$$D = \frac{m}{V}$$

$$D = \frac{15 \text{ grams}}{10 \text{ cubic centimeters}}$$

$$D = 1.5 \frac{\text{grams}}{\text{cubic centimeter}} = 1.5 \text{ grams per cubic centimeter}$$

Changes in temperature have a considerable effect on the volume of a liquid or of a gas. The density of a liquid or a gas is therefore dependent on temperature. In our discussion of density, we will use room temperature (about 20°C) as a convenient reference point.

In studying the density of liquids, we generally use the density of water as the standard. The density of water is 1 gram per cubic centimeter in the metric system.

Fluids of greater density exert more force on a particular surface than those of lesser density. For example, mercury has a density of 13.6 grams per cubic centimeter. As a result, mercury exerts 13.6 times as much force on a given surface as does the same volume of water. Table 12–1 gives the densities of some other common liquids.

**Table 12–1. Density of Common Liquids
(At Room Temperature)**

Liquid	Density (grams per cubic centimeter)
Gasoline	0.68
Ethyl alcohol	0.79
Water	1.00
Seawater	1.025
Mercury	13.6

PRESSURE OF LIQUIDS

Liquids have weight and, like solids, they exert pressure. You are probably familiar with water pressure because of its effect on your ears when you swim underwater. As you go deeper in the water, the pressure increases and may cause discomfort to your eardrums. The pressure of water at great depths is so enormous that submarines and bathyscaphs are especially constructed to withstand it.

Experimentation has shown that, at different depths, the pressure of a liquid depends on two factors: the height of the liquid and its density. Consequently, the pressure exerted by a liquid is expressed by the equation

$$\text{pressure} = \text{height} \times \text{density}$$

When P is pressure, h is height, and D is density,

$$P = h \times D$$

Suppose an open cylinder contains a column of water 300 centimeters high (Fig. 12–3). To find the pressure of the water on the bottom of the cylinder, we recall that the density of water is 1 gram per cubic centimeter. By substituting this value for density,

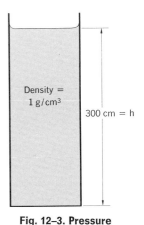

Density = 1 g/cm³

300 cm = h

$$P = h \times D$$

$$P = 300 \text{ centimeters} \times \frac{1 \text{ gram}}{\text{cubic centimeter}}$$

$$P = 300 \text{ grams per square centimeter}$$

Note that to calculate the units, we may write cubic centimeter as centimeter × centimeter × centimeter. (When we cube a number, we multiply it by itself three times.) Thus,

Fig. 12–3. Pressure exerted by a liquid.

$$P = 300 \text{ centimeters} \times 1 \frac{\text{gram}}{\text{centimeter} \times \text{centimeter} \times \text{centimeter}}$$

$$P = 300 \frac{\text{grams}}{\text{centimeter} \times \text{centimeter}}$$

$$P = \frac{300 \text{ grams}}{\text{square centimeter}} \text{ or } 300 \text{ grams per square centimeter}$$

A few simple experiments disclose some important characteristics of the pressure exerted by liquids.

1. *The pressure exerted by a liquid acts equally in all directions and is dependent on depth.* The can in Fig. 12–4a, page 218, has holes drilled in the bottom and at different levels in the side. When the can is filled with fine dry sand, a little sand runs out of the side holes, most

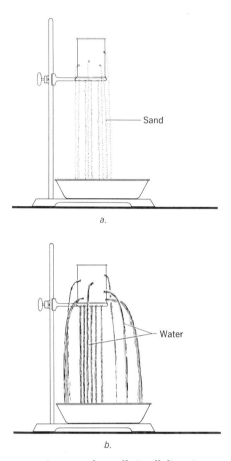

Fig. 12–4. Liquid pressure is exerted equally in all directions and depends on depth.

of the sand runs out of the bottom holes. Why? When the can is filled with water, the water runs out of the side holes as well as the bottom holes (Fig. 12–4b). This indicates that water, as well as sand, exerts a pressure in all directions. Note that water from the lowest side hole travels outward the farthest distance. This shows that the pressure exerted by a liquid depends on its depth; the greater the depth, the greater is the pressure.

The apparatus in Fig. 12–5 further confirms this. The apparatus consists of a thistle tube that is covered by a rubber membrane and connected to a pressure indicator. The indicator shows that, at any one depth, the pressure is equal, regardless of the direction in which the membrane is aimed. When the membrane is lowered, the pressure

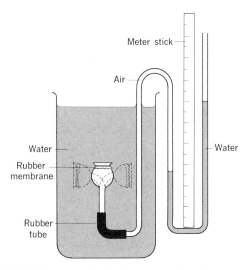

Fig. 12–5. An apparatus that measures liquid pressure.

at the new depth is again equal regardless of the direction the membrane faces. However, the pressure at
the lower level is greater than before.

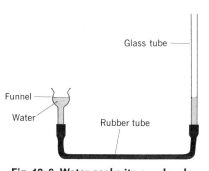

2. *Liquids seek their own level.* By
means of a long rubber tube, connect
a funnel to a long, straight glass tube
(Fig. 12–6). Pour water into the funnel until the glass tube is about one-
third full of water. As the funnel is
raised or lowered, the level of water

Fig. 12–6. Water seeks its own level.

in the glass tube always matches the level in the funnel.

When a system of glass tubes of different shapes and diameters is
connected as shown in Fig. 12–7 and water is poured into one tube,

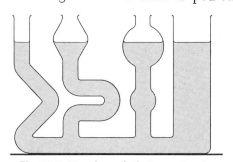

Fig. 12–7. Liquids seek their own level.

the level of water in all the tubes reaches the same height. Since the height (depth) of a liquid column determines its pressure, the liquid flows into each tube until the levels, and therefore the pressures, are equal.

3. *The pressure of a liquid is independent of the shape of its container.* The devices shown in Fig. 12–8 are called Pascal's vases. The dimensions of the bottom of each vase are the same, but their other dimensions differ. When the vases are filled to the same height with the same liquid, the dials indicate that the pressure at the bottom of all the vases is the same. Thus, we can see that the pressure of a liquid column depends on its height, rather than on the shape of its container.

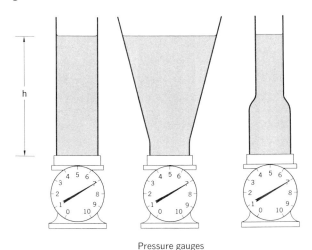

Pressure gauges
Fig. 12–8. Pascal's vases.

4. *Pressure is transferred throughout a liquid.* In a closed container filled with a liquid, any additional pressure applied to the liquid is transmitted without loss to all other parts of the liquid. Here too, the pressure acts equally in all directions. This statement, known as *Pascal's law,* can be demonstrated as follows:

Fill a tall bottle *completely* with water, and insert a glass stopper. The excess water flows out, and no air remains in the bottle. When you strike the stopper gently with a mallet, the bottom of the bottle cracks. Had the bottle been empty, the only result of the blow would have been to force the stopper farther in. Because the bottle is full of water, the pressure from the blow is transmitted without loss through the liquid in all directions. Since the area of the bottom of the bottle is larger than the area of the stopper, the *total force* on the bottom of the bottle increases considerably and, as a result, the bottle shatters.

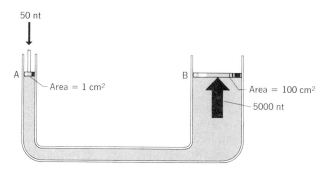

Fig. 12–9. A hydraulic press.

Fig. 12–9 shows how the hydraulic press operates. If 50 newtons per square centimeter of pressure is exerted on the small piston (A), this pressure is transmitted to every square centimeter of the large piston (B). Since the area of the large piston is 100 times that of the small piston, 50 newtons of effort on the small piston can move a resistance of 5000 newtons on the large piston. (50 newtons per square centimeter = 5000 newtons per 100 square centimeters.) As in all machines, the work done on both sides is the same. To move the 5000-newton resistance upward 1 centimeter, the small piston must move downward 100 centimeters.

PRESSURE OF GASES

Although their densities are very small, gases exert pressure for the same reasons that liquids do. We can best understand gas pressure by concerning ourselves with the common mixture of gases called air. We live at the bottom of an ocean of air, the atmosphere.

The characteristics of air pressure (atmospheric pressure) are:

1. *Air pressure decreases as the altitude increases.* Recall that the pressure exerted by a liquid depends upon the height of the liquid. This is also true for air pressure. Air pressure is greatest at the bottom of the atmosphere, which is at the altitude of sea level. As we ascend in the atmosphere by climbing a mountain or by flying in an airplane, the height of the column of air above us becomes smaller. As a result, the air pressure at any altitude above sea level is less than that at sea level.

At sea level and 0°C, the air pressure is 10.13 newtons per square centimeter. This pressure is also called 1 *atmosphere*.

Just as changes in water pressure may cause discomfort to our ears when we swim, changes in air pressure often have the same effect. This may occur when we travel rapidly up or down a tall building in an elevator.

2. *Air exerts pressure equally in all directions.* Like liquids, gases exert pressure equally in all directions. The fact that plants, animals, and inanimate objects are not crushed by the tremendous weight of the air gives evidence that this statement is true.

For example, consider a leaf attached by a thin stalk to a branch. The leaf may have an area of 65 square centimeters. Since the air pressure is about 10 newtons per square centimeter at sea level, the total weight of air on this leaf is about 650 newtons (10 newtons per square centimeter × 65 square centimeters = 650 newtons). This is about 66 kilograms. Ordinarily, such a great weight would snap the stalk and crush the leaf. However, since air exerts pressure equally in all directions, the same force (650 newtons) is acting upward from the underside of the leaf. The upward force balances the downward force, and the leaf remains intact.

3. *An increase in pressure reduces the volume of gases.* Unlike liquids and solids, gases can be compressed. *Robert Boyle,* in 1660, showed that when pressure is applied to a gas in a closed container (the temperature remaining constant), the volume of the gas decreases. As the pressure becomes greater, the volume occupied by the gas becomes smaller. Stated otherwise, the volume of a gas at constant temperature varies inversely with the pressure on it. This statement is part of *Boyle's law.*

For example, when the pressure exerted on a gas is doubled, the volume of the gas is reduced to one-half its original volume (Fig. 12–10). By the same token, when the pressure on the gas is reduced to one-half of what it was, the volume of the gas doubles. Remember that, in all of these cases, the temperature must remain unchanged.

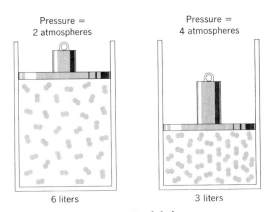

Fig. 12–10. Boyle's law.

MEASURING AIR PRESSURE

Air pressure is measured with an instrument called a *barometer*. There are two major types of barometers: the mercury barometer and the aneroid barometer.

The Mercury Barometer

The mercury barometer was first constructed in 1643 by the Italian scientist, *Evangelista Torricelli*. This device, which is still in use today, consists of an 81-centimeter length of glass tubing that is closed at one end. The glass tube is first filled with mercury and then inverted in a dish of mercury (Fig. 12–11). The mercury column falls but stops when its height reaches about 76 centimeters, or 760 millimeters, at sea level and 0°C. This is the maximum amount of mercury that the air pressing down on the dish can support. Air pressure under these conditions is called *standard pressure*. Since one millimeter of mercury is also referred to as a *torr*, at sea level standard pressure equals 760 torr. (If the mercury column were 1 square centimeter in cross-section, the mercury in the tube would weigh 10.13 newtons. This weight would exactly balance a normal atmospheric pressure of 10.13 newtons per square centimeter, or 1 atmosphere.)

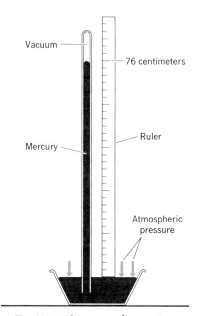

Fig. 12–11. A mercury barometer.

As the mercury in the tube moves downward, a partial vacuum is created in the 5 centimeters of space above it. When the atmospheric pressure increases, the mercury in the tube rises. (The greater air pressure will support a greater weight, or higher column, of mercury.) When the atmospheric pressure decreases, the mercury in the tube descends.

The Aneroid Barometer

The aneroid barometer (Fig. 12–12, page 224) consists of a corrugated metal box from which most of the air has been removed. When

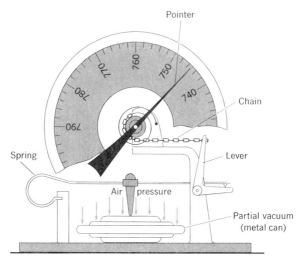

Fig. 12–12. An aneroid barometer.

the air pressure increases, it pushes the top of the box downward, causing the pointer to move in one direction by means of a spring, a lever, and a chain. When air pressure decreases, the top of the box moves upward, causing the pointer to move in the opposite direction.

MAKING USE OF AIR PRESSURE

Such simple devices as the medicine dropper (Fig. 12–13*a*), the soda straw (Fig. 12–13*b*), and the vacuum cleaner operate by reducing the air pressure inside them and allowing the outside air, under its own pressure, to push something into the device.

Devices such as a bicycle tire pump, sprayers, and blowers operate by increasing the air pressure within a closed space. In these cases, pistons are usually used to force air into the closed space and then compress the air.

A bicycle pump (Fig. 12–14, page 226) operates as follows: On the upstroke of the piston, the volume of air in the pump chamber increases. According to Boyle's law, the pressure of the air in the chamber decreases. Air from the outside rushes into the chamber to balance the pressure in the chamber. On the downstroke, the volume of air in the pump chamber decreases, increasing the pressure of the air. This forces air out of the pump. A set of valves opens and closes at the proper time to admit or to expel air. On the upstroke, valve A closes, and air enters valve B. On the downstroke, valve B closes, and compressed air is expelled through valve A.

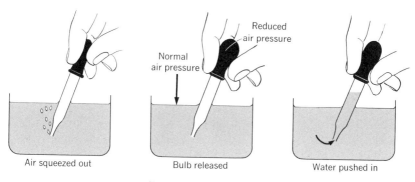

a. How a medicine dropper works

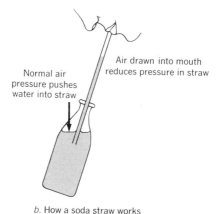

b. How a soda straw works

Fig. 12–13. Air pressure in use.

EFFECTS OF FLUIDS IN MOTION

In the eighteenth century, *Daniel Bernoulli*, a Swiss scientist, observed that the pressure exerted by a fluid in motion is less than that exerted by the same fluid at rest. This observation is now called *Bernoulli's principle.*

Bernoulli's principle is demonstrated by water flowing through a tube that varies in diameter (Fig. 12–15, page 226). Since the same amount of water passes through different parts of the tube in the same time interval, the water passes through the narrower part at a higher speed, or velocity. In section A of the tube, where the velocity of the water is low, the pressure of the water against the tube is high. In section B, where the velocity of the water is greater, the pressure on the tube is lower. In section C, where the water slows down again, the pressure on the tube increases again.

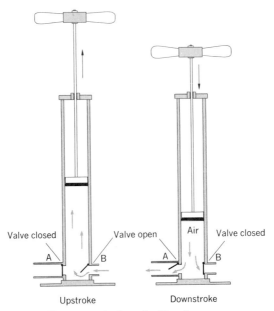

Fig. 12–14. Action of a bicycle pump.

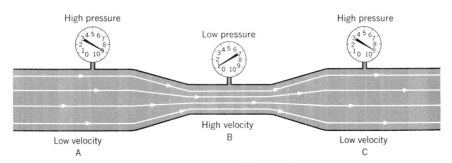

Fig. 12–15. Bernoulli's principle.

Bernoulli's principle, which applies to gases as well as liquids, can also be demonstrated by suspending two ping-pong balls on strings about 5 centimeters apart (Fig. 12–16). When we blow air between the two ping-pong balls, they move toward each other. This occurs because the rapidly moving air between the balls exerts less pressure than the air on the outer sides of the balls. As a result, the ping-pong balls are pushed together by the pressure of the surrounding air, which is not in motion.

The ability of an airplane to fly depends on Bernoulli's principle. The forward motion of the airplane forces air to flow over and under

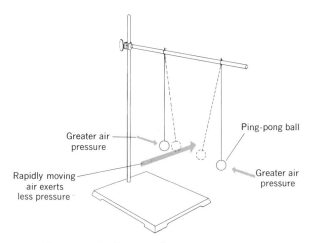

Fig. 12–16. Application of Bernoulli's principle.

the wings of the plane. As shown in Fig. 12–17, the upper surface of a wing is curved and therefore somewhat longer than the lower surface, which is almost flat. The moving air above the wing must cover a greater distance in the same time as the air below the wing. Consequently, the velocity of the air above the wing is greater than that below, and the pressure on the upper surface decreases. At the same time, the pressure of the air below the wing becomes relatively greater than that above the wing. This difference in the air pressure above and below the wing creates an upward force called *lift*, which raises the airplane from the ground.

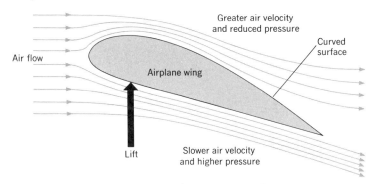

Fig. 12–17. How does an airplane fly?

EFFECTS OF FLUIDS AT REST

We have learned that a liquid, not in motion, exerts pressure in all directions because of its weight. This helps us to understand why objects appear to lose weight when they are immersed in water. For any object to lose weight, the downward force exerted by gravity must be opposed by an upward force. Since water exerts pressure in all directions, its upward pressure produces a force that is called *buoyant force*. This force opposes the weight of an object and makes it appear to lose weight.

We become aware of the buoyant force of water when we attempt to lift a friend who is immersed in water. It is this same buoyant force that supports ships in water and balloons in air. To find the buoyant force of water on an object, we need only find the difference between the weight of an object in air and its weight in water.

Archimedes' Principle

When we place an object in water, the object pushes aside, or *displaces*, some water. The volume of water that is displaced is equal to the volume that the submerged part of the object itself occupies. Thus, the buoyant force upon the object is the upward pressure of the remaining water on the object. This pressure is found to be equal to the weight of the displaced water. This weight, in turn, is equal to the weight that the object appears to lose.

These observations, first described by the ancient Greek mathematician *Archimedes*, are summarized in what we now call *Archimedes' principle*. Archimedes' principle states that an object immersed in a liquid seems to lose the same amount of weight as the weight of the liquid that the object displaces.

In the laboratory experience, you discovered Archimedes' principle for yourself. When you lowered the stone into the water-filled overflow can, the weight of the water that was displaced into the catch bucket equaled the weight that the stone appeared to lose in water.

Why Some Objects Float

Archimedes' principle applies not only to bodies that sink in water, but also to bodies that float. In the laboratory experience, when you used a block of wood instead of a stone, you found that the block sank only a little, until the weight of the displaced water equaled the weight of the wood in air. This observation illustrated the *law of flotation*, which states that a floating object displaces a weight of liquid equal to its own weight. Thus, a 100-gram block of wood floats in water with just enough of its volume underwater to displace 100 grams of water.

If a flat sheet of metal were dropped into a pail of water, the metal would sink. The sheet displaces a volume of water equal to its own volume. However, the displaced water would weigh less than the sheet. (By Archimedes' principle, we know that the weight of the displaced water equals the loss of weight of the metal.)

When the same sheet of metal is shaped into a box or a boat and is dropped into water, the metal will float. The little boat now has a greater volume than when the metal was in the form of a flat sheet because it now encloses a volume of air. In this form, the same amount of metal displaces an additional volume of water. The total volume of water displaced now equals the weight of the metal and, therefore, the object floats.

This principle is applied in the construction of ships. In order for a 10,000-ton ship to float, it must be constructed so that it displaces 10,000 tons of water. Similarly, if a balloon is to float in air, it must be large enough to displace an amount of air whose weight is equal to the weight of the balloon.

Specific Gravity

We can determine whether an object will sink or float by determining its *specific gravity*. The specific gravity of a substance is the ratio of the density of the substance to the density of water. Thus, specific gravity can be found according to the formula

$$\text{specific gravity} = \frac{\text{density of substance}}{\text{density of water}}$$

We know that the density of mercury is 13.6 grams per cubic centimeter, whereas the density of water is 1 gram per cubic centimeter. Thus, the specific gravity of mercury is 13.6:

$$\text{specific gravity} = \frac{\text{density of mercury}}{\text{density of water}}$$

$$\text{specific gravity} = \frac{13.6 \text{ grams per cubic centimeter}}{1 \text{ gram per cubic centimeter}}$$

$$\text{specific gravity} = 13.6$$

Note that specific gravity has no units.

If the specific gravity of a substance is greater than 1, the substance will sink in water. However, if the specific gravity of a substance is less than 1 (wood, for example, has a specific gravity of about 0.6), the substance will float in water.

Looking Back

All matter has weight and therefore exerts pressure. The pressure of fluids (liquids and gases) acts equally in all directions. Pressures are stated as force units (newtons) divided by area units (square centimeters).

When an outside pressure is applied to an enclosed liquid, the additional pressure is transmitted throughout the liquid. This effect is employed in hydraulic machines. Differences in air pressure operate devices such as the barometer, bicycle pump, water pump, medicine dropper, soda straw, and airplane wing.

Archimedes' principle explains why some objects sink in fluids, whereas other objects float. A knowledge of specific gravity will enable us to make this prediction.

Looking Ahead

When work is done, an object moves. The movement of many different objects is important in daily life. Moving objects have certain useful characteristics, which we will study in the next chapter.

Multiple-Choice Questions

1. The term fluid applies
   a. only to liquids
   b. only to gases
   c. only to solids
   d. to liquids and gases
2. Density is determined by the formula
   a. $\dfrac{m}{V}$ b. $\dfrac{V}{m}$ c. $m \times V$ d. $m + V$
3. An object with a mass of 20 grams and a volume of 4 cubic centimeters has a density of
   a. 5 grams
   b. 5 grams per cubic centimeter
   c. 20 grams per cubic centimeter
   d. 80 grams per cubic centimeter
4. When fluids of greater density are compared to those of lesser density, the fluid with greater density
   a. can exert more force
   b. exerts less force
   c. exerts less pressure
   d. has a lower specific gravity
5. The ratio of force per unit area describes
   a. density   b. specific gravity   c. power   d. pressure

6. Liquid pressure depends upon the product of the density of the liquid and its
   a. volume   b. mass   c. height   d. specific gravity
7. When open glass tubes of different diameters are connected, and a liquid is poured into one tube, the liquid levels are
   a. higher in the thin tubes and lower in the thick tubes
   b. at the same height in all tubes
   c. lower in the thin tubes than the thick tubes
   d. unrelated
8. When pressure is applied to a liquid in a closed container, the added pressure
   a. is lost
   b. is transmitted throughout the liquid
   c. affects only the part of the liquid to which the pressure is applied
   d. bursts the container
9. Pascal's law is applied in a
   a. hydraulic press   b. lever   c. wheel-and-axle   d. Pascal's vase
10. As the altitude increases, air pressure
    a. increases   c. decreases
    b. increases then decreases   d. remains the same
11. At sea level, air pressure is
    a. 1 atmosphere   c. 10.13 atmospheres
    b. 2 atmospheres   d. 100 atmospheres
12. When the pressure on a gas is increased, and the temperature remains unchanged, the volume of the gas
    a. increases   c. decreases then increases
    b. decreases   d. remains the same
13. Air pressure can be measured with an instrument called
    a. a thermometer   c. a barometer
    b. a lever   d. an indicator
14. At sea level, air pressure can support a column of mercury whose height is
    a. 10.13 centimeters   c. 76 centimeters
    b. 30 centimeters   d. 81 centimeters
15. Of the following, the device that does *not* use air pressure to function is a
    a. hydraulic press   c. soda straw
    b. medicine dropper   d. vacuum cleaner
16. When the velocity of a moving fluid increases, the pressure of the fluid
    a. increases   c. increases then decreases
    b. decreases   d. remains the same
17. When air is blown between two ping-pong balls that are suspended next to each other, the balls
    a. move together   c. are unaffected
    b. move apart   d. rotate in space
18. When a metallic object attached to a spring scale is lowered into water, the object appears to
    a. lose volume   b. gain volume   c. gain weight   d. lose weight

19. To find the buoyant force of water on an object, we
    a. multiply the weight of the object in air by its weight in water
    b. find the difference between the object's weight in air and its weight in water
    c. add the weights in air and water
    d. multiply the weight of the object by its density
20. When a metallic object is submerged in water, the water displaced
    a. is equal in volume to that of the object
    b. is equal in weight to that of the object
    c. has a greater volume than the object
    d. has a greater weight than the object
21. A floating object in water displaces
    a. a weight of water greater than its own weight
    b. no water
    c. a weight of water equal to its own weight
    d. a weight of water smaller than its own weight
22. In order for a 15,000-ton ship to float, it must displace an amount of water equal to
    a. 10,000 tons   b. 15,000 tons   c. 20,000 tons   d. 30,000 tons
23. A floating object generally has a specific gravity that is
    a. greater than 1   b. 1   c. less than 1   d. 2

Modified True-False Questions

1. In the metric system, the density of water is 13.6 *grams* per cubic centimeter.
2. The force per unit area exerted by a substance is called *pressure.*
3. The pressure exerted by a liquid acts *equally in all directions.*
4. That pressure can be transferred throughout a liquid is stated in *Boyle's law.*
5. The popping of our ears as we travel up and down in an elevator results from changes in *force.*
6. Air exerts pressure *equally* in all directions.
7. As the pressure on a gas increases, the volume of the gas *increases.*
8. The fact that the volume of a gas at constant temperature varies inversely with the pressure on it is known as *Newton's law.*
9. The mercury barometer was first constructed by the scientist *Torricelli.*
10. The aneroid barometer is used to measure *density.*
11. That the pressure exerted by a fluid in motion is less than that exerted by the same fluid at rest is stated in *Pascal's law.*
12. An upward force created by the differences in air pressure above and below an airplane wing is known as *lift.*
13. The upward force of water against an object placed into it is called the *buoyant force.*
14. The ratio between the density of a substance and the density of water is known as *pressure.*

Thought Questions

1. Define each of the following terms:
   a. density
   b. pressure
   c. buoyant force
   d. specific gravity
   e. Pascal's law
2. Find the density of a substance whose mass is 28 grams and whose volume is 4 cubic centimeters.
3. a. Find the pressure exerted by an object that exerts a force of 180 newtons on an area of 10 square centimeters.
   b. Find the pressure exerted by a column of water 7 meters high.
4. List four characteristics of liquid pressure.
5. List three characteristics of air pressure.
6. Explain how Bernoulli's principle enables an airplane to fly.
7. a. Why do objects appear to lose weight in water?
   b. Explain how an iron ship must be constructed if it is to float on water.
8. An object floats in water. Will the same object float higher or lower in mercury than it does in water? Explain.

CHAPTER 13
WHAT ARE THE CHARACTERISTICS OF MOVING OBJECTS?

When you have completed this chapter, you should be able to:

1. *Relate* motion to speed, velocity, and acceleration.
2. *Use* simple formulas about moving objects to calculate distance, velocity, acceleration, and momentum.
3. *Describe* Galileo's contribution to the study of moving objects.
4. *State* Newton's laws of motion.
5. *Discuss* the motions involved in artificial satellites, the Apollo program, and Skylab.
6. *Distinguish* between (*a*) inertia and momentum (*b*) centripetal force and centrifugal reaction (*c*) apogee and perigee.

In the laboratory experience that follows, you will study the motion of an object that is acted on by varying forces.

Laboratory Experience

HOW ARE MASSES AFFECTED BY FORCES ACTING ON THEM?

A. Weigh a Hall's carriage on a balance.
    1. How much does the carriage weigh?
B. Place a board (about 1 meter long) and the Hall's carriage on a table as shown in Fig. 13–1. Place weights totaling 500 grams in the carriage.
    2. What is the total weight of the carriage and its contents?
C. Slowly raise one end of the board (at A), forming an inclined plane, just enough to overcome the friction that keeps the carriage stationary; that is, raise the carriage until it begins to move slowly. Wedge a book or some other object under the board to maintain the incline. Hold the carriage.

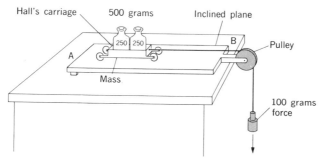

Fig. 13–1.

D. Hang a 100-gram weight on the end of the string that passes from the carriage and over the pulley on the end of the inclined plane. Move the carriage to the raised end of the inclined plane. Release the carriage and, using a stopwatch, measure the time it takes for the carriage to reach the pulley. Copy the table below into your notebook, and enter the time in it.

Mass of Carriage	Mass of Weights	Total Mass	Force on String	Time
grams	500 grams	grams	100 grams	
grams	500 grams	grams	200 grams	
grams	500 grams	grams	300 grams	

E. Add another 100-gram weight to the string, and repeat part D. Record the time in the table.
F. Add a third 100-gram weight to the string, and repeat part D again. Record the time in the table.
  3. In each step of parts D, E, and F, which factor was kept constant?
  4. Which factor was varied?
  5. What effect did the variation have on the speed of the carriage?
G. Remove all the weights from the string, and remove the 500-gram weight from the carriage. Place a 100-gram weight in the carriage and a 100-gram weight on the end of the string. Move the carriage to the raised end of the inclined plane. Release the carriage and, using a stopwatch, measure the time it takes for the carriage to reach the pulley. Copy the second table, on the next page, and enter the time in it.
H. Add another 100-gram weight to the weight already in the carriage, and repeat part G. Record the time in the table.

Mass of Carriage	Mass of Weights	Total Mass	Force on String	Time
grams	100 grams	grams	100 grams	
grams	200 grams	grams	100 grams	
grams	300 grams	grams	100 grams	

I. Add a third 100-gram weight to the carriage, and repeat part G again. Record the time in the table.
   6. In each step of parts G, H, and I, which factor was kept constant?
   7. Which factor was varied?
   8. What effect did the variation have on the speed of the carriage?
   9. Summarize the observations you recorded in the two tables.

Introduction

When we use the term motion, we generally mean the movement of an object from one point to another. Our school bus obviously moves as it takes us to school. But is our school moving? As we look out of a window, we see no evidence of this movement. Yet our earth is turning about its axis at a speed of about 1600 kilometers per hour, and is also revolving around the sun at a speed of over 96,000 kilometers per hour. Since our school is on the earth, it must also be moving. We are not aware of this motion because, relative to what we see around us, the building does not move.

A passenger seated on a moving bus appears to be moving when viewed by someone in the street; but, when viewed by another seated passenger on the bus, the first passenger appears to be at rest. The scientific meaning of *motion* is a change in position relative to an object assumed to be at rest—that is, an object that is not moving.

CHARACTERISTICS OF MOTION

All objects in the universe move only when some unbalanced force acts upon them. If the magnitude of the force acting on the object does not change, the speed of the object remains unchanged. If the force acting on the object continues to change, the speed of movement changes. In this case, we say the object is accelerating. The characteristics of motion can be described in terms of *speed, direction, distance, time,* and *acceleration.*

SPEED AND VELOCITY

Although the terms speed and velocity are generally used inter-changeably, they have somewhat different meanings.

Speed is the distance traveled by an object in a unit of time. In other words, speed is the rate of change of the position of the object. For example, when a car travels a distance of 80 kilometers in a period of 1 hour, we say that the speed of the car is 80 kilometers per hour. However, this statement tells us nothing about the direction in which the car is traveling. If we start a trip in New York City and travel at a speed of 80 kilometers per hour, at the end of 1 hour we could be in New Jersey, Connecticut, or Long Island, depending on the direction in which we have traveled. Since no direction is involved, speed is a scalar quantity (see Chapter 10, page 169); that is, speed is a measure of quantity, or magnitude, only.

Velocity, on the other hand, is a vector quantity (see Chapter 10, page 169); that is, it indicates direction as well as magnitude. Velocity is the *distance* traveled by an object in a unit of *time* in a specific *direction*. Thus, if we travel 80 kilometers per hour northeastward from New York City, in 1 hour we will be somewhere in Connecticut. If we travel in a westerly direction, we will be in New Jersey.

HOW VELOCITY, DISTANCE, AND TIME ARE RELATED

When we take a trip by bus or car, we are aware that the velocity of the vehicle is constantly changing because of traffic, pedestrians, stop signs, and traffic lights. However, we can determine the *average velocity* for the trip if we know the distance we have traveled and the time it has taken to travel this distance. The average velocity is determined by dividing the distance covered by the time taken for the trip. Thus,

$$\text{average velocity} = \frac{\text{distance}}{\text{time}}$$

When average velocity is represented by v_{av}, distance by d, and time by t, this equation is written

$$v_{av} = \frac{d}{t}$$

For example, suppose we complete a 400-kilometer trip from Washington, D.C., to New York City in 5 hours. To determine the average velocity for our trip, we divide the distance (400 kilometers) by the time (5 hours) and find that the average velocity for the trip is 80 kilometers per hour:

$$v_{av} = \frac{d}{t}$$

$$v_{av} = \frac{400 \text{ kilometers}}{5 \text{ hours}}$$

$$v_{av} = \frac{80 \text{ kilometers}}{\text{hour}} = 80 \text{ kilometers per hour}$$

This does not mean that we traveled 5 hours at a steady 80 kilometers per hour. We may have slowed down when traffic built up, or we may have stopped completely to refill the gas tank. Since our speed during these intervals was considerably less than 80 kilometers per hour, we would have had to increase our speed at times to maintain the average speed of 80 kilometers per hour.

If the distance and average velocity are known, we can find the time by using another equivalent of the same formula:

$$t = \frac{d}{v_{av}}$$

Thus, if we are planning a trip of 400 kilometers and expect to maintain an average velocity of 80 kilometers per hour, we can expect the trip to take a total of 5 hours.

$$t = \frac{400 \text{ ~~kilometers~~}}{80 \text{ ~~kilometers~~ per hour}}$$

$$t = 5 \text{ hours}$$

ACCELERATION

As we know, the velocity of a moving car seldom remains the same for any length of time. We decrease the velocity when traffic causes us to slow down; we increase it after a stop. Changes in velocity are called *acceleration*. (A decrease in velocity is also acceleration, but it is often called *deceleration*.)

The scientific definition states that acceleration is the rate of change of velocity (speed or direction). Thus, acceleration is the change in velocity divided by the time it takes to make this change. If an object either speeds up or slows down at a constant rate, we say it is accelerating uniformly.

To find the acceleration of an object, we divide the change in its velocity by the time it takes to make the change. The change in velocity is found by subtracting the velocity at the beginning of the acceleration from the velocity at the end of the acceleration. Thus,

$$\text{acceleration} = \frac{\text{final velocity} - \text{starting velocity}}{\text{time}}$$

If we represent acceleration as a, final velocity as v_f, and starting velocity as v_s, then the equation is written as

$$a = \frac{v_f - v_s}{t}$$

Acceleration can be described in units such as kilometers per hour *per second*, kilometers per hour *per minute*, meters per second *per second* (or *meters per second²*), and centimeters per second *per second* (or *centimeters per second²*).

Calculating Acceleration

Suppose a driver accelerates a car from a velocity of 30 kilometers per hour to a velocity of 80 kilometers per hour in a time of 5 seconds. To find the acceleration of this car, we subtract the starting velocity (30 kph) from the final velocity (80 kph) and divide this change in velocity by 5 seconds:

$$a = \frac{v_f - v_s}{t}$$

$$a = \frac{80 \text{ kph} - 30 \text{ kph}}{5 \text{ seconds}}$$

$$a = \frac{50 \text{ kph}}{5 \text{ seconds}}$$

$$a = 10 \frac{\text{kph}}{\text{second}} = 10 \text{ kilometers per hour per second}$$

We find that the car accelerates 10 kilometers per hour every second. This means that at the end of each second of acceleration, the velocity

of the car has increased by 10 kilometers per hour. Thus, at the end
of one second of acceleration, the car would be traveling at a velocity
of 40 kilometers per hour. At the end of 2 seconds, the car's velocity
would be 50 kilometers per hour, and so on, until, at the end of 5
seconds, it would reach 80 kilometers per hour.

Calculating Final Velocity

When we know that an object is accelerating uniformly and the
length of time during which the acceleration takes place, we can readily
compute the final velocity:

$$\text{final velocity} = \text{acceleration} \times \text{time}$$

$$v_f = a \times t$$

From this equation we can determine the final velocity for any object
that starts from rest and accelerates.

For example, suppose an object starting from rest is accelerated
at a rate of 16 kilometers per hour per second for 7 seconds. To find
the final velocity of the object at the end of 7 seconds, we need only
multiply the acceleration (16 kilometers per hour per second) by the
time (7 seconds). The final velocity is 112 kilometers per hour:

$$v_f = a \times t$$

$$v_f = 16 \text{ kilometers per hour per second} \times 7 \text{ seconds}$$

$$v_f = 112 \frac{\text{kilometers per hour}}{\cancel{\text{second}}} \times \cancel{\text{second}}$$

$$v_f = 112 \text{ kilometers per hour}$$

If the object were not at rest but were traveling at some velocity before
it started to accelerate, we must account for this starting velocity when
calculating final velocity. For example, if the object in our problem
were traveling at 24 kilometers per hour before it started to accelerate,
then the final velocity would be the sum of the starting velocity (v_s) and
the product of $a \times t$. Thus, the final velocity of a uniformly accelerating
body having a starting velocity is found from the equation

$$v_f = v_s + (a \times t)$$

In our problem, the final velocity is 136 kilometers per hour:

$$v_f = v_s + (a \times t)$$

$$v_f = 24\,\text{kph} + (16\,\text{kph per second} \times 7\,\text{seconds})$$

$$v_f = 24\,\text{kph} + (16\,\frac{\text{kph}}{\text{second}} \times 7\,\text{seconds})$$

$$v_f = 24\,\text{kph} + 112\,\text{kph} = 136\,\text{kph}$$

HOW FORCE AND ACCELERATION ARE RELATED

In 1590, *Galileo*, an Italian scientist, was one of the first scientists to study objects whose velocities changed because additional forces acted upon them. That is, he studied the effects of acceleration on objects. He performed experiments to determine how distance, velocity, time, and acceleration are related.

One of Galileo's experiments, shown in Fig. 13–2, concerned the motion of a metal ball rolling down an inclined plane under the influence of the force of gravity. Galileo found that the distance covered by the ball was related to the square of the time during which the ball accelerated uniformly. (He ignored friction in all his calculations.) If the conditions were such that the ball rolled 1 centimeter in the first second, he found that it rolled 4 centimeters by the end of the second second ($2^2 = 4$), and 9 centimeters by the end of the third second ($3^2 = 9$).

The relationship between distance and acceleration can be stated as follows: The distance covered by an object that starts from rest and is uniformly accelerated depends upon the average acceleration and upon the square of the time period during which the accelerating force acts. (It is necessary to use the average acceleration here because the acceleration ranges from zero at the starting point to some maximum at the end of the time period. We find the average by dividing the final acceleration by 2.) As an equation, this relationship is expressed as:

$$\text{distance} = \frac{1}{2}\,\text{acceleration} \times \text{time}^2$$

$$d = \frac{1}{2}\,a \times t^2$$

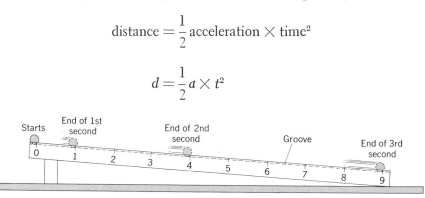

Fig. 13–2. Galileo's experiment.

At times, the various formulas for objects in motion can be very confusing. Table 13–1 can help you to determine which formula to use in a given situation. It displays the unknown quantities, the known quantities, and the appropriate formula.

Table 13–1. Motion Formulas

Unknown Quantity	Known Quantities	Formula
Average velocity	Distance, time	$v_{av} = \dfrac{d}{t}$
Distance	Average velocity, time	$d = v_{av} \times t$
Time	Distance, average velocity	$t = \dfrac{d}{v_{av}}$
Acceleration	Final velocity, starting velocity, time	$a = \dfrac{v_f - v_s}{t}$
Final velocity (object initially at rest)	Acceleration, time	$v_f = a \times t$
Final velocity	Acceleration, time, starting velocity	$v_f = v_s + (a \times t)$
Distance	Acceleration, time	$d = \dfrac{1}{2} a \times t^2$

Acceleration by Gravity

The carriage in your laboratory experience and the metal ball in Galileo's experiment were both at rest initially. Both accelerated as a result of the force of gravity (which pulls the objects down the incline) and the force of friction (which holds the objects back). It seems reasonable to conclude that the force of gravity will be greatest—and the force of friction will be least—when the object falls freely to the ground. This is the situation when an inclined plane is in a vertical position or when the object is dropped from a height.

By carefully measuring the acceleration given to a freely falling object by gravitational force, scientists have found that this acceleration is 980 centimeters per second every second. (An object will fall freely if it is dense and has a small surface area.) Galileo hypothesized that the acceleration produced by gravity is the same for all objects regardless of their density. However, when he tested this hypothesis, he found that objects of greater density often fell faster than some objects of lesser density. Galileo reasoned that the exceptions to his hypothesis must be related to the effect of air resistance on the falling bodies.

Therefore, in a vacuum, all objects should fall at the same rate.

Galileo's idea was proven to be true by scientists using a "coin and feather" tube (Fig. 13–3). When air is present in the tube and we allow the coin and the feather to fall at the same time, the coin accelerates faster than the feather and reaches the bottom of the tube first. The feather flutters down more slowly because of the resistance of the air to its motion. However, when the air is removed from the tube, leaving a vacuum in it, both the coin and the feather reach the bottom of the tube at the same time. The astronauts on the moon (where there is no air) also verified Galileo's idea.

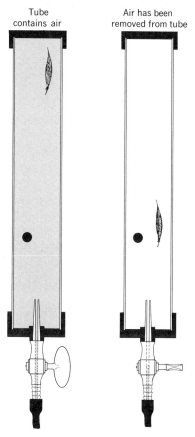

Fig. 13–3. The "coin and feather" experiment.

Calculations Concerning Falling Bodies

If we wish to calculate the velocity, distance, or time concerning falling objects, we can use the appropriate formula from Table 13–1. Since the acceleration caused by gravity, g, is uniform ($g = 980$ centimeters per second per second), we can substitute this value for acceleration in any of the formulas.

For example, find the final velocity of an object, initially at rest, that falls freely for 3 seconds. Referring to Table 13–1,

$$v_f = a \times t$$

Replacing a with g,

$$v_f = g \times t$$

$v_f = 980$ centimeters per second per second $\times$ 3 seconds

$$v_f = 2940 \; \frac{\text{centimeters per second}}{\text{second}} \times \text{second}$$

$v_f = 2940$ centimeters (29.4 meters) per second

Knowing the value of g enables us to find the height of a building if we know how long it takes for an object dropped from its top to strike the ground. For example, find the height of a tower if an object dropped from the top reaches the ground in 10 seconds. Since the unknown quantity is the distance traveled by the freely falling object, and we know the acceleration and the time, we use the formula

$$d = \frac{1}{2} a \times t^2$$

Replacing *a* with *g*,

$$d = \frac{1}{2} g \times t^2$$

$$d = \frac{1}{2} \times 980 \text{ centimeters per second per second} \times (10 \text{ seconds})^2$$

$$d = 490 \frac{\text{centimeters}}{\text{second} \times \text{second}} \times 10 \text{ seconds} \times 10 \text{ seconds}$$

$$d = 490 \text{ centimeters} \times 100$$

$$d = 49{,}000 \text{ centimeters } (490 \text{ meters})$$

NEWTON'S LAWS OF MOTION

During the seventeenth century, Sir *Issac Newton* carefully investigated motion. From his observations, Newton formulated three fundamental laws which have contributed to our understanding of moving objects. These laws deal with *inertia*, *acceleration*, and *action and reaction*.

Law of Inertia

The law of inertia states that an object at rest tends to remain at rest, and an object in motion tends to remain in motion in a straight line, unless the object is acted upon by an unbalanced force.

We can demonstrate the law of inertia by performing the simple experiment shown in Fig. 13–4. Place a card on a glass tumbler and a coin on the card. In this position, both the card and the coin are at rest. When we exert a force on the card by sharply flicking it with

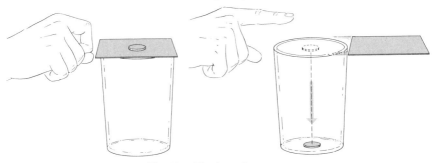

Fig. 13–4. The law of inertia.

a finger, the card begins to move outward in a straight line as a result of the one-sided (unbalanced) force that acted on it. Then, as gravity acts on the card, it falls downward in a curved path. Meanwhile, the coin drops straight downward into the glass. Originally the coin was at rest, and it remains that way until the flicking force is exerted on the card. The coin tends to remain in its original position because the horizontal flicking force is exerted on the card and not on the coin. When the card moves outward and the supporting force that keeps the coin in its original position disappears, the coin keeps its horizontal position and moves only vertically.

Inertia is experienced daily by passengers in vehicles. When standing in a bus or train, people often lurch forward as the vehicle stops. As the brakes are applied to the vehicle, it slows down. However, by the law of inertia, the people continue to move forward in a straight line at the same rate of speed.

Law of Acceleration

An unbalanced force applied to an object in motion changes the velocity of the object—that is, causes the object to accelerate. How great the acceleration is depends upon the strength (magnitude) of the force and the mass, or weight, of the object. The relationship of force and mass to acceleration is expressed in Newton's second law, the law of acceleration. This law states that the acceleration of an object depends on the ratio of the acting force to the mass of the object. The law is represented as

$$\text{acceleration} = \frac{\text{force}}{\text{mass}}$$

$$a = \frac{f}{m}$$

An example of the relationship expressed in Newton's second law is a bus that starts and stops. When starting the bus, the driver depresses the gas pedal, causing the engine to exert force on the mass of the bus. This causes the bus to accelerate. When 20 additional people board the bus, thereby increasing its mass, and the driver gives the engine as much gas as before, the bus accelerates more slowly than before. In order to accelerate a loaded bus as rapidly as an empty one, the engine requires more gas in order to increase the force acting on the mass of the bus. In other words, as the mass increases, the force must also increase, if the acceleration is to remain the same. Your laboratory experience can help you come to this same conclusion.

Law of Action and Reaction

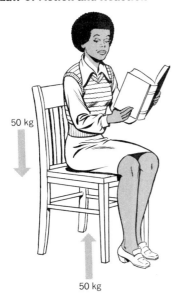

50 kg

50 kg

Fig. 13–5. Equal and opposite forces.

We have learned that when a force is exerted on an object, the object moves unless another force, acting in the opposite direction, balances the first. When a girl sits in a chair (Fig. 13–5) or places a book on a table, both the girl and the book no longer move even though both exert a downward force called weight. The chair exerts an upward force equal to the weight of the girl, and the table exerts an upward force equal to the weight of the book.

In each of these situations, we are dealing with two objects. In the first case, it is the chair and the girl; in the second case, it is the book and the table. In each case, the force exerted by one object is balanced by a force exerted by the other. Newton stated his observations of similar situations in his third law, the law of action and reaction. This law states that whenever an object exerts a force (action) on a second object, the second exerts an equal and opposite force (reaction) on the first.

The same law holds true for objects that are free to move. For example, if a girl steps from an untied rowboat to the shore, she exerts a force against the boat as she moves forward onto the shore. At the same time, the boat exerts an equal force against the girl, but in the opposite direction, and it moves away from the shore (Fig. 13–6). Similarly, when a rifle is fired, the explosive force of the gunpowder

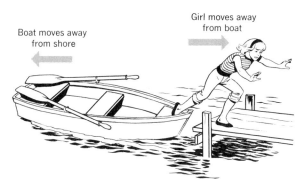

Boat moves away from shore

Girl moves away from boat

Fig. 13–6. Action and reaction.

causes the bullet to move out of the barrel. At the same time, the bullet exerts an opposite force, and the rifle recoils against the shoulder.

The law of action and reaction also operates in jet and rocket engines. When a jet engine is started and when a rocket is fired, rapidly expanding gases exert a force on them, while they exert equal but opposite forces on the gases. The gases move backward and the jet or rocket moves forward or upward (Fig. 13–7).

MOMENTUM

Closely associated with the acceleration, mass, and speed of moving objects is the idea of *momentum*. Momentum (M) is the force acquired by a moving object as a result of its motion. This force depends upon the mass of the object and the velocity with which the object moves:

$$momentum = mass \times velocity$$

$$M = m \times v$$

For example, a rifle bullet weighing 25 grams is fired, leaving the rifle barrel at a velocity of 30,000 centimeters per second. What is the momentum of the bullet at the moment it leaves the rifle?

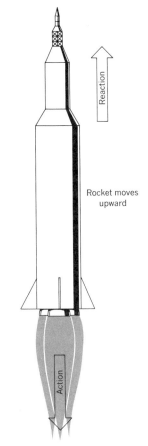

Reaction

Rocket moves upward

Action

Hot gases forced downward

Fig. 13–7. What lifts a rocket?

$$M = m \times v$$

$$M = 25 \text{ grams} \times 30{,}000 \, \frac{\text{centimeters}}{\text{second}}$$

$$M = 750{,}000 \, \frac{\text{grams} \times \text{centimeters}}{\text{second}}$$

The unit $\dfrac{\text{grams} \times \text{centimeters}}{\text{second}}$ is usually expressed as gram-centimeters/ second. Thus,

$$\text{momentum} = 750{,}000 \text{ gram-centimeters/second}$$

An object weighing 30,000 grams and moving at a velocity of 25 centi-meters per second would have the same momentum. Thus, the momentum force can be increased by increasing the mass or the velocity of the moving object (or by increasing both).

Conservation of Momentum

A rolling bowling ball acquires momentum because it has mass and rolls with a specific velocity. When a moving bowling ball strikes a line of five other bowling balls, the momentum that it imparts causes only the last bowling ball in the line to move (Fig. 13–8). Careful measurements of the velocities of the incoming ball and the outgoing ball show that these velocities are equal. Since the two balls also have the same mass, the momentum of the outgoing ball is the same as that of the incoming ball.

In general, when two objects collide, the momentum of one object is completely transferred to the second. This observation is known as *conservation of momentum*. The conservation of momentum means that the total momentum entering a system is equal to the total momentum leaving the system.

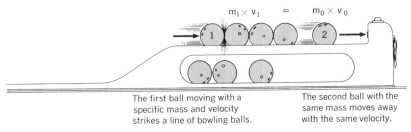

The first ball moving with a
specific mass and velocity
strikes a line of bowling balls.

The second ball with the
same mass moves away
with the same velocity.

Fig. 13–8. Conservation of momentum.

The conservation of momentum can be expressed as

$$\text{momentum (incoming)} = \text{momentum (outgoing)}$$

Since momentum is the product of mass multiplied by velocity, then

$$\begin{matrix} \text{mass} \\ \text{(incoming)} \end{matrix} \times \begin{matrix} \text{velocity} \\ \text{(incoming)} \end{matrix} = \begin{matrix} \text{mass} \\ \text{(outgoing)} \end{matrix} \times \begin{matrix} \text{velocity} \\ \text{(outgoing)} \end{matrix}$$

$$m_i \times v_i = m_o \times v_o$$

Calculations Involving Momentum

Suppose a 10-gram bullet is fired from a 2000-gram rifle with a velocity of 50,000 centimeters per second. At what velocity does the rifle recoil against the rifleman's shoulder? To solve this problem, we substitute these values in the equation:

$$m_i \times v_i = m_o \times v_o$$

$$2000 \text{ grams} \times v_i = 10 \text{ grams} \times 50,000 \text{ centimeters per second}$$

$$v_i = \frac{10 \text{ grams} \times 50,000 \text{ centimeters per second}}{2000 \text{ grams}}$$

$$v_i = 250 \text{ centimeters per second}$$

We find that the rifle recoils at a velocity of 250 centimeters per second.

Essentially, the conservation of momentum is similar to Newton's law of action and reaction. A common example of conservation takes place during the game of billiards. Recall that when one object exerts a force on a second object, the second object exerts an equal but opposite force on the first. Thus, when one billiard ball collides squarely with another, the first ball exerts a force on the second ball. As a result, the second ball moves forward at the same velocity as the first. At the same time, the second ball exerts an equal but opposite force on the first ball, causing the first ball to stop.

CIRCULAR MOTION

Our previous discussion of motion has concerned itself with objects moving in a straight line. Such objects as orbiting space vehicles, revolving wheels, or the clothes in a washing machine during its "spin" cycle exhibit motion in a curved or circular path. When these objects move at a constant speed along a curved path of constant radius, the motion is called *uniform circular motion.*

Suppose we tie a string to a small stone and then twirl the stone. The object moves in a circular path because of the force the string exerts on the stone. This force, called *centripetal* (center-seeking) force, pulls the moving stone toward the center of its curved path. At the same time, the stone also exerts a force on the string. This is the reaction to the center-seeking force and is called the *centrifugal* (center-fleeing) reaction. If the string were to snap, the stone would fly off in a straight line. Since no centripetal force exists when the string breaks, there is no centrifugal reaction. According to Newton's first law, an object in motion continues in motion in a straight line.

Newton's laws of motion help us to understand the movement of objects on earth. These same laws govern the movement of objects in space.

Artificial Satellites

A stone attached to a piece of string hangs vertically from the string because gravity attracts the stone. The only force acting on the stone is its weight, pulling it downward. An object dropped from any height within the earth's gravitational pull is also pulled downward. If the stone is twirled rapidly, the centrifugal reaction force counterbalances the centripetal (gravitational) force, and the stone moves in a circular path.

If the stone could be propelled outward with sufficient velocity in a path parallel to the surface of the earth, the stone would move in a circular path around the earth. If proper conditions were present, the stone would continue to move around and around the earth. Under these conditions, the path of such an object is called an *orbit.* If the object orbits around the earth, the object is called a *satellite.*

The moon is a natural satellite which orbits eastward around the earth. Since the building of high-powered rockets, about 3000 artificial satellites have been launched and are now orbiting the earth.

An artificial satellite must be lifted vertically to an altitude of at least 160 kilometers. (Because of the tremendous friction generated, orbiting through the earth's atmosphere would burn up the satellite. At an altitude of 160 kilometers, the effect of friction from the earth's atmosphere is greatly decreased.) The satellite is lifted to this altitude by the reaction force generated by rocket engines. The direction of flight of the satellite is then changed to a path that is parallel to the earth's surface. Then the rocket engines cause the satellite to attain a horizontal velocity of about 28,800 kilometers per hour, or about 8 kilometers per second. This is called the *orbiting velocity*. At this velocity, the forward push of the rocket engines is just sufficient to counterbalance the earth's gravitational pull, and the satellite goes into orbit.

As the satellite moves forward at this tremendous speed, two forces are acting on the satellite. Pushed by the rocket, it is moving outward, away from the earth. At the same time, gravity is pulling the satellite toward the earth. Since the surface of the earth is rounded, the earth continues to curve away from the falling satellite. It is as though the earth is "falling away" from the satellite. When the two forces are in balance, the satellite is in a stable orbit. At this point, the rocket engines can be shut down. According to the law of inertia, the moving satellite will continue to move in the same path as long as there is no force opposing its motion.

If the velocity of the satellite is correct, and if the satellite is traveling perfectly parallel to the surface of the earth, its orbit will be circular. Since there is some air resistance, even at an altitude of 500 kilometers, it is almost impossible to have the satellite traveling with the correct velocity in the exact direction. The orbit of the satellite becomes flattened and follows an elliptical path.

At different points in an elliptical orbit, the velocity of the satellite and the distance of the satellite from the earth vary. The farthest point from the earth is called the *apogee* of the orbit, while the point closest to the surface of the earth is called the *perigee* (Fig. 13–9).

As the satellite approaches the earth from apogee, the satellite accelerates because of the increased influence of gravity. Thus, the velocity of the satellite increases. As the satellite leaves perigee, the satellite moves away from the earth, against the gravitational pull, and the velocity of the satellite decreases.

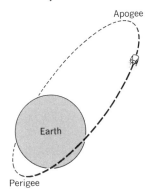

Fig. 13–9. Orbiting the earth.

Space Travel

Propelling a space vehicle to the moon is very much like launching a satellite. The orbit of the satellite around the earth is an ellipse. If the ellipse can be stretched sufficiently, the location of the apogee can be at the moon.

A space vehicle going to the moon is first placed into earth orbit. At the proper altitude and time (calculated by computers on the spacecraft), the velocity of the vehicle is increased to about 40,000 kilometers per hour, or about 11 kilometers per second. This is the velocity required to overcome the earth's gravity completely and is called the *escape velocity*. When this velocity has been attained, smaller rockets on the space vehicle direct it into the proper elliptical orbit, with the moon at its apogee. Once the space vehicle is in orbit, from Newton's law of inertia, very little rocket power is required to reach the moon owing to the small amount of friction with the earth's atmosphere. In addition, the farther away from the earth a space vehicle is, the smaller is the gravitational pull of the earth on the space vehicle.

On July 20, 1969, three American astronauts, Neil Armstrong, Edwin Aldrin, Jr., and Michael Collins, reached the moon. This was the Apollo 11 space mission. The specially designed space vehicle consisted of two sections, one called a command module, and the other, the lunar excursion module (LEM). These sections were separated when the vehicle was a small distance above the moon. While the command module, piloted by Collins, continued to orbit the moon 96 kilometers above its surface, the LEM, with Armstrong and Aldrin in it, descended to the moon. Several months later, using the same techniques, three other American astronauts reached the moon. Since that time, four more Apollo flights have landed men on the moon.

Whether the same procedures can be utilized for interplanetary travel in the future remains to be seen. In any event, the first words uttered by Neil Armstrong, on setting foot on the moon, will long be remembered:

> "That's one small step for a man,
> one giant leap for mankind."

Skylab

Skylab is a large artificial satellite that is an orbiting space station and laboratory. The satellite flies in a 95-minute circular orbit around the earth about 386 kilometers above it. Inside Skylab are living and sleeping quarters, facilities for food preparation, personal hygiene equipment, and laboratory instruments. Mounted on the outside of Skylab are numerous solar cells for generating needed electricity.

In May 1973, three astronauts, Charles Conrad, Jr., Joseph P. Kerwin, and Paul Weitz, rocketed to Skylab and entered it. In their first few days aboard Skylab, these men repaired equipment that had been broken when Skylab was launched. They spent a total of 28 days in the weightless condition aboard Skylab before they returned safely to earth. Later in the year, they were followed by other crews that remained aboard Skylab much longer. None of the astronauts seems to have suffered any serious ill effects from weightlessness.

As Skylab orbits the earth, astronauts have carried out many experiments related to research in biology, medicine, and space. Some of their research activities have included studies of X-ray and ultraviolet emissions from the sun, studies of the weather, and surveys of resources on the earth. It is expected that many more experiments will be carried out by future astronaut crews. Some of these experiments will likely deal with the feasibility of using the space station as a launching point for spaceships that will explore the solar system further.

Looking Back

Characteristics of a moving object are velocity, or speed and direction of motion, and acceleration, or change in velocity caused by an unbalanced force acting on the object. These characteristics are embodied in Newton's three laws of motion. Knowledge and application of these laws have made space travel possible.

Looking Ahead

So far, our studies of motion and machines have concentrated on nonliving objects. In the next chapter, we will study animal movement.

Multiple-Choice Questions

1. A change in position relative to an object assumed to be at rest is called
   a. motion   b. momentum   c. inertia   d. acceleration
2. Of the following, the term that is *not* used to describe motion is
   a. distance   b. time   c. acceleration   d. force
3. A term that is a vector quantity is
   a. distance   b. direction   c. velocity   d. speed
4. The average velocity can be determined from the formula

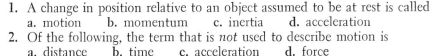

   a. $\dfrac{time}{distance}$ b. $\dfrac{time}{acceleration}$ c. $\dfrac{distance}{time}$ d. distance × time

5. The distance covered by a car traveling at an average velocity of 50 kph for 5 hours is
   a. 10 kilometers   c. 55 kilometers
   b. 45 kilometers   d. 250 kilometers
6. The rate of change of velocity is called
   a. acceleration   b. motion   c. momentum   d. inertia
7. Final velocity is equal to
   a. $\dfrac{v_{av}}{t}$ b. $\dfrac{t}{a}$ c. $\dfrac{a}{t}$ d. $a \times t$

8. Consider a ball rolling down an inclined plane: The greatest acceleration occurs when the plane is at an angle of
   a. 0°   b. 30°   c. 60°   d. 90°

9. The acceleration caused by gravity has been found to be
   a. 9.8 cm/sec   b. 980 cm/sec   c. 980 cm/sec²   d. 980 m/sec²

10. The scientist who hypothesized that the acceleration produced by gravity is the same for all objects is
    a. Galileo   b. Newton   c. Copernicus   d. Archimedes

11. In a "coin and feather" tube, the feather falls at a slower rate than the coin because of
    a. inertia   b. buoyant force   c. momentum   d. air resistance

12. The symbol used to represent the gravitational constant for falling objects is
    a. a b. v c. g d. t

13. That an object at rest tends to remain at rest and an object in motion tends to remain in motion, unless acted upon by an unbalanced force, is stated in the law of
    a. motion   b. inertia   c. momentum   d. action and reaction

14. A moving bus comes to a sudden stop, and the passengers lurch forward. What happens to the passengers is an example of
    a. inertia   b. momentum   c. acceleration   d. deceleration

15. As the force acting on an object decreases, the acceleration of the object
    a. increases   c. remains the same
    b. decreases   d. increases then decreases

16. As the mass of an object increases, the acceleration of that object
    a. increases   c. remains the same
    b. decreases   d. increases then decreases

17. The momentum of an object is the product of the mass of the body and its
    a. acceleration   b. distance   c. speed   d. velocity

18. The motion of a jet aircraft is based primarily on the law of
    a. action and reaction   c. momentum
    b. inertia   d. conservation of energy

19. A group of bowling balls is at rest in a rack. When a moving ball rolls into the group,
    a. the last ball moves out of the pack
    b. two balls move out of the pack
    c. no change is observed
    d. all the balls are set in motion

20. An inward force created by uniform circular motion is called
    a. buoyant force   c. centripetal force
    b. centrifugal reaction   d. gravity

21. In earth orbit, the point in the orbit that is closest to the earth is called the
    a. apogee   b. center   c. ellipse   d. perigee

22. Escape velocity from earth orbit is approximately
    a. 18,000 kph   b. 20,000 kph   c. 28,000 kph   d. 40,000 kph

Modified True-False Questions

1. The distance traveled by an object in a unit of time is called *speed*.
2. The slowing down of a car in a given time is called *velocity*.
3. Acceleration can be described in *kilometers per hour*.
4. One of the first scientists to study the effect of force on velocity was *Newton*.
5. In air, gravitational acceleration is affected by *surface area*.
6. The gravitational acceleration *varies* for every object studied.
7. The force acquired by a moving object because of its motion is called *inertia*.
8. Newton's third law is also known as the law of *acceleration*.
9. The velocity required for a spacecraft to break free of the earth's gravity is called *orbital velocity*.
10. A rocket's flight is explained by the law of *action and reaction*.

Thought Questions

1. Define each of the following terms:
   a. motion
   b. velocity
   c. acceleration
   d. inertia
   e. momentum
2. Compute the acceleration of a car that starts from rest and reaches a velocity of 80 kilometers per hour in 10 seconds.
3. A car, starting from rest, accelerates at 10 kph per second. What is the velocity of the car at the end of 4 seconds?
4. a. A stone that is dropped from the top of a building strikes the ground in 10 seconds. Compute the height of the building.
   b. What is the velocity of the stone at the end of the 7th second?
5. Find the acceleration of an object if its weight is 250 newtons and it is being acted upon by an unbalanced force of 1000 newtons.
6. Explain how a rocket engine lifts a spaceship, such as the type used in the Apollo program.
7. A 10-gram bullet is fired from a 3000-gram rifle with a velocity of 60,000 centimeters per second. With what velocity does the rifle recoil?
8. Does an orbiting body require the application of an unbalanced force? Explain.
9. What are some possible benefits of the Skylab program?

CHAPTER 14

HOW DO THE SKELETON AND MUSCLES ENABLE ANIMALS TO MOVE?

When you have completed this chapter, you should be able to:

1. *Relate* simple machines to the levers in the body of a living thing.
2. *State* the major ways in which the skeleton and muscles are important to the human body.
3. *Describe* the main divisions and joints of the skeleton.
4. *Distinguish* between (*a*) ligaments and tendons (*b*) voluntary and involuntary muscles.
5. *Discuss* some basic rules for caring for the skeleton and muscles.

In the laboratory experience that follows, you will determine how muscles and bones enable an animal to move parts of its body.

Laboratory Experience

WHAT MAKES A CHICKEN'S TOES MOVE?

A. Get a fresh chicken leg and examine the end that has been cut (Fig. 14–1). With forceps touch the different tissues that lie under the skin. The hard material is bone. The oval, tubelike structure that lies to one side of the bone is a *sheath* (or covering) that encloses several tendons.

B. Using dissecting scissors, slit the sheath lengthwise for a distance of about 3 centimeters. Look for a group of shiny white bands of tissue. With forceps pick up these bands and fold them toward you. Each band is a *tendon.*

C. On the side of the leg opposite the tendons you have just exposed, slit the skin lengthwise for a distance of about 5 centimeters. Inside the slit skin, find at least one single tendon, and bring its end outside the slit.

D. Firmly grasp the single tendon with your forceps, and pull the tendon upward.

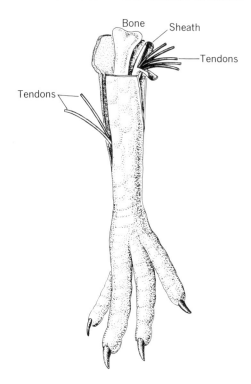

Bone   Sheath

Tendons

Tendons

Fig. 14–1.

    1. What happens to the chicken's toes?
E. Release the tendon.
    2. What happens to the chicken's toes?
F. Firmly grasp the group of tendons on the opposite side of the leg, and pull all of them upward at one time.
    3. Describe what happens.
G. Pull each tendon of the group separately.
    4. Describe what happens.
    5. In a live chicken, what body structures pull on these tendons?
H. Try to tear one of the tendons.
    6. Describe one outstanding property of a tendon.

Introduction

    Animals move from place to place as they obtain what they need from the environment for survival. We can observe the movements of animals as they breathe and seek food and water. Animals also move from place to place in seeking shelter and escaping from their enemies. These movements usually involve the entire body of the animal. In some activities, an animal moves only a part of its body. For example, when a cow chews, it moves mainly its lower jaw and tongue; when a squirrel digs, it moves its forelegs.

LEVERS ARE INVOLVED IN BODY MOVEMENTS

Whether the animal is a bird that flies, a fish that swims, or a human that walks, the body of the animal is engaged in physical work. In other words, matter (the animal body) is moved from one place to another through a particular distance. Both the skeleton and the muscles enable the animal's body to carry out this work. By contracting, muscles move the bones of the skeleton to which the muscles are attached. The bones are levers that move only when muscles exert a pulling force on them. Recall that a lever is a type of simple machine consisting of a rigid bar (in this case a bone) which can turn about a fulcrum.

In the body of an animal, many different joints act as fulcrums for different bony levers. The muscles attached to a bony lever provide the force that makes it move. Like other machines, levers in the body make it possible to accomplish work with less effort, or to increase speed, or to magnify small movements.

The levers in a body are of several types. One type is illustrated in chewing. In this activity, the bone of the lower jaw is the lever (Fig. 14-2). The joints of the jaw are fulcrums for this curved lever. When muscles attached to the lower jaw and to the skull contract, they pull the lower jaw upward. This action crushes food between the teeth. The food that is crushed is the resistance. The muscles that extend from the lower jaw to the skull provide the effort force. In effect, the jaw is a third-class lever (see Chapter 11, page 198).

Another type of lever is illustrated when we use a hammer. In the act of hammering, the bones of the forearm are the lever that raises the hand and hammer. The elbow joint is the fulcrum for this lever. Certain muscles of the upper arm, which are attached to the bones of the forearm and to the shoulder, contract. This action pulls the bones of the forearm and raises the forearm, hand, and hammer.

THE HUMAN SKELETON

All the levers in the body that enable us to move either a part of the body or the entire body are parts of the skeleton. The skeleton is important to the body in four major ways:

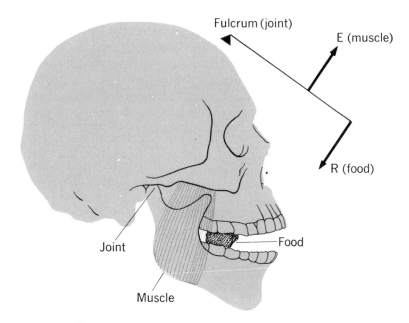

Fig. 14–2. How lever and fulcrum work in chewing.

1. *Movement.* Together with the muscles, the skeleton enables the body to carry out its movements.

2. *Support.* Because the material of which the bones are made is stiff and strong, the skeleton acts as a framework that supports the rest of the body.

3. *Protection.* Since the skeleton is hard and tough, it keeps many delicate organs inside the body from being injured by blows. The skull bones protect the brain; the rib bones protect the heart and lungs.

4. *Formation of blood cells.* The only place in the body where red blood cells are made is in the *marrow* of certain bones. Marrow is the soft tissue in the center of each of the long bones of the skeleton. As red blood cells wear out, the marrow forms new ones.

The human skeleton (Fig. 14–3, page 261) consists of 206 bones, in three chief divisions: the *skull*, the *spine*, and the *limbs* (arms and legs).

Skull

The skull consists of several curved bones that are interlocked at their edges. These bones form a hollow case that encloses the brain. Indentations in the front part of the skull form the cavities in which the eyes lie. Chambers in the sides of the skull house the inner parts of the ears. A framework of bone and *cartilage* (a tissue that is softer than bone) and a bony passageway form the nose. The skull rests on the upper end of the spine.

Spine

The spine (or *backbone*) consists of thirty-three bones, called *vertebrae*. These bones are separated from one another by disk-shaped pads of cartilage. This arrangement of bones and disks gives the spine some flexibility. The vertebrae and pads form a hollow tube that encases the delicate nerve tissue of the spinal cord. The spine and the muscles attached to it keep the trunk and head erect.

Beginning at shoulder level, there are twelve pairs of *ribs* attached to the spine. Most of the ribs meet in front of the body at the *breastbone*. The ribs and breastbone form the chest cavity, in which the heart and the lungs lie. Muscles attached to the ribs raise and lower the ribs during breathing.

Limbs

The bones of the arm consist of a single bone from the shoulder to the elbow; two bones between the elbow and the wrist; eight wrist bones; five palm bones; two bones in the thumb; and three bones in each of the other fingers. The arm is connected to the rest of the skeleton by a socket formed by the group of bones that includes the collarbone and the shoulder blade.

The bones of the leg consist of a single thigh bone; two bones between the thigh and the ankle; seven ankle bones; five foot bones; two bones in the big toe; and three bones in each of the other toes. The leg is connected to the rest of the skeleton by a socket formed by the bones that make up the hip.

JOINTS

A *joint* is the place where two bones meet (Fig. 14–4). Some joints, such as those in the skull, cannot be moved. These are called *immovable joints*. Other joints act as fulcrums and enable bony levers to move around them. A *ball-and-socket joint*, such as the shoulder joint, allows the limb to move in all directions. A *hinge joint*, such as the knee joint, allows the lower leg to move backward and to return.

CARTILAGE

Cartilage tissue is strong, softer than bone, slippery, and somewhat elastic. Cartilage supports the outer ear and part of the nose. This tissue

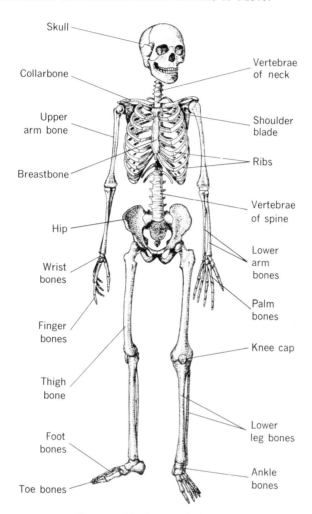

Skull

Collarbone

Upper
arm bone

Breastbone

Hip

Wrist
bones

Finger
bones

Thigh
bone

Foot
bones

Toe bones

Vertebrae
of neck

Shoulder
blade

Ribs

Vertebrae
of spine

Lower
arm
bones

Palm
bones

Knee cap

Lower
leg bones

Ankle
bones

Fig. 14–3. The human skeleton.

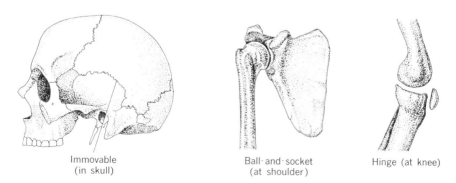

Immovable
(in skull)

Ball-and-socket
(at shoulder)

Hinge (at knee)

Fig. 14–4. Kinds of joints in the human skeleton.

also covers the ends of bones at movable joints. There, the slipperiness of the cartilage, along with a special fluid, helps to reduce friction and thus to promote easy movement of bone levers about their fulcrums.

LIGAMENTS AND TENDONS

The structures that bind the individual bones of the skeleton together and that bind muscles to bones are composed of very tough fibers. *Ligaments* are bands of tissue that bind one bone to another. *Tendons* are bands of tissue that bind a muscle to a bone.

In your laboratory experience, you discovered how tough tendons are and how a force that pulls a tendon moves the bone to which the tendon is attached.

THE MUSCLES

All normal, healthy muscles exert a pulling force when they contract. This is the muscular force that enables the bone levers and other body structures to move and to carry on their normal activities. Muscles enable the body to carry out two types of movement: *involuntary movement* and *voluntary movement*.

Involuntary Movement

Movement that we cannot control is called involuntary movement. Usually we are not aware that such movements are taking place. Involuntary movements go on inside the body at all times—even during sleep. Examples of involuntary movement include the pumping action of the heart and the pushing of food along the food canal. Involuntary movements within the body are carried on by involuntary muscle tissue. The muscles that make up the walls of the heart, the blood vessels, and the food tube are composed of involuntary muscle tissue.

Voluntary Movement

Movement that we can control is called voluntary movement. Such movement does not occur unless we want it to occur. We can control this type of movement and are usually aware of it. Examples of voluntary movement include opening a book and turning on a TV set. Voluntary movements are carried on by the muscles that are attached to every bone of the skeleton.

HOW MUSCLES MOVE BONES

A bone can move from a given position only when the muscle attached to the bone contracts. When the muscle contracts, it shortens and forcefully pulls on the bone. The bone then moves, with its joint serving as its fulcrum. When the muscle relaxes, it lengthens and releases its pull on the bone. At the same time that this muscle relaxes, another muscle on the opposite side of the bone contracts. These actions then restore the bone to its original position.

For example, when a person bends an outstretched arm upward, the *biceps* muscle, located on the upper side of the arm between the elbow and the shoulder, contracts (Fig. 14–5). At the same moment, the *triceps* muscle, located on the opposite side of the arm, relaxes. When a person straightens a bent arm, the triceps muscle contracts as the biceps muscle relaxes.

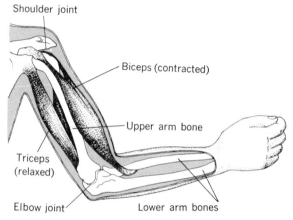

Fig. 14–5. Muscle action in the upper arm.

The action of muscles on bones was demonstrated in your laboratory experience. Pulling on one set of tendons causes the chicken's toes to curl inward. Pulling on the other set causes the toes to straighten. The force you exerted when you pulled on these tendons produces the same toe movements that the muscles of a live chicken ordinarily produce.

CARE OF THE SKELETON AND THE MUSCLES

Good health and body development depend to a large extent on the proper care of your bones and muscles. Some basic rules for this care follow.

1. *Eat properly.* Proteins, the mineral elements calcium and phosphorus, and vitamin D are all required for the normal growth of bone. Calcium is also required for muscles to contract normally. Proteins supply the building material for muscle growth. A well-balanced diet, which includes all the nutrients, helps normal growth and keeps the skeleton and muscles in good condition.

2. *Practice good posture.* Good posture lessens muscle fatigue because it keeps the weight of different parts of the body in balance. It also helps the body grow correctly. Good posture can be practiced by holding the head and trunk erectly at all times—even when sitting.

3. *Exercise regularly.* The contraction and relaxation of muscles improves the circulation of blood through them. Better circulation brings more food and oxygen to the cells, removes wastes from them, and thus aids their growth. Regular exercise also keeps the muscles and joints in good condition. Although regular exercise is good for the body, the exercise should be moderate and should be preceded by a warm-up period. Sudden, violent exercise can injure muscles, tendons, ligaments, and joints.

4. *Relax regularly.* All muscles must have periods of rest. During such periods, accumulated wastes are removed from muscle cells, and energy-producing nutrients are restored to them.

5. *Get adequate sleep.* The body is most relaxed during sleep. Most people require about 8 hours of sleep daily. The bed should be comfortable, large enough, and firm enough to keep the muscles and skeleton from being cramped.

6. *Wear shoes that fit.* Standing and walking in shoes that do not fit well may throw the skeleton out of balance. Over a period of time, poor posture, foot discomfort, pain, and excessive fatigue can result.

Looking Back

The skeleton and the muscles attached to it enable animals to move. Many bones of the skeleton are levers. The fulcrum of each bone lever is the joint between two movable bones, which are held together by ligaments. Muscles, which are attached to bones by tendons, supply the effort force that moves the levers.

Looking Ahead

Forces are important to us because they produce movement in our environment. In Chapter 15, we will learn how forces in the earth change our environment.

Multiple-Choice Questions

1. Which two body systems, acting together, enable an animal to move and find food?
   a. muscular and digestive systems
   b. digestive and skeletal systems
   c. skeletal and respiratory systems
   d. skeletal and muscular systems

2. The lungs are protected by the part of the skeleton called the
   a. vertebra   b. spine   c. rib cage   d. shoulder blade

3. Blows to the head usually do not harm the eye because this sensitive organ is protected by the
   a. upper eyelid   c. bones of the skull
   b. lower eyelid   d. eyebrows

4. The force that enables body levers to move is supplied by the
   a. brain   b. kidneys   c. heart   d. muscles

5. Long bones manufacture the cells of the tissue called
   a. cartilage   b. heart muscle   c. blood   d. smooth muscle

6. The bones of the skeleton can be grouped into three main divisions, which are
   a. spine, skull, arms   c. limbs, hip, skull
   b. skull, spine, limbs   d. legs, collarbone, shoulder blade

7. Bones in the body move only when the
   a. bones attached to ligaments contract
   b. muscles attached to bones contract
   c. nerves attached to muscles contract
   d. bones attached to muscles contract

8. The nerve tissue of the spinal cord is covered by a
   a. solid bony tube
   b. bony tube composed of separate vertebrae and disks of cartilage
   c. bony tube composed of only separate vertebrae
   d. disks of cartilage

9. In the human, the number of bones present between the right elbow and the right wrist is
   a. 2   b. 5   c. 8   d. 13

10. Involuntary muscle is located in the
    a. heart, blood vessels, and food tube
    b. arm, leg, and ear
    c. heart, knee, and toe
    d. finger, tongue, and lip

11. Several immovable joints are present in the
    a. thumb   b. wrist   c. shoulder   d. skull

12. The joint at the elbow is of the type called
    a. hinge   b. ball-and-socket   c. lever   d. immovable

13. The beating of the heart during sleep is an example of
    a. voluntary movement   c. triceps action
    b. tendon contraction   d. involuntary movement

14. The number of bones in the left leg between the hip joint and the knee joint is

    a. 1   **b.** 2   **c.** 5   **d.** 7

15. Which type of muscle is directly used in throwing a ball?

    a. involuntary   **b.** voluntary   **c.** heart   **d.** automatic

Modified True-False Questions

1. A joint between two movable bones often acts as *a fulcrum.*
2. The framework of the human body consists mainly of *cartilage.*
3. Marrow is located in the center of many *teeth.*
4. The space enclosed by the breastbone and the ribs is the *chest* cavity.
5. The outer ear is supported by *tiny ear bones.*
6. The bones of the hand are held together by *tendons.*
7. For the skeleton to stay healthy, two mineral elements needed are phosphorus and *copper.*
8. Vitamin D and *iron* are needed for the building of strong bones.
9. *Tendons* bind the muscles of the leg to bony levers.
10. Wastes are removed from muscle cells when the cells *contract.*

Thought Questions

1. Explain the difference between the two terms in each of the following pairs:

    a. bone and cartilage

    b. hinge joint and ball-and-socket joint

    c. tendon and ligament

    d. lever and fulcrum

    e. biceps muscle and triceps muscle

2. This is a diagram of an arm and shoulder.

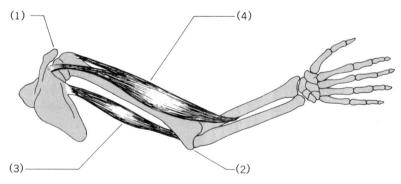

    a. What type of joint is present at (1)?

    b. What type of joint is present at (2)?

    c. When muscle (3) contracts, what happens to muscle (4)?

    d. When muscle (3) contracts, what happens to the arm?

CHAPTER 15

HOW ARE THE FEATURES OF THE ENVIRONMENT AFFECTED BY MOVEMENT OF THE EARTH'S CRUST?

When you have completed this chapter, you should be able to:

1. *Discuss* the causes of earthquakes.
2. *Describe* the location of earthquake belts and the damage done by earthquakes.
3. *Explain* how earthquakes are located and how they are used to study the structure of the earth.
4. *Relate* crustal movements to faults, shock waves, tsunamis, and some types of mountains.
5. *Compare* the types of volcanoes and volcanic mountains.
6. *Define* batholith, sill, plateau, plain, peneplain, syncline, anticline.
7. *State* the theory of continental drift.

In the laboratory experience that follows, you will study a map to locate the major earthquake belts.

Laboratory Experience

WHERE ARE THE MAJOR EARTHQUAKE ZONES?

A. The places where earthquakes have occurred most frequently are listed below. These places are shown on the map of the world (Fig. 15–1, page 269). Trace this map on a clean sheet of paper; be sure to include the little circles. Locate each place on the map, and darken the circle near each place.

Places Having Frequent Earthquakes

Acapulco	Arica	Costa Rica
Aleutian Islands	Athens	Ecuador
Anchorage	Auckland	Fiji Islands
Ankara	Concepción	Hokkaido

Java	Magellan Straits	Shanghai
Juneau	New Guinea	Sicily
Kamchatka	Portland	Sumatra
Karachi	Puerto Rico	Tehran
Los Angeles	San Francisco	Yokohama

B. Between the meridians of 100°E and 60°W longitude, draw a line connecting the circles you have filled in.

   1. Describe any pattern or patterns you see between these meridians.

C. Between the meridians of 80°W and 80°E longitude, draw similar lines connecting the circles you have filled in.

   2. In what ways, if any, do the patterns in this region differ from the pattern(s) in part B?

D. Using a map of the world as a guide, place an X on your map where each of the following volcanoes is located:

Fujiyama (Japan)	Krakatoa (Java)
Mauna Kea (Hawaii)	Parícutin (Mexico)
Mt. Pelée (Martinique)	Popocatepetl (Mexico)
Mt. Rainier (Washington)	Mt. Shasta (California)
Taal (Philippines)	Vesuvius (Italy)

   3. What relation do you observe between the location of these volcanoes and earthquake zones? Explain.

   4. What can you conclude concerning the geologic features in certain parts of the world and the occurrence of earthquakes?

Introduction

The crust of the earth is composed of masses of igneous rock, sedimentary rock, and metamorphic rock. *Igneous rock* is formed as the result of the cooling of molten materials. *Sedimentary rock* is formed after small rock particles settle under water and then become compressed or cemented together. *Metamorphic rock* is formed from other rocks by the action of heat and pressure.

The masses of rock that make up the crust of the earth move continuously—up, down, and sideways—as a result of natural underground forces. Most of the movement is so slight that we are unaware of it. At times, however, the force produced by the movement of the earth's crust is great and sudden. The ground trembles, cracks appear in the earth's crust, landslides occur, and buildings fall. Whether these move-

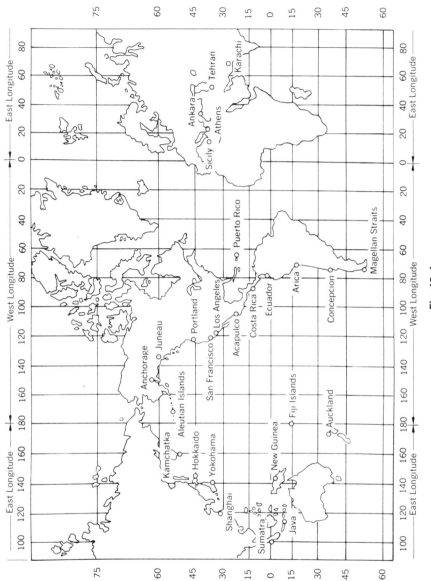

Fig. 15–1.

ments of the crust are slight or great, they are called *earthquakes*. Strong earthquakes are deadly. They can destroy an entire village or city in minutes, taking thousands of lives and leaving thousands of people homeless. In this century alone, over 500,000 people have been killed by earthquakes. Unfortunately, as yet, earthquakes cannot be predicted with great reliability.

Apart from earthquakes, the movements of the earth's crust are very slow and barely detectable by the most sensitive instruments. Over a very long period of time, however, these gradual movements produce results that are far more impressive than the sudden movements of earthquakes. For example, we often find the remains of extinct sea animals in the rocks on tops of mountains. This means that what are now mountaintops were once on the floor of the ocean. Besides mountains, other land features such as plateaus and plains are the result of movements of the earth's crust.

EARTHQUAKES

About one million earthquakes occur every year. However, fewer than 1% of these earthquakes destroy property or injure anyone. Geologists who study earthquakes have learned what causes them and where they are most likely to occur. In addition, through their study of earthquakes, geologists have learned a great deal about the interior of the earth.

Cause of Earthquakes

According to the modern theory of the behavior of the earth's crust, the crust is not one large, unbroken layer of rock. Rather, the crust is divided into at least six large, semirigid slabs, or *plates*. Each continent and the ocean floor near it are parts of a plate. The plates float on denser, hot material beneath them and move very gradually (about 8 centimeters per year) with respect to one another. This theory is called the *plate tectonics theory*, or the *continental drift theory*.

The plate tectonics theory states that new crust forms along extensive underwater ridges (mountain chains) located near the middle of each large ocean. At each ridge, hot, molten material from under the crust rises to the ocean floor. This material spreads out, cools, and becomes part of the crust as the plates on either side of the ridge move away in opposite directions from the ridge and from each other. In regions where the underwater plates reach plates bearing continents, the underwater plates are forced downward. In such regions, forces strong enough to cause earthquakes and volcanoes are produced.

These forces are always exerting pressure against the rocks that make up the crust. When these pressures become too great, the crust will

Fig. 15–2. What causes earthquakes?

break, or *fracture* (Fig. 15–2). The fracture relieves the pressure on the crust for a time.

Much the same thing happens when you take a twig in your hands and bend it. As you exert a bending force on the ends of the twig, the twig bends more and more. If you exert enough force, the twig snaps in two. As the twig breaks, the bent ends suddenly straighten out again. As they straighten out, the ends of the twig vibrate. In fact, the snapping noise you hear when the twig breaks is caused by the vibrations of the ends of the twig.

When the crust of the earth fractures, the broken sections vibrate as they adjust to their new positions. What we call an earthquake is this vibration, or trembling, of the crust.

Weak Spots in the Earth's Crust

The place where the crust fractures is called a *fault* (Fig. 15–2). The fault is a weak spot in the crust. If the pressure builds up again in the same part of the crust, it is very likely that the pressure will relieve itself by a movement, or *slippage*, of the rocks on either side of the same fault. Many of the most violent earthquakes on record have taken place along faults in this way.

Less violent earthquakes are also caused by erupting volcanoes and by underground explosions purposely set off by geologists. Such explosions are set off in order to produce *shock waves*, or vibrations, in the crust (Fig. 15–3, page 272). Instruments at the surface of the earth record these shock waves. By studying the instrument recordings, geologists can determine the structure of the rocks in the crust.

LOCATING EARTHQUAKES

When an earthquake occurs anywhere in the world, *seismologists* (scientists who study earthquakes) thousands of kilometers away can

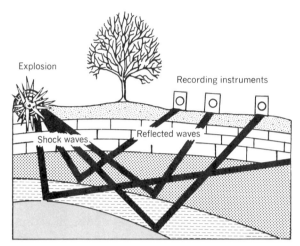

Fig. 15–3. An earthquake may be set off purposely.

detect its shock waves. They can detect and record the effects of the earthquake with the aid of a sensitive instrument called a *seismograph* (Fig. 15–4).

The basic part of a seismograph is a suspended weight with a pen attached to it. The pen writes on a chart attached to a drum. The base of the instrument is attached to solid bedrock. Vibrations in the bedrock cause the drum to vibrate against the stationary pen. As the drum vibrates, the pen traces a wavy line on the drum.

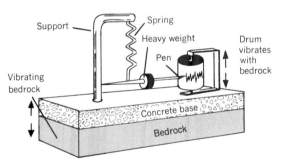

Fig. 15–4. A seismograph.

How Earthquakes Are Located

The center of an earthquake is called the *focus*. A point on the surface directly above the focus is called the *epicenter*. If three seismograph stations detect the same earthquake, seismologists can calculate the exact location on the surface of the earth (the epicenter) under which the earthquake originated. This is possible because each type of shock wave travels through the earth at a certain speed. Consequently, shock waves will reach different seismograph stations at different times, depending on how far each station is from the earthquake.

Seismologists in Chicago, for example, can locate the distance of an earthquake from their seismograph station by first calculating how long it took the shock waves to reach the station. They then draw a circle on a map with the station at the center of the circle. The diameter of the circle represents the distance of the earthquake from the station.

The seismologists know that the earthquake occurred somewhere on the circle they have drawn, but they do not know the direction of the earthquake from the station. However, by finding out the sizes of the circles drawn by other seismologists at stations such as El Paso and Phoenix, they can combine all these circles on one map (Fig. 15–5). The circles will cross at one point. That point is the epicenter of the earthquake.

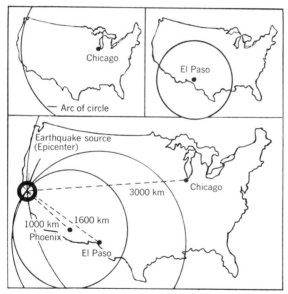

Fig. 15–5. Locating an earthquake.

The depth at which an earthquake occurs is determined in a way similar to that used for locating an epicenter on the surface of the earth. Most earthquakes, including the most destructive, occur within 50 kilometers of the surface. Some earthquakes, however, occur as far as 700 kilometers below the surface.

Earthquake Regions

Although earthquakes may occur any place in the world, most earthquakes occur in two regions called *earthquake belts*. You studied the locations of these belts in your laboratory experience. One earthquake belt borders the Pacific Ocean; the other runs from the Mediterranean Sea, across Asia, and from there to the Pacific Ocean (Fig. 15-6). These earthquake belts are in regions of the earth where we also find many active volcanoes and mountains that contain many faults in their rocks.

Alaska and California are two states that have had violent earthquakes in the past and are likely to have more earthquakes in the future. Both of these states lie in the earthquake belt that borders the Pacific Ocean. California's earthquakes are caused primarily by slippages of the earth's crust along a fault almost 1000 kilometers long, known as the San Andreas fault (Fig. 15-7). The San Andreas fault runs from Cape Mendocino in northwestern California, through San Francisco, to the Mohave Desert in the southeastern part of the state.

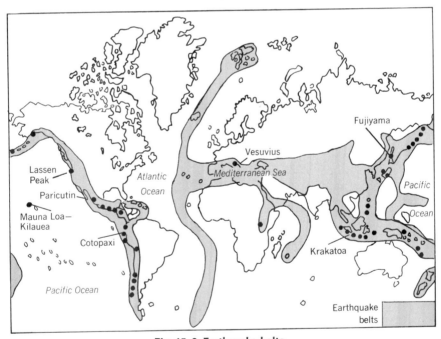

Fig. 15-6. Earthquake belts.

EFFECTS OF EARTHQUAKES

A study of the earthquake belts reveals that earthquakes may occur on land and under the oceans. In both regions, the earthquakes can be very destructive.

Fig. 15–7. San Andreas fault.

Earthquakes on Land

How much the crust moves as the result of an earthquake can readily be observed in many places. For example, after the San Francisco earthquake of 1906, measurements of displaced sections of highways showed that the crust had moved more than 6 meters. After an earthquake in Alaska in 1899, investigators found that a section of the shore that had been underwater before the earthquake was raised nearly 15 meters above sea level. The actual effect of an earthquake can be seen in Fig. 15–8, page 276. A wrecked building rests on a section of the earth that has dropped almost 4 meters below the section in the left half of the picture.

The damage to buildings caused by an earthquake depends on a number of factors, including the intensity of the earthquake and the type of material on which the buildings rest.

Strange as it may seem, a building resting on solid bedrock is less likely to be destroyed by an earthquake than a building resting on loose earth. A building whose foundations rest on bedrock can ride out an earthquake because the shock waves produced by the movement of the crust pass through the bedrock without setting up destructive vibrations. On the other hand, a building resting on loose earth shakes and slides because the earth underneath the building vibrates.

Fig. 15–8. Earthquake damage.

You can see how this happens if you spread a thin layer of sand on top of a heavy table. When you tap the table sharply with a hammer, the loose grains of sand will jump and move about violently, while the table top itself vibrates only slightly.

Earthquakes Under Water

Earthquakes that occur on the ocean floor often produce destructive ocean waves called *tsunamis*. Tsunamis are also produced by underwater volcanic eruptions and by coastal landslides. A tsunami can move across thousands of kilometers of ocean at speeds up to 800 kilometers per hour. On the open ocean, the waves of a tsunami are many kilometers from crest to crest, and the waves are so low they are usually unnoticed. However, when a tsunami reaches the shallow waters of a coastal area, its waves pile up on the shore. The waves are usually less than 20 meters high when they strike the land, although one tsunami was estimated to have waves 63 meters high. Some tsunamis are so weak that they pass unnoticed when they reach the shore.

A tsunami often takes more lives and causes more destruction than the earthquake, landslide, or volcanic eruption that produced it. In 1896, a tsunami nearly 30 meters high crashed onto the coast of Japan. Over 10,000 houses were swept away, more than 27,000 people were killed, and thousands of others were injured. In 1946, a tsunami struck

Hawaii and took 159 lives. This tsunami tore railroad tracks from their beds, washed houses out to sea, and destroyed entire beaches.

A tsunami usually gives warning before it reaches shore. Minutes before a large tsunami strikes, the water moves rapidly away from the beach, as if it were being sucked out to sea. Parts of the beach that have always been below sea level now stand high and dry. Then, with a great hissing sound, the giant wave moves in at high speed and rushes across the waterless beach. As the first wave strikes the shore, a roaring noise is produced. Since tsunamis come in series, the waves may continue their destruction for several hours.

Shock Waves Produced by Earthquakes

When rocks fracture or slip along a fault, the earth vibrates. The vibrations travel through the crust as shock waves (Fig. 15–9). Some shock waves travel along the surface of the earth. Other shock waves travel through the interior of the earth. Both surface and internal shock waves travel outward in all directions from the source of the earthquake but at different speeds. The differences in speed depend upon the type of shock wave produced, differences in the density of the material through which the shock waves travel, and on the paths the shock waves take through these materials.

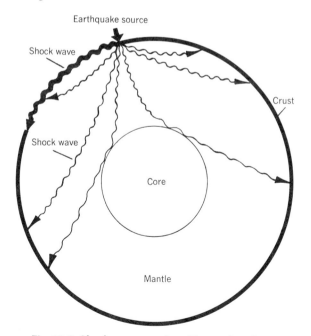

Fig. 15–9. Shock waves produced by earthquakes.

The earth consists of a series of zones that vary from the solid state to the liquid state. Geologists have obtained this picture of the interior of the earth by studying the speeds and paths followed by the shock waves of a great many earthquakes.

SLOW MOVEMENTS OF THE CRUST

We have learned that forces within the crust of the earth cause earthquakes. Earthquakes in turn cause other parts of the crust to move suddenly and violently. Forces within the earth may also cause the crust to move very gradually and over a very long period of time. Because these movements are so slow, they can be observed only by examining records extending over a period of hundreds of years.

There are many pieces of evidence showing how slowly the earth's crust moves.

1. Many mountains consist of sedimentary rocks. These rocks may contain the remains of animals or plants that once lived underwater. Since sedimentary rocks ordinarily form after small rock particles have settled underwater, these remains indicate that the rocks were originally submerged and that they then rose above sea level (Fig. 15–10).

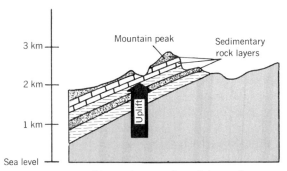

Fig. 15–10. Mountains may form from rocks that were once under water.

2. The continents consist of rocks that are less dense than the rocks on which they rest. This means that the continents "float" on top of this denser rock material. As weathering and erosion remove rock material from the top of a mountain, and the mountaintop loses mass, it rises slowly. At the same time, the region to which the rock has been transported becomes heavier and sinks slowly. Note that a change in one vertical direction is offset by a change in the opposite direction. This state of balance is called *isostasy*. It is for this reason that the surface of the earth is not completely level.

3. Cuts made in the sides of mountains during roadbuilding operations have exposed many layers of sedimentary rock having wavy patterns called *folds*. Since sedimentary rocks are formed as horizontal layers, this means that some force has deformed the original layers into folds.

4. As we saw in our study of earthquakes, many faults exist in the earth's crust. From this and other evidence, we can conclude that faults have always existed in the crust and that these faults caused slippages of the crust in the far distant past as well as in the present.

5. The outlines of the continents that border the Atlantic Ocean seem to match each other like the pieces of a jigsaw puzzle (Fig. 15–11). Furthermore, the rocks in these continents are alike in a number of ways. From this evidence, many geologists have concluded that these continents were once joined together. Today, as you know, the Atlantic Ocean separates Europe and Africa from North America and South America. Thus, if this theory (continental drift, or plate tectonics) is true, these continents have moved thousands of kilometers apart.

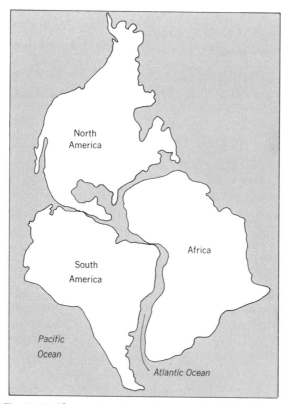

Fig. 15–11. The continents as they once might have been.

Some of the features on the earth's surface that have been formed by movements of the crust are *mountains, plateaus,* and *plains.*

FORMATION OF MOUNTAINS

Those parts of the earth's crust in which the rocks are tilted away from the horizontal and rise high above the surrounding terrain are called mountains. Although there are mountains that rise more than 6000 meters above sea level, and these mountains seem high to us, they are actually only slight bumps on the surface of the earth, compared to the size of the entire earth.

Mountains are classified according to the forces that produced them. Here we will discuss the formation of two types—*fold mountains* and *fault-block mountains.*

Fold Mountains

Movements of the crust may cause layers of sedimentary rocks in the crust to fold into wavelike patterns. Mountains formed in this way are called fold mountains.

You can see how folds are produced in layers of sedimentary rocks if you lay several strips of different-colored clay on top of one another (Fig. 15–12). These strips represent layers of sedimentary rocks within the crust. Holding the ends of the strips with your hands, slowly push the ends toward each other. The pressure applied to the clay will cause the layers to fold.

Rocks that have been folded upward produce formations called *anticlines* (Fig. 15–13). Rocks that have been folded downward produce formations called *synclines.* Anticlines form great ridges on the surface of the earth, with the synclines forming deep valleys between the ridges. The Appalachian Mountains, the Rocky Mountains, and the Alps all show evidence of folding.

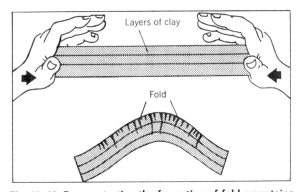

Fig. 15–12. Demonstrating the formation of fold mountains.

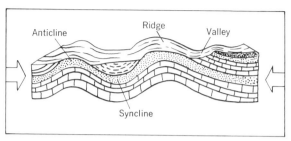

Fig. 15–13. Anticlines and synclines.

The agents of weathering and erosion continually wear away the ridges. After millions of years, ridges may be worn as flat as the original sedimentary layers. When a folded region is worn almost flat by erosion, the region is called a *peneplain*.

Fault-Block Mountains

A mountain that is the result of the fracturing and lifting up or dropping of a large block of the crust is called a fault-block mountain (Fig. 15–14). Fault-block mountains are usually long, rectangular-shaped blocks that have been tilted upward by pressures in the crust. The Sierra Nevada is the largest chain of fault-block mountains in the continental United States. These mountains are over 600 kilometers long and from 80 to 130 kilometers wide. In some places, the uppermost edges of the blocks rise nearly 3 kilometers above the surrounding terrain. Smaller fault-block mountains are located east of the Sierra Nevada in the Great Basin area of Utah, Nevada, and Oregon.

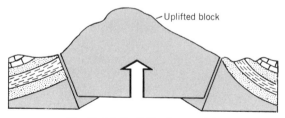

Fig. 15–14. Fault-block mountain.

FORMATION OF PLATEAUS

A plateau is a broad, flat region that has been raised hundreds or thousands of feet above sea level. A plateau may form when a large section of the crust rises without being folded or broken. The Appalachian Plateau, which extends from New York to Alabama on the western side of the Appalachian Mountains, was formed in this way.

In the western United States, the Colorado Plateau was formed millions of years ago when tens of thousands of square kilometers of the earth's crust rose more than 1500 meters above sea level. As the plateau rose, the Colorado River, which flows across this region, slowly carved the Grand Canyon deep into the rocks that make up the plateau (Fig. 15–15).

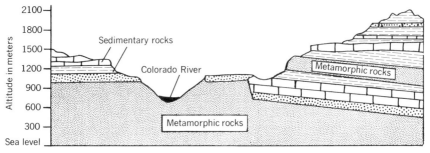

Fig. 15–15. The Grand Canyon.

Plateaus are often referred to as mountains. For example, the region of the Catskill Mountains in New York State is a plateau that has been deeply carved by erosion. Although the Catskill region looks mountainous, it is basically a plateau. The simplest way of describing the difference between a plateau and a mountain is that the rocks in a mountain are tilted away from the horizontal, while in a plateau the rocks are horizontal.

FORMATION OF PLAINS

Like a plateau, a plain is a broad, flat region. It is not usually as high as a plateau. Plains are classified into a number of different types, according to the sediments or rocks of which the plains are made. We will limit our discussion to *marine plains, lake plains,* and *glacial plains.* (Although glacial plains are not the result of crustal movement, we include them here because they resemble other plains.)

Marine Plains

Marine plains, or ocean plains, form when shallow parts of the ocean rise above sea level. The Atlantic Coastal Plain, which extends from New Jersey to Florida, and the Gulf Coastal Plain, which borders the Gulf of Mexico, are examples of marine plains. The Great Plains of the United States and Canada were originally marine plains. The Great Plains rose out of a shallow inland sea that once extended from Hudson Bay to the Gulf of Mexico.

Lake Plains

Lake plains are the dry beds of former lakes. The Great Salt Lake Desert in Utah is a lake plain that was once the bed of the ancient lake called Lake Bonneville.

Lake Ontario, between the United States and Canada, once covered a large part of what is now upper New York State. At the end of the last ice age, a large portion of the water drained away. The former bottom of the ancient lake is now flat farmland.

The greatest lake plain in North America today was once the bottom of a huge lake called Lake Agassiz (Fig. 15–16). During the ice age, this lake covered about 250,000 square kilometers of what is now Minnesota, North Dakota, and Central Canada—an area larger than all the Great Lakes put together. Fertile farmland and several small lakes are all that remain of Lake Agassiz.

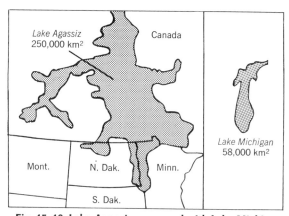

Fig. 15–16. Lake Agassiz compared with Lake Michigan.

Glacial Plains

Glacial plains are formed from the deposits left behind by glaciers. For example, the southern half of Long Island, New York, is a glacial plain.

Fig. 15–17, page 284, shows various land features that are formed by movements and other changes of the earth's crust.

UNDERSTANDING VOLCANOES

The hot, molten (liquid) rock that lies beneath the solid crust of the earth is called *magma*. When magma moves through the crust or emerges to the surface of the earth, this activity is known as *vulcanism*.

When magma emerges to the surface, the opening is called a *volcano*.

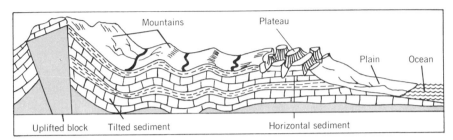

Fig. 15–17. Plains, plateaus, and mountains.

Sometimes the magma emerges through a break or crack in the crust called a *fissure*. A *volcanic mountain* is built up by successive deposits of magma around a volcano.

Volcanoes are classified according to whether or not magma still erupts from them. *Active volcanoes* still erupt from time to time. Volcanoes that have been known to erupt in modern times, but not very recently, are called *dormant volcanoes*. *Extinct volcanoes* are volcanoes that have never erupted since the beginning of human history.

VOLCANIC ERUPTIONS

The bowl-shaped opening at the top of a volcano is called a *crater*. The crater of a dormant volcano is often covered by a thin layer of solidified lava. (*Lava* is magma that has emerged from the earth.) When the pressure of the molten lava inside a dormant volcano builds up enough, the volcano *erupts*; that is, the molten lava shatters the thin layer of hardened lava. The lava then either flows quietly from breaks in the crater or volcano walls (a *quiet eruption*), or it explodes out of the crater (an *explosive eruption*). Molten lava may flow many kilometers down the slopes of the volcano.

The eruption of a volcano can be both spectacular and disastrous. Clouds of volcanic cinders, ashes, dust, and poisonous gases erupting from explosive volcanoes have wiped out entire cities. In 1902 the eruption of Mt. Pelée in the West Indies took 30,000 lives in nearby towns and villages. One of the most explosive eruptions ever recorded took place on the Indonesian island of Krakatoa in 1883. A large part of the island was blown to bits. The sound of the explosion was heard well over 4000 kilometers away. Part of the island that had been about 800 meters above sea level was left 270 meters under water.

VOLCANIC MOUNTAINS

Vulcanism has resulted in the formation of some of the world's best-known mountains. Eruptions of molten lava have built up these mountains into the form of cones. Among these volcanic mountains are Mt. Rainier in the State of Washington, Mt. Fuji in Japan, and Mt. Vesuvius in Italy. The islands of Hawaii are a group of volcanic mountains.

Volcanic mountains differ according to the way they were formed—as the result of a quiet eruption, an explosive eruption, or a combination of the two. Each type of eruption forms a different type of volcano—a *shield volcano*, a *cinder cone volcano*, or a *composite volcano* (Fig. 15–18).

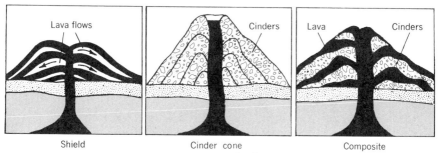

Fig. 15–18. Types of volcanoes.

Shield Volcanoes

Shield volcanoes, also called *lava cones*, form when rivers of lava flow out of the earth's crust. The hot lava spreads out over the surface of the earth like heavy syrup before it cools and hardens. When a series of these lava flows occurs over a period of many years, the lava forms a broad, cone-shaped mountain with gentle slopes. Examples of shield volcanoes include Mauna Loa and Mauna Kea, the largest of five shield volcanoes that make up the island of Hawaii. Both of these volcanoes have peaks about 4200 meters above sea level. At its base on the sea floor, Mauna Loa, the world's largest volcano, is about 120 kilometers long and 100 kilometers wide.

Cinder Cone Volcanoes

Cinder cone volcanoes form when hot, liquid lava is hurled high into the air during an explosive volcanic eruption. The lava breaks up into small drops which cool and harden into particles of dust and cinders before falling back to earth. The hardened particles can form a mountain-sized cone in less than a year. The cone is relatively steep and is seldom more than 450 meters high.

In February, 1943, for example, a number of earthquake shocks shook the small village of Parícutin, Mexico. Hot gases, lava, and cinders began to spew from a crevice in a cornfield near the village. By September, seven months later, a mountain 450 meters high stood where the cornfield had been. In addition, the entire region within several kilometers of the volcano was buried under a layer of ashes several meters deep.

Composite Volcanoes

Composite volcanoes are built up of layers of both cinder falls and lava flows. Well-known composite volcanoes include Mt. Rainier in Washington, Mt. Shasta in California, Mt. Fuji in Japan, Popocatepetl in Mexico, and Mt. Vesuvius in Italy.

DOME MOUNTAINS

Dome mountains form when large quantities of magma force their way through horizontal layers of sedimentary rock. The upper layers of rock are forced upward. These raised layers form mountains that resemble inverted cups, or the domes of buildings (Fig. 15–19). In time, the top layers of rock are eroded and the solidified magma (*igneous rock*) is exposed at the surface. Dome mountains are sometimes 250 kilometers in diameter. Examples of dome mountains are the Henry Mountains of Utah and the Orange Mountains of New Jersey.

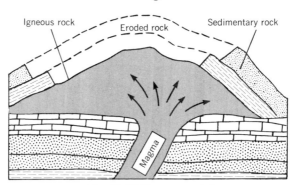

Igneous rock   Eroded rock   Sedimentary rock

Magma

Fig. 15–19. Dome mountain.

VULCANISM INSIDE THE EARTH'S CRUST

Vulcanism is responsible for underground geologic features as well as for above-ground features such as mountains and lava flows. These underground features cannot be seen unless they have been exposed by erosion or some other natural process. Two such underground features are *batholiths* and *sills*. These features are formed when magma, which has worked its way into cracks or layers in the rocks, eventually solidifies (Fig. 15–20).

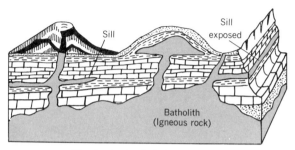

Fig. 15–20. Batholiths and sills.

Batholiths

Batholiths form the cores of many of the world's dome mountains. Some batholiths cover areas larger than most of our states. The largest batholith in North America, the Coast Range batholith along the Pacific coast of Canada, is about 1600 kilometers long and 240 kilometers wide. Other great batholiths are in the Sierra Nevada in California, and in the Rocky Mountains in Idaho.

Sills

When magma works its way into layers of horizontal sediments and then hardens, the magma forms a thick layer of solid rock that may be many kilometers long and hundreds of meters thick. The hardened magma is called a sill. An outstanding example of an exposed sill is the Palisades, which are cliffs that tower along the New Jersey side of the Hudson River opposite New York City.

Looking Back

All movement, including crustal movement, is the result of the action of unbalanced forces. The environment is constantly changing as a result of very gradual as well as very sudden movements of the earth's crust. Such movements are responsible for earthquakes and the formation of mountains and other features of our environment.

Looking Ahead

In Unit I, we studied the properties and reactions of the nonliving matter of the environment. In Unit II, we have learned how the forces of the environment produce motion and otherwise affect living and nonliving things. In Unit III, we will study how living things manage to survive from generation to generation in a changing environment.

Multiple-Choice Questions

1. Of the million earthquakes that occur every year, the number that cause any noticeable destruction is about
   a. 1%   b. 10%   c. 20%   d. 50%

2. Earthquakes usually occur when huge blocks of rock slip along breaks in the bedrock called
   a. joints   b. faults   c. fractures   d. zones

3. The region of the earth that is *least* likely to experience strong earthquakes is the
   a. Atlantic Ocean   c. Mediterranean Sea
   b. Pacific Ocean   d. Asian continent

4. The regions of the earth where earthquakes are most likely to occur are called earthquake
   a. lines   b. zones   c. belts   d. rims

5. The length of the San Andreas fault in California is about
   a. 10 kilometers   c. 500 kilometers
   b. 100 kilometers   d. 1000 kilometers

6. Tsunamis reach their greatest height between trough and crest when they
   a. first form
   b. are in the middle of the ocean
   c. move onto the land
   d. travel across a calm part of the ocean

7. The first sign that a tsunami is approaching a shore is
   a. a hissing and roaring noise
   b. the movement of water away from the shore
   c. a sudden flattening of the waves
   d. the appearance of a wall of water on the horizon

8. The study of earthquake shock waves has shown that the internal structure of the earth is largely
   a. liquid   b. solid   c. liquid and gas   d. gas

9. In order to function properly, a seismograph must be
   a. attached to bedrock
   b. located in the basement of a large building
   c. attached to the foundation of a building
   d. resting on loose earth

10. The minimum number of circles ordinarily needed to locate the epicenter of an earthquake is
    a. 1   b. 2   c. 3   d. 4

11. The maximum depth at which earthquakes occur is about
    a. 10 kilometers   c. 250 kilometers
    b. 50 kilometers   d. 700 kilometers

12. Evidence that the continents were once joined is found partly in the
    a. location of reefs off the continents
    b. location of rivers along the coasts of continents
    c. locations of mountains
    d. shapes of the coastlines of opposing continents

13. Mountains in which sedimentary rocks have been forced into wavelike patterns are called
    a. fold mountains   **c.** fault-block mountains
    b. dome mountains   **d.** volcanic mountains
14. An example of a volcanic mountain is
    a. Mt. Washington   **c.** Mt. Rainier
    b. the Matterhorn   **d.** the Sierra Nevada
15. The theory that explains the cause of many earthquakes is called
    a. continental uplift   **c.** isostasy
    b. volcanic eruptions   **d.** plate tectonics

Modified True-False Questions

1. The most violent earthquakes are caused by *landslides.*
2. In the United States, earthquakes are most likely to occur in the states near the *Pacific* Ocean.
3. Regions of the earth in which there are both *active volcanoes* and high mountains are most likely to experience earthquakes.
4. The earth's *crust* may move as much as 15 meters as the result of an earthquake.
5. The destructive waves that are produced by underwater earthquakes are properly called *tidal waves.*
6. The shock waves produced in the earth's crust by earthquakes *cannot* travel through those parts of the earth that are below the crust.
7. The different types of shock waves produced by an earthquake travel through the earth at *the same* speeds.
8. The instrument used by geologists to detect earthquakes is the *seismograph.*
9. The point on the earth's surface under which an earthquake originates is called the *focus* of the earthquake.
10. Most earthquakes occur within 50 *kilometers* of the earth's surface.
11. The presence of *sedimentary* rocks on the tops of mountains is evidence that these rocks were probably formed beneath the sea and have since been uplifted.
12. An upward fold in rocks is called *a syncline.*
13. The remains of a mountain range that has been worn flat by erosion are called *a peneplain.*
14. *Dome* mountains are the result of the eruption of molten substances.
15. *Cinder cone* volcanoes result from the slow hardening of molten lava.

Thought Questions

1. Account for the presence of a fossil sea animal in the rocks on top of a plateau that is one kilometer above sea level.
2. Explain how most strong earthquakes occur.
3. Describe the land formations that are most likely to be found in an earthquake zone.

4. The skyscrapers on the island of Manhattan are built on solid bedrock—the remainder of an ancient system of mountains. Give two reasons why these skyscrapers are unlikely to be affected by earthquakes.

5. If you were at the seashore and noticed that the water suddenly moved away from the shore much more rapidly than usual, why would it be wise for you to go inland and remain there for several hours?

6. Explain the difference between fold mountains and fault-block mountains.

7. Explain why it is possible that the area of the Hawaiian islands may double in the future.

8. By studying the shock-wave patterns produced by earthquakes, geologists have learned a great deal about the inner structure of the earth. These shock waves move at a faster rate of speed through dense rocks; they move at a slower rate of speed through rocks that are less dense. In addition, as these shock waves travel through the earth, they gradually become weaker. Geologists also know that the deeper rocks in the earth are denser than the rocks closer to the surface. Using this information and Fig. 15–9 (page 277), answer the questions that follow.

    a. Where is the densest part of the earth?

    b. Where should the strongest shock waves be located?

    c. If the shock waves penetrated all parts of the earth, through which part would the waves travel most slowly?

    d. Should the shock waves traveling from mantle to crust increase or decrease in speed?

Overview

Humans and all other living things are affected in many ways by the environment. Recall that the environment includes living things, nonliving things, natural forces, and different forms of energy. You are now familiar with the elements and compounds of the environment, how and why they react as they do, how they affect living things, and how we use the elements and compounds in our daily lives. You are acquainted with some of the natural forces of the environment, how they affect living things, and how we use the forces in making our lives more comfortable.

The law of conservation of matter and energy teaches us that neither matter nor energy can be created or destroyed but that both can be changed in form. As humans take the matter they need from the environment, they use some form of energy and change the matter and energy to some other forms. Thus, with the aid of geologists, chemists, and engineers, humans take iron from the earth and convert it into steel to be used in automobile bodies. When the automobile is no longer serviceable, they junk it. Rarely do humans return the iron in it to the earth. Seldom do they take pains to reuse the iron and other materials in the automobile. As a result, the store of iron and other valuable resources steadily decreases.

Under natural conditions, every kind of plant and animal requires for its survival some type of energy, food, and other materials. Every living thing obtains these requirements from its environment. As plants and animals carry on the life activities necessary for survival, they take into their bodies some substances present in the environment. At the same time, they also return other substances, such as wastes, to the environment. In time, the wastes change to usable materials which then become available for living things once more.

Unlike nonliving things, living things can replenish the environment and keep the number of living things on earth fairly constant. This is possible because of the process of *reproduction*. In this process, each type of living thing makes more of its own kind. In this unit, we will study how living things reproduce.

CHAPTER 16

HOW DO CELLS AND
SIMPLE ORGANISMS REPLENISH
THE ENVIRONMENT?

When you have completed this chapter, you should be able to:

1. *Define* asexual reproduction, chromosomes, regeneration, scion, stock.
2. *Discuss* the work of Redi in disproving spontaneous generation.
3. *Relate* the importance of genes to cell division, mitosis, and reproduction.
4. *Distinguish* between binary fission, budding, and sporing.
5. *Describe*, with examples, natural and artificial methods of vegetative reproduction.

In the laboratory experience that follows, you will observe reproduction in the bread mold.

Laboratory Experience

HOW DOES BREAD MOLD PRODUCE MORE
BREAD MOLD?

This laboratory experience requires about two weeks before observations can be completed.

Use your textbook or other sources of information to become familiar with a bread mold plant and the conditions this plant needs in order to grow.

A. Study the dish of bread mold you receive, first without and then with a magnifying glass or a dissecting microscope. Do not uncover the dish.

    1. Sketch or describe the appearance of a small portion of the mold as it appears magnified.

B. Place a blotter in a clean dish. Moisten the blotter. Obtain a quarter-slice of fresh white bread, and set it in the middle of the blotter.

Now, uncover the dish of mold and, with the tip of a toothpick, touch a few of the black spots present. Cover the dish again.

Gently draw the tip of the toothpick over the surface of the fresh bread. Discard the toothpick. Cover the dish containing the bread, and set it aside in a warm (about 30°C), dimly lighted or dark place. At intervals of three days, examine the bread with the magnifying glass. Whenever you see something different, sketch or describe what you see.

C. When black spots appear, prepare another piece of bread as you did in step B, and touch the spots with a clean toothpick. Draw the toothpick over the new piece of bread. Cover both dishes, and set the new dish in the warm place. At the end of a week, sketch or describe what you observe.

2. What happened in each of the dishes you prepared?

3. What family relationship exists between the three sets of mold plants? Explain.

4. Although you probably saw very little, if anything, on the toothpicks, what did you really do when you touched each toothpick to a fresh piece of bread?

5. Explain what made it possible for you to grow one generation of mold after the other.

6. In this experiment, how many parents did each generation of mold have?

Introduction

People once believed that new generations of living things arose from nonliving matter. For example, snakes were believed to arise from horsehairs and flies from decaying meat. This false idea about the production of living things was called *spontaneous generation*. It was not until late in the seventeenth century that *Francesco Redi*, an Italian physician, experimented and became the first to disprove that flies arose from decaying meat.

Redi placed slices of meat in three sets of jars (Fig. 16–1, page 294) and then observed what happened. His procedures and observations were:

1. The jars of the first set were left uncovered. In a short time, he saw flies entering and leaving the jars. A few days later, he saw wormlike organisms crawling about the meat. In a few more days, he saw these organisms develop into flies.

2. The jars of the second set were covered with cloth netting that allowed odors to escape from the jars, but prevented flies from entering

Meat

Open jars   Cloth netting   Sealed jars

Fig. 16–1. Redi's experiment.

the jars. At first, he noticed that flies gathered on the cloth. Some time afterward, he found wormlike organisms crawling around the meat in the jars. In a few days, he saw the organisms develop into flies.

3. The jars of the third set were tightly sealed with a material that prevented odors from escaping. He found neither flies nor wormlike organisms in or around these jars.

Redi reasoned that the odor of the decaying meat in the open jars and in the cloth-covered jars attracted adult flies. In the first set of jars, these flies laid eggs on or near the meat. In the second set of jars, the eggs fell through the holes of the netting and reached the meat. The eggs developed into wormlike organisms and then into flies. Since no odor escaped from the sealed jars, flies never came to them and never laid eggs near them. His conclusion was that each generation of flies comes from eggs laid by a preceding generation like itself.

Today we know that all living things give rise to offspring like themselves by the process of *reproduction.*

REPRODUCTION

In the course of living, every organism grows old, fights off germs, adjusts to its environment, escapes enemies, and competes for food with other organisms. In other words, organisms struggle to exist. Eventually, every organism loses the struggle and dies. If, before their death, the members of a species did not reproduce, the entire species would die out and become extinct. Although an individual need not reproduce in order to exist, some individuals must reproduce in order for the species to continue. Reproduction is the way in which organisms replenish the environment with more organisms of the same species.

Cell Division

Every organism, whether composed of one cell or many cells, begins life as a single cell. Cells increase in number by dividing into two.

By the same act, a one-celled organism reproduces as it divides and produces another one-called organism just like itself. In this case, the processes of cell division and reproduction are identical.

When a cell of a many-celled organism divides, the cell produces another just like itself but it does not reproduce the entire organism. In this case, cell division and reproduction are not identical processes. In our discussion, we will use the term reproduction to mean the production of new generations of organisms. We will use the term *cell division* to mean the production of another cell.

Genes

Among the most important cell structures are the *nucleus, nucleolus, cytoplasm,* and *cell membrane* (Fig. 16–2, page 296). The nucleus controls reproduction and all other cell activities. The nucleus is able to control the cell because the nucleus contains *genes*. These bodies control the hereditary traits of organisms and carry the traits from the old generation to the new one.

Chemically, genes are composed of a protein combined with DNA (*deoxyribonucleic acid*). DNA molecules are the only molecules known that can construct copies of themselves.

When molecules of DNA construct copies of themselves, new sets of genes are produced. The nucleus then divides, and one set of genes passes into each daughter nucleus. The nucleus divides in a series of complex steps called *mitosis*. This process is followed by a division of the cytoplasm. After the nucleus and the cytoplasm have divided, two cells are present where before there was one.

Steps in Mitosis

By the time a cell begins to divide, the new copies of its genes have been formed. Thus, two sets of genes are present—the original set and an exact copy. The sets of genes are located in microscopic threads called *chromosomes*. At first, the chromosomes are long and thin and hard to see (Fig. 16–2a, page 296). Soon they shorten and thicken, changing to dense rods (Fig. 16–2b). Each dense rod is really a double rod composed of an original set of genes and a copied set of genes.

The number and the kind of chromosomes formed are definite for each kind of organism. For example, sixteen chromosomes are formed in an onion cell, whereas forty-six chromosomes are formed in a human cell. Although different organisms may have the same chromosome number, the genes within their chromosomes are different.

While the chromosomes are forming within the nucleus, the nucleolus disappears. Fibers form on either side of the nucleus. The nuclear membrane disappears (Fig. 16–2c). Some fibers from the ends of the

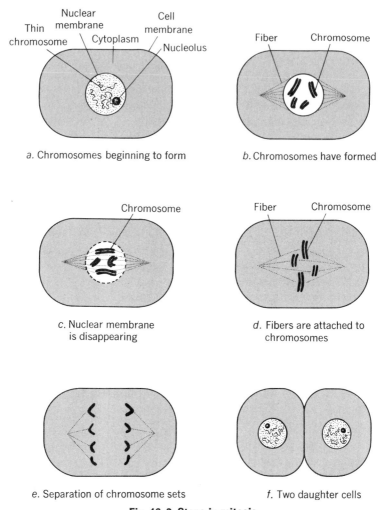

a. Chromosomes beginning to form   b. Chromosomes have formed

c. Nuclear membrane   d. Fibers are attached to
   is disappearing   chromosomes

e. Separation of chromosome sets   f. Two daughter cells

Fig. 16–2. Steps in mitosis.

cell become attached to each doubled chromosome (Fig. 16–2d). The doubled chromosomes line up in the center of the cell and are then pulled apart by the fibers. This action separates each original part of a chromosome from its copy (Fig. 16–2e). A new cell membrane forms between these two sets of chromosomes, isolating one set of chromosomes in each of the two *daughter cells*. In a short time, the chromosomes thin out, the nucleolus and nuclear membrane reappear, and two complete cells are produced (Fig. 16–2f).

After the genes in each set of chromosomes are copied again, each cell may increase in size and may divide once more. Thus, one cell becomes two; the two, four; and so on. As cell divisions continue, the organism grows.

TYPES OF REPRODUCTION

There are two basic types of reproduction. In *asexual reproduction,* only one parent is necessary. In *sexual reproduction,* two parents are necessary. Most simple organisms and some complex organisms can reproduce asexually. Most organisms, however, reproduce sexually. We will discuss asexual reproduction in this chapter and sexual reproduction in the next.

There are several types of asexual reproduction, but all have one characteristic in common—a set of genes from only one parent passes into the next generation. Consequently, the offspring usually have traits exactly like those of the parent and like those of one another.

BINARY FISSION

Binary fission is the splitting of an organism into two equal parts. It is the simplest type of reproduction. This process occurs in such simple one-celled organisms as the ameba, the paramecium, the bacterium, and the euglena.

After an ameba feeds, grows, and reaches full size, its nucleus divides by mitosis into two equal parts (Fig. 16–3). At the same time, the cytoplasm thins out in the middle, pinches in, and separates into two equal parts. Each of these parts has one nucleus in it. Each of the two new individuals, or daughter cells, is smaller than the parent cell. Both daughter cells have the same genes.

BUDDING

Budding is the splitting of an organism into two unequal parts. At the beginning of this process, the new generation grows out of the

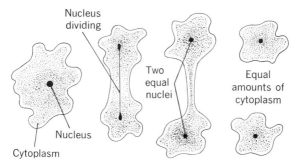

Fig. 16–3. Binary fission in the ameba.

parent and goes through its early development while still clinging to the parent. Organisms that reproduce by budding include yeast (a one-celled organism) and the hydra (a many-celled organism).

Budding in Yeast

In a yeast cell that is about to bud, the cytoplasm, which is always in motion, carries the nucleus over to one side of the cell (Fig. 16–4). Then the nucleus divides by mitosis into two equal parts. The cytoplasm and the cell wall close to the nucleus push out and form a small projection, the *bud*. One of the nuclei moves into the offspring cell, the bud. The other nucleus stays inside the older cell, or parent. Eventually, the cell wall grows in and separates the bud from the parent. Although the new cell is smaller than the parent cell, both cells have identical genes. A bud may produce a bud of its own before breaking away from the parent. This is the way in which a mass of attached yeast cells, called a *colony*, develops.

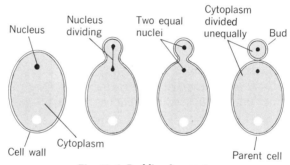

Fig. 16–4. Budding in yeast.

Budding in the Hydra

When the hydra reproduces, a small projection, the bud, forms on the body below the arms (tentacles) of the hydra (Fig. 16–5). The bud consists of numerous cells. As the bud matures, it develops a mouth and small tentacles. In time, the bud becomes detached from the older hydra and continues to grow on its own.

SPORING

Sporing is like binary fission except that instead of two cells being formed, many small cells of equal size are formed. These cells are *spores*. Spores are able to resist dryness and other unfavorable conditions. In those plants in which sporing is a method of reproduction, the spores are usually formed in sacs called *spore cases*.

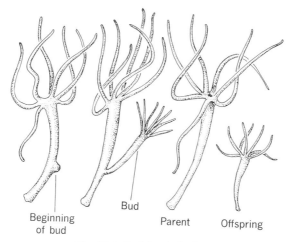

Fig. 16–5. Budding in hydra.

Organisms that reproduce by sporing include bread mold. In your laboratory experience, you transferred spores from a parent plant of bread mold to a fresh piece of bread and watched a new generation of plants develop.

When a bread-mold plant has food and moisture, it grows rapidly and spreads over its food. The free ends of many of its upright branches become swollen. The living material within each swollen tip then divides into many cells. Each cell becomes a spore (Fig. 16–6). The cell wall of the enlarged tip is now the spore case. Eventually, the spore case breaks open, and the spores are freed. Since the spores are tiny and very light in weight, air currents readily scatter them. Spores that land on moist organic material such as bread begin to grow into a new mold plant.

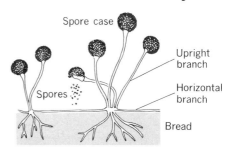

Fig. 16–6. Bread mold (enlarged).

VEGETATIVE REPRODUCTION

An organ of a plant that makes, transports, or stores food is called a *vegetative organ*. Leaves, buds, roots, and stems are the major vegetative organs of a plant. When these organs give rise to new organisms of the same kind, the type of reproduction is called *vegetative reproduction* (or *vegetative propagation*).

Tubers

Some stems develop underground and become swollen with excess food. Such a stem that has buds projecting from it is called a *tuber*. (Fig. 16–7). A white-potato plant produces several tubers. The buds on tubers are called "eyes."

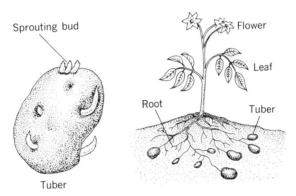

Fig. 16–7. Vegetative reproduction—tuber (white potato).

A potato tuber can be used to produce several potato plants. The tuber is cut into cubes, each bearing one "eye" on its outer surface. When the "eyes" are planted, a complete potato plant grows from each "eye." Each of these potato plants usually forms several new potatoes. Thus, many new independent potato plants can be reproduced from a vegetative organ (the tuber) of the potato plant. Potato farmers use this method of vegetative reproduction when they grow potatoes for market.

Bulbs

A bud that develops underground and has thick leaves full of excess food is called a *bulb* (Fig. 16–8). Such plants as the garlic, the onion, and the lily form several attached bulbs below the soil line. When the bulbs become separated, each one can develop into a complete, independent plant.

Stem Cuttings

A *stem cutting* (Fig. 16–9) is a piece of stem or branch that has been cut from a growing plant and then planted. After the cutting forms roots and its buds open into leaves, the cutting becomes established as a new plant. Such plants as the lilac, the geranium, and the begonia are often grown from cuttings.

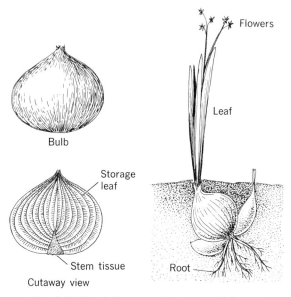

Fig. 16–8. Vegetative reproduction—bulb (onion).

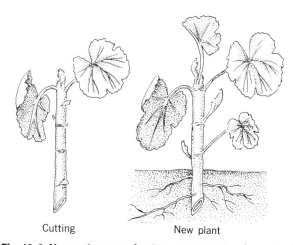

Fig. 16–9. Vegetative reproduction—stem cutting (geranium).

Fleshy Roots

A *fleshy root* is a root that becomes enlarged with stored food (Fig. 16–10, page 302). When a fleshy root is planted, it can develop leaves and a stem and form a complete plant. Such plants as the carrot and the sweet potato can be grown from their fleshy roots.

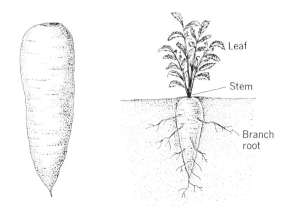

Fig. 16–10. Vegetative reproduction—fleshy root (carrot).

GRAFTING

Grafting is a type of vegetative reproduction that occurs only with human help. When grafting is carried out, part of one plant, either a twig or a bud, is cut off and transferred to another plant. The part of the first plant that has been cut off and is being transferred to the other plant is called the *scion*. The second plant, which has roots and receives the scion, is called the *stock* (Fig. 16–11).

Good grafts are usually obtained when the stock and the scion are of plants that are closely related. The closer the relationship between the plants, the better is the chance for the conducting tissue and the growing tissue of both plants to make good contact. Such contact

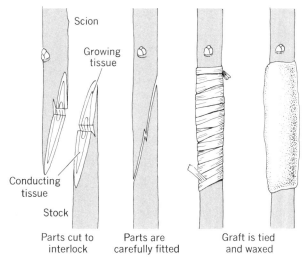

Fig. 16–11. Vegetative reproduction—grafting.

enables minerals, water, and food to pass between the grafted parts. The growing layers of both parts can then grow together and form a permanent attachment.

Ordinarily, grafting cannot be used to produce new breeds of fruits or flowers. Both the scion and the stock continue to grow as they did before being grafted. For example, if a branch from a purple-flowered lilac (the scion) is grafted to a white-flowered lilac (the stock), the scion continues bearing purple flowers, and the stock continues to bear white flowers.

REGENERATION

Regeneration is the process by which an organism grows back a part of its body that has been lost. In plants, regeneration is often the same as vegetative reproduction because complete plants are formed. In animals, regeneration also occurs, but to a limited extent. Hardly any animals reproduce naturally by regeneration.

Some animals have great powers of regeneration, others little. If a starfish is chopped into five equal parts, each part can grow into a new starfish. A lobster can regrow a leg that has been broken off, but the leg cannot regrow the rest of a lobster. The body of humans can repair small surface injuries, but it cannot grow back an appendix that has been surgically removed.

HOW ASEXUAL REPRODUCTION IN PLANTS IS VALUABLE TO HUMANS

Asexual reproduction in plants is valuable to humans for the following reasons:

1. One parent can produce new organisms.

2. All the new plants have the same characteristics as the parent variety.

3. Offspring are produced more rapidly by this type of reproduction than by sexual methods.

4. Offspring can be produced from seedless varieties of plants.

Looking Back

One-celled and other simple organisms replenish the environment by the process of reproduction. Many of these organisms reproduce asexually and give rise to one or more offspring exactly like themselves. Cell division by mitosis is important in this process.

Common methods of asexual reproduction include binary fission, budding, sporing, and vegetative reproduction.

Looking Ahead

Many simple organisms can reproduce either asexually or sexually. Most complex organisms can reproduce only sexually under natural conditions. Sexual reproduction in animals and plants is described in Chapter 17.

Multiple-Choice Questions

1. Where do cockroaches come from?
    a. eggs   b. garbage   c. worms   d. flies
2. Before a cell divides, the genes in the nucleus
    a. are halved   c. move to the surface
    b. are copied   d. move into the nucleolus
3. The number of parents that take part in asexual reproduction is
    a. none   b. 1   c. 2   d. 3
4. Two amebas that came from one parent are likely to have
    a. different genes
    b. the same genes
    c. the same number but not the same kind of genes
    d. the same kind of genes but not the same number
5. Which is the simplest type of reproduction?
    a. fertilization   c. binary fission
    b. sexual reproduction   d. grafting
6. In binary fission, the nucleus divides equally by the process of
    a. cell division   b. mitosis   c. sporing   d. budding
7. Unequal division of an organism occurs during the process of
    a. sporing   b. fission   c. spontaneous generation   d. budding
8. A plant and an animal that reproduce by budding are
    a. the euglena and the starfish   c. the yeast and the bread mold
    b. the yeast and the starfish   d. the yeast and the hydra
9. The asexual reproductive bodies of a mold plant are called
    a. buds   b. grafts   c. spores   d. scions
10. A plant that bears spores inside spore cases is the
    a. bacterium   b. bread mold   c. euglena   d. hydra
11. A mold plant growing on bread was probably brought to the bread by
    a. an air current   b. a water current   c. a bird   d. a worm
12. A vegetative part of a plant is a structure ordinarily used by the plant for
    a. reproduction   b. nourishment   c. locomotion   d. digestion
13. Lilies are usually grown by gardeners from
    a. stocks   b. grafts   c. bulbs   d. tubers

14. When a plant is grown from a stem cutting, the missing plant structures that grow back soon are the
    a. roots   **b.** buds   **c.** spores   **d.** seeds
15. The "eye" of a potato is a
    a. root   **b.** stem   **c.** bud   **d.** seed
16. An example of a fleshy root that can grow into a complete plant is the
    a. sweet potato   **b.** lilac   **c.** geranium   **d.** white potato
17. The part of a seedless grapefruit plant that could be used to produce more plants is the
    a. "eye"   **b.** seed   **c.** stem   **d.** leaf
18. The fruits that would be expected to grow on a plum twig that has been grafted to a peach tree are
    a. plums   **b.** peaches   **c.** nectarines   **d.** plums and peaches
19. Successful plant grafts depend mainly on direct contact between the layers of conducting cells and
    a. the root   **b.** bulbs   **c.** bark   **d.** dividing cells
20. An advantage of asexual reproduction is
    a. similarity of offspring
    b. the chance to improve the parent variety
    c. better offspring
    d. different offspring

Modified True-False Questions

1. *Regeneration* is the life process by which offspring are produced.
2. That flies seen around decaying meat did not come from the meat was proved by *Francesco Redi.*
3. The belief that horsehairs can turn into snakes or worms is called *spontaneous generation.*
4. *Reproduction* is the life process necessary for a species, but not an individual, to continue its existence.
5. A lobster can regrow a claw by the process of *binary fission.*
6. A plant that produces bulbs is the *onion.*
7. One advantage of *grafting* is that this process does not produce new types of fruit.
8. More seedless oranges can be produced by *planting seeds.*
9. An animal that can grow back a limb that has been lost is the *starfish.*
10. When yeast plants stick together after reproducing, they form *a spore.*
11. In Redi's experiment, flies appeared only in the jars that were either uncovered or covered by *netting.*
12. Offspring formed as a result of *binary fission* are equal in size.
13. If the *bud* of an ameba were cut out, the ameba would be unable to reproduce by binary fission.
14. A white potato is *a root.*
15. Onions can be reproduced more rapidly by *vegetative* reproduction than by sexual reproduction.

Thought Questions

1. Give the difference in meaning between the members of each of the following pairs of terms:
   a. scion and stock   c. tuber and stem cutting
   b. bulb and fleshy root   d. binary fission and budding
2. In addition to the examples given in this chapter, find two other examples of plants that can reproduce or be propagated by each of the following methods:
   a. binary fission   d. cuttings
   b. spore formation   e. grafting
   c. bulbs
3. By means of clearly labeled diagrams, show how budding in yeast differs from binary fission in the ameba.
4. When a lobster loses a claw, the lobster regenerates (regrows) the missing part. Why isn't this ability to regenerate considered a method of reproduction?
5. Explain why and how you would employ grafting in the following case: The roots of European grape vines, which bear sweet fruit, are destroyed by parasites when they are planted in American soil. The roots of the wild American grape vines, which bear sour fruit, are immune to parasites.
6. Newspaper advertisements often offer for sale a single tree that bears McIntosh, Delicious, and other apple varieties. Explain the reason for believing that the advertisement could be true.
7. Describe an experiment that you could perform to tell whether mosquitoes come from standing water.

CHAPTER 17

HOW DO COMPLEX ORGANISMS
REPLENISH THE ENVIRONMENT?

When you have completed this chapter, you should be able to:

1. *Distinguish* between (*a*) asexual and sexual reproduction (*b*) internal and external fertilization (*c*) a seed and a fruit.
2. *Trace* animal sex cells and plant sex cells from the structures that produce them until fertilization occurs.
3. *Describe* the early stages in the development of animal embryos.
4. *Compare* (*a*) the life cycle of a fish with that of a frog (*b*) the life cycle of a grasshopper with that of a moth.
5. *Contrast* the development of a bird embryo with that of a mammal embryo.
6. *Identify* and give the function of each part of a flower.
7. *Relate* the ability of offspring to survive to (*a*) the place of fertilization (*b*) the number of offspring produced (*c*) the amount of parental care.
8. *Indicate* how the adaptations for survival of a plant embryo differ from those of a bird embryo.

In the laboratory experience that follows, you will trace the path of sex cells in the reproductive systems of frogs.

Laboratory Experience

HOW DO THE REPRODUCTIVE SYSTEMS OF
MALE AND FEMALE FROGS DIFFER?

A. Your team will receive freshly killed male and female frogs, but you will not be told which is which. Place both frogs, backs uppermost, in a dissecting pan, and examine them carefully. Turn both frogs over, and continue your examination.
   1. Record any differences between the two frogs, such as color, length of body, thickness of body, size of toes, and so on.

B. Turn each frog on its back, and pin down its legs. With forceps, lift the skin near the crotch. With scissors, make a small incision (cut) in the raised skin. Insert the forceps into the cut, lift the muscular body wall, and cut into it too. Now insert the blunt-pointed blade of the scissors through both incisions, and cut through the body wall and skin, as indicated by the dotted lines in Fig. 17–1. Fold back and pin down the flaps of the body wall.

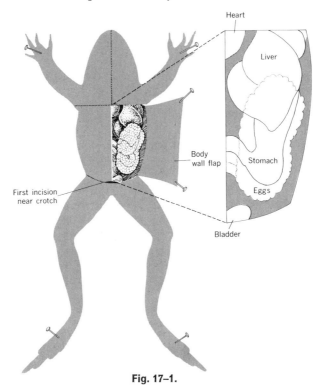

Fig. 17–1.

When you cut open the body wall of the female frog, you will find two large masses of small blackish spheres. Each mass is an *ovary*; each sphere is an *egg cell*. These structures are not present in the male.

C. Remove the eggs from the female, and put them aside temporarily. In both the female and the male, push aside the intestines, and study the remaining organs. Then consult Fig. 17–2, and compare your dissections with it. Identify the following female structures: *ovaries, eggs,* and *oviducts*. Identify the following male structures: *testes* and tiny *sperm ducts*.

　2. What external differences are there between the male and female frog?

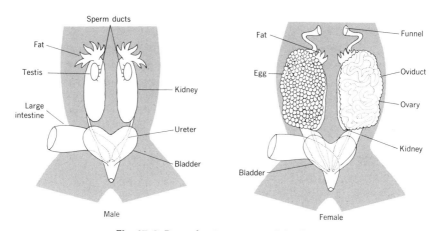

Fig. 17–2. Reproductive organs of the frog.

3. What internal differences are there?
4. What structures in the female frog do the eggs pass through on their way to the outside of the body? Name them in order.
5. What structures in the male frog do the sperms pass through on their way to the outside of the body? Name them in order.

D. Place one egg in a dish of Ringer's solution (a solution of salts like those in the body fluid of the frog), and examine the egg with a magnifying glass.

6. Describe the appearance of the egg.

E. Your teacher will mash a testis of the male frog in a little Ringer's solution and will place a drop of the mixture under the microscope.

7. Describe the appearance and behavior of a sperm.

Introduction

As we learned in the preceding chapter, asexual reproduction requires only one parent. In sexual reproduction, two parents are needed in order to produce offspring. One of these parents is the female and the other, the male. In the reproductive process, each parent contributes a special cell, called a *sex cell*. When the male sex cell unites with the female sex cell, the new offspring comes into being.

SEXUAL REPRODUCTION IN ANIMALS

Some simple animals, such as the hydra, can reproduce either asexually or sexually. All higher animals, such as the dog, reproduce only sexually.

Sex Glands

Sex cells are produced by special glands, called the *sex glands*. The sex gland of the male is called the *testis*; the sex gland of the female, the *ovary*. The sex cells produced by the testis are the *sperm cells*; the sex cells produced by the ovary are the *egg cells*.

The sperm cells leave the body of the male by way of delicate tubes called *sperm ducts*. The egg cells leave the body of the female by way of thick tubes called *oviducts*.

You observed all of these parts of the reproductive system in the frog in your laboratory experience (see Fig. 17–2, page 309).

Sperm and Egg Cells

In any particular kind of animal, the nucleus of a sperm cell and that of an egg cell are similar. In other respects, these sex cells are markedly different (Fig. 17–3).

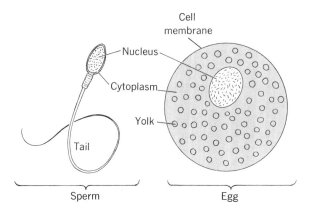

Fig. 17–3. The sex cells.

You have observed living sperm cells of a frog in your laboratory experience. The microscope reveals that a sperm cell is very small. One end of this cell is composed of a nucleus and a very small amount of cytoplasm. The rest of the cell is a long, whiplike tail. By lashing this tail back and forth, the sperm cell can move (swim) in water or body fluid. The male animal produces many more sperm cells than a female produces egg cells.

When you dissected the female frog, the eggs lying in the body cavity were readily visible to the unaided eye. An egg cell is usually round and is always much larger than a sperm cell. The egg cell is composed of a nucleus and a large amount of cytoplasm. The cytoplasm contains stored food, called *yolk*. The size of an egg cell depends upon the amount of yolk in it. The egg cell of birds (the "yellow") contains more yolk than that of other animals. The egg cell of mammals lacks yolk and is microscopic in size. Unlike the sperm cell, the egg cell has no structure for movement.

Fertilization

The new generation starts when a sperm cell enters an egg cell and unites with it. The union of a sperm cell and an egg cell is called *fertilization*. The combined cell that results from the union of the sperm and egg cells is called a *fertilized egg*. Fertilization may take place outside or inside the body of the female.

In water-dwellers, such as fishes, the eggs of the female usually pass out of her body into the water. The sperm cells then swim to these eggs and unite with them. This type of fertilization outside the body of the female is called *external fertilization*.

In some water-dwellers and in most land-dwellers, the eggs of the female are kept inside her body (within the oviducts). The sperms are deposited inside an oviduct, swim in the fluid present there, and unite with the eggs. This type of fertilization inside the body of the female is called *internal fertilization*. Internal fertilization occurs in birds, insects, mammals, and other animals.

Development of the Young

In some kinds of animals, the young organism develops outside of the mother's body. This type of development, called *external development*, is common in animals that fertilize externally, such as fishes. In other kinds of animals, the young develop inside the mother's body. This type of development, called *internal development*, is commonly seen among mammals.

In birds and insects, fertilization occurs internally, but development occurs externally. In mammals, both fertilization and development generally take place internally.

Whether fertilized externally or internally, the fertilized egg divides many times and forms an undeveloped organism called an *embryo*. Fig. 17–4, page 312, shows the early stages in the development of an embryo. These stages are much the same in all kinds of animals.

At first, the fertilized egg divides into two cells, forming a two-celled embryo. The two-celled embryo divides into four cells, the four cells into eight, and so on, until a ball of cells is formed. Later, as still more cells form, this ball becomes hollow, and one of its sides folds inward. At this stage, the embryo consists of two layers of cells. Shortly afterward, a third layer of cells forms between the other two layers.

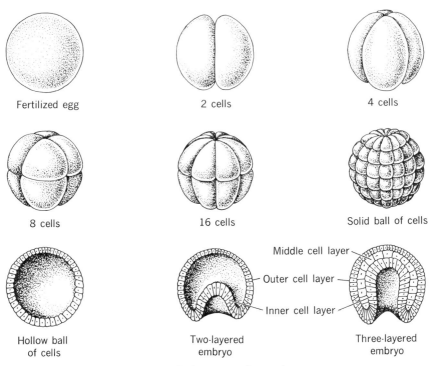

Fertilized egg   2 cells   4 cells

8 cells   16 cells   Solid ball of cells

Middle cell layer

Outer cell layer

Inner cell layer

Hollow ball   Two-layered   Three-layered
of cells   embryo   embryo

Fig. 17–4. Early stages of an embryo.

It is from these three layers that all of the organs of the new individual grow and take shape.

LIFE CYCLES OF SOME ANIMALS

The stages in the development of an organism from the time it is an egg until it grows to adulthood and takes part in reproduction itself is called its *life cycle*.

Life Cycle of a Fish

In the process called *spawning*, a female fish lays numerous eggs in the water, and the male sprays them with sperm cells. After fertilization, the developing embryo is nourished by the yolk of the egg. Before the yolk supply is exhausted, the embryo hatches into a tiny fish. At first, this fish feeds on the remaining yolk. When the yolk is used up, the fish gets its own food. The young fish grows. When its sex organs have developed, the fish finds a mate and reproduces (Fig. 17–5).

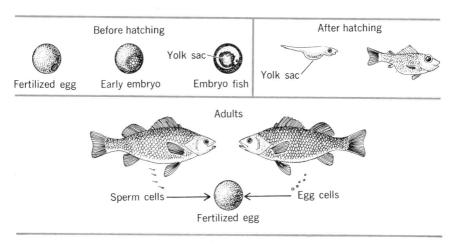

Fig. 17–5. Life cycle of a fish.

Life Cycle of a Frog

In the frog, as in the fish, both the fertilization of the egg and the development of the embryo are external and take place in shallow water. After fertilization, layers of protective jelly form around the fertilized egg, which is then warmed by the sun. The developing embryo is nourished by yolk. Before long, the embryo hatches into a *tadpole*, which gets its own food, grows, and undergoes a series of bodily changes. Eventually, the tadpole is transformed into a frog. This series of changes from egg to tadpole to adult is shown in Fig. 17–6, page 314.

The tadpole, which lives in water, breathes by means of gills and swims by means of a flat tail. As the tadpole grows, hind legs appear; later, forelegs appear. Meanwhile, the body of the tadpole absorbs the tail; lungs form and replace the gills. By this time, the tadpole has become a frog and can hop out of the water and onto land. When its sex organs are fully developed, the frog finds a mate and reproduces.

Life Cycle of a Bird

In birds, the fertilization of the egg is internal. A sperm may fertilize an egg cell (the yellow portion of the egg) within the oviduct of the female. Whether fertilized or not, the egg moves down the oviduct and becomes coated with albumen (the white), membranes, and a shell (Fig. 17–7, page 314).

After eggs have been laid in some sort of nest provided by the parent birds, the parents *incubate* the eggs (sit on them). In this way, the fertilized eggs are warmed by the body heat of the parents. Unless a

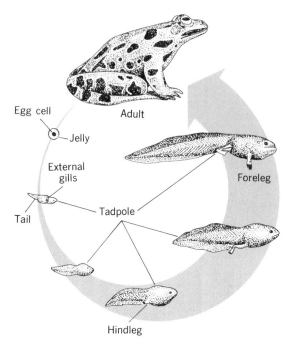

Fig. 17–6. Development of a frog.

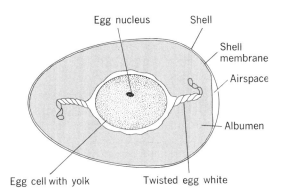

Fig. 17–7. Egg of a bird.

fertilized egg is kept warm, the embryo does not develop. Birds usually guard their eggs and take care of their young until the young can fly or can get their own food.

During the incubation period, the embryo bird develops near the center of the egg. Membranes that develop around the embryo produce a fluid which cushions the embryo. One of these membranes aids the respiration of the embryo. Oxygen and carbon dioxide are exchanged between the embryo and the outside by diffusion through this membrane and the pores that exist in the shell. At first, the embryo is nourished by the yolk, later by the "white." In a few weeks the young bird cracks the shell from within and hatches. When the young bird grows to adulthood, it finds a mate and reproduces.

Life Cycle of a Mammal

In mammals, both the fertilization of the egg and the development of the young are internal. The very young embryo becomes attached to a special part of the mother's oviduct, called the *uterus* (Fig. 17–8).

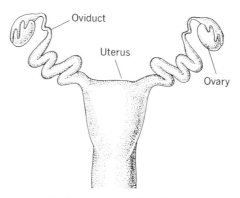

Fig. 17–8. Female reproductive organs.

Inside the uterus (Fig. 17–9, page 316), a special organ, called the *placenta*, develops. This organ exchanges food, oxygen, and wastes between the embryo and the mother. These materials are exchanged by way of two separate sets of capillaries. One set is connected to the circulatory system of the embryo and the other set to the circulatory system of the mother. The two sets are not directly connected. Nutrients and oxygen from the blood of the mother's capillaries diffuse into the embryo's capillaries. Similarly, wastes from the embryo pass into the mother's bloodstream and are eventually excreted by her kidneys.

As the embryo grows, the uterus, which has elastic, muscular walls, is stretched and becomes larger. At birth, the walls of the uterus automatically contract, pushing the young mammal out of the body of the parent. The young mammal is then fed on milk. Parent mammals care for their young until the young become independent. When it has fully developed, the young mammal finds a mate and reproduces.

Life Cycle of an Insect

In insects, the fertilization of the egg is internal, but the development of the young is external. The female deposits the fertilized eggs close

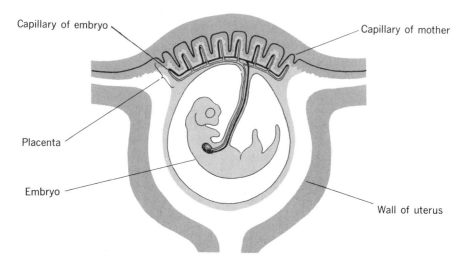

Capillary of embryo

Capillary of mother

Placenta

Embryo

Wall of uterus

Fig. 17–9. Embryo of a mammal.

to food that will be available to the young when they hatch. Except for a few types of insects, such as ants and bees, no other care is provided for the young. Before hatching, the embryo feeds on yolk within the egg. After hatching, the young insect feeds on plant or animal material. Like frogs, insects undergo a change in body form as they develop.

Insects, like other jointed animals, are covered by a shell-like skeleton that limits their growth. In the process called *molting*, the skeleton is shed and then formed anew. This happens several times. Before each new skeleton hardens, the insect grows rapidly. After the final molting, the insect is an adult and grows no more.

Some types of insects, such as the grasshopper, undergo a gradual change during their development. In these insects, the young resembles the adult but cannot fly because its wings are not fully developed. There are three stages in the life cycle of such insects—*egg, nymph,* and *adult* (Fig. 17–10a).

Other types of insects, such as the moth, undergo a complete change during their development. In these insects, the young is very different from the adult. There are four stages in the life cycle of such insects—*egg, larva, pupa,* and *adult* (Fig. 17–10b).

SEXUAL REPRODUCTION IN PLANTS

Some simple plants reproduce asexually. However, most plants have two stages in their life cycles. One is an asexual stage (spore formation), and the other is a sexual stage in which eggs are fertilized by sperms.

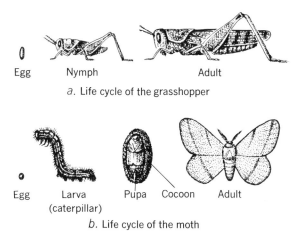

Egg   Nymph   Adult

a. Life cycle of the grasshopper

Egg   Larva   Pupa   Cocoon   Adult
       (caterpillar)

b. Life cycle of the moth

Fig. 17–10. Growth stages of insects.

In the familiar flowering plants, egg cells and sperm cells are produced within the *flower.*

Structure of a Flower

Most flowers have four groups of parts—*sepals, petals, stamens,* and *pistils* (Fig. 17–11).

Sepals are the leaflike outermost structures that are located in a circle at the base of a flower. Sepals are usually green and carry out photosynthesis, the food-making process, as leaves do. Since the sepals surround and cover the delicate flower before it is fully developed, they also protect it.

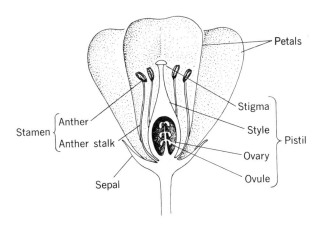

Fig. 17–11. Parts of a flower.

Petals are the parts that are usually brightly colored. They are leaflike in structure and are located just within the circle of sepals. Special cells near the bottom of the petals produce a fluid, called *nectar*. The nectar contains sugar and substances that give flowers their characteristic odor. The color, odor, and nectar of flowers are attractive to insects and other animals.

The stamens are organs that produce the male sex cells of the plant. Each stamen has two important parts:

1. The *anther stalk* is a slender structure that supports the anther.

2. The *anther* is a sac which contains *pollen grains*. Eventually, a pollen grain produces sperms.

The pistil is the organ that produces the female sex cells of the plant. In some kinds of plants, the flower has several pistils; in others, it has only one. A pistil consists of the following parts:

1. The *stigma*, which is the topmost part of the pistil, is sticky and often hairy. It can catch and hold pollen grains.

2. The *style*, which is below the stigma, connects the stigma to the ovary.

3. The *ovary*, which is the enlarged base of the pistil, contains one or more round bodies, called *ovules*. Eventually, each ovule produces an egg.

Pollination of a Flower

The first step in bringing together the eggs and sperms of flowers is *pollination*. In this process, pollen grains are transferred from an anther to a stigma. *Self-pollination* is the transfer of pollen from an anther of a flower to a stigma of the same flower. *Cross-pollination* is the transfer of pollen by some agent from an anther of one flower to a stigma of a flower on another plant of the same kind. Natural agents of cross-pollination include insects, wind, water, and some birds. *Artificial pollination* is the transfer of pollen by humans.

Fertilization in a Flower

As a result of pollination, several pollen grains may stick to a stigma. Then an extension grows out of each pollen grain. This extension is called a *pollen tube* (Fig. 17–12a). The tube grows down through the tissues of the stigma, the style, and the ovary and enters a tiny opening in an ovule. As the pollen tube enters the ovule, the end of the pollen tube dissolves.

By the time a pollen tube reaches an ovule, two sperm cells have

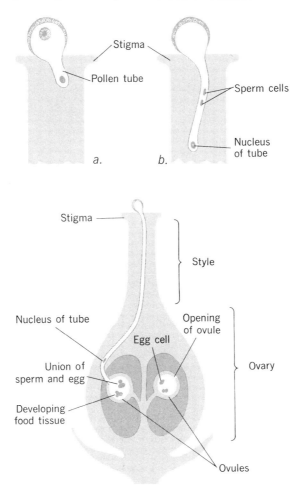

Fig. 17–12. Steps in the fertilization of a flower.

formed inside the pollen tube (Fig. 17–12b), and one egg cell has formed inside an ovule. The sperms move out of the pollen tube into the tissue of the ovule (Fig. 17–12c). One sperm unites with the egg, forming a fertilized egg cell that soon develops into an embryo plant. A food tissue then develops around the embryo.

Embryo and Seed

As the fertilized egg in an ovule develops and grows, the ovule itself grows. As the ovule enlarges, its outer covering hardens. The ripe ovule and its contents are called a *seed*. A seed is composed of a hard wall (called the *seed coat*), an embryo, and food tissue (Fig. 17–13, page 320).

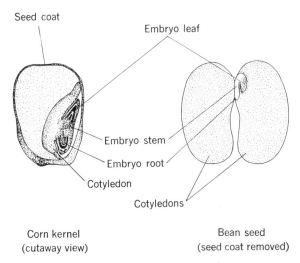

Fig. 17-13. Two types of seeds.

The major parts of a plant embryo are the *embryo tip*, the *embryo stem*, the *embryo root*, and either one or two *cotyledons*. The embryo tip eventually gives rise to the first leaves, buds (which later give rise to other leaves), and the growing point of the stem. The embryo stem gives rise to the middle part of the stem and its branches. The embryo root gives rise to the root and its branches. The cotyledons contain stored food which is used by the young plant when it begins to grow. When its own chloroplasts develop, the young plant can make its own food by photosynthesis.

Fruit

After the ovules inside an ovary have been fertilized, they grow. At the same time, the ovary itself enlarges. A ripened ovary, which encloses seeds and any flower parts still attached to it, is called a *fruit*. In some plants, the fruit is juicy and sweet; in others, it is hard and dry and unpleasant tasting.

A fruit usually contains many seeds. When its seeds are ripe, a fruit scatters its seeds. By being scattered, the seeds are separated from one another. Those seeds that land in favorable soil have a good chance of growing successfully, if they are not overcrowded.

The way in which seeds are scattered differs with the kind of plant (Fig. 17-14). The fruits of some plants possess wings or feathery parachutes. These structures enable the wind to scatter the seeds. The fruits of other plants have hooks that catch onto fur. These structures enable animals to scatter the seeds. The fruits of a few plants are balloonlike

Maple—by wind   Cocklebur—by animals   Squirting cucumber— by explosion

Fig. 17–14. Types of seed dispersal.

sacs that are under pressure. When these sacs explode, the seeds are shot out and scattered in many directions.

The Sprouting of Seeds

After seeds leave the parent plant, they lie inactive until the next growing season. When environmental conditions are suitable—that is, when adequate moisture, oxygen, and warmth are present—the embryo within the seed begins to sprout, or *germinate*. The stages in the germination of seeds are shown in Fig. 17–15.

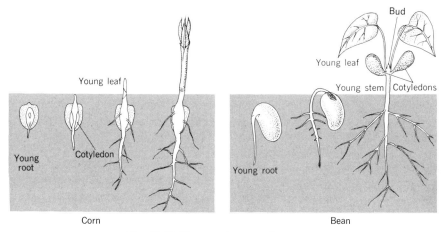

Corn   Bean

Fig. 17–15. The germination of seeds.

CARE OF THE YOUNG BY PARENTS

As we have learned before, some of the young of a species must live long enough to reproduce if the species is to continue. The survival of some offspring until they are old enough to reproduce can come about in one of two ways: (1) by producing so many offspring that, even without care, some of them are likely to live until they mate, or (2) by producing comparatively few offspring and taking very good care of them until they grow up.

In lower animals, both the fertilization of the eggs and the development of the young are external. In these cases, a very large number of eggs is produced, and many of them are fertilized, but they are then abandoned by the parents. Very often, other animals eat most of the fertilized eggs. This occurs in most species of fishes and amphibians. A few offspring, however, do manage to reach adulthood and reproduce.

In higher animals, the fertilization of the eggs is internal. In many species, the development of the young is also internal. These animals produce only a few eggs, most of which are fertilized. The young that develop are cared for by one or both parents for some period of time. This type of care occurs in birds and mammals. In humans, usually only one egg is produced at a time and is successfully fertilized. After birth, the young human is cared for by its parents for many years.

Many flowering plants produce large numbers of offspring and also provide for their growth. The parent plant produces many seeds and stores food within them for the young plants. The parent plant also produces structures that help in scattering the seeds. Then, when the seeds begin to grow, the new plants do not crowd one another to death.

HOW SEXUAL REPRODUCTION IN ORGANISMS IS VALUABLE TO HUMANS

In sexual reproduction, genes from two parents take part in controlling the inherited traits of the offspring. When these genes come together and mix in the fertilized egg, there is a chance for the offspring to inherit some favorable traits from each of its parents.

These facts enable humans to develop breeds of plants and animals having specific desired features. Sperm cells (or pollen grains, which form sperm cells) from males that have some desired characteristic are used to fertilize egg cells from females that have another desired characteristic. The offspring that develop often have both desired characteristics. Examples of organisms that have been developed in this fashion are the corn plant and the mule. More information on this subject is given in Chapter 19, pages 353–356.

Looking Back

By sexual reproduction, complex animals and plants replenish the environment with other organisms like themselves. Sexual reproduction requires two parents. In this process, a sperm and an egg unite, forming a single cell that develops into an offspring. In general, parents that reproduce sexually care for their offspring to some extent until the offspring can obtain food and otherwise care for itself.

Looking Ahead

In both asexual and sexual reproduction, the offspring produced are like their parents because the offspring receive their traits from their parents. How the traits are passed on from parent to offspring is the subject of Chapter 18.

Multiple-Choice Questions

1. A cell contributed by each of two parents to the next generation is called a
   a. spore cell   b. sex cell   c. pollen grain   d. fertilized egg
2. A jellyfish can reproduce either asexually or sexually, but a cat can reproduce only
   a. asexually   b. by regeneration   c. sexually   d. by incubation
3. Sperms are produced by the
   a. testis   b. ovary   c. sperm duct   d. oviduct
4. The tubes through which frog eggs leave the body of the parent are the
   a. sperm ducts   b. yolk ducts   c. pollen ducts   d. oviducts
5. Sperm cells are able to swim in a fluid because they have
   a. testes   b. yolk   c. tails   d. ducts
6. Stored food in a fish egg is called
   a. starch   b. cotyledon   c. sugar   d. yolk
7. Which two structures unite in sexual reproduction?
   a. fertilized eggs   c. egg and sperm
   b. albumen and yolk   d. ovary and testis
8. During internal fertilization in a bird, sperms are deposited in which organ of the female?
   a. ovary   b. egg   c. oviduct   d. placenta
9. Internal fertilization and external development occur in
   a. most fishes   c. most mammals
   b. most amphibians   d. all birds
10. The eggs of birds have
    a. no protective covering   c. a jellylike covering
    b. a hard covering   d. a leathery covering
11. As a fertilized egg develops into an offspring, the egg undergoes
    a. tremendous growth in size   c. three cell divisions
    b. shrinkage   d. many cell divisions

12. Before hatching, the young organism is called
    a. an ovule   **b.** a baby   **c.** a spawn   **d.** an embryo
13. The young animal that hatches from a frog's egg is called a
    a. nymph   **b.** pupa   **c.** tadpole   **d.** fertilized egg
14. A tadpole would soon die if its
    a. nostrils were plugged with wax   **c.** lungs were removed
    b. gills were cut off   **d.** tail were held out of water
15. The organ that grows first, as a tadpole changes form into a frog, is the
    a. hind leg   **b.** foreleg   **c.** tail   **d.** lung
16. A chick cannot develop inside a hen's egg unless the egg is
    a. fertilized and kept warm   **c.** laid in a nest
    b. unfertilized and kept warm   **d.** kept warm in a nest
17. A chick embryo inside the egg gets oxygen through
    a. the placenta   **b.** its lungs   **c.** pores in the shell   **d.** its gills
18. In which structure does the embryo of a rabbit develop?
    a. uterus   **b.** stomach   **c.** ovary   **d.** intestine
19. The embryo of a cow gets rid of its waste carbon dioxide through
    a. its lungs   **c.** the placenta
    b. the cow's large intestine   **d.** the cow's stomach
20. The embryo of an insect feeds on
    a. blood   **b.** yolk   **c.** grass   **d.** frogs
21. The stages in the life of a grasshopper are
    a. egg, nymph, adult   **c.** egg, pollen, seed
    b. egg, larva, pupa, adult   **d.** egg, caterpillar, adult
22. The sex cells of a flowering plant are located in the
    a. sepals and petals   **c.** stigma and nectar
    b. fruit and seed   **d.** stamens and pistils
23. In order to reach an ovule, a pollen tube grows through the
    a. stigma, stamen, petal   **c.** sepals, stamen, stigma
    b. stigma, style, ovary   **d.** cotyledon, style, ovule
24. The egg of a lettuce plant develops in the
    a. pollen grain   **b.** ovule   **c.** stigma   **d.** fruit
25. The sperm of a potato plant develops in the
    a. testis   **b.** sperm tube   **c.** pollen   **d.** pollen tube
26. The part of the flower that becomes the seed is the
    a. petal   **b.** ovule   **c.** sepal   **d.** ovary
27. A ripened ovary of a flower is called the
    a. embryo   **b.** seed   **c.** pistil   **d.** fruit
28. Maple seeds are scattered by
    a. wind   **b.** insects   **c.** humans   **d.** water
29. In order to start growing, most seeds need
    a. water, oxygen, minerals   **c.** yolk, water, light
    b. water, oxygen, warmth   **d.** light, pollen, nectar
30. The greatest amount of parental care is found among organisms that
    a. reproduce asexually   **c.** produce many offspring
    b. have external fertilization   **d.** produce few offspring

Modified True-False Questions

1. Two parents are required in *vegetative* reproduction.
2. Egg cells are produced in the *ovaries*.
3. The smaller of the two sex cells is the *yolk* cell.
4. In general, *more* sperm cells are produced than egg cells.
5. *External* fertilization is characteristic of fishes.
6. *External* development is characteristic of mammals.
7. Embryo fish and very young fish feed on *yolk*.
8. When laid, frog eggs are covered by *a shell*.
9. The true egg cell of a chicken is the *white* of the egg.
10. When a grasshopper molts, it sheds the *skeleton*.

Thought Questions

1. Give a scientific explanation for each of the following true statements:
   a. In the spring, a farmer sprayed his apple orchard with DDT in order to get rid of flies and mosquitoes. That year he had no apple crop.
   b. If both cotyledons are removed from a bean seed and the young plant is then covered with soil, a new plant fails to grow. However, if one cotyledon is removed and the young plant is then covered with soil, a new plant grows for a few weeks.
   c. Breeders who are trying to develop a new variety of tulip sometimes cover the tulip flowers with plastic bags.
   d. Although the juicy part of a cherry cannot nourish the embryo cherry plant that is in the seed, the juicy part is valuable to the embryo in some other way.
   e. Codfish may produce as many as 5 million eggs in one mating season, but fewer than ten offspring are likely to grow to adulthood.
2. Compare a sperm cell with an egg cell with respect to:
   a. the nucleus that each contains
   b. the amount of cytoplasm in each
   c. the ability of each to move

CHAPTER 18

HOW ARE TRAITS PASSED FROM GENERATION TO GENERATION?

When you have completed this chapter, you should be able to:

1. *Define* reduction division, dominant trait, recessive trait, gene, pure-bred, hybrid, mutation, DNA.
2. *Distinguish* between (*a*) complete and incomplete dominance (*b*) acquired and inherited characteristics.
3. *Discuss* each of the following kinds of cells, including the number of chromosomes found in each: body cells, sex cells, fertilized egg cells, polar bodies.
4. *State* Mendel's three laws of heredity.
5. *Predict* the types of offspring produced by parents whose heredity is known.
6. *Summarize* the contributions to our knowledge of mutation by De Vries, Morgan, and Muller.

In the laboratory experience that follows, you will investigate how picking combinations affects heredity.

Laboratory Experience

WHAT DETERMINES THE WAY IN WHICH YOU PICK PAIRS?

A. You will receive 50 red and 50 white "pop-it" beads in separate bowls. Assume that each bead represents a gene carried in the nucleus of a sex cell. Let the contents of one bowl represent the eggs produced by a female and the contents of the other bowl the sperms produced by a male.

Draw one bead from the "female" bowl. This bead represents a gene in an egg cell. Draw one bead from the "male" bowl, and

attach it to the first bead. The second bead represents a gene in a sperm cell. The pair of beads you have picked then represents the two genes in a fertilized egg—one from the female parent and the other from the male parent. In the same fashion, draw ten more pairs of beads.
1. What color combination(s) did you get?
2. If you continued drawing pairs, what combinations could result? Explain.
3. Why is it impossible to get any other color combinations?
B. Separate the beads you have joined and replace them in their bowls. Mix your 50 white and 50 red beads in one bowl. You will be working together with one of your classmates, whose sets of beads should be mixed together in another bowl. You now have two bowls, each containing both red and white beads.

Assume that one bowl is a female organism that produces 100 eggs. Each of 50 of these eggs carries a gene for redness, and each of the other 50 eggs carries a gene for whiteness. The other bowl, a male, contains 100 sperms, 50 carrying a gene for redness and 50 carrying a gene for whiteness.
4. If you picked one bead from the egg bowl and one from the sperm bowl, what color combination(s) could you get?
5. Which combination should appear most often? Why?
6. What are the chances of picking a red–white combination as compared to either red–red or white–white? Explain.
C. Copy the table below into your notebook. Thoroughly mix the beads in the male bowl. Do the same for the female bowl. With your eyes closed, draw a bead from the male bowl and one from the female bowl at the same time. Pop them together, and hand the pair to your partner, who will tally the pair in the table. Continue this procedure until all the beads have been used up.

	Red–Red	Red–White	White–White
First student			
Second student			
Total			

D. Separate all the pairs of beads, placing 50 red ones and 50 white ones in one bowl and the others in the second bowl. Repeat the procedure of picking pairs, this time letting your partner pick the pairs as you keep the tally. Total the results.
7. Are your results different from your partner's?

8. Explain why the totals are not in a perfect ratio of 1:2:1 (50 red–red:100 red–white:50 white–white).
9. Under what conditions would the picking of pairs result in a perfect 1:2:1 ratio?

Introduction

Organisms that have survived in a particular environment possess certain traits suitable for their way of life. When the organisms reproduce, these traits are passed on to their offspring. By this means, the offspring come to have traits that are suitable for the same way of life as that of their parents.

The development of the traits in each new generation of offspring is controlled by the genes that the offspring inherit. As explained in our discussion of mitosis (see Chapter 16, pages 295–296), genes are located in chromosomes.

SIMILARITIES AND DIFFERENCES BETWEEN GENERATIONS

In organisms that reproduce by an asexual method, inheritance is relatively simple because mitosis is the major process involved in reproduction. During mitosis, the genes in the set of chromosomes in a parent cell make copies of themselves, forming two sets. Then, one set of chromosomes passes into one daughter cell, and the second set into the other daughter cell. Since the genes in the offspring cells are identical, the offspring develop the same traits as the parent had.

In organisms that reproduce sexually, inheritance is complicated because other processes, in addition to mitosis, are involved. As a result of these processes, the offspring are rarely exactly alike. Although they resemble one another and their parents, the offspring differ not only from one another, but also from their parents. The differences that are present among all organisms of the same species are called *variations*.

Variations sometimes appear in organisms that reproduce asexually. However, variations occur much more often in organisms that reproduce sexually. This happens because one set of chromosomes, containing genes from the male parent, and a second set of chromosomes, containing genes from the female parent, pass into one offspring. This combination of two sets of genes makes it possible for the offspring to resemble its parents in some respects and differ from them in other respects.

In order to understand how this comes about, we must first follow the steps in the formation of the sperm cells and the egg cells. Then we will be able to see how the chromosomes in the sperm cells and in the egg cells reach the next generation.

CHROMOSOME NUMBERS IN CELLS

In many-celled organisms that reproduce by means of fertilization, only some cells take a direct part in the process. The cells that take no direct part in fertilization are called *body cells*. Examples of such cells are the cells of muscle, nerve, and skin. The nucleus of each body cell contains chromosomes (which contain the genes).

The number of chromosomes present in body cells is the same for all organisms of a particular species. However, the number of chromosomes is different in different species. For example, each of the body cells of all fruit flies has 8 chromosomes (or 4 pairs); of pea plants, 14 chromosomes (or 7 pairs); and of humans, 46 chromosomes (or 23 pairs). The chromosome number that is characteristic of the body cells of a species is called the *species number* of chromosomes.

The cells that take direct part in fertilization are called *sex cells*. These cells are the egg cells and the sperm cells. The nuclei of these cells contain chromosomes, but the number of chromosomes in the nucleus of a sex cell is one-half the number in the nucleus of a body cell. For example, in the fruit fly, which has 8 chromosomes in its body cells, the sex cells contain only 4 chromosomes; in the pea plant, which has 14 chromosomes in its body cells, the sex cells contain only 7 chromosomes; and in the human, which has 46 chromosomes in its body cells, the sex cells contain only 23 chromosomes. The chromosome number that is characteristic of the sex cells of a species is one-half the species number of chromosomes. The change in the chromosome number from the species number to one-half that number takes place when sex cells are formed.

The fruit fly is used as an example in the following discussion because it has a small number of chromosomes.

The Chromosomes of Sperm Cells

Immature sperm cells in the male reproductive glands (the testes) at first contain the species number of chromosomes (Fig. 18–1a, page 330). As these cells develop, they go through a special cell division. In this division, two new cells of equal size are formed, and one-half of the species number of chromosomes enters each cell. This type of division, which reduces the chromosome number to one-half the species number, is called *reduction division*. For example, when a cell having a species number of 8 chromosomes undergoes reduction division, each of the two new cells that are formed has 4 chromosomes.

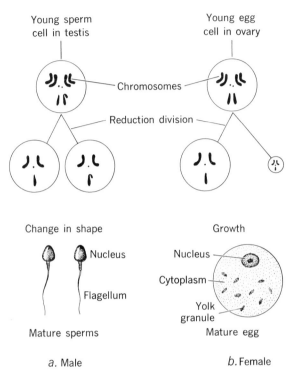

Fig. 18–1. Formation of sperm and egg cells.

After the reduction division has taken place, the shape of each developing sperm cell changes. The cytoplasm of the cell shrinks, and a *flagellum* (a whiplike tail) forms. The cell that is produced is a mature (ripe) sperm cell which can move and which contains one-half the species number of chromosomes. Mature sperm cells can leave the testes.

The Chromosomes of Egg Cells

Immature egg cells, which are located in the female reproductive glands (the ovaries), first contain the species number of chromosomes (Fig. 18–1b). Like the developing sperm cells, the young egg cells go through reduction division. As a result, the cells that are formed have one-half the species number of chromosomes.

Unlike the cells produced in the male, which are of equal size, the cells produced by the reduction division in the female are of unequal size. One cell is large and contains a great deal of cytoplasm; the other is tiny and contains very little cytoplasm. However, both cells have one-half the species number of chromosomes. The large cells are unripe egg cells, which develop further. The tiny cells eventually disappear and take no part in reproduction.

Yolk (made from nutrients brought to the ovary by the blood) then accumulates in the large cell and, as a result, the cell grows. When growth is complete, a mature egg cell is formed. This cell contains food and, like the mature sperm cell, has one-half the species number of chromosomes. When mature, the cells are released from the ovaries.

The Chromosomes of Fertilized Egg Cells

In the process of fertilization, a sperm cell meets and enters an egg cell. Then the nuclei of the two sex cells become transformed into chromosomes, which remain in the fertilized egg. This is what happens when a sperm cell of a fruit fly, containing 4 chromosomes (one-half the species number), and an egg cell, also containing 4 chromosomes (one-half the species number), meet (Fig. 18–2).

After the sperm enters the egg, the fertilized egg contains 8 chromosomes, which is the original species number of the fruit fly. The fertilized egg cell then divides many times and becomes an embryo. Since all the cell divisions in this process involve only mitosis, every body cell that eventually develops in this new individual also contains the species number of chromosomes. Upon reaching adulthood, the new individual's ovaries or testes form the sex cells for the next generation.

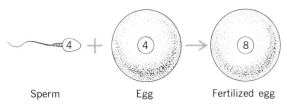

Sperm   Egg   Fertilized egg

Fig. 18–2. Fertilization in the fruit fly.

We can now see that half the number of chromosomes and genes in a fertilized egg come from the male parent and half from the female parent. As each trait of the offspring develops, it is influenced by two genes—one from the male parent and one from the female.

In the rest of this chapter, we will study the reactions between these two genes and the development of traits that may resemble or differ from those of one or both parents.

EXPERIMENTS IN HEREDITY

The study of how organisms inherit similarities and differences is called *heredity*. An Austrian monk, *Gregor Mendel* (1822–1884), carried on many experiments with the garden pea plant. As a result of his experiments, Mendel was the first to succeed in explaining heredity. He did this even before chromosomes and genes had been discovered.

Among the inherited traits of the pea plant that Mendel studied were the length of the stem, the color of the flower, the form of the seed, and the color of the seed. He observed that there were opposite (or contrasting) characters for each of these traits. For example, some stems were tall, and others were short; some flowers were purple, and others were white.

Mendel started his experiments with *purebred strains*; that is, all the offspring were just like their ancestors. For example, he had short pea plants that came from short ancestors, and tall plants that came from tall ancestors. He transferred pollen from the anthers of some purebred tall plants to the pistils of other purebred tall plants. He also allowed each purebred tall plant to self-pollinate. After collecting all the seeds that developed, he planted them. He found that all the seeds grew into tall plants like their parents. In other words, 100% of the offspring were tall. When Mendel pollinated purebred short plants in a similar experiment, he found that purebred short parents produced all (100%) short offspring.

Mendel then artificially placed pollen from purebred tall plants on the pistils of purebred short plants. Similarly, he placed pollen from purebred short plants on the pistils of purebred tall plants. All of the offspring that resulted from these crosses were as tall as their tall parents. Only tallness, the contrasting character to shortness, appeared in the first generation offspring, or F_1. Mendel called the characteristic that appeared in the F_1 the *dominant character*. The character that did not appear in the F_1 Mendel called the *recessive character*. Such offspring of contrasting parents, which exhibited only the dominant character, he called *hybrids*.

Mendel found that there were three fundamental laws that determine how heredity operates. It has since been found that *Mendel's laws* generally apply to all organisms, including humans. These three laws are known as the *law of dominance*, the *law of segregation and recombination*, and the *law of independent assortment*.

LAW OF DOMINANCE

From the results of numerous experiments, Mendel was able to state the first law of heredity, known as the law of dominance: When two parents that are pure for contrasting characters are crossed, the dominant character appears in the hybrid, and the recessive character is hidden.

Modern Explanation of Dominance

Each body cell and each immature sex cell of pure-strain parents, such as tall pea plants, has two sets of chromosomes—the species number of chromosomes. Therefore, each of these cells contains two genes for tallness. As we have seen, when a parent produces sex cells, the number of genes (or chromosomes) is reduced to one-half of what it was. Thus, every sex cell contains one-half the species number of chromosomes and only one gene for tallness.

After the egg and sperm cells unite, the fertilized egg contains a gene for tallness from one parent and another gene for tallness from the other parent. When the fertilized egg develops into the offspring, each offspring—having a combination of two genes for tallness—grows up to be like its parents. It is the chemical reactions controlled by the DNA of the genes that determine the final appearance of the offspring. When an offspring has two like genes for a trait, the offspring is said to be purebred.

In the first part of the laboratory experience, you picked from separate bowls only red beads and only white beads and then paired them. In this case, each pair of picked beads represents a hybrid offspring having one dominant and one recessive gene. As the offspring grows, some chemical reaction between the dominant and recessive genes enables only one of the genes—the dominant one—to show its effect.

In the case of Mendel's peas, then, the dominant gene controlled the development of a long stem in each hybrid individual. The recessive gene is still present in every hybrid, but it is inactive and is overshadowed by the dominant gene. Hybrids have two unlike genes for each trait, in contrast to purebreds, which have two like genes for each trait.

Examples of the Law of Dominance

By using a few symbols and a diagram called the *Punnett square,* it becomes easy to see the relationships between the combination of genes that an organism inherits and its final appearance. The Punnett square method is also useful in working out problems in heredity. In this method, letters are used to represent genes: a capital letter (such as T) for the dominant gene and a small letter (such as t) for the recessive gene. These symbols are explained in a key at the beginning of the problem.

Example 1. Cross two pure tall pea plants, showing the gene combinations and the appearance of their offspring.

Key: Let T = gene for tallness (dominant)
t = gene for shortness (recessive)

	Female		*Male*
Parents:	pure tall	$\times$	pure tall
Genes of Parents:	TT	$\times$	TT
Genes in Sex Cells:	T		T

Possible Fertilizations:

Sperms
T

Eggs   T | TT |

Offspring (F_1):

Gene Combinations	*Appearance*
all TT	100% tall (pure)

Thus, we readily see that Mendel obtained all tall pea plants from parents that were purebred tall because the sex cells of the parents contained only genes for tallness.

Example 2. Cross two pure short pea plants, showing the gene combinations and the appearance of their offspring.

Key: Same as in Example 1.

	Female		*Male*
Parents:	pure short	$\times$	pure short
Genes of Parents:	tt	$\times$	tt
Genes in Sex Cells:	t		t

Possible Fertilizations:

Sperms
t

Eggs   t | tt |

Offspring (F_1):

Gene Combinations	*Appearance*
all tt	100% short (pure)

Thus, we readily see that Mendel obtained all short pea plants from parents that were purebred short because the sex cells of the parents contained only genes for shortness.

Example 3. Cross a pure tall pea plant with a pure short pea plant, showing the gene combinations and the appearance of their offspring.

Key: Same as in Example 1.

	Female		*Male*
Parents:	pure tall	$\times$	pure short
Genes of Parents:	*TT*	$\times$	*tt*
Genes in Sex Cells:	*T*		*t*

Possible Fertilizations:

Sperms

t

Eggs   *T* $\boxed{Tt}$

Offspring (F_1):

Gene Combinations	*Appearance*
all *Tt*	100% tall (hybrid)

Thus, we see that Mendel obtained all tall offspring from crossing parents with contrasting characters because the only possible combination of genes at fertilization was *Tt*—one dominant gene from the pure tall parent and one recessive gene from the pure short parent.

LAW OF SEGREGATION AND RECOMBINATION

Mendel crossed many first-generation hybrid tall pea plants and obtained their seeds. After planting these seeds, Mendel found that some plants of this second generation (or F_2) were tall, whereas others were short. When he counted the numbers of tall and short offspring, he found that the ratio of plants showing the dominant character to those showing the recessive character was 3:1.

From the results of many experiments of this type, Mendel was able to state the second law of heredity, known as the law of segregation and recombination: When two hybrids are crossed, the recessive character, which had been hidden in the F_1 generation, is segregated (separated) from the dominant character. At fertilization, there is a chance for the recessive characters to recombine (come together again) and appear in some members of the F_2 generation.

Modern Explanation of Segregation and Combination

As sex cells mature and reduction division occurs, the two sets of chromosomes in the immature sex cells separate, and one set of chromosomes moves into each new cell. As a result, every egg and sperm cell contains only one of any pair of genes. When fertilization takes place, there are chances for like or unlike genes to meet.

What Are the Chances?

In the second part of the laboratory experience, you picked red and white beads together from bowls containing both red and white beads. In this case, each pair you picked was one of these three types of combinations: red–red, red–white, white–white. You found that, by chance, the red–white combination appeared more often than either the red–red or white–white combinations.

In the same way that only chance determined the possible combinations of beads you picked, chance also determines the combinations of genes that are possible when a sperm fertilizes an egg. These possible combinations are:

1. If a sperm having a dominant gene unites with an egg having a dominant gene, the offspring has two dominant genes and shows the dominant character (pure).

2. If a sperm having a dominant gene unites with an egg having a recessive gene, the offspring has one dominant gene and one recessive gene and shows the dominant character (hybrid).

3. If a sperm having a recessive gene unites with an egg having a dominant gene, the offspring has one dominant gene and one recessive gene and shows the dominant character (hybrid).

4. If a sperm having a recessive gene unites with an egg having a recessive gene, the offspring has two recessive genes and shows the recessive character (pure).

Thus, there are three chances that an offspring will show the dominant character to one chance that it will show the recessive character (Fig. 18–3).

Note that what Mendel called *segregation* takes place during what we now call *reduction division*; and what he called *recombination* takes place at *fertilization*.

The reason for the 3:1 ratio becomes clearer when we work out a cross of two hybrids with a Punnett square.

Key: Let T = gene for tallness (dominant)
t = gene for shortness (recessive)

	Female		*Male*
Parents (F_1):	hybrid tall	$\times$	hybrid tall
Genes of Parents:	Tt	$\times$	Tt
Genes in Sex Cells:	T or t		T or t

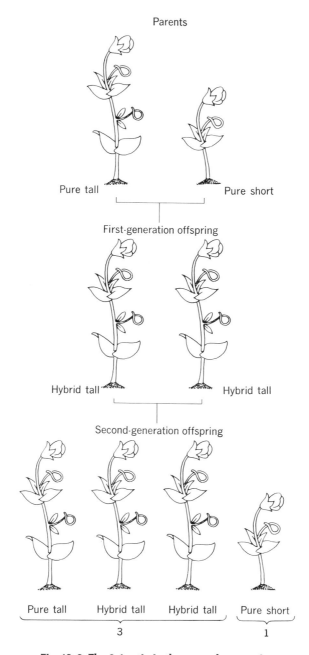

Fig. 18–3. The 3:1 ratio in the second generation.

Possible Fertilizations:

Sperms

		T	t
Eggs	T	TT	Tt
	t	Tt	tt

Offspring (F_2):

Gene Combinations	Appearance
$\frac{1}{4}$ TT	25% tall (pure)
$\frac{2}{4}$ Tt	50% tall (hybrid)
$\frac{1}{4}$ tt	25% short (pure)

The fraction $\frac{1}{4}$ means 1 out of 4 possible gene combinations; $\frac{2}{4}$ means 2 out of 4 possible gene combinations. Note that the ratio of the different gene combinations ($\frac{1}{4}$ TT: $\frac{2}{4}$ Tt: $\frac{1}{4}$ tt) is 1:2:1. Note further that since all tall plants look alike, regardless of the genes within them, there are really 75% tall plants and 25% short plants. This ratio, 75%:25% (or 3:1), is the ratio of the appearance of tall to short plants, whereas 1:2:1 is the ratio of the gene combinations in the same F_2 generation.

LAW OF INDEPENDENT ASSORTMENT

In some of his experiments, Mendel used plants that were hybrid for two traits. For example, he crossed plants that were hybrid tall and had hybrid yellow seeds with others of the same type. He found that the ratio relating to the appearance of the offspring was 9:3:3:1. That is, out of every 16 offspring, 9 were tall and yellow-seeded; 3 were tall and green-seeded; 3 were short and yellow-seeded; and 1 was short and green-seeded.

From the results of many such experiments, Mendel was able to state the third law of heredity, known as the law of independent assortment (or unit characters): Each character behaves as a unit and is inherited independently of any other character.

Modern Explanation of Independent Assortment

It is now known that, in peas, the genes for height (tallness or shortness) and the genes for seed color (yellowness or greenness) lie in different pairs of chromosomes of the two sets of chromosomes present in body cells and in young sex cells. When the immature sex cells undergo reduction division, their two sets of chromosomes and genes move apart and enter separate egg cells and sperm cells. At fertilization, several different gene combinations can occur.

What Are the Chances?

The appearance ratio for combinations of two independent traits is $9 : 3 : 3 : 1$. This ratio represents 16 $(9 + 3 + 3 + 1)$ possible gene combinations at fertilization. Fully written out, this means that of the 16 possibilities, $\frac{9}{16}$ are tall plants with yellow seeds, $\frac{3}{16}$ are tall plants with green seeds, $\frac{3}{16}$ are short plants with yellow seeds, and $\frac{1}{16}$ are short plants with green seeds. By separately adding up all the tall and all the short plants, we find that there are twelve tall plants to four short plants—a ratio of $3 : 1$. By separately adding up all the yellow-seeded plants and all the green-seeded plants, we find that there are twelve yellow to four green—another ratio of $3 : 1$.

These ratios show that the ratio for height has no effect on the ratio for seed color and that the genes for height have no effect upon the genes for seed color. In other words, although the genes for height and the genes for color are inherited at the same time, they act independently of each other. The two ratios of $3 : 1$ show that the $9 : 3 : 3 : 1$ ratio is a combination of two separate $3 : 1$ ratios.

INCOMPLETE DOMINANCE

Since Mendel's time, it has been discovered that, in some cases, there are exceptions to the law of dominance. The appearance of the offspring's trait was between that of the contrasting characters of its purebred parents. In these cases, the reaction between the contrasting genes resulted in a blended trait that did not resemble the trait of either parent. This type of inheritance is called *blending inheritance*, or *incomplete dominance*.

When purebred red-flowered four-o'clock plants are crossed with purebred white-flowered four-o'clock plants, their offspring have pink flowers. Although these offspring are pink, the genes for redness and whiteness do not change. This is readily seen by working out the crosses.

Example 1. Cross a red-flowered four-o'clock plant with a white-flowered four-o'clock plant, showing the gene combinations and the appearance of their offspring.
  Key: Let R = gene for red flower
          W = gene for white flower
      Neither gene is dominant.

	Female		*Male*
Parents:	pure red	×	pure white
Genes of Parents:	RR	×	WW
Genes in Sex Cells:	R		W

Possible Fertilizations:

$$\text{Sperms}$$
$$W$$
$$\text{Eggs} \quad R \quad \boxed{RW}$$

Offspring (F_1):

Gene Combinations	*Appearance*
all RW	100% pink (hybrid)

Example 2. Cross two pink four-o'clock plants, showing the gene combinations and the appearance of their offspring.

	Female		*Male*
Parents (F_1):	hybrid pink	×	hybrid pink
Genes of Parents:	RW	×	RW
Genes in Sex Cells:	R or W		R or W

Possible Fertilizations:

$$\text{Sperms}$$

		R	W
Eggs	R	RR	RW
	W	RW	WW

Offspring (F_2):

Gene Combinations	*Appearance*
$\frac{1}{4}$ RR	25% red (pure)
$\frac{2}{4}$ RW	50% pink (hybrid)
$\frac{1}{4}$ WW	25% white (pure)

Note that in the F_2 offspring, the ratios of both the gene combinations and the appearance of the offspring are the same, that is, 1 : 2 : 1. Therefore, this case really does not conflict with Mendel's law of segregation and recombination.

Another example of incomplete dominance occurs in Andalusian fowl. In this variety of chicken, the crossing of black chickens with white chickens results in offspring that are a mixture of black and white that appears bluish.

ACQUIRED AND INHERITED CHARACTERS

The study of heredity shows that differences among organisms of the same species and even of the same family can result from the normal operation of the laws of heredity. It is also true that differences unrelated to heredity do occur. Such different characters, which are acquired during the lifetime of individuals, are due to ordinary differences in their environment. These different characters are called *acquired characters.*

For example, if one member of a set of identical boy twins trains as a weight lifter and the other does not, the weight lifter develops stronger muscles than his brother. The development of strong muscles affects only body cells. Such acquired characters are not inherited because they do not affect the genes in the sex cells. Therefore, the trait for large muscles cannot reach the next generation.

Sometimes, new characters that can be passed to offspring do develop. This type of character is called an *inherited character.* New inherited characters result from a change in one or more genes in a sex cell of at least one of the parents. When such a change in genes occurs, it is permanent and is passed on to succeeding generations.

MUTATIONS

Permanent changes in genes (or chromosomes) may occur naturally and suddenly. These changes are called *mutations.* The individual that bears such a new trait is called a *mutant.* For example, in a species of green frog, white offspring sometimes arise. When such frogs are bred, the white color is found to be inherited. In this case, the new color is a mutation. The white frog (an *albino*) is a mutant.

Hugo De Vries (1848–1935) was the first to study mutations systematically. He experimented with mutant evening primrose plants that had flowers much larger than normal. He found that their descendants continued to bear large flowers.

Thomas Hunt Morgan (1866–1945) discovered such mutations as white eyes in the fruit fly. In addition, Morgan and his coworkers proved that mutations could result from breaks in chromosomes.

Hermann J. Muller (1890–1967) discovered that penetrating radiations, such as X rays, could cause genes to change permanently. Muller's work has also shown that rays from radioactive material can reach the reproductive cells and cause their genes to change more frequently than usual. Additional studies of radiations indicate that excessive radioactive fallout from nuclear explosions can present a hazard to future generations.

Looking Back

In organisms that reproduce asexually, traits pass from one generation to the next when the chromosomes (and the genes in them) duplicate and then move into newly formed cells.

In organisms that reproduce sexually, traits pass to the new generation by way of the chromosomes (and the genes in them) that are carried in each sex cell (egg or sperm). As the sex cells of a parent mature, the number of chromosomes in an immature sex cell is reduced to one-half. When the sex cells unite at fertilization, the original number of chromosomes is restored. As a result, the offspring receives a set of genes (in chromosomes) from each parent.

The gene combinations formed during reproduction help explain the fundamental principles of heredity, namely, complete dominance, incomplete dominance, segregation and recombination, independent assortment, and mutation.

Looking Ahead

In this chapter, we have discussed mainly the inheritance of traits in the fruit fly and the garden pea. In Chapter 19, we will concentrate on hereditary traits of humans and some other organisms.

Multiple-Choice Questions

1. The group that includes only body cells is
   a. oviduct cells and egg cells   c. sperm duct cells and sperm cells
   b. sperm cells and egg cells   d. oviduct cells and sperm duct cells
2. The normal, or species, number of chromosomes in the human is
   a. 23   b. 24   c. 46   d. 48

3. If the species number of chromosomes is 4, how many chromosomes does a sperm cell of the species have?
   a. 1   b. 2   c. 4   d. 8

4. When a cell of the testis ripens into a sperm, the cell
   a. undergoes division and then enlarges
   b. changes shape and then enlarges
   c. undergoes division and then changes shape
   d. undergoes division and then enters the ovary

5. If the number of chromosomes in an egg cell is 4, the species number of chromosomes is
   a. 2   b. 4   c. 8   d. 16

6. In animals, when egg cells form from cells of an ovary, another type of cell produced at the same time is
   a. an egg cell that disappears   c. a yolk cell that gathers food
   b. a sperm cell that fertilizes it   d. a tiny cell that disappears

7. In a fertilized egg that has 4 chromosomes,
   a. 2 came from the mother and 2 from the father
   b. 3 came from the mother and 1 from the father
   c. 4 came from the mother and 4 from the father
   d. 4 came from the mother and 0 from the father

8. The laws of heredity were first stated by
   a. Thomas Morgan   c. Gregor Mendel
   b. Hermann Muller   d. Hugo De Vries

9. When purebred yellow-seeded pea plants are crossed with other pure-bred yellow-seeded pea plants, the plants of the next generation have seeds
   a. all of which are yellow   c. all of which are white
   b. all of which are green   d. some of which are yellow

10. The offspring of parents that are pure for opposite traits are called
    a. hybrids   b. dominants   c. recessives   d. blends

11. The crossing of pure tall pea plants with pure short pea plants produces offspring that are
    a. 50% tall and 50% short   c. 100% medium
    b. 100% short   d. 100% tall

12. When pure white guinea pigs are crossed with other pure white guinea pigs, we can expect their offspring to be
    a. 100% gray   c. 100% white
    b. 100% black   d. 50% black and 50% white

13. When do genes of a pair normally separate?
    a. during all cell divisions   c. only during reduction division
    b. only during mitosis   d. during fertilization

14. The chemical compound in genes that controls the development of the inherited traits of an organism is
    a. DDT   b. DNA   c. ATP   d. ACTH

15. White mice mated with white mice normally produce only white mice because the genes for color in the parents are
    a. hybrid   b. the same   c. weak   d. different

16. If one parent has the gene combination AA and the other *aa*, the gene combination in the offspring will be
    a. AA   b. A*a*   c. *aa*   d. AA*aa*

17. A 3:1 ratio in offspring is the result of the law of
    a. dominance   c. segregation and recombination
    b. recessiveness   d. independent assortment

18. Although genes separate before reproduction, they have a chance to come together again in different combinations during the process of
    a. fertilization   b. mitosis   c. segregation   d. spore formation

19. A student tossed two pennies at a time for 100 times. Her results were: both heads—25; one head and one tail—46; both tails—29. Which cross could result in a similar ratio?
    a. A*a* × A*a*   b. A*a* × *aa*   c. A*a* × AA   d. AA × *aa*

20. If a plant having red flowers is cross-pollinated with one having yellow flowers and their offspring produce orange flowers, the color change was probably the result of
    a. dominance   b. recessiveness   c. unit characters   d. blending

21. That X rays could reach the genes of sex cells and cause mutations was discovered by
    a. Morgan   b. Mendel   c. Muller   d. De Vries

22. The crossing of parents that are double hybrids would most likely result in a ratio of
    a. 12:1   b. 9:3:3:1   c. 9:1   d. 1:1

23. In guinea pigs, rough fur is dominant over smooth fur. If two hybrid rough guinea pigs are mated and have six offspring,
    a. all of them should have rough fur
    b. some of them should have rough fur and some should have smooth fur
    c. all of them should have smooth fur
    d. all of them should be hybrid smooth

24. Two pink four-o'clock hybrids are cross-pollinated. Of their offspring
    a. all should be pink   c. all should be white
    b. all should be red   d. some should be white

25. An albino deer is rare. This color probably occurs as a result of
    a. a natural mutation   c. an artificial mutation
    b. an artificial breeding   d. a dominant trait

26. A male dog is trained to sit up and beg. It is then mated with a female that has been trained the same way. Puppies born to these dogs should be able to do the same tricks
    a. immediately   c. with the same training
    b. without any training   d. sooner than the parents

27. A pure breed of roses always produces red flowers. The sudden appearance of a yellow rose on this plant would be evidence of
    a. blending   b. mutation   c. dominance   d. segregation

28. A breed of animals that illustrates incomplete dominance is the
    a. blue Andalusian chicken   c. white rat
    b. black guinea pig   d. black panther

29. Harmful changes in the genes of sex cells can be caused by
   a. crossing hybrids
   b. incomplete dominance
   c. fertilization by three sperms
   d. radioactivity
30. Percentages of 75% to 25% are the same as the ratio
   a. 1:1   b. 2:1   c. 3:1   d. 4:1

Modified True-False Questions

1. The traits of organisms that reproduce either sexually or asexually are controlled by *chloroplasts*.
2. Offspring of one parent are more likely to be *the same* than are the offspring of two parents.
3. Cells of an organism not directly involved in sexual reproduction are called *body* cells.
4. A gene that is overshadowed by a dominant gene is called *an incomplete* gene.
5. If BB represents a purebred, and *bb* the opposite purebred, then Bb represents a hybrid.
6. That every trait is inherited independently of every other trait is a statement related to the law of *unit characters*.
7. After eating wild onions, cows give milk that has the odor of onions. This is an example of *an inherited* character.
8. *Gregor Mendel* discovered mutations in the evening primrose plant.
9. A change in a gene produces a new *acquired* character.
10. In both asexual and sexual reproduction, *radioactive fallout* can endanger the next generation.

Thought Questions

1. Write the number of the proper choice. Check your answer with a Punnett square.
   a. If all of a large number of offspring of a garden pea cross are *Tt*, the parents were most likely
     (1) *Tt × Tt*   (2) *TT × tt*   (3) *TT × Tt*   (4) *Tt × tt*
   b. When red and pink four-o'clocks are crossed, the color of the offspring will be
     (1) some pink, some white   (3) some red, some pink
     (2) all pink   (4) all red
   c. If many tall pea plants are crossed, which result would be the *least* likely?
     (1) 100% pure tall
     (2) 50% pure tall, 50% hybrid tall
     (3) 50% short, 50% tall
     (4) 25% short, 75% tall

d. A cattleman buys a black bull supposed to be a thoroughbred (pure
   black). Knowing that black color in cattle is dominant over red color,
   he decides to make sure that the black bull is purebred by mating it
   with several red cows. If the bull is pure, the offspring should be
   (1) all black   (3) 3 black : 1 red
   (2) all red   (4) 1 black : 1 red
2. Write the appropriate chromosome number for each of the circles in the
   diagram (a-e), and write the term that belongs in each of the blanks
   (f-j).

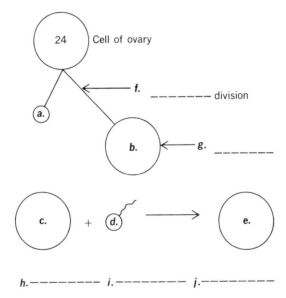

CHAPTER 19

HOW DOES HEREDITY HELP US UNDERSTAND OURSELVES AND OTHER ORGANISMS?

When you have completed this chapter, you should be able to:

1. *List* some human hereditary traits.
2. *Explain* how the sex of an individual is determined.
3. *Describe* the way in which sex-linked traits are inherited.
4. *Indicate* the extent to which the sex of an unborn child can be predicted.
5. *Compare* the origin and heredity of identical and fraternal twins.
6. *Discuss* how environment affects heredity.
7. *State*, with examples, the methods used in improving plants and animals.
8. *Understand* what is meant by genetic engineering.

In the laboratory experience that follows, you will investigate the heredity of a trait in your family.

Laboratory Experience

WHAT IS ONE PATTERN OF HEREDITY IN YOUR FAMILY?

You are going to survey the hair form, or hair shape, of yourself and your close relatives. For this purpose, consider hair to be either naturally wavy or straight. All types of wavy hair, such as curly, should be considered as wavy.

A. Observe the hair form of your brother(s), sister(s), parents, uncle(s), aunt(s), and, if possible, your grandparents on your mother's side and on your father's side. Copy the following table into your notebook, and record your observations in it.

Relative	Hair Form	Relative	Hair Form
Self		Uncle(s) (mother's side)	
Brother(s)		Aunt(s) (mother's side)	
Sister(s)		Grandfather (father's side)	
Father		Grandmother (father's side)	
Mother		Grandfather (mother's side)	
Uncle(s) (father's side)		Grandmother (mother's side)	
Aunt(s) (father's side)		Other relatives	

B. Examine the family history (pedigree) chart (Fig. 19–1). Copy into your notebook the sections labeled Grandparents, Parents, and Your Generation. Add symbols as necessary for your brothers and sisters and your parents' brothers and sisters. Inside each symbol record W for those relatives who have wavy hair and w for those who have straight hair.

C. Using the pedigree chart as you have filled it in for your family, answer the following questions:

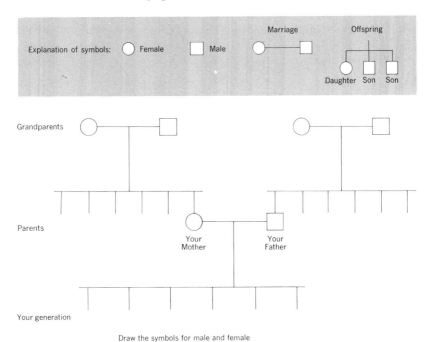

Draw the symbols for male and female

Fig. 19–1. Family history chart.

1. What evidence is there in your family that hair form is inherited?
2. Which hair form appears to be dominant? Explain your answer.
3. What gene combination for hair form do you probably have? Explain your reasoning.
4. What gene combination for hair form does your *mother* probably have? What gene combination for hair form does your *father* probably have? Explain your reasoning in both cases.
5. What gene combinations for hair form did each of your *grandparents* probably have?

Introduction

Although human inheritance is more complex than that of other organisms, scientists have accumulated many facts about human hereditary traits. What is known about a few of these traits is shown in Table 19–1. These conclusions have been reached after scientists studied numerous family histories (like the one you prepared in the laboratory experience) and large numbers of hospital and medical records.

Table 19–1. Some Inherited Traits in Humans

Trait	Type of Inheritance
Color of eyes	Dark dominant over light
Color of hair	Dark dominant over light
Distribution of hair color	White forelock dominant over normal
Amount of hair	Complete hairlessness dominant over normal
Form of hair	Wavy dominant over straight
Speed of blood-clotting	Normal dominant over slow (hemophilia: sex-linked)
Blood type	Rh positive dominant over Rh negative
	A dominant over O
	B dominant over O
	AB, blend of A and B
Type of hemoglobin in red blood cells	Normal dominant over defective hemoglobin (sickle-cell anemia—red blood cells collapse into crescent, or sickle, shape when oxygen supply is low)
Ability to see colors	Normal dominant over colorblindness (both red and green appear gray: sex-linked)
Color of skin	Normal color dominant over no color (albino)
Number of toes	Extra toe (a mutation) dominant over five toes
Mentality	Normal dominant over some kinds of feeble-mindedness
Tasting the chemical PTC	Bitter dominant over no taste

INHERITANCE AND SEX

A person's sex, like eye color, is inherited. However, the pattern of sex inheritance is somewhat different from that of other inherited traits.

What Determines Sex?

The sex of an offspring is determined by genes that lie in a particular pair of chromosomes, called the *sex chromosomes*. In one sex, the two sex chromosomes are alike in appearance; in the other, they are unlike.

In the human female, as in the female of the fruit fly and other organisms, the two sex chromosomes are alike (Fig. 19–2). Each of these sex chromosomes is called an X chromosome. Thus, a female has two X chromosomes, or XX. In the male of the human, as in the male of the fruit fly and other organisms, one sex chromosome looks like an X chromosome of the female, and the other is noticeably different. This different chromosome is called the Y chromosome. Thus, a male has both an X and a Y chromosome, or XY.

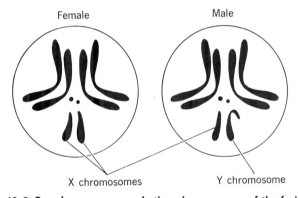

Fig. 19–2. Sex chromosomes and other chromosomes of the fruit fly.

In the preceding chapter, we learned that every body cell and every immature sex cell has the species number (or two sets) of chromosomes. After reduction division, each of the sex cells that is formed has one set of chromosomes. In an adult female, every young egg cell has the XX combination of chromosomes. As a result of reduction division, every mature egg cell has only one X chromosome. In an adult male, every young sperm cell has the XY combination of chromosomes. As a result of reduction division, some mature sperm cells have an X chromosome, and some have a Y chromosome.

When a sperm cell and an egg cell unite in the process of fertilization, the combination of chromosomes that results determines whether the new individual will be a male or a female. The egg, having an X chromosome from the mother, may unite with a sperm that carries either an X or a Y chromosome from the father. If the chromosome combination happens to be XX, the offspring will be a female. If the combination happens to be XY, the offspring will be a male. Which combination occurs is a matter of chance. That this is so is readily seen by working out the Punnett square:

Key: Let XX = female
XY = male

Parents:	female	×	male
Sex Chromosomes:	XX	×	XY
Chromosomes in Sex Cells:	X		X or Y

Possible Fertilizations:

Sperms

		X	Y
Eggs	X	XX	XY

Offspring:

Chromosome Combinations	Sex
$\frac{1}{2}$ XX	50% females
$\frac{1}{2}$ XY	50% males

The ratio of 50% females to 50% males is a 1 : 1 ratio. This ratio can result only when there are a very large number of fertilizations. Where there is only one offspring, there is a fifty-fifty chance for it to be a male or a female. Where there are four girls in a family, the X and X combination at fertilization occurred four times, whereas the X and Y combination did not, by chance, occur at all. In a family that has all boys, the opposite could have occurred. However, in the world population as a whole, the ratio of males to females is very close to a 1 : 1 ratio. That is, the numbers of males and females are approximately equal.

Some Traits Are Linked With Sex

The sex chromosomes, like other chromosomes, carry specific genes. In humans, the sex chromosomes carry such genes as those that determine color vision and blood-clotting. Since the genes for these traits are carried on the sex chromosomes, the traits controlled by the genes are called *sex-linked traits*. Normal color vision is dominant over color blindness, which is the inability to distinguish between red and green. Normal blood-clotting is dominant over hemophilia (bleeder's disease), or delayed clotting time. In general, colorblindness and hemophilia occur more often in males than in females.

THE HEREDITY OF TWINS

In most kinds of animals, the female produces many eggs at one time. After fertilization, the eggs develop at the same time into many offspring. In humans, one offspring is usually produced at a time. In some instances, two or more offspring may be born at the same time. The tendency to produce more than one offspring at a time seems to be inherited. The production of more than one offspring can result either from the development of two or more fertilized eggs into separate embryos or from the splitting of a single young embryo into two or more embryos.

Identical Twins

Sometimes, after an egg has been fertilized, it develops into a two-celled embryo, and the two daughter cells separate instead of staying together. Then, each daughter cell undergoes many cell divisions, forming two separate embryos. In this manner, two individuals, called *identical twins*, are produced (Fig. 19–3a). Such twins are identical because they arise from the same egg and sperm. As a result, they have the same genes, look alike, and are of the same sex.

There have been many cases in which identical twins have been separated in infancy and brought up in different environments by different foster parents. When these twins grew up, they looked alike but showed some differences in character, ability, and personality. Identical

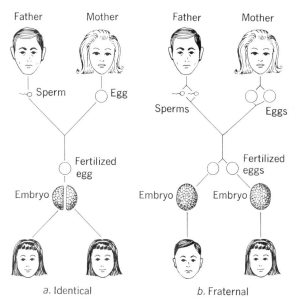

Fig. 19–3. Human twins.

twins who have been brought up together by the same parents are much more alike in these traits.

Fraternal Twins

Occasionally, a human ovary releases two eggs at a time. Each egg is then fertilized separately, and two separate embryos that become twin individuals develop (Fig. 19–3b). Since such twin offspring arise from two different fertilized eggs, they have different combinations of genes, do not look any more alike than any other brothers and sisters, and may be of different sexes. These twins are called *fraternal twins*.

Fraternal twins that have been brought up together in the same environment by their own parents are as different as any two children in a family.

HEREDITY AND ENVIRONMENT

Physical traits, such as height, eye color, and skin color, are controlled by genes and are therefore inherited. Studies of the heredity of human twins and of the offspring of many kinds of organisms show that, in addition to physical traits, some types of behavior are controlled by genes. Examples of such traits are reflexes and instincts.

Studies also show that the development of some characteristics depends upon the environment as well as heredity. Although an organism may inherit the ability to develop strong bones and to grow to a large size, a poor diet can lead to rickets and stunted growth. Similarly, basic mental ability and special talent appear to be inherited, but both of these traits require a suitable environment for their fullest development. Thus, a talented child exposed to music has a chance of becoming a musician.

A favorable environment aids the development of desirable traits not only in humans, but also in the plants and animals that are important to humans. For example, when wheat plants of the same pure breed are grown in fertile soil, they produce more grain than when they are grown in poor soil. Cows that are well fed and kept free of disease and annoying insects produce better and more milk than do cows of the same breed that are neglected.

IMPROVING PLANTS AND ANIMALS THROUGH HEREDITY

Many breeds of plants and animals are necessary for human well-being. By using a knowledge of heredity, humans have improved and are continuing to improve many breeds of plants and animals. In carrying out these improvements, plant and animal breeders use a number of different methods.

Selection

Selection, or *selective breeding*, means that breeders choose for mating only those organisms that possess the best characteristics. Such selection is carried out generation after generation until the desired type of organism is produced. Examples of species that have been improved by means of selection are wheat and horses.

A breed of wheat that resists the disease called wheat rust originated from a few disease-resistant seeds. The plants that grew from these seeds did not produce much grain. For many generations thereafter, only those plants that gave the largest crops were crossed. Eventually, a new improved breed, called Kanred wheat, was established. This breed resists the rust disease and yields a large quantity of grain per unit of land.

In a similar fashion, speedier race horses were developed. Generation after generation, breeders selected as parents only the swiftest horses.

Hybridization

Hybridization, or *crossbreeding*, means that organisms of different breeds, each having a desirable trait, are crossed. Very often, hybrid organisms grow to larger size and are more vigorous than either of the parental breeds. Two examples are *hybrid corn* and the *mule*.

Hybrid corn, which is the major type of corn grown in the United States, is developed from four pure types of corn plants. One type produces large ears; another, straight rows of kernels; a third, many kernels per ear; and a fourth, strong stalks. In producing hybrid corn, two of these types are cross-pollinated and, at the same time, the other two types are also cross-pollinated. Then, the offspring of the first crossing are cross-pollinated with those of the second. When the seeds that result are planted, they grow into hybrid corn.

The mule, which is the hybrid offspring of male donkeys and female horses, combines the traits of both parents. Mules combine the size of the horse with the surefootedness and strength of the donkey. Mules are less stubborn and more intelligent than donkeys and can be trained as easily as horses.

Inbreeding

Inbreeding, or *close breeding*, means that breeders mate only closely related organisms. The breeding of many successive generations of such related organisms often produces a breed in which all the offspring are very much alike. In other words, the breed becomes pure because the genes of every organism are very much like those of others of the same breed. Inbreeding is usually used after a breed has been improved by some other method.

Inbreeding has been used to improve the garden pea and Holstein cattle. After breeders produced the sweet, green garden pea, they allowed the plants to inbreed. Since peas are normally self-pollinated, the process of inbreeding continues to produce plants of the same variety. Holstein cows, which are noted for the large volume of milk they produce, are bred only with Holstein bulls in order to produce more offspring with the same desirable characteristics.

Utilizing Mutations

Some mutations, useful to humans, are given special care by breeders. Seedless oranges and hornless cattle are examples of valuable breeds that arose by mutation.

Seedlessness in oranges arose as a mutation on a tree that had previously produced only oranges with seeds. This mutation caused the bud to grow into a branch bearing only seedless oranges. By grafting twigs from this branch to stems of young seeded orange trees, breeders have produced many trees that now bear seedless oranges.

Hornlessness in cattle originated as a result of a mutation in a breed that had always had long horns. (Long horns are sawed off by cattle ranchers in order to prevent injury to the cattle and the cattle workers.) Breeding experiments showed that the hornless condition was dominant and that the development of horns was recessive. After a few hornless individuals were obtained, they were inbred. By continued inbreeding, a new breed of hornless cattle was established.

At the Brookhaven (New York) laboratories of the Energy Research and Development Administration, many experiments are carried out in order to increase the rate at which mutations arise in plants that are important to humans. As mutants appear, they are examined for their possible value in improving existing kinds of plants. If the mutants seem valuable, they are crossed with an existing breed. An example of a plant improved by this method is the rust-resistant oat plant.

IMPROVING HUMAN HEREDITY

Medical treatments to help people who have inherited defective traits such as hemophilia and sickle-cell anemia are available. However, the treatments are often uncomfortable and expensive. Could the methods used by breeders for animals be used to improve human heredity and so wipe out inherited defective traits and reduce human misery? Although this is theoretically possible, we might find it undesirable in a democratic society to control people in their selection of mates or their right to have children.

Genetic Engineering

Some geneticists believe that it may be possible some day to work with genes in such a way as to prevent or cure serious genetic defects. Such work with genes is called *genetic engineering*. The geneticists have come to this belief as a result of certain experiments done with viruses and bacteria. These experiments reveal that viruses can carry genes from one bacterium to another. As a result, the heredity of the receiving bacterium is changed. For example, one bacterium may lack a gene that enables the bacterium to manufacture an enzyme necessary for a life process. Another bacterium possesses the gene and lives normally. Upon transfer of the gene into the first bacterium from the second, the first bacterium lives normally, as do all of its descendants.

Genetic Engineering in Humans

Could such a gene transfer be accomplished in humans? Could a normal gene from another organism be substituted for a defective human gene? Could we by such means permanently rid humans of conditions such as diabetes and hemophilia?

Genetic engineering may also pose various kinds of problems for humanity. Let us suppose that through gene transfer a gene made a common type of bacteria resistant to all known antibiotics. What would happen if such bacteria escaped from a laboratory and multiplied throughout the human race? Or who is to decide whether it would be "good" or "bad" for all human beings to be the same height or have blue eyes?

The answers to some of these questions are not yet available. For others, there may never be any simple answers. At present many investigations are being carried on to study the benefits as well as the dangers involved in genetic engineering.

Looking Back

In this unit, we have learned how living things replenish the environment with offspring by means of either asexual or sexual reproduction. As a result of heredity, offspring resemble their parents in most respects. Studies have shown that the proper development of many traits in an organism depends both on the organism's heredity and on its environment.

Looking Ahead

Since a favorable environment is important to the lives of all organisms, we will devote our last unit to learning about the environments of the past, the present, and the future.

Multiple-Choice Questions

1. A human condition that is not inherited is
   a. hemophilia   b. rickets   c. colorblindness   d. albinism
2. A human disease that is inherited is
   a. rickets   b. Rh positive blood   c. hemophilia   d. PTC
3. The sex of an animal is determined by the
   a. chromosomes contributed by the parents
   b. diet of the mother
   c. chromosomes of the grandparents
   d. number of male offspring already born
4. Every egg cell of the fruit fly and the human has
   a. one Y chromosome   c. one X and one Y chromosome
   b. two X chromosomes   d. one X chromosome
5. Whether an offspring will be male or female is determined by chance at the moment of
   a. cell division   c. fertilization
   b. reduction division   d. birth
6. Which statement about sex determination is true?
   a. XY chromosomes are found only in males.
   b. XY chromosomes are found only in females.
   c. More females are born than are males.
   d. What the mother reads influences the sex of a child before birth.
7. Red-green colorblindness is most common in
   a. females   b. males   c. sickle-cell anemia   d. albinos
8. Whether identical twins will be born depends on what happens to
   a. the divisions of the egg cell after fertilization
   b. the X and Y chromosomes
   c. the mother's diet
   d. the sperm cells
9. A person's character is determined by his or her
   a. heredity   c. environment and heredity together
   b. education   d. genes
10. A human condition in which red blood cells may collapse and change shape is
    a. hairlessness   c. white forelock
    b. sickle-cell anemia   d. feeblemindedness
11. Twins born from two eggs fertilized at the same time are known as
    a. identical twins   c. Siamese twins
    b. hybrid twins   d. fraternal twins
12. When a breeder chooses only the best animals or plants for mating, he makes use of the method of
    a. crossbreeding   b. sex linkage   c. mutation   d. selection
13. Inbreeding is used to
    a. produce new types   c. cause mutations
    b. maintain existing types   d. increase variation
14. The desirable characteristics of two wheat plants of different breeds may be combined in the offspring by
    a. selection   b. grafting   c. cross-pollination   d. mutation

15. A cat breeder can determine that a tailless cat is a mutation if the cat
   a. does not grow a tail for 5 years
   b. remains tailless after its diet is changed
   c. is mated to a tailed cat and the offspring are tailless
   d. grows more fur than its parents

Modified True-False Questions

1. The chromosome combination of X and Y is found in the *males* of fruit flies.
2. In a large population, the number of males to females is in a ratio of approximately *1 : 2*.
3. *Fraternal* twins are always of the same sex.
4. An *instinct* is an example of behavior that is inherited.
5. Kanred wheat is an example of a plant that has been improved by *selection* and inbreeding.
6. Hybrid corn was developed through *inbreeding*.
7. A horse mated to *a lion* can produce a mule.
8. Holstein cows are noted for their ability to produce *large quantities of milk*.
9. The breed of seedless oranges arose as *a mutation*.
10. Natural hornless animals have been known to arise as a result of *reduction division*.

Thought Questions

1. Use the Punnett square method to answer each of the following questions:
   a. What is the probability that a child will be born a boy rather than a girl?
   b. If two individuals having hereditary feeblemindedness marry, why is it likely that all of their offspring will be feebleminded? (Feeblemindedness is recessive.)
   c. The gene combination of a person who cannot taste a certain chemical is *tt*, whereas that of a taster may be either *TT* or *Tt*. What are the chances that the offspring of parents who are *tt* and *Tt* will be tasters?
2. Discuss possible benefits and dangers of genetic engineering.
3. A potato breeder developed a breed that produced large and tasty potatoes. He found that these potatoes often rotted before he could harvest all of them. Another breeder had small potatoes that never rotted before harvesting. Using your knowledge of how flowering plants reproduce and of heredity, explain what the breeders could have done to improve their potato crop.
4. Two brown-eyed parents had four children, of which three were blue-eyed and one was brown-eyed. (Blue is recessive.) Give a reasonable explanation of this situation and show by means of a Punnett square that it can happen.

UNIT IV
Environments:
Present, Past, and Future

Overview

The environment has not always been the same. It is changing very, very slowly at this moment just as it has changed in the past. Erosion, the rise of mountains, the sinking of land, earthquakes, and ice ages—all products of natural forces—are signs of changes in the environment.

Living things did not always exist on earth. When the earth was very young, there were no living things on it—the environment consisted entirely of nonliving matter. At that time, the environment was unfavorable to living things as we know them. The temperature was high; the radiant energy from the sun was very intense; the air had little or no oxygen in it. In time, as the environment changed further, living things developed.

Until the relatively recent appearance on earth of humans, living things adjusted to their environment and lived in a balanced state with it. When humans appeared and their population increased, they began to explore the earth and to change the environment for their own purposes. They did this to get more adequate shelter and warmth, to get more food for an increasing population, and to increase their comfort. In the recent past, humans have changed the natural environment more and more. As a result of human activities, the environment may become so different that living things will cease to exist.

Will humans be able to solve the problems they have created in their earthly environment? Will it be necessary for humans to look elsewhere in the universe for a suitable environment? What will the problems be in an environment such as that on the moon?

In this unit, we will seek some answers to these questions as we study how we locate places on the earth, the relationship between the earth and some of the heavenly bodies that affect it and, also, the complicated relationships between each living thing and its environment. These relationships are the subject of *ecology*, which we will study in detail later. We will also consider the environment as it was in prehistoric times and the problem of traveling to environments distant from the earth.

CHAPTER 20

HOW DO WE LOCATE
PLACES ON EARTH?

When you have completed this chapter, you should be able to:

1. *Distinguish* between (*a*) latitude and longitude (*b*) parallels and meridians.
2. *Relate* Greenwich time to local time.
3. *Explain* how to locate a place on earth with the aid of instruments.
4. *Contrast* Mercator and conic map projections.
5. *Interpret* and use topographic maps.

In the laboratory experience that follows, you will show how the shape of a round object is represented on a flat surface, as is done on a topographic map.

Laboratory Experience

HOW CAN WE SHOW THE FORM OF A ROUND OBJECT ON A FLAT SURFACE?

A. Inspect the bowl at your desk. Describe its shape.
B. Using a ruler, find the dimensions of the bowl.
    1. What is the diameter of the bowl?
    2. What is the height of the bowl?
C. Place the bowl upside-down over a sheet of blank paper (Fig. 20–1). With a grease pencil, draw a circle around the rim of the bowl where it meets the sheet of paper. Label this line 0 (zero) mm on the bowl.
D. Draw another line all around the bowl at a height of 10 millimeters above the rim. This line should circle the bowl completely and be parallel to the rim. Label this line 10 mm.
E. Draw another line all around the bowl at a height of 20 millimeters above the rim. Continue drawing lines around the bowl at 10-millimeter intervals until you can go no higher. Label each line according to its height above the rim.

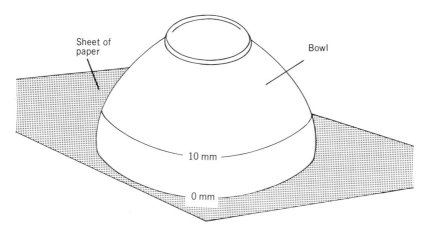

Fig. 20–1.

F. From above, look directly down on the inverted bowl.
   3. Describe the appearance of the lines.
   4. Why aren't the lines evenly spaced even though you drew them at equal 10-millimeter intervals?
   5. Why don't the lines ever cross each other?

G. Remove the bowl from the paper. There should be a circle on the paper with the same diameter as the maximum diameter of the bowl.
   6. What is the diameter of the circle?

H. Using a compass, and looking down on the inverted bowl as a guide, try to copy the circles on the bowl by drawing circles of the same radii on the sheet of paper.
   7. Measure the distances between the circles on the sheet of paper. What do you find?
   8. How do you explain the fact that the circles on the sheet of paper are not 10 millimeters apart?

I. Draw a line through the center of your drawing, dividing the circles in half. Set the bowl aside where you cannot see it.

From the circles drawn on the sheet of paper, try to draw a diagram showing what a side view of the bowl looks like.
   9. Compare your drawing with the actual bowl. How accurate is your drawing?

Introduction

The surface of the earth on which we and all other living things make our homes is very large. The earth is a huge sphere with a circumference of 40,000 kilometers at the equator. The area of the earth's surface is more than 500 million square kilometers. This tremendous area is inhabited by about 4 billion humans and many billions of organisms of other species.

The earth's surface is huge. Therefore, it is essential to be able to locate a given position or to know how to reach different locations. Humans have devised maps that help locate specific places quickly and easily. Maps also enable people to find their way in regions they never visited before.

A map is usually a flat sheet of paper on which a part of the earth's surface has been drawn. This drawing of the earth's surface cannot be perfectly accurate because it is impossible to show the curvature of the earth on a flat sheet of paper without distorting the appearance of the earth.

In spite of this limitation—which applies to all maps—different types of maps have been invented that have proven very useful. For example, a road map tells us what road to take and in what direction to travel to reach a particular destination. A road map also helps us to determine the distance between one city and another. Topographic maps, which are used by geologists and other earth scientists, not only show distances and directions but also show very accurately the size, shape, and location of natural features on the surface of the earth.

DIRECTIONS AND DISTANCES ON THE EARTH

To enable us to locate places on the earth, map makers have devised a system of *reference lines*. First, the surface of the earth is divided by a number of equally spaced lines (or half-circles, since the earth is spherical) that extend north and south and meet one another at the North Pole and the South Pole. These lines are called *meridians* (Fig. 20–2). Second, the surface of the earth is divided by another group of equally spaced lines (or circles) that completely circle the earth in an east-west direction. These lines, which are parallel to the equator, are called *parallels* (Fig. 20–3).

Individual meridians and parallels can be located easily on a globe because each meridian and each parallel has been assigned its own particular number (Fig. 20–4, page 364) In addition, each parallel is assigned a letter—either N or S—which indicates that the parallel is in the Northern Hemisphere or the Southern Hemisphere. Each meridian is assigned a letter also—either E or W—which indicates that the meridian is east or west of Greenwich, England, formerly the site of the Royal Observatory. You should note that the meridians east and west of Greenwich do not end at 90°; instead they continue behind the globe to 180°.

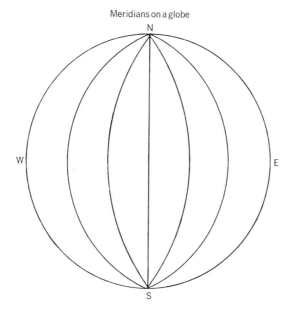

Fig. 20–2. Meridians.

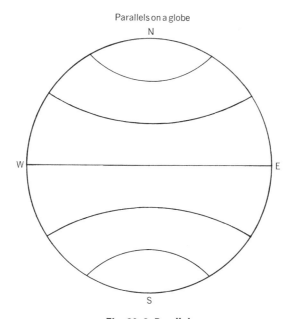

Fig. 20–3. Parallels.

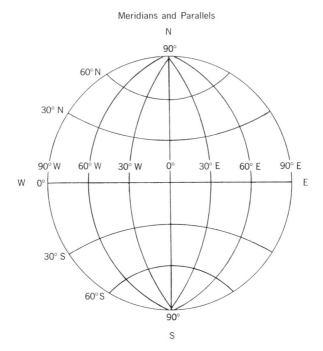

Fig. 20–4. Meridians and parallels on a globe.

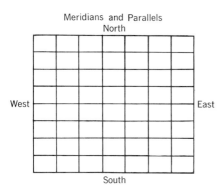

Fig. 20–5. Meridians and parallels on a map.

On a flat surface, such as a map, meridians and parallels can be shown as straight lines which cross each other as shown in Fig. 20–5.

MERIDIANS OF LONGITUDE

If you divide the distance around the equator into 360 equal parts, or *meridians of longitude,* each meridian will measure 1/360th of the earth's circumference. The distance measured off by 1/360th of the earth's circumference is called a *degree of longitude.* (This same system of dividing a circle into 360 equal parts, or degrees, is used to mark off the scale on a protractor.)

Each degree of longitude is subdivided into 60 equal parts called *minutes.* Each minute is subdivided into 60 smaller equal parts called *seconds.*

Length of a Degree of Longitude

At the equator, one degree of longitude represents a distance of about 110 kilometers (Fig. 20–6). However, as you travel toward the North Pole or South Pole, the circumference of the earth becomes smaller and, therefore, the distance represented by one degree of longitude becomes less than 110 kilometers. The farther you travel from the equator, the shorter this distance becomes. For example, in the northern states of the United States, one degree of longitude is equal to about 80 kilometers. At either the North Pole or the South Pole, all the meridians of longitude meet at the same point. Thus, at the poles the distance between two meridians of longitude is zero.

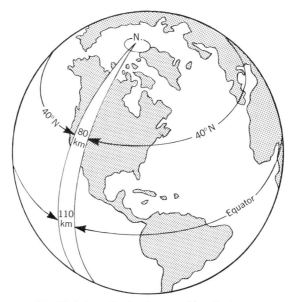

Fig. 20–6. Length of a degree of longitude.

Measuring Distances in Longitude

Meridians of longitude are measured in *degrees east* or *degrees west*, according to their distances from the *prime meridian*, which is located at Greenwich, England. The prime meridian of longitude at Greenwich has been assigned the number 0.

If two people travel halfway around the world in opposite directions, one person going east and the other person going west from Greenwich, the farthest distance either of them can travel from Greenwich is halfway around the earth, or 180 degrees of a circle.

The person traveling toward the east would always be east of

Greenwich until he reached the 180th meridian of longitude. Thus, all places east of the prime meridian at Greenwich up to the 180th meridian are said to have *east longitude*. For example, Rome, Italy, is located at about 12° E longitude. That is, Rome is 12 degrees east from the prime meridian at Greenwich. Traveling farther east from Greenwich, Athens, Greece, is located at about 24° E longitude (Fig. 20–7).

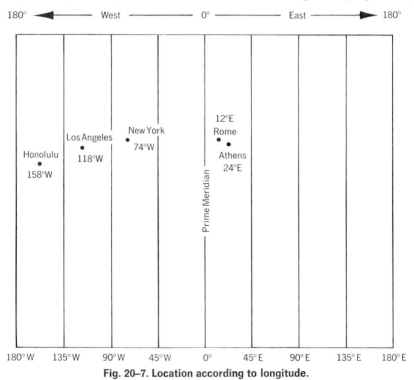

Fig. 20–7. Location according to longitude.

Places on the earth west of Greenwich up to the 180th meridian are said to have *west longitude*. For example, New York City is located at about 74° W longitude, and Los Angeles, which is farther west from Greenwich than is New York, is located at about 118° W longitude. Still farther west is Honolulu at 158° W longitude.

Determining Longitude

Longitude is measured in degrees east or west of the prime meridian. Finding the longitude (and latitude) of a ship or an airplane is the job of a *navigator*. The navigator determines longitude by comparing the time at Greenwich with the time at the navigator's location.

A special clock, called a *chronometer*, always shows the time at

Greenwich. When it is noon at the navigator's longitude, the navigator notes the time at Greenwich according to the chronometer. If the time at Greenwich is later than 12:00 noon, the navigator is west of Greenwich. The sun has already passed the zenith (overhead position) at Greenwich; therefore, it must be at its zenith at some point farther west (Fig. 20–8a). If the time at Greenwich is earlier than 12:00 noon, the navigator is east of Greenwich. The sun has not yet reached the zenith at Greenwich; therefore, it must be at its zenith at some point farther east (Fig. 20–8b).

Since there are 360 degrees of meridian and 24 hours in a day, each hour of time difference is equal to 15° of longitude ($360° \div 24 = 15°$). Thus, for example, if Greenwich time is 5 P.M., while it is noon at the navigator's position, the navigator is $5 \times 15°$ or 75° west of Greenwich (75°W). Similarly, if Greenwich time is 10 A.M., while it is noon at the navigator's position, the navigator is $2 \times 15°$, or 30°, east of Greenwich (30°E).

PARALLELS OF LATITUDE

If you divide the distance from the equator to either the North or South Pole into 90 equal parts, or *parallels of latitude*, each parallel will

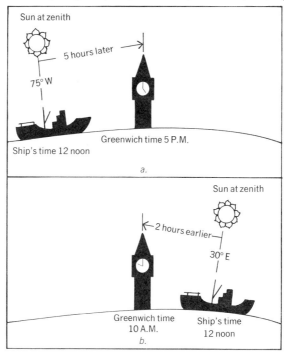

Fig. 20–8. Determining longitude.

represent 1/360th of the earth's circumference (about 110 kilometers). Unlike the meridians of longitude, the distances between the parallels of latitude remain the same as you travel from the equator to either the North or South Pole.

The numbers assigned to the parallels of latitude increase from 0° at the equator to 90° at each pole (Fig. 20–9). For example, Honolulu is located at about 21° N latitude, Los Angeles is located at about 34° N latitude, and New York City is located at about 41° N latitude. In Europe, Athens is at 38° N, and Rome is at 42° N.

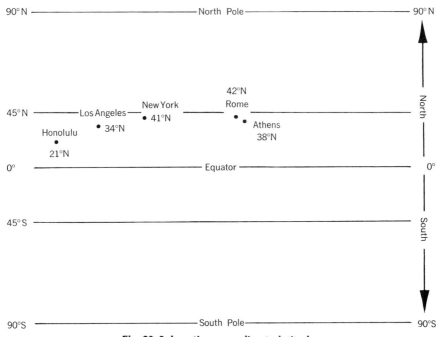

Fig. 20–9. Location according to latitude.

To locate a specific place, it is necessary to know both the longitude and the latitude of that place. Fig. 20–10 shows a map on which the cities previously mentioned are pinpointed according to their longitudes and latitudes. (This kind of map, called a Mercator, is discussed more fully on page 372.)

Measuring Distances in Latitude

Unlike meridians of longitude, parallels of latitude always represent the same surface distance. The distance represented by one degree of latitude is about 110 kilometers anywhere on the earth's surface. Like degrees of longitude, degrees of latitude are subdivided into 60 minutes,

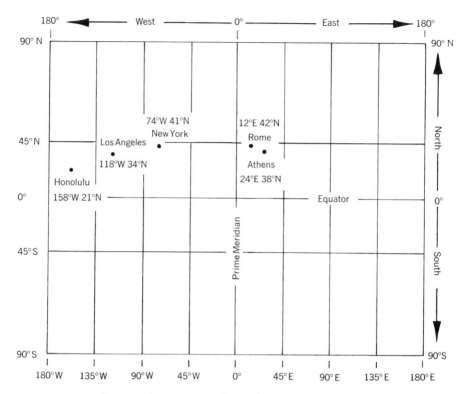

Fig. 20–10. Location according to longitude and latitude.

and each minute is subdivided into 60 seconds. One minute of latitude is less than 2 kilometers long; one second of latitude is about 30 meters long.

Determining Latitude

Recall that latitude is measured in degrees north or degrees south of the equator. The equator is the same as 0° latitude, and the North Pole is the same as 90° north latitude. Thus, there are 90° of latitude between the equator and the North Pole. A place that is halfway between the equator and the North Pole is at 45° latitude.

In finding latitude, a navigator uses an instrument called a *sextant*. Basically, the sextant consists of a telescope, a system of mirrors, and a scale (Fig. 20–11, page 370).

To determine a latitude in the Northern Hemisphere, a navigator first locates the North Star in the telescope. The system of mirrors aligns the incoming starlight until the image of the star appears to rest on the earth's horizon. The altitude, or the number of degrees the

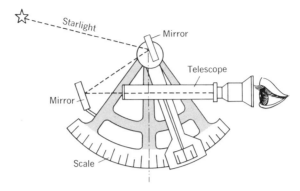

Fig. 20–11. A sextant.

North Star is above the horizon, is then read off on the scale.

The altitude of the North Star, in degrees above the horizon, is the same as the navigator's latitude. At the North Pole, the North Star would appear straight overhead; its altitude would be 90° above the horizon. At the equator, the North Star would appear just at the horizon; its altitude would be 0°.

The closer a navigator is to the North Pole, the greater is the altitude of the North Star (Fig. 20–12). Thus, the North Star appears higher in the sky to a navigator near the U.S.-Canadian border than it does to a navigator near the U.S.-Mexican border. The altitude of the North Star near the Canadian border is about 52° above the horizon. Along the Mexican border, the altitude of the North Star is about 30°.

Finding North by Simple Methods

The direction of the North Pole can be found by several different methods. In the daytime, in the Northern Hemisphere, if you face

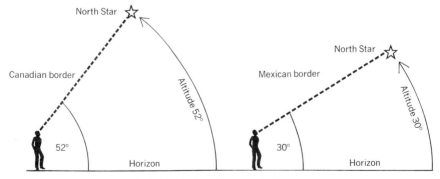

Fig. 20–12. Determination of latitude.

the sun at noon, north is behind you. At night, in the Northern Hemisphere, north is determined by locating the North Star, which is the last star in the handle of the Little Dipper. The Little Dipper can be located readily by following the two pointer stars of the Big Dipper (Fig. 20–13).

North can also be found using a *magnetic compass*. However, the needle of a magnetic compass does not usually point to the true North Pole; it points to the magnetic north pole, which is in the Hudson Bay region of Canada. True north is determined with a magnetic compass by finding magnetic north and then referring to government charts that contain a correction factor.

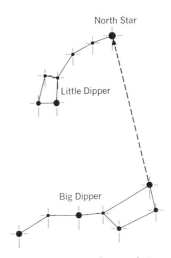

Fig. 20–13. Finding the North Star.

The *radio compass* and *gyrocompass* are used in airplanes and ships. The radio compass is really a radio receiver that locates north automatically by determining the direction of incoming radio signals transmitted from radio stations whose locations are known.

When set spinning, a gyroscope always keeps its axis facing in the same direction. The gyrocompasses used in airplanes and ships are kept spinning by small motors. They continue to face in the same direction regardless of the course followed by the airplane or ship.

Once the direction of the North Pole is established, the other compass directions—south, east, and west—are easily determined. If you face north, south is behind you, east is on your right, and west is on your left.

MAKING MAPS

Map making is complicated because neither a sphere, such as the earth, nor a mountain on that sphere, such as Mt. Everest, can be drawn on a flat sheet of paper without stretching the sphere or the mountain out of shape. You can readily see why this is so if you try to wrap a thin sheet of clear plastic wrapper around a ball. In order to make the sheet of plastic follow the curve of the ball exactly, you must either fold and wrinkle the plastic or stretch the plastic.

If you try to make the sheet of plastic fit the ball by wrinkling the plastic, you will notice that small sections of the plastic appear to be quite smooth. In the same way, maps of small sections of the earth can be drawn fairly accurately on a flat sheet of paper, while maps of very large areas distort the appearance of the large area. The larger the area covered by a map, the more inaccurate the map becomes.

Transferring the features on the surface of the earth to a flat sheet of paper is done by a process called *projection*. Two types of map projection commonly used by map makers are the *Mercator projection* and the *conic projection*.

Mercator Projection

The basic idea behind the Mercator projection is shown in Fig. 20–14, where a cylinder of paper is wrapped around a transparent model of the earth. If a lamp were shining inside the model, the earth's parallels and meridians would be projected onto the cylinder. A small section of the cylinder is also shown in Fig. 20–14. Note how the regions farthest from the equator become spread out and, therefore, distorted.

If you examine a map of the world drawn according to the Mercator projection, you will find that Greenland is so distorted that it appears only a little smaller than North America (Fig. 20–15). Actually, North America has about 12 times the surface area of Greenland.

In spite of this type of inaccuracy, a map drawn according to the Mercator projection is useful to navigators because any straight line drawn on the map shows the true direction of the line. On a Mercator map, all parallels of latitude run due east and west, and all meridians of longitude run due north and south.

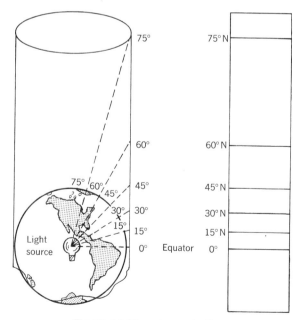

Fig. 20–14. Mercator projection.

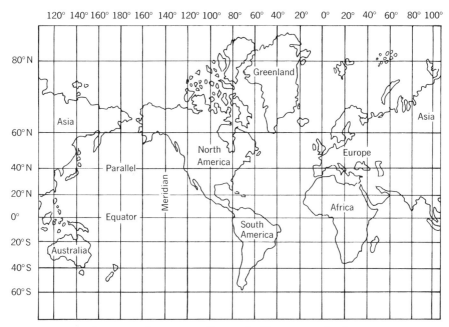

Fig. 20–15. A map according to the Mercator projection.

Conic Projection

The basic idea behind a conic projection is shown in Fig. 20–16, where paper cones are placed over a transparent model of the earth. A lamp inside the model projects the earth's meridians and parallels onto the cone. A small strip of the cone, where the cone touches the model, represents the shape of the earth quite accurately. Maps made according to this conic projection are more accurate than maps made according to the Mercator projection because the narrow strip of the cone matches the curvature of the earth much better than does a cylinder.

A section of the world, drawn according to a conic projection, is shown in Fig. 20–17, page 374. Note that Greenland is now much smaller than North America, as it should be.

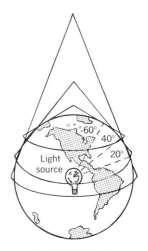

Fig. 20–16. Conic projection.

Although it is true that no type of projection produces a completely accurate map, a nearly accurate map can be made if the map shows only a small, limited area on the earth's surface. An example of such a map is the *topographic map*. Topographic maps are produced by means of the conic projection.

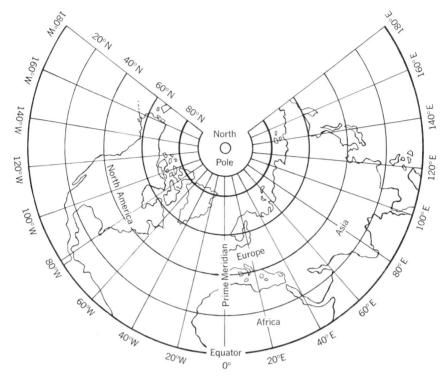

Fig. 20–17. A map according to the conic projection.

MAPS OF SURFACE FEATURES

A topographic map shows the *physical features* and *relief* of a small section of the earth's surface. Physical features include valleys, hills, mountains, rivers, lakes, swamps, and so on. Relief refers to the differences in elevation, or the height of the land above sea level. Topographic maps also show features created by humans, such as highways, bridges, railroads, and buildings. Different symbols are used to represent different types of features. Topographic maps are used by geologists, engineers, aviators, hikers, the military, nature lovers, and anyone else who needs or wants information about the shape of the land in any particular region.

Understanding Topographic Maps

A topographic map may look confusing at first, but the map becomes easy to understand if you learn the meanings of the lines and symbols. The information shown in a topographic map is obtained by *surveyors* on the ground and from *aerial photographs*.

Area Shown on a Map

Most topographic maps show an area on the ground that is much less than one degree from north to south (latitude) and from east to west (longitude). Maps drawn by the *United States Geologic Survey* usually cover an area that is 7½ minutes, 15 minutes, or 30 minutes in both latitude and longitude. At the equator, a 7½-minute map shows an area of about 200 square kilometers; a 15-minute map shows an area of about 800 square kilometers; a 30-minute map shows an area of about 3200 square kilometers.

The fewer the number of minutes of area shown on a map, the greater is the detail with which the features of the area can be shown on the map (Fig. 20–18). For example, since a 15-minute map covers only one-quarter the area of a 30-minute map, the 15-minute map shows much more detail than the 30-minute map. However, the 15-minute map cannot show as much of an entire region as the 30-minute map can show.

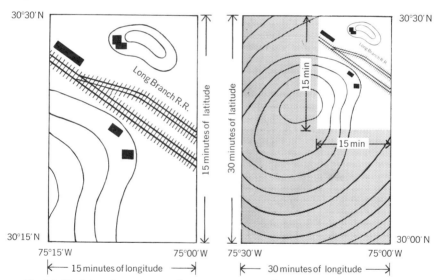

Fig. 20–18. A 15-minute map and a 30-minute map (features not drawn to scale).

Map Scales

Most maps include a scale that tells us how the size of the map compares to the actual size of the earth. On many maps, the scale is stated both verbally and graphically. Somewhere on the map it may read: "1 centimeter to 1 kilometer" or "1 centimeter to 1500 meters." This statement is called a *verbal scale*. A line drawn along the border of the map that is marked off in units of length, such as kilometers, is called a *graphic scale*.

Many maps also have their scales expressed numerically. A *numerical scale* may read: "1:100,000" or "1:250,000" or "1:1,000,000." A scale of 1:100,000 means that one unit on the map represents 100,000 of the same units on the earth. We can also say that the map shows the earth 100,000 times smaller than it is. On maps drawn to a scale of 1:100,000, one centimeter on the map is equal to one kilometer on earth (one kilometer equals 1000 meters, or 100,000 centimeters).

CONTOUR LINES AND THE SHAPE OF THE LAND

In your laboratory experience, you drew a number of lines completely around a bowl. The lines you drew are called *contour lines*. Together, they represent the shape and size of the bowl.

Imagine now that the bowl disappears, leaving the contour lines suspended in space. Even though the bowl is gone, you still know what it looked like because the contour lines are there to show you the shape and size of the bowl.

Imagine further that these contour lines drop straight down onto a sheet of paper. The lines are now only concentric circles (circles having a common center point) on the sheet of paper. However, the lines still represent the shape and size of the original bowl. By exercising your imagination as you look at the circles, you can easily reconstruct the appearance of the bowl in your mind.

On a topographic map, the shape of the land is shown by contour lines in the same way that the shape of the bowl in our imaginary experiment is shown by the concentric circles. Because contour lines on topographic maps represent the shape, or form, of land, topographic maps are also called *contour maps*. Fig. 20–19 shows the shapes of three different hills by means of contour lines.

Elevation of the Land

In constructing a contour map of a particular region, surveyors measure the exact height, or elevation, above sea level of many points in that region. They note the elevation of each point and leave a record of the measurement stamped on a metal plate fastened to a marker at each point. Such markers are called *bench marks*. On a map, bench marks are shown by the letters *BM* followed by small numbers printed in black, which give the exact elevation of the bench marks.

After surveyors have measured many horizontal and vertical distances, they plot the information on an outline map. When all the points having the same elevation are connected by a line, the line becomes

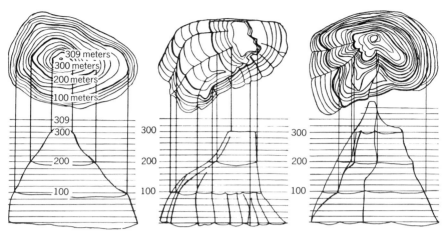

Fig. 20–19. Contour lines show the shapes of hills.

a contour line. Thus, contour lines indicate elevations as well as the shape of the land.

Contour Intervals

The difference in elevation between two contour lines is called the *contour interval*. In the top right section of Fig. 20–20, page 378, there are five spaces between the 100-meter line and the 200-meter line. A total elevation of 100 meters divided by five tells us that the distance between any two adjacent contour lines is 20 meters. Therefore, the contour interval is 20 meters.

The surveyors decide whether the interval between contour lines will represent a change in elevation of 1, 5, 10, 20, 50, or 100 meters. The interval they finally select will depend on the slope of the land. For gently sloping or nearly level land, they may choose a contour interval of 1, 5, or 10 meters. For mountainous and very steep slopes, they may choose a contour interval of 50 or 100 meters.

As you can see in Fig. 20–20, the distance between contour lines helps you visualize the steepness of the land. Where High Hill is steepest, the contour lines are closest together. Where the hill is less steep, the contour lines are farther apart.

When using a contour map to find the elevation of a particular spot, a bench mark may not be shown. In such a case, you can determine the approximate elevation by using the contour interval. For example, in Fig. 20–20, recall that the contour interval is 20 meters. To find the height of High Hill, we count contour lines, starting from the one labeled 300. We find that High Hill is between 460 and 480 meters

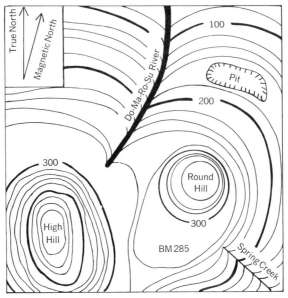

Fig. 20–20. Contour map.

high. If High Hill were more than 480 meters high, the map would show another contour line. Similarly, we can deduce that the summit of Round Hill is somewhere between 360 and 380 meters high.

To make the reading of contour maps easier, every fifth contour line is made heavier, and the elevation of the line is printed on the line. In addition, the contour interval may be stated on the bottom of the map.

Depressions

When climbing a hill, you may find depressions such as holes or pits in your path. A contour map of the area would show these depressions as contour lines having *hachures*, which are tiny comblike lines that extend from the contour lines in the direction of the bottom of the depression. Contour lines with hachures are called *depression contours*.

The hachure lines in the top right part of Fig. 20–20 represent a pit. This depression, indicated by the closed contour lines with hachures, has the same elevation as the normal contour line just below it, namely, 160 meters.

River Valleys

In Fig. 20–20, note that contour lines bend in an uphill direction when they cross a river valley (Do-Ma-Ro-Su River). The amount of the bend shows the shape of the river valley. When contour lines cross a narrow river valley, the lines bend sharply, in the shape of a V. When the contour lines cross a wide river valley, the lines bend gradually, in the shape of a U.

SYMBOLS USED ON TOPOGRAPHIC MAPS

To help you learn to interpret topographic maps, a number of the most common symbols used on the maps are shown in Fig. 20–21.

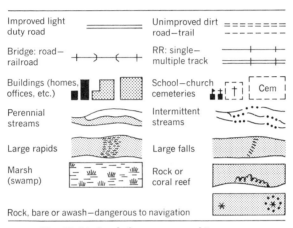

Fig. 20–21. Symbols on topographic maps.

Looking Back

We locate different features or places on the earth by means of the reference lines called meridians of longitude and parallels of latitude. Distances between meridians are measured in degrees east and degrees west of the prime meridian located in Greenwich, England. Distances between parallels are measured in degrees north and degrees south of the equator.

Different types of maps have been devised to show more than just the distances between surface features. Mercator and conic projection maps show the outline of bodies of land. Topographic maps show the elevation and shape of particular areas. Map scales enable us to calculate the size of areas.

Looking Ahead

Maps help us understand the surface environment of the earth. However, they give us no information about how heavenly bodies beyond the earth affect our environment. We will study the effects of these bodies in the next chapter.

Multiple-Choice Questions

1. An accurate representation of the earth's surface can be made on a
   a. piece of paper   b. cylinder   c. cone   d. sphere
2. The distance between any two meridians is measured in degrees of
   a. latitude   b. longitude   c. magnitude   d. altitude
3. The latitude of an observer who measures the altitude of the North Star as 30° is
   a. 0°   b. 30°   c. 45°   d. 60°
4. The clock that is used by navigators to determine their longitude is called a
   a. sextant   b. compass   c. chronometer   d. hachure
5. If a navigator on a ship determines that Greenwich time is 12:00 noon and that the local time is 8:00 A.M., the longitude of the ship is
   a. 15° E   b. 60° E   c. 15° W   d. 60° W
6. The maximum distance, in degrees of longitude, that a person can travel east from Greenwich, England, is
   a. 60   b. 90   c. 180   d. 360
7. One degree of longitude equals a distance of zero kilometers at
   a. Greenwich, England   c. the International Date Line
   b. the equator   d. the North Pole
8. One degree of latitude equals about
   a. 2 kilometers   c. 110 kilometers
   b. 80 kilometers   d. 200 kilometers
9. The scale on a map tells us
   a. where true north is
   b. the height of the land
   c. how the size of the map compares with the actual size of the land area
   d. the shape of the land areas
10. Which of the following ratios states that one centimeter equals one kilometer?
    a. 1:1000   b. 1:10,000   c. 1:100,000   d. 1:250,000
11. Contour lines that are very close together indicate that the land is very
    a. steep   b. high   c. wide   d. flat
12. A known height on a map is indicated by
    a. dots   b. *H*   c. *MT*   d. *BM*
13. A contour line that has tiny comblike lines along the inner edge indicates the presence of a
    a. mountain   c. river valley
    b. steep cliff   d. depression in the ground

Modified True-False Questions

1. On maps drawn according to the Mercator projection, Greenland appears much *smaller* than the United States.
2. Imaginary lines that encircle the earth and pass through both the North and South Poles are called *meridians.*
3. The distance, in degrees, from a parallel to the equator is called *longitude.*

4. Greenwich, England, is located on the *180°* meridian of longitude.
5. At the equator, 1° of longitude is equal to about *1000* kilometers.
6. A 15-minute map represents *a smaller* area of the earth's surface than does a 30-minute map of the same size.
7. To an observer at the *equator*, the North Star appears to be on the horizon.
8. If you are located west of Greenwich, England, your local time is *earlier* than the time at Greenwich.
9. When you face north, *west* is on your right.
10. Points on a map that are the same height above sea level are connected by the same line, which is called *a contour* line.
11. The letters "*BM*" on a map indicate the measured elevation of that part of the land.
12. Contour lines bend *downstream* when they cross a river valley.

Thought Questions

1. Explain why the number of kilometers between any two parallels always remains the same, while the number of kilometers between any two meridians can vary greatly.
2. What is the difference between a 7½-minute topographic map and a 15-minute topographic map?
3. Study the map below and then answer the questions that follow. (The contour lines are marked in meters.)

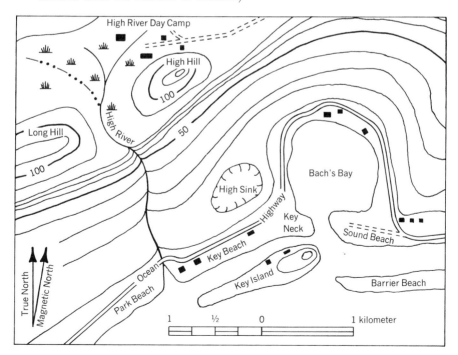

   a. What is the contour interval on the map?

   b. What is the height of the contour lines that outline the shape of the coast?

   c. What is the shortest distance between Key Island and Sound Beach?

   d. All of Barrier Beach lies below what altitude?

   e. At approximately what elevation does High River flow most rapidly?

   f. Name the feature that is a depression.

   g. In which direction would you move in order to travel from Park Beach to Key Beach along the Ocean Highway?

   h. What is the highest possible altitude of High Hill?

   i. Where is an intermittent stream located?

4. Describe how you might determine your latitude at night.

5. Describe three different ways in which you can locate true north.

CHAPTER 21

HOW DO HEAVENLY BODIES
AFFECT OUR EARTHLY ENVIRONMENT?

When you have completed this chapter, you should be able to:

1. *Define* umbra, penumbra, revolution of the earth, solstice, equinox.
2. *Relate* (*a*) the rotation of the earth to night and day (*b*) the axis of the earth to the change in the length of day (*c*) our time system to the sun (*d*) our calendar system to the moon.
3. *Explain* the cause of the seasons.
4. *Account* for the time zones of the United States.
5. *Discuss* the phases of the moon and tides.
6. *Distinguish* between the causes of lunar and solar eclipses.

In the laboratory experience that follows, you will investigate the effect of the angle of light rays on a surface. This will help you understand the effect of the sun's rays on the earth during each season.

Laboratory Experience

WHAT EFFECT DOES THE ANGLE OF A BEAM OF LIGHT HAVE ON A SURFACE RECEIVING THE LIGHT?

A. Attach a cardboard tube to a flashlight (Fig. 21–1, page 384). Direct the flashlight beam onto a sheet of paper as shown in position A. Draw a pencil line around the pattern of light that is produced on the paper. Repeat the procedure for positions B and C.

   1. In which position is the beam of light most concentrated?

B. Place a radiometer on your desk. Using the flashlight with the cardboard tube attached, direct the beam of light as shown in position D in Fig. 21–2. The flashlight should be from 30–60 centimeters from the radiometer. Count the number of turns the vanes of the radiometer make in one minute. Record the number. Repeat the procedure for positions E and F.

   2. In which position of the flashlight did the vanes of the radiometer turn most rapidly?

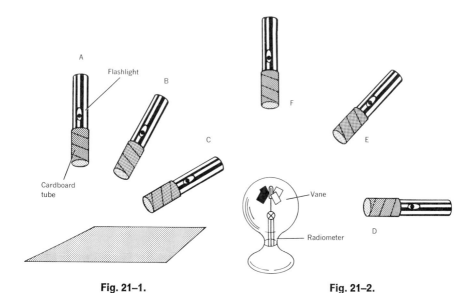

Fig. 21–1.   **Fig. 21–2.**

3. Which position in Fig. 21–2 is similar to position *D* in Fig. 21–1?

4. In which positions in Figs. 21–1 and 21–2 are the beams of light most concentrated? Least concentrated?

C. Study Fig. 21–3, which shows rays of light coming from the sun to the earth.

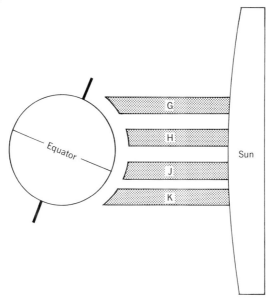

Fig. 21–3.

5. Which ray of sunlight in the Northern Hemisphere is most like beam D in Fig. 21–2?
6. Which ray of sunlight is most like beam E?
7. Which ray of sunlight shining on the earth would you expect to be most concentrated? Explain.
8. From your observations in activities A, B, and C, explain how the angle of sunlight affects the amount of heat delivered to different parts of the earth.

Introduction

Because of gravity, all heavenly bodies—the sun, moon, and earth—exert a force on one another. At the same time, the motion of one heavenly body affects the motion of another. These motions are responsible for the regular, repeated changes in our environment. Among such changes are night and day, the seasons, and tides.

The changes in the lengths of night and day and the seasons affect every living thing. Thus, the supply of food and oxygen for animals depends upon the exposure of green plants to light, which enables the plants to carry on photosynthesis. The ability of many plants to produce flowers and seeds, and of many land animals to mate and reproduce, depends on the coming of the proper season and on the presence of the correct amount of light. In a somewhat similar way, the changing tides are essential to the well-being of water-dwelling plants and animals.

EFFECTS OF MOTIONS OF THE EARTH

Living on the surface of the earth as we do, we are always moving in several different directions at the same time. As the earth rotates, or spins on its axis, the earth carries us around in a circle as if we were on a giant merry-go-round. This motion is called *rotation*. At the same time, the earth also revolves in an orbit around the sun, carrying us along as if we were on a giant spaceship. Each orbit around the sun is called a *revolution*.

Furthermore, because it is part of the solar system, the earth is also moving with the solar system in a still larger orbit around the center of our galaxy, the Milky Way. Finally, our galaxy is moving away from the other galaxies in the universe, and we are part of this movement as well. Fig. 21–4, page 386, illustrates all of these motions taking place at the same time.

The motions of the earth, especially its rotation on its axis and its revolution around the sun, are important to us in a number of ways. These two motions are responsible for the daily succession of night

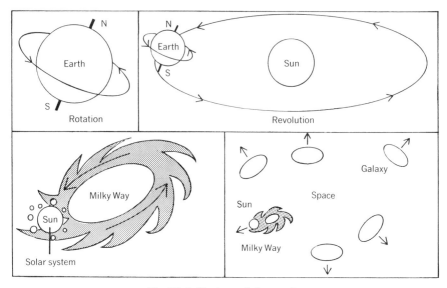

Fig. 21–4. Motions of the earth.

and day and the annual change of seasons. Two units of time, the *day* and the *year*, are also based on these two movements of the earth. In addition, the frequency of the tides is, in part, due to the rotation of the earth.

ROTATION CAUSES NIGHT AND DAY

Since the earth is a sphere, only half of it can be fully lighted by the sun at one time. As a result, one half of the earth is always in sunlight, and the other half is always in darkness.

The rotation of the earth on its axis allows the sun to shine on every part of the earth in turn. Since there are 24 hours in a day, we might expect that there would be 12 hours of daylight followed by 12 hours of darkness every day in the year. Actually, this happens only at the equator. In the middle latitudes, in which most Americans live, the hours of daylight and darkness vary greatly throughout the year. For example, you know that summer days are long and winter days are short. In summer, the hours of daylight may extend from about 6:00 in the morning until about 9:00 in the evening; in winter, the hours of daylight may extend from about 7:00 in the morning until about 5:00 in the evening. The farther you live from the equator, the longer the sun shines in the summer and the longer are the nights in the winter.

Why the Length of the Day Changes

There are two reasons why the lengths of the days and nights differ throughout the year: (1) The axis of the earth is inclined (or tilted) $23\frac{1}{2}°$ from the vertical in relation to its path around the sun. (2) The direction in which the axis of the earth points does not change as the earth rotates and continues to revolve around the sun.

Imagine that you have a top that is spinning in a large circle around you. The top represents the earth traveling in its orbit, and you represent the sun. Imagine further that the top is tilted $23\frac{1}{2}°$ as it spins. The top will always point in the same direction in the sky as it continues to circle around you. This behavior of the earth's axis is called *parallelism* (Fig. 21–5).

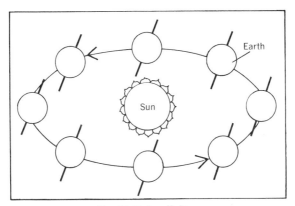

Fig. 21–5. Parallelism.

Length of the Day in Summer

On the first day of summer in the Northern Hemisphere, the relation between the earth and the sun is such that the earth's axis is tilted $23\frac{1}{2}°$ from the vertical *toward* the sun (Fig. 21–6, page 388). More than one-half of the Northern Hemisphere (the dashed line) is exposed to the sun. This means that the Northern Hemisphere has more hours of daylight than hours of darkness. In addition, you can see that the farther north you are, the greater will be the number of hours of daylight. For example, the equator has 12 hours of daylight and 12 hours of darkness (night). Farther north, at mid-latitudes, daylight is about 15 hours long, and darkness is about 9 hours long. Still farther north, the area from the Arctic Circle to the North Pole remains in daylight for 24 hours. That is, if you were living above the Arctic Circle on June 21, you would see the sun in the sky throughout the 24-hour period.

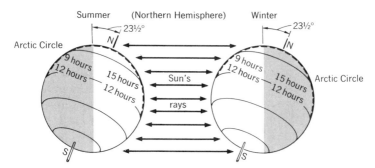

Fig. 21–6. Length of day in summer and winter.

Length of the Day in Winter

The relation between the earth and the sun on the first day of winter in the Northern Hemisphere is such that the northern tip of the earth's axis is tilted *away* from the sun (Fig. 21–6). This means that the Northern Hemisphere has more hours of darkness than of daylight. On the first day of winter, the area above the Arctic Circle has 24 hours of darkness and no daylight; the mid-latitudes have about 15 hours of darkness and 9 hours of daylight; and the days and nights at the equator continue to be of equal length.

The Arctic night is not as dark as are the nights in the United States. The Arctic night is more like our late twilight because the atmosphere refracts (bends) into the Arctic region some of the sunlight that passes through the earth's atmosphere.

Length of the Day in Spring and Fall

On the first day of spring and on the first day of fall, the earth's axis points neither toward nor away from the sun (Fig. 21–7). On

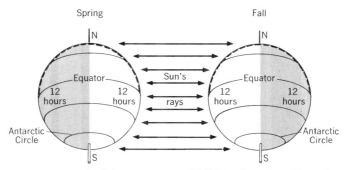

Fig. 21–7. Length of day in spring and fall (N pole is tipped into the page at an angle of 23½°).

these two days, the direction of the earth's axis, in relation to the sun, is such that the sun shines for 12 hours on every part of the earth. Thus, as the earth rotates on its axis, all parts have 12 hours of daylight and 12 hours of darkness.

REVOLUTION CAUSES THE SEASONS

The inclination of the earth's axis causes not only variations in the lengths of the days and nights, but also the annual change of the seasons.

Summer and Winter

Recall that the axis of the earth is always inclined in the same direction in space, regardless of the location of the earth in its orbit around the sun. Thus, the northern tip of the earth's axis is tilted toward the sun during the summer and away from the sun during the winter (Fig. 21–6). With each passing day, as the earth revolves around the sun, each of the hemispheres leans closer to or farther away from the sun. In the Northern Hemisphere, the tilt of the earth's axis causes the days to be longer by about six hours in the summer than they are in the winter. At the equator, in the summer or winter, day and night are equal in length.

The Northern Hemisphere, therefore, receives more of the sun's rays during the summer than it receives during the winter. Also, since nights are shorter in the summer, there are fewer hours available during which the earth can radiate its heat back into space. As a result, in summer, the Northern Hemisphere accumulates more heat than it does during the winter.

The angle at which the sun's rays strike the surface of the earth is most important. As you discovered in the laboratory, the more directly the sun's rays strike the surface of the earth, the more heat the surface absorbs. The sun's rays strike the Northern Hemisphere more directly in the summer than they do in the winter (see Fig. 21–6). The sun's rays strike the Northern Hemisphere directly during the summer but obliquely (at a slant) during the winter. Thus, the inclination of the earth's axis accounts for the seasons. The inclination also explains why the seasons are reversed in the Northern Hemisphere and the Southern Hemisphere. When it is summer in North America, it is winter in South America.

Note that the Northern Hemisphere is about 5 million kilometers farther from the sun during the summer than it is in winter (Fig. 21–8, page 390). Thus, distance from the sun to the earth has nothing to do with seasonal changes.

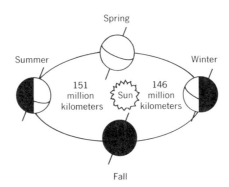

Fig. 21–8. The seasons.

Spring and Fall

During the spring and fall, the earth's axis points neither toward nor away from the sun (Fig. 21–8). At these times of the year, all parts of the earth have days and nights of nearly equal length. The sun's rays fall directly on the earth only at the equator (Fig. 21–7, page 388). Hence, the temperatures of the upper and middle latitudes of the Northern and Southern Hemispheres lie between the winter and summer temperatures of these latitudes.

Since the space between the earth and the sun is almost a vacuum, the sun's rays travel through space almost completely unchanged. Therefore, it is the position of the earth in its orbit that is the cause of the seasons, not the distance of the earth from the sun.

Solstices

Astronomers call the moment that summer begins the *summer solstice*. The moment that winter begins is called the *winter solstice*.

In the Northern Hemisphere, the summer solstice occurs on or about June 21. On this date, the sun's vertical rays fall directly on the *Tropic of Cancer* in the Northern Hemisphere, $23\frac{1}{2}°$ north of the equator. At the summer solstice, the northern tip of the earth's axis (that is, the North Pole) is inclined farther toward the sun than at any other time of year. Therefore, this day, which is the first day of summer, is also the longest day of the year.

In the Northern Hemisphere, the winter solstice occurs on or about December 21. On this date, the vertical rays of the sun fall on the *Tropic of Capricorn* in the Southern Hemisphere ($23\frac{1}{2}°$ south of the equator). At the winter solstice, the northern tip of the earth's axis is inclined farther away from the sun than at any other time. Therefore, this day, which is the first day of winter in the Northern Hemisphere, is also the shortest day of the year. The beginning of winter in the Northern Hemisphere marks the beginning of summer in the Southern Hemisphere.

Equinoxes

Equinox comes from two Latin words that mean "nights of equal length." The equinoxes occur twice a year, when the rays of the sun fall directly on the equator.

The *fall equinox* occurs when the vertical rays of the sun cross the equator as the sun appears to move south toward the Tropic of Capricorn. The fall equinox, which is the first day of fall, occurs on or about September 23.

The *spring equinox* occurs when the vertical rays of the sun cross the equator as the sun appears to move north toward the Tropic of Cancer. The spring equinox, which is the first day of spring, occurs on or about March 21.

RELATION OF TIME TO THE SUN

The clocks we use in our daily lives are based on the amount of time it takes the earth to rotate on its axis and revolve around the sun. Both of these motions are very regular year after year. When we adjust the hands of a clock, what we are really doing is adjusting the clock according to the position of the earth in space.

Until 1687, when the minute hand was invented, clocks had only an hour hand. The dials of these first clocks were divided into hours and quarter hours. In contrast, finely made modern clocks and watches are accurate to within a few seconds a week. The most accurate clocks used in scientific work today are atomic clocks, which are accurate to within one second in 300 years.

The Year

A year is the amount of time it takes the earth to make one complete revolution around the sun. A year is about 365¼ days long. This means that the earth rotates on its axis 365¼ times in the time it takes to make one complete revolution about the sun.

The Day

A day is the amount of time it takes the earth to make one complete rotation on its axis. The 24-hour day that we use in our daily lives is based on the *solar day*. Each day, the sun appears to travel across the sky, that is, the sun seems to rise in the east, move across the sky, and set in the west. In reality, it is the rotation of the earth on its axis that is responsible for the apparent motion of the sun. We see the sun appear to rise above the eastern horizon because the earth rotates from west to east, carrying us along toward the sun. As the earth continues to carry us along during the day, the sun appears to set below the western horizon because we are being carried away from the sun.

From sunrise to sunset, then, the sun appears to trace a curved path across the sky (Fig. 21–9). When the sun is directly overhead, it is at its highest point in the curve. At this point, the sun is said to *cross the meridian*. At this moment, the time is said to be "exactly noon, local time."

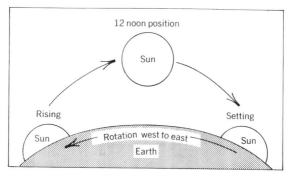

Fig. 21–9. 12 noon.

Because the earth's position changes and its speed varies every day, the length of the solar day can vary by as much as 16 minutes. To avoid complications, our clocks run on *mean solar time*, which is the average length of all the solar days throughout the year. In this system, each day is exactly as long as any other day, regardless of the position of the sun.

The twelve hours that pass each day before the sun reaches your local meridian are called A.M., for *ante meridiem*, which in Latin means "before the meridian." The twelve hours that pass after the sun has crossed your meridian are called P.M., for *post meridiem*, which means "after the meridian." To differentiate between 12:00 noon and 12:00 midnight, we may use 12 A.M. for noon and 12 P.M. for midnight.

TIME ZONES

Up to the end of the nineteenth century, people set their clocks by the noonday sun. Noon was the moment when the sun was at its highest point in the sky. This method of keeping time was satisfactory until railroads and the telegraph spread across the United States in the nineteenth century. The railroads, especially, had great difficulty setting up train schedules because towns and cities only 100 miles away from each other often had official times that differed from one another by 1 to 8 minutes. To avoid this confusion, the railroads agreed in 1883 to divide the United States into four standard *time zones*. Within each zone, all the clocks were set to the same *standard time*.

Eventually, the entire world adopted standard time, and the earth was divided into 24 time zones. Each time zone extends through $\frac{1}{24}$ of a circle, or 15° of longitude $(\frac{360°}{24} = 15°)$. In theory, the lines were to be drawn straight north and south along meridians of longitude. However, where a large town or city, or a political subdivision such as a state or county, was divided in two by the time zone, the line separating the time zones was shifted in order not to split the community or political subdivision into two zones. Imagine the confusion that would result if the time in one part of your city was an hour behind the same time in another part of your city.

Time Zones of the United States

The continental United States is divided into four standard time zones. These are called the *Eastern, Central, Mountain,* and *Pacific* standard time zones (Fig. 21–10). As you travel from east to west across the United States, the time in each zone you enter is one hour earlier than the time in the zone you just left. Thus, when it is 7 A.M. in the Eastern standard time zone, it is 6 A.M. in the Central standard

Pacific standard time   Mountain standard time   Central standard time   Eastern standard time

Fig. 21–10. Time zones.

time zone, 5 A.M. in the Mountain standard time zone, and 4 A.M. in the Pacific standard time zone. Therefore, the difference in time between the east coast and the west coast of the United States is three hours. For example, when it is 5 P.M. in Boston, it is 2 P.M. in Los Angeles.

During the months when days are longer, most states change from standard time to *daylight saving time*. On a given date in the spring, all clocks are set one hour ahead of standard time. This enables people to gain an extra hour of daylight in the evening (instead of early in the morning). In the fall, the clocks are set back to standard time again.

International Date Line

We have seen that, if you travel westward around the earth, you set your watch back (or gain) one hour for each 15° of longitude. If you travel all around the earth, you will gain 24 hours. This means that it is now a full day earlier than it was when you started. If you traveled eastward around the earth, it would be one day later. To avoid this confusion, the day is changed at the 180th meridian, called the *international date line*. This line runs in a north-south direction through the middle of the Pacific Ocean. A new day always begins on the western side of the line.

For example, if it is Tuesday on the eastern side of the international date line, it is Wednesday on the western side of the line. Thus, if a ship sails westward across the line at 12 noon Tuesday, Tuesday is crossed out on the ship's calendar, and the time becomes 12 noon Wednesday. On the other hand, a ship traveling in the opposite direction, from west to east, on crossing the line, would set its calendar back one day, from 12 noon Wednesday to 12 noon Tuesday.

EFFECTS OF MOTIONS OF THE MOON

The division of the year into months had its beginning thousands of years ago when men noted that a fully lighted moon, or *full moon*, appears in the sky once every 29½ days, approximately. Between full moons, the moon is lighted only partially or not at all. After the appearance of the full moon, the lighted portion of the moon slowly *wanes*, or grows smaller. About 15 days later, it becomes only a thin sliver of curved light before disappearing completely. Shortly afterward, the *new moon* reappears as a thin sliver of light. Its illuminated portion continues to grow, or *wax*, for 14 to 15 days until it is fully lighted once again. These regular changes in the moon's appearance are called *phases*.

Phases of the Moon

Today we know that the moon is a natural satellite of the earth. A satellite, you will recall, is a body that revolves in a regular orbit around a planet. The phases of the moon depend on the position of the moon, in relation to both the earth and the sun, as the moon revolves around the earth.

As the moon revolves around the earth, its position with respect to the earth and the sun is constantly changing (Fig. 21–11). The amount of sunlight that we see reflected from the surface of the moon depends on its position with respect to the earth and the sun.

When the sun, moon, and earth are directly in line with one another, the moon is seen either fully lighted (a full moon) or almost darkened (a new moon). As you can see in Fig. 21–11, a full moon is visible only to an observer on the nighttime side of the earth. When the moon is on the daytime side of the earth, the dark side of the moon faces the earth. A new moon is visible only on the daytime side of the earth.

Let us follow the path of the moon through its monthly orbit around the earth.

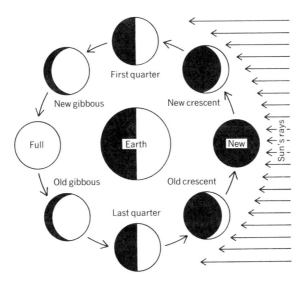

Fig. 21–11. Phases of the moon.

A few days after a new moon, we see only a small curved portion of its surface. This lighted portion is called a *new crescent*. About 7 days after the new moon, we see a quarter of the moon's illuminated surface. This is called the *first quarter phase*. As the moon continues to move around the earth, we see more of its illuminated surface in the phase called the *new gibbous phase*. This phase occurs during the time after the first quarter phase and before the full moon phase.

After the full moon phase, we see less of the lighted surface in the *old gibbous phase*. A few days later, we see a quarter of the moon, called the *last quarter phase*. After passing through the *old crescent phase*, the moon again becomes a new moon.

Although the full moon appears every $29\frac{1}{2}$ days, the moon actually revolves around the earth once every $27\frac{1}{3}$ days. We see a full moon every $29\frac{1}{2}$ days because, as the moon orbits the earth, both the earth and moon are orbiting the sun. Although the moon completes one revolution around the earth every $27\frac{1}{3}$ days, at the end of this time the moon, earth, and sun are not in a direct line with one another. It takes about 2 days more for the moon to travel far enough in its orbit to line up directly with the sun and the earth, just as it was $29\frac{1}{2}$ days earlier.

The Moon and Our Calendar

A calendar is a device or system used to mark off long periods of time, such as a month and a year. Our modern calendar had its origin in moon calendars used thousands of years ago that were constructed according to the phases of the moon. These moon calendars lost about ten days every year because twelve lunar months of $29\frac{1}{2}$ days are about ten days shorter than a solar year of 365 days.

Julian Calendar

In 46 B.C., Julius Caesar adopted the calendar now called the *Julian calendar*. The Julian calendar was based on a year of $365\frac{1}{4}$ days, the time it takes for the earth to make one revolution around the sun. The year was divided into 12 months of varying lengths that had a total of 365 days. Every fourth year, called a *leap year*, an extra day was added to the calendar.

The Julian calendar was better than the old moon calendars because it assured that any given day of any month would fall at the expected time in its season. However, the Julian calendar had a slight inaccuracy, which began to show up after it had been in use for several hundred years. The fault in the Julian calendar was that it was based on a year of exactly $365\frac{1}{4}$ days. Since the year is actually 11 minutes, 14 seconds shorter, the Julian year was just a little too long. After 128 years, the calendar was lagging behind the seasons by about one day.

Gregorian Calendar

By the year 1582, the spring equinox, which had been set at March 21, arrived on March 11, according to the Julian calendar. In that year,

Pope Gregory XIII ordered that the calendar be adjusted by dropping the 10 extra days. To make up for the slight lag that still existed between the Julian calendar and the progression of the seasons, he also ordered that 3 leap year days be eliminated every 400 years. These days were eliminated by a simple rule—a century year (that is, 1600, 1700, 1800, 1900, and so on) becomes a leap year only if its first two digits are divisible by 4. Thus, the years 1700, 1800, and 1900 were not counted as leap years, but the year 1600 was a leap year and the year 2000 will be a leap year. This revision of the Julian calendar is called the *Gregorian calendar*. It is more accurate than the Julian calendar, and it is the calendar we use today.

THE MOON AND ECLIPSES

Because the earth and the moon are solid objects, they block sunlight and cast a shadow into space. Actually, each body casts two shadows, one contained within the other. The darker, shorter, inner shadow, which covers a cone-shaped space completely shut off from the sun's rays, is called the *umbra*. The lighter, longer, outer shadow, which covers a gradually widening space partially shut off from the sun's rays, is called the *penumbra* (Fig. 21–12).

The earth's umbra extends about 1,375,000 kilometers into space; the moon's umbra extends about 373,000 kilometers into space. The length of the moon's shadow is about one-quarter the length of the earth's shadow because the moon's diameter is about one-quarter of the earth's diameter.

At times, as the moon orbits the earth, the earth comes between

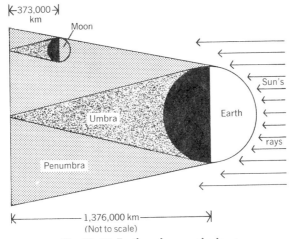

Fig. 21–12. Earth and moon shadows.

the sun and the moon (Fig. 21–12, page 397). The earth's shadow is cast on the moon, and the moon appears darkened. We call this a *lunar eclipse*. At other times, the moon passes between the earth and the sun. The moon's shadow is cast on the earth, and the sun appears darkened. We call this a *solar eclipse*.

Lunar Eclipses

Since the earth moves between the sun and the moon once a month, we might expect that the moon would be eclipsed once every month. Actually, however, lunar eclipses occur only 2 to 5 times a year. The reason that lunar eclipses do not occur 12 times a year is that the moon's orbit is at an angle to the earth's orbit, and therefore the moon does not pass through the earth's shadow every month (Fig. 21–13). Because the moon's orbit is at an angle to the earth's orbit, the moon usually passes outside the earth's shadow.

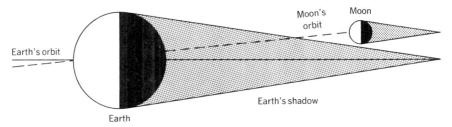

Fig. 21–13. The moon's orbit is at an angle to the earth's orbit.

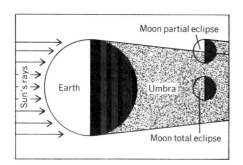

Fig. 21–14. Lunar eclipse.

When the moon is on the dark side of the earth but not in the earth's shadow, it appears as a full moon because the whole of its lighted half is visible from the earth. If the moon moves into the earth's shadow, it receives less light from the sun and is thus eclipsed (Fig. 21–14). The eclipse is said to be *total* when the moon enters the earth's umbra completely. The eclipse is said to be *partial* when the moon enters the earth's umbra only partially.

During a total lunar eclipse, the moon does not disappear from view completely because the red rays of sunlight traveling through the earth's atmosphere are bent, or refracted, into the earth's shadow. For this reason, the moon appears to shine with a dull red or copper color.

Solar Eclipses

When the moon's shadow falls on the earth, a solar eclipse occurs. In order for the moon's shadow to fall on the earth, not only must the moon pass directly between the sun and the earth, but the moon must be close enough to the earth for its umbra to reach the earth.

As the moon orbits the earth, its distance from the earth varies. At its closest approach to the earth, the moon is about 360,000 kilometers away. In this position, the moon is said to be at *perigee*. At its farthest distance from the earth, the moon is about 405,000 kilometers away. In this position, the moon is said to be at *apogee*. The average distance of the moon from the earth is about 380,000 kilometers.

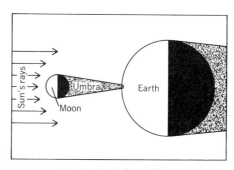

Fig. 21–15. Solar eclipse.

You will recall that the moon's umbra is about 373,000 kilometers long. When the moon is less than this distance from the earth, at perigee, its umbra is long enough to reach the earth. When the moon's umbra does fall upon the earth, the sun cannot be seen from that part of the earth covered by the umbra—it is eclipsed (Fig. 21–15).

Solar eclipses occur 2 to 5 times a year at different locations on the earth. The moon's umbra, when cast on the earth, covers an area up to about 270 kilometers in diameter. For this reason, a total solar eclipse can be seen only along the narrow band of darkness about 270 kilometers wide cast on the earth by the moon's umbra. A partial eclipse of the sun may be seen by those outside of the moon's umbra.

When the sun is totally eclipsed, a halo of light (the sun's *corona*) is seen around the dark disk of the moon. The area on the earth that is within the moon's umbra becomes as dark as night for about 5 minutes, and the stars can be seen.

THE MOON AND TIDES

We know that the earth completes one orbit of the sun in 365¼ days and rotates on its axis once every 24 hours. In the discussion that follows, we will disregard both of these motions in order to visualize more clearly a third motion of the earth, one which contributes to the tides.

You recall that the moon revolves around the earth approximately once a month. Actually, the earth and the moon revolve around a common center of gravity (point of balance) like the opposite ends of a bottle that has been set spinning. The narrow end of the bottle (the moon), being lighter, spins in a larger circumference than the heavier wide end (the earth). The ends of the bottle spin around the center of gravity of the bottle, which is a point inside the bottle and nearer the bottom (heavier portion). Since the earth is about 81 times as massive as the moon, the common center of gravity of the earth-moon system lies inside the earth, about 1600 kilometers below the surface (Fig. 21–16).

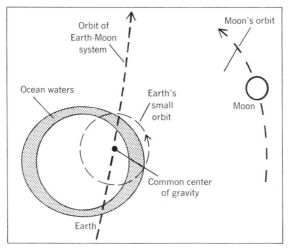

Fig. 21–16. Causes of tides.

Two forces, acting together, make the earth travel in its small orbit around the earth-moon common center of gravity, and also account for the tides. One of these forces is the gravitational attraction of the moon. This force draws the earth and its waters toward the moon. The other force is produced as a result of the earth-moon system's spinning about the common center of gravity. This force causes the ocean waters on the opposite side of the earth, that is, away from the moon, to bulge upward.

The resulting tide-producing forces on opposite sides of the earth cause the water to swell up in two tidal bulges. Between the two tidal bulges, the ocean is lower than at the bulges. Each bulge is called a *high tide*, and each depression is called a *low tide*. Fig. 21–17 shows the positions of high and low tides relative to the moon.

High Tide and Low Tide

On the open ocean, when the moon is overhead, the water beneath it bulges upward as much as one meter. As the earth rotates, shore areas pass beneath the moon, and the bulging ocean moves onto the

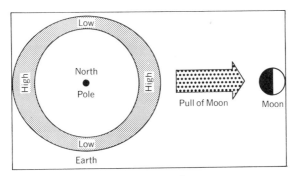

Fig. 21–17. Tides.

shore. This is an incoming, or *flood*, tide. As the earth continues to rotate, the tide reaches a peak, called high tide, and then begins to recede, forming an *ebb* tide. A few hours later, the tide falls to its lowest level, or low tide, before it begins to rise once more.

Since one rotation of the earth takes 24 hours, one might expect that the tides would be six hours apart, two high and two low. Actually the tides are about 6 hours and 13 minutes apart. The reason for the difference is that, as the earth rotates, the moon moves ahead in its orbit. After 24 hours, the moon is ahead of the point over the earth which it had occupied 24 hours earlier. It takes the earth an additional 52 minutes (or an additional 13 minutes added to each 6-hour period) to "catch up" with the moon. Thus, if high tide occurs at 12 midnight, low tide will occur at 6:13 A.M., and the next high tide will occur at 12:26 P.M.

The height of the tides is greatly affected by the shape of the coast, the shape of the ocean floor, and the depth of the coastal waters. These factors also influence the time at which the tides occur. In general, the water level along a shoreline will rise at least 60 centimeters at high tide. Inland seas and lakes have little or no tide.

The range between high and low tide along the shore of the ocean can vary greatly. For example, in Honolulu the water may rise a maximum of 60 centimeters; in the Bay of Fundy (Nova Scotia), because of the way the bay narrows, the water may rise about 18 meters.

Recording Tides

The regular rise and fall of the ocean waters can be recorded by means of a special float. The float is placed in a protected enclosure which has an outlet to the ocean. The water in the enclosure rises and falls in the same way as do the ocean waters. However, the water in the enclosure does not have waves in it as does the ocean. Instead, the surface of the water upon which the float rests is quiet, or still. By means of a special mechanism, the float is attached to a pen which rests on a chart. As the float moves up and down, the pen traces the same movements on the chart. The resulting pattern of lines appears as shown in Fig. 21–18, which shows the tidal charts of Los Angeles and New York for one month.

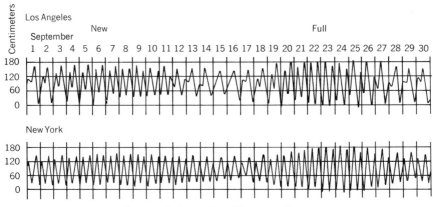

Fig. 21–18. Recording tides on a chart.

Neap Tides

Twice a month, when the moon is in a quarter phase, the moon and the sun form a right angle to each other, relative to the earth. At these times, the sun's gravitational pull opposes the moon's gravitational pull (Fig. 21–19). As a result, the tidal bulge produced by the moon is smaller than usual. At these two times, the tides are neither as high nor as low as they normally are. These very weak tides are called *neap tides.*

Spring Tides

Twice a month, the sun, the moon, and the earth are in a direct line with one another (see page 395). At these times, the sun, which has about half the gravitational attraction of the moon on the earth, adds its pull to the moon's (Fig. 21–20). At these two times, the combined pull of the sun and the moon causes the high tide to be much higher and the low tide to be much lower than normal. These extreme tides are called *spring tides.*

Looking Back

Our environment on earth is affected by the rotation of the earth on its tilted axis, the revolution of the earth around the sun, and the

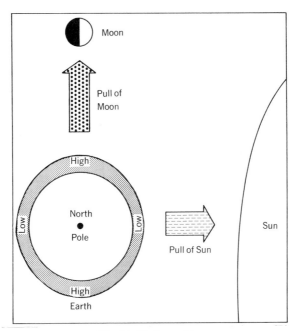

Fig. 21–19. Neap tides.

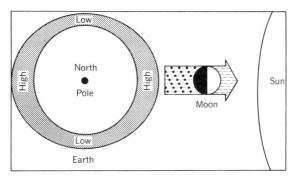

Fig. 21–20. Spring tides.

revolution of the moon around the earth. The rotation of the earth is responsible for night and day. The revolution of the earth around the sun is responsible for the changing seasons. The length of night and day changes with the seasons.

We base our time system on the time it takes for the earth to rotate on its axis and the time it takes for the earth to revolve around the sun. We base our calendar system on the time it takes for the moon to revolve around the earth.

The position of the moon in its orbit around the earth is responsible for the amount of light the moon reflects to us, for solar and lunar eclipses, and for the changing tides.

Looking Ahead

Scientists have accumulated knowledge of the effects of the sun and moon on the earth through observations made here on earth. Since 1969, astronauts and scientists have added to this knowledge by means of direct human explorations of space and the moon. We will describe these explorations in Chapter 22.

Multiple-Choice Questions

1. The only regions on earth that have about the same number of daylight and nighttime hours every day in the year are located
   a. within the Arctic and Antarctic Circles
   b. along the Tropics of Cancer and Capricorn
   c. at the North and South Poles
   d. along the equator
2. In the Western Hemisphere, the parts of the earth that have about 15 hours of daylight and 9 hours of darkness in the summer are located
   a. above the Arctic Circle
   b. in northern Canada below the Arctic Circle
   c. in the northern parts of the United States
   d. along the Gulf of Mexico
3. During the spring and fall, the greatest concentration of sunlight falls on the
   a. equator   c. Tropic of Capricorn
   b. Tropic of Cancer   d. Antarctic Circle
4. The vertical rays of the sun are shining directly on the Tropic of Capricorn on or about
   a. December 21   b. June 21   c. September 21   d. March 21
5. The beginnings of spring and fall are called the
   a. equinoxes   c. seasonal progressions
   b. solstices   d. Tropics of Cancer and Capricorn
6. The number of time zones into which the world has been divided is
   a. 4   b. 12   c. 24   d. 36
7. When it is 12:00 midnight on the east coast of the United States, the time on the west coast of the United States is
   a. 9:00 P.M.   b. 1:00 A.M.   c. 3:00 A.M.   d. 5:00 A.M.
8. The purpose of the international date line is to
   a. separate the Eastern and Western Hemispheres
   b. separate one day from another day
   c. provide a standard of time for the world
   d. define the 180° of longitude

9. There can be a new moon only about once
   a. every week   b. a month   c. a year   d. every century
10. Since the year is actually about $365\frac{1}{4}$ days long, the calendar is adjusted every four years by
    a. adding $\frac{1}{4}$ day
    b. subtracting one day
    c. adding one day
    d. subtracting one day in century years only
11. The length of the moon's umbra is about
    a. 270 kilometers   c. 1,375,000 kilometers
    b. 373,000 kilometers   d. 5,000,000 kilometers
12. Lunar eclipses occur only 2 to 5 times a year because
    a. the moon comes close enough to the earth only 2 to 5 times a year
    b. the earth is usually between the sun and the moon
    c. the moon travels in an orbit that is at an angle to the earth's orbit around the sun
    d. the dark side of the moon is rarely between the earth and the sun
13. The moon's shadow falling on the earth produces a
    a. solar eclipse   b. lunar eclipse   c. partial eclipse   d. vernal eclipse
14. The regular rise and fall of the tides usually occurs at intervals of
    a. 6 hours   c. 6 hours and 13 minutes
    b. 24 hours   d. 24 hours and 26 minutes
15. When the sun and the moon are in direct line with each other and with earth, the tides that are produced are called
    a. neap tides   b. flood tides   c. ebb tides   d. spring tides
16. The number of times in one month that the moon and the sun are at right angles to each other in relation to the earth is
    a. 1   b. 2   c. 3   d. 4
17. The lowest tides occur when the moon is in its
    a. quarter phases   c. full and quarter phases
    b. full and new phases   d. new phase only

Modified True-False Questions

1. During the summer, the region above the Arctic Circle experiences 24 hours of *daylight*.
2. The sun's rays shine nearly vertically on the equator during the first week of *summer*.
3. The moment that summer or winter begins is called the *solstice*.
4. When summer begins in the Northern Hemisphere, *fall* is beginning in the Southern Hemisphere.
5. The apparent motion of the sun across the sky each day is caused by the earth's *revolution*.
6. The period of twelve hours that passes before the sun is at its highest point in the sky is called *A.M.*
7. The world is divided into 24 time zones, each being *one degree* wide.
8. During *a full* moon, the moon and the sun are on opposite sides of the earth.

9. The moon makes one complete revolution around the earth every 27⅓ days.
10. According to the Gregorian calendar, a century year becomes a leap year if the first two digits in the year are divisible by *four*.
11. The shadow cast by the moon is much shorter than the shadow cast by the earth because of the earth's *atmosphere*.
12. Tidal bulges appear in the oceans because of the combined action of the moon's gravitational pull and *the earth's magnetic field*.

Matching Questions

Column A   Column B

1. solstice   a. the highest tides
2. equinox   b. tides that are neither very high nor very low
3. penumbra   c. the beginning of summer or winter
4. lunar   d. the beginning of spring or fall
5. solar   e. lighter shadow
6. spring tide   f. tides that occur only in the springtime
7. neap tide   g. type of eclipse produced when the moon passes through the earth's darker shadow
                     h. type of eclipse produced when the moon blocks out the sun's light from the earth

Thought Questions

1. Explain why, in the United States, there are more hours of daylight during the summer than during the winter.
2. Why are there 24 hours of sunlight during the summer at all places above the Arctic Circle?
3. Name the seasons during which the *vertical* rays of the sun are shining on the following regions of the earth:
   a. the equator   b. Tropic of Capricorn   c. Tropic of Cancer
4. How are the following units of time derived from the motions of the earth in space?
   a. hour   b. day   c. year
5. By means of diagrams, show the positions of the sun, the earth, and the moon during the following phases of the moon:
   a. new moon   c. first or last quarter
   b. full moon   d. new or old gibbous
6. How do you account for the fact that, although the moon revolves around the earth once every 27⅓ days, we see a full moon every 29½ days?
7. Explain why we have leap years.
8. By means of diagrams, show the positions of the sun, the earth, and the moon during a solar eclipse and a lunar eclipse.
9. Explain why there are usually two high tides and two low tides over a period of about 25 hours.
10. Explain the causes of spring tides and neap tides.

CHAPTER 22

HOW DO WE EXPLORE ENVIRONMENTS AWAY FROM THE EARTH?

When you have completed this chapter, you should be able to:

1. *Discuss* how the following life requirements are met in a spaceship: oxygen, air pressure, food, water, waste disposal, normal force of gravity and blood circulation, protection against harmful radiation, temperature.
2. *Compare* the following types of engines: jet, rocket, ion-propulsion, photon.
3. *Distinguish* between escape and orbiting velocities.
4. *Relate* Newton's third law of motion to space flights.
5. *Describe* the features of the moon seen through telescopes and by moon explorers.
6. *Explain* the evidence for the presence or absence of life on the moon.
7. *List* and describe the devices that could detect life on distant heavenly bodies.

In the laboratory experience that follows, you will study how Newton's third law of motion applies to a propelled object.

Laboratory Experience

HOW IS AN OBJECT PROPELLED BY THE FORCE OF REACTION?

Note: This experiment should be performed as a teacher demonstration.

A. Study the parts of the apparatus shown in Fig. 22–1, page 408. Note the position of the rubber band, the weight to be propelled, and the position of the backstop. The backstop (a wastebasket) is a safety device that will stop the weight when it is propelled backward.

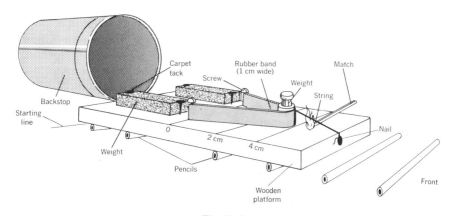

Fig. 22–1.

B. To prepare the apparatus for firing, follow these steps:

(1) Tie one end of a piece of string (about 30 centimeters long) to the rubber band, using a double knot.

(2) Pull the rubber band back with one hand, and pull the string back with the other hand. Have a classmate hold the platform in place. Holding the rubber band at the first mark, pull the string tight, and wind the loose end of the string about 10 or 12 times around the nail. Tuck in the loose end of the string.

(3) Place the platform on 4 round pencils or dowels, as shown in Fig. 22–1. Position several more pencils in front of the platform.

(4) Place the lighter of two weights inside the rubber band.

(5) Light a match, set it down on the string, stand back, and observe what happens.

(6) When the platform has stopped moving, blow out the match.

(7) Measure the distance the platform has traveled. Copy the table below, and record your results in it.

(8) Cut the burned string, and remove it from the platform.

(9) Repeat steps 1 to 8. This time, however, pull the rubber band to the second mark. Record your observations.

(10) Repeat steps 1 to 9 using the heavier of the two weights. Be sure to fire the weight twice—once from the first mark and once from the second mark. Record the results in your table.

Weight	Stretched Rubber Band	Distance Platform Travels
Light	First mark (2 cm)	
Light	Second mark (4 cm)	
Heavy	First mark (2 cm)	
Heavy	Second mark (4 cm)	

1. Describe the effect on the platform when
   a. the rubber band is stretched a greater distance.
   b. a heavier weight is propelled.
2. List two factors that affect the distance the platform travels.
3. If weights of the platform and the propelled weight remain the same, how can you get the platform to travel a greater distance?
4. In this experiment, you studied the relation between action and reaction.
   a. In terms of the experiment, describe the action.
   b. In terms of the experiment, describe the reaction.
   c. How are action and reaction related?

Introduction

The earthly environment supports millions of species of living things. Can the environment of Jupiter, Mars, Venus, and other heavenly bodies also support life? If life does exist elsewhere in the universe, what state of development has that life reached? How does the environment inside a spaceship or spacesuit provide for the life activities of the astronauts who dare to explore space and the moon?

Whether traveling to the moon or exploring unknown parts of the earth, all voyagers into the unknown must overcome similar difficulties. First, the explorers must have some sort of a vehicle that can carry them and a sufficient amount of supplies to sustain their life activities. Second, they must be able to navigate from one point to another.

Throughout history, explorers have depended mainly on their knowledge of the stars to find their way. Many explorers have also been aided by instruments such as magnetic compasses, sextants, and chronom-

eters to determine their position. But astronauts encounter problems—
of which navigation is only one—which are unknown to explorers who
move only on the earth.

PROBLEMS OF SURVIVAL IN SPACE

Without special equipment, it is impossible for an earthly organism,
particularly a human, to exist in space because the space environment
is so different from that at the surface of the earth. Among the major
life requirements that create problems for human survival in space are
oxygen, adequate air pressure, food, water, removal of body wastes, adequate blood circulation, protection against excessive radiation, adequate
environmental temperature, and adjustment to the weightless condition.

Oxygen and Air Pressure Suitable for Humans

Here on the earth's surface, about 20% of the atmosphere is oxygen,
and the pressure of the atmosphere is about 1 kilogram per square
centimeter. As the altitude increases, both the oxygen content and the
pressure of the atmosphere decrease. Under these conditions, normal
breathing is difficult, and the amount of oxygen inhaled is insufficient
for normal oxidation in the body. Outside the earth's atmosphere, in
space, there is so little oxygen that oxidation cannot go on at all. Furthermore, since normal breathing depends upon a difference between the
pressure on the outside of the body and that within the lungs, the
absence of pressure in space makes breathing impossible.

At sea level, it is normal for such gases as nitrogen to be dissolved in
the blood. When a rapid decrease in atmospheric pressure occurs, as
it does when a spaceship is rocketed into space, the nitrogen in the
blood tends to form bubbles. Such gas bubbles in the bloodstream plug
small blood vessels and block circulation.

All of these problems are overcome by means of special equipment
that provides oxygen and also pressurizes spacesuits or the interior of
the spaceship.

Food, Water, and Disposal of Wastes

Experimentation has shown that an astronaut can exist on a daily
supply of about $2\frac{1}{2}$ liters of water and about a half-kilogram of food.
For short space trips, adequate stores of water and concentrated food
are readily carried in a spaceship.

In a flight to the moon, a person subsisting on $2\frac{1}{2}$ liters of water and
$\frac{1}{2}$ kilogram of concentrated food a day produces about 1 kilogram of
carbon dioxide, about 3 liters of water, and about 85 grams of solid

wastes. Exhaled carbon dioxide is removed by special chemical filters. Exhaled water vapor is condensed by a device that is similar to an air conditioner. Urine and intestinal wastes are collected in special plastic containers, which are disposed of after the spaceship returns to the earth.

For long trips that may take more than 120 days in space, carrying a load of food, water, and oxygen is not practical. A spaceship carrying so heavy a load of these supplies would be difficult to launch. It is planned to overcome this problem by making the ship self-sustaining.

The plan involves using green algae, such as chlorella (a one-celled plant), as a source of food and oxygen. The algae would produce these materials; the humans would consume them. The algae, in turn, would make use of excess carbon dioxide. Thus, the plants and humans in the ship would depend on one another and would work together as a *closed environmental system* (Fig. 22–2). This system would operate in a manner similar to the balance between fish and plants in a balanced aquarium.

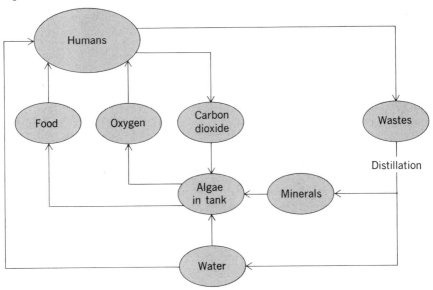

Fig. 22–2. Scheme of a closed environmental system.

Within the spaceship, the algae would be cultured in a tank exposed to light. The plants would absorb the carbon dioxide given off by the passengers and use it in photosynthesis (food-making). As a result of this process, oxygen would be released and used by the passengers. As the algae carried out photosynthesis, they would grow and reproduce. Some of the plants would be removed from the tank and, after suitable treatment and preparation, would be eaten by the passengers. Thus, a cycle would be established—the algae would provide food and oxygen for the humans who, in turn, would provide carbon dioxide for the algae.

A constant water supply would be maintained for both plants and humans by reclaiming and reusing the water that is present in exhaled air, perspiration, and urine. Water vapor, from exhaled air and evaporated perspiration, would be condensed. This water, together with urine, would be distilled. In the process of distillation, the impure water would be heated in a chamber until the water boiled and evaporated. The water vapor produced would then be led to a cold chamber in which the vapor would condense and become liquid water. The impurities (mainly mineral matter), which do not evaporate, would remain in the first chamber. The resulting distilled water would be chemically pure, germ-free, and suitable for human consumption.

In order to carry out photosynthesis and other life activities, green plants require minerals. As a result of the distillation process aboard the spaceship, the minerals that remain in the first chamber could be collected and supplied to the plants in the culture tank.

Maintaining Normal Blood Circulation

The human circulatory system is able to supply blood to all the body organs when the effects of gravity and other forces are relatively constant, as they are on the surface of the earth. When a spaceship blasts off, the astronaut's body is suddenly subjected to forces that may be as much as ten times the force of gravity. Ordinarily, such conditions would cause a person to lose consciousness because the heart cannot pump enough blood to the brain to enable it to operate normally. This problem is met in a spaceship by providing passengers with pressurized suits and with specially shaped supports. Both the pressure within the suit and the shape of the support enable each passenger to lie in a position that permits the circulatory system to withstand the excessive blast-off forces.

Protection Against Radiations

Few harmful radiations from space reach the surface of the earth because the thick envelope of air around the earth filters out most of the radiations. As the altitude increases, the strength of dangerous radiations also increases. Among such radiations are ultraviolet, alpha, and cosmic rays. In addition, there exists a doughnut-shaped zone of penetrating rays, called the *Van Allen radiation belt*. This belt surrounds the equator, beginning about 4000 kilometers above it and extending outward to a distance of about 64,000 kilometers.

Spacesuits and the walls of the spaceships that have orbited the earth have provided some protection against radiation other than that in the Van Allen belt. After several space flights, space scientists have found that the Van Allen belt does not present a serious threat to their operations.

Temperature Suitable for Humans

The human body works best when the temperature of the environment is near 20°C. As a result of the burning of rocket fuel, the heat that results from friction, and the absorption of radiation from the sun, the walls of a spaceship may reach a temperature of several hundred degrees. However, the temperature within the ship is kept at safe levels by means of insulation, of refrigeration units, and of coatings that reflect radiation.

Weightlessness

Humans have become adjusted to the force of gravity of the earth; that is, they have learned to react to their own weight and to that of the objects they handle. This adjustment is automatic and rarely requires conscious effort.

When the force of blast-off propels the spacecraft away from the earth, and when the spacecraft attains a stable orbit, the force of gravity is not noticeable. Under such conditions, neither the spacecraft nor its occupants appear to have any weight.

It has been found that weightlessness upsets a person's sense of balance, coordination, and adjustment to the environment. Before astronauts are able to carry out delicate, coordinated tasks in a condition of weightlessness, they must be given special training. Since even food, water, and their containers become weightless, eating and drinking aboard a spaceship cannot be carried out as they are on earth. To overcome this difficulty, "squeeze-bottles" that enable a person to force liquids and pastelike foods directly into the mouth are used.

TRAVELING IN SPACE

Spaceships are able to leave and return to earth because they are propelled by *rockets*. Rockets have a history that goes back almost 1000 years. The Chinese are believed to have built rockets as early as 1040. The Chinese used rockets propelled by gunpowder as weapons and for fireworks displays. Rockets are used for these purposes even today.

In 1926, *Robert H. Goddard* (1882–1945), an American physicist, built the first rocket propelled by a liquid fuel. In 1930, Goddard built a liquid-fueled rocket that reached a velocity of 800 kilometers per hour and that soared to a height of 600 meters. German scientists were also active in rocket design during this period. During World War II, the Germans developed a liquid-fueled rocket that could travel at a speed of 4800 kilometers per hour and carry a ton of explosives to targets 240 kilometers away. They used these rockets, called V-2's, to bomb London. After World War II, the United States and Russia succeeded in building rockets with enough power to leave the earth.

In October 1957, Russian scientists launched the first artificial satellite, called *Sputnik I*, into orbit around the earth. In February 1958, the United States placed its first artificial satellite, *Explorer I*, in orbit around the earth. The first person to orbit the earth, in April 1961, was Yuri Gagarin in the spacecraft *Vostok I*.

By 1977, the United States and the Soviet Union had launched approximately 3,000 satellites and spacecraft. Some of the satellites carried instruments that collected data concerning the weather, the earth's magnetism, solar radiations, meteoroids, and conditions in space. Unmanned spacecraft have traveled to Mercury, Mars, Venus, and Jupiter. Both unmanned and manned spacecraft have reached the moon. As a result, we have learned a great deal about these bodies.

Jet Engines and Rocket Engines

You already know that it is the pull of the earth's gravity that keeps objects on the earth from flying off into space. In order for any object on earth to leave the earth, gravity must be overcome.

When a high jumper leaps into the air, he moves upward against the pull of gravity. The harder he jumps, the higher he can go. However, once he is in the air he can no longer exert any upward force. Consequently, the pull of gravity overcomes his upward motion, and he falls back to earth. Even a supersonic jet airplane speeding along at 3000 kilometers per hour does not have enough force to overcome the pull of gravity and fly off into space. If its jet engines stopped, the airplane would fall toward the earth.

If jet engines could be made more powerful, they could move an airplane faster, but they could not move the airplane away from the earth completely. At heights above 30 kilometers above the earth, the air has so little oxygen that the fuel in most jet engines will not burn. The engines, therefore, would stop. If the airplane were equipped with rocket engines, however, it could fly higher above the earth. Let us see why.

The basic difference between a jet engine and a rocket engine is that a jet engine takes in oxygen from the air, while a rocket carries its supply of oxygen with it. The jet engine is an "air-breather." It sucks

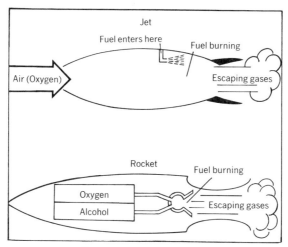

Fig. 22–3. Jets and rockets.

in air and uses the oxygen in the air to burn a fuel such as kerosene (Fig. 22–3). Fuels commonly used in rocket engines are alcohol and gasoline. A rocket engine carries its own supply of oxygen along with it in the form of liquid oxygen. Thus, the rocket is ideally suited for travel into outer space where there is no oxygen. In addition, rocket engines are the only engines yet developed that can provide a force great enough to overcome the pull of the earth's gravity.

How Rockets Work

A rocket moves forward in one direction by propelling gases backward in the opposite direction. A simple device that demonstrates this principle is an ordinary toy balloon. When a toy balloon is inflated with air and its mouth is closed, the air inside the balloon pushes against every part of the balloon's interior with the same force (Fig. 22–4, page 416). Since the push of the air is the same in every direction, the forces inside the balloon are balanced. When the mouth of the balloon is opened suddenly, the escaping air upsets the balance of forces within the balloon. The force exerted against the mouth rapidly diminishes as the air rushes out. The forces inside the balloon are now unbalanced. As a result, the air pressure on the forward inside wall of the balloon pushes it through the air.

This type of movement is an example of Newton's third law of motion (pages 246–247), which states that for every action there is an equal and opposite reaction. In the case of the balloon, the action is represented by the air escaping through the mouth. The reaction is the movement of the balloon in the opposite direction.

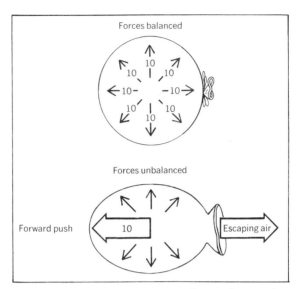

Fig. 22–4. Demonstration showing how rockets work.

Imagine that you have a cannon, securely mounted, on a raft in the middle of a lake. What will happen to the raft when you fire the cannon? As the cannon fires, the reaction to the forward motion of the cannonball pushes the raft in the opposite direction. If the cannon continues to fire, the continued reaction will push the raft across the lake. Recall from your laboratory experience how the movable platform was propelled. This is another example of Newton's third law.

Rocket engines produce a reaction force in the same way as a toy balloon from which the air is escaping. In a rocket engine, fuel is burned inside a combustion chamber (Fig. 22–5). The burning fuel releases a large quantity of hot, expanding gases. These gases are under pressure, and they push against the walls of the combustion chamber. The gases rush out at high speed from the rear of the rocket engine. The pressure at the open end of the combustion chamber is greatly reduced; as a result, the forces inside the combustion chamber become

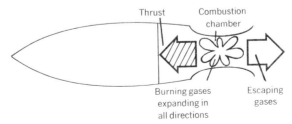

Fig. 22–5. Thrust in a rocket engine.

unbalanced. The expanding gases pushing against the front (closed end) of the combustion chamber produce a forward-directed force.

The forward-directed force is called *thrust*. The amount of thrust produced depends largely on the pressure inside the combustion chamber and the speed at which the gases are ejected from the nozzle. The greater the velocity of the ejected gases, the greater is the thrust.

The most common type of rocket is a *chemical rocket*. Chemical rockets are the only rockets that are powerful enough to lift a spacecraft into orbit. They get their thrust by burning fuel in a combustion chamber and then expelling the gases that are formed through an exhaust nozzle. A chemical rocket may have either a liquid propellant or a solid propellant as a fuel.

Solid-Propellant Rockets

A *solid-propellant rocket* is very similar to the rockets used in fireworks displays. Fireworks rockets consist of paper cylinders stuffed with gunpowder and closed at one end. The gunpowder consists of a fuel and an oxidizing agent, or *oxidizer*. (An oxidizing agent is a chemical that permits the burning of a fuel.) When the fuel burns, it gives off very hot gases. These gases rush out the open end of the paper cylinder. The modern solid-propellant rocket is a metal cylinder filled with a special blend of fuel and oxidizer.

Advantages of solid-propellant rockets are: (1) the rockets can be stored indefinitely, and (2) the engines have so few moving parts that the chances of any malfunction occurring are greatly reduced.

Disadvantages of solid-propellant rockets are: (1) the engines cannot be turned off once they are ignited, (2) the engines provide less thrust than liquid-propellant engines, and (3) since fuel and oxidizer are always in contact with each other, the likelihood of an explosion or uncontrolled burning is increased.

Liquid-Propellant Rockets

Outwardly, rockets containing liquid propellants look like rockets that contain solid propellants. However, in a *liquid-propellant rocket*, shown in Fig. 22–3, page 415, the fuel and the oxidizing agent are kept in separate tanks. A complicated system of pipes, valves, and pumps brings the fuel and the oxidizing agent together in the combustion chamber, where they are ignited.

Fuels used in liquid rockets include gasoline, alcohol, kerosene, and liquid hydrogen. The oxidizing agent may be liquid oxygen, nitric acid, or liquid fluorine.

The advantages of liquid-propellant rockets are: (1) for a given weight of fuel, they produce more thrust than solid-propellant rockets, and (2) the system of pipes, valves, and pumps makes it possible to turn the rocket engine off and on and to control the rate at which the fuel is burned.

Among the disadvantages of liquid-propellant rockets are: (1) the complicated system of pipes and valves increases the chances of trouble with the engine, and (2) the rocket cannot be stored for long periods because the propellants must be kept refrigerated at temperatures as low as $-270°C$ to prevent them from exploding.

Other Types of Rockets

Although liquid- and solid-propellant rockets are highly satisfactory for launching satellites and spacecraft, they are not practical for extended voyages through space. This is because these rockets use up their fuels very rapidly, and, compared to the total weight of a space vehicle, their propellants make up too much of the weight. For these reasons, rocket engineers hope to develop rocket engines that are light and that can produce small amounts of thrust for very long periods of time. Examples of these engines are the *ion-propulsion engine* and the *photon engine.*

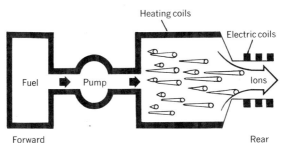

Fig. 22–6. Ion propulsion.

The ion-propulsion engine (Fig. 22–6) uses heated metals, such as cesium or rubidium, which can be easily changed into charged particles, called *ions.* These ions behave like the escaping gases in an ordinary rocket. The rapid movement of these ions out of the rear of the engine produces thrust.

The photon engine would be propelled by light. A photon rocket would be constructed with huge "sails." Sunlight striking these sails would push the rocket forward. Since sunlight travels at 300,000 kilometers per second, the photon rocket could theoretically approach the speed of light.

The powerful thrust that can be obtained from a chemical rocket would be used to launch a spacecraft, and the weaker but longer-lasting thrust of an ion-propelled or light-propelled rocket would then be used to propel the ship at high speeds in outer space.

Nuclear rockets, which would use atomic energy as some submarines and aircraft carriers do, are also planned. If nuclear rocket engines are perfected, they should be able to propel very heavy spacecraft to all the other planets in our solar system.

Launching Rockets Into Space

The Saturn V rocket, which launched *Apollo 11* into orbit, stands about 90 meters high and weighs about 2,700,000 kilograms. Its five giant engines can lift the rocket off the ground because they produce a combined thrust of 3,400,000 kilograms (over 30,000,000 newtons).

The farther away the rocket travels from the ground, the more effective its thrust becomes. This is true for the following reasons:

1. The rocket uses up tons of fuel during every second of its operation. After several seconds, the rocket is many tons lighter. As the rocket becomes lighter, the engines have less mass to push, and the rocket travels faster and farther.

2. The farther an object is from the center of the earth, the smaller is the pull of the earth's gravity on the object. For example, you weigh less on the top of a mountain than you do at sea level.

The force of gravity at sea level is referred to as 1 g, where g is the acceleration due to gravity. About 2500 kilometers above the earth, the force of gravity is about $\frac{1}{2}$ g. At this altitude, you would weigh $\frac{1}{2}$ your weight at sea level. At an altitude of 25,000 kilometers, the force of gravity is about $\frac{1}{25}$ g, and you would weigh $\frac{1}{25}$ your weight at sea level.

3. When a rocket reaches the thinner air of very high altitudes, there is less resistance to its forward movement.

4. The thin air at higher altitudes offers less resistance to the gases escaping from the nozzles of the engines than does the denser air at lower altitudes. For this reason, the thrust increases as the altitude of the rocket increases.

Keeping Rockets in Space

At a height of several hundred kilometers above the earth, a rocket must keep moving at a speed of almost 30,000 kilometers per hour, or about 8 kilometers per second, to keep from falling back to earth. If it is moving at the proper velocity, the rocket becomes an artificial satellite and begins to orbit the earth (Fig. 22–7). Although a satellite in orbit is being pulled continuously to the earth by gravity, the speed at which the satellite is moving balances the force of gravity that is pulling it toward the earth. When the satellite is in a stable orbit, it continues to follow a curved path around the earth.

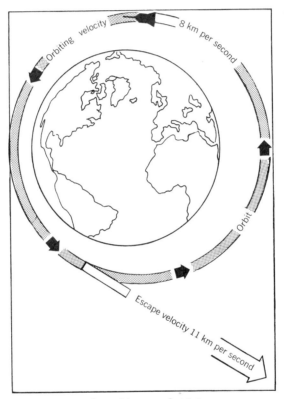

Fig. 22–7. Launching a rocket into space.

A satellite or spacecraft in orbit can leave its orbit if it speeds up or slows down. The speed is decreased by applying a thrust in a direction opposite to the direction in which the satellite is moving. Such *reverse thrust* is applied by firing *retro-rockets*, which act against the forward motion of the satellite. As the satellite slows down, it loses altitude. In time, it will reenter the atmosphere and be slowed up even more by friction with air. Friction with the earth's atmosphere may cause the satellite to burn up like a meteor. Returning spacecraft, such as the *Apollo* command modules, have heat shields that protect the spacecraft and their crews as they descend into the atmosphere.

The speed of a satellite or spacecraft in orbit can be increased by firing its rocket engines. This is done when it is desired to break away from the pull of the earth's gravity entirely. When the spacecraft's velocity reaches 40,000 kilometers per hour, or 11 kilometers per second, it is moving fast enough to escape the earth's gravity (Fig. 22–7). This speed is called *escape velocity*.

To achieve the great speeds needed to orbit the earth and to achieve escape velocity, the engines of a launching rocket are fired in stages (Fig. 22–8). Firing rocket engines in stages has two great advantages: (1) when the first stage has used up all of its fuel and its engine burns out, the first stage is released from the rocket, reducing the overall weight of the rocket; (2) the thrust of the second-stage engine adds to the speed already imparted by the first stage, which increases the speed of the rocket still further. The same effect is achieved by a third stage.

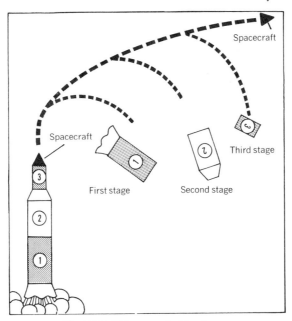

Fig. 22–8. Firing a rocket in stages.

NAVIGATION THROUGH SPACE

Navigating through space is more complicated than navigating on earth. On earth, navigation is two-dimensional. The navigator of a ship, for example, need find only the latitude and longitude of the ship. Navigating through space is three-dimensional; the navigator must find the location of a craft in space by reference to three points.

A small navigational error on earth may put a ship or an airplane several kilometers off course. A similar error in the enormous distances of space may put a spacecraft thousands or even millions of kilometers off course.

An *inertial guidance system* is used to guide spacecraft through space. This system makes use of computers, gyroscopes, and other devices to make the calculations necessary to guide the spacecraft accurately. The inertial guidance system records the spacecraft's position relative to the earth, the moon, and the stars. Once the spacecraft is set on its course, the inertial guidance system automatically keeps it on course. Without this system, space travel would be impossible.

One feature that space navigation has borrowed from earth navigation is the system of lines of latitude and longitude. To visualize these lines, imagine the earth as a small sphere at the center of a huge hollow sphere, which has been called the *celestial sphere*. The stars appear as pinpoints of light on the inside of the celestial sphere. The North and South Poles, the equator, and all the parallels of latitude and meridians of longitude are imagined to extend from the earth to the inside of the celestial sphere.

In navigating through space, the navigator fixes the position of a spacecraft within the celestial sphere, using a sextant or automatic star-tracking device. With the help of a computer, the navigator then calculates the course that the spacecraft must follow in order to reach its destination.

EXPLORING THE MOON

Before astronauts orbited the earth and landed on the moon, our knowledge about the moon was obtained by means of telescopes, spectroscopes, and other instruments. As a result of the moon flights and the work of the astronauts, our knowledge of the moon's features and composition has grown. In addition, we have a better understanding of how to support life in the moon environment.

General Features of the Moon

The diameter of the moon is about 3500 kilometers, which is a little more than one-fourth the diameter of the earth. The moon looks small because it is so far from us. You will recall that the average distance from the earth to the moon is about 380,000 kilometers. The mass of the moon is $\frac{1}{81}$ the mass of the earth, and the force of gravity on the surface of the moon is only $\frac{1}{6}$ the force of gravity on the surface of the earth.

The moon has no atmosphere, nor has water been detected on the surface of the moon. Lacking water and an atmosphere, the moon has no weather. Because the moon lacks the protective covering of an atmosphere, surface temperatures may be more than 100°C on its sunlit side and less than −150°C on its dark side.

The Surface of the Moon

The moon's surface is covered with fine, dustlike particles. In some places, the particles are packed about as densely as soil on the earth. In addition to the fine particles, larger particles, including boulders of various sizes, are present. A photograph taken by Lunar Orbiter V shows a dislodged boulder about 18 meters in diameter that has rolled down a slope, leaving a trail more than 200 meters long.

The outstanding characteristic of the moon's appearance is the presence of thousands of *craters*. The craters range in size from less than a meter in diameter to more than 270 kilometers in diameter.

Two well-known craters are *Tycho*, which is about 80 kilometers in diameter, and *Copernicus*, which is almost 100 kilometers in diameter. Both craters are named after famous astronomers. Tycho is surrounded by mountains that rise about 4800 meters above the floor of the crater. The floor of Copernicus is about 3300 meters deep. Many very small craters appear to extend only a short distance into the lunar surface.

Some craters appear to have been filled by lava flows. Other craters appear to be filled by the fine particles that make up the lunar surface. Scientists believe that some of the craters may have been formed by the impacts of meteorites, while other craters may have been formed by volcanic eruptions. A system of starlike lines, or *rays*, extends hundreds of miles outward from some craters. These rays are believed to consist of debris thrown out from the craters by the force of the impacting meteorites.

Some of the mountains on the moon reach great heights. For example, the Doerfels are about 5400 meters high, and the Apennines are about 5100 meters high. According to some estimates, lunar mountains are as high as 7500 meters, comparable to some of the earth's highest mountains.

The moon also has large dark areas called *maria*, or seas. The Latin word *maria* (singular, *mare*) was first applied to these areas by Galileo, who thought that they resembled the seas on earth. The maria are actually relatively smooth plains and, of course, contain no water (Fig. 22–9, page 424).

Fig. 22–9. Mare (or sea) and craters of the moon.

In the vicinity of the Apollo 11 landing spot, the moon's loose surface materials consist of fragmented debris about 3 to 6 meters deep. The particles range in size from microscopic particles to blocks more than a meter across. Among the fragmented materials are basaltic igneous rocks, crystalline fragments, glassy fragments, and meteorites. The fragments on the surface of the moon were probably formed from the moon's crust as a result of being bombarded by particles from space.

Chemical Nature of the Moon

The moon rocks brought back to earth by the Apollo moon flights have been examined carefully. Also, rockets equipped with special instruments have been landed on the surface of the moon. These instruments perform chemical analyses and radio the results back to earth.

In general, scientists have found that samples of the moon's surface are quite similar in composition to the rocks in the earth's crust. Thus, the composition of the moon's soil is like that of powdered basalt, which is one of the most common rocks of the earth's crust. Further analysis of the moon's surface indicates the presence of many elements, including iron, carbon, oxygen, sodium, aluminum, magnesium, silicon, and calcium. The most abundant of these elements on the moon, as on earth, are oxygen, silica, and aluminum.

Compared to earth rocks, all moon rocks have higher concentrations of certain elements, such as scandium, titanium, and zirconium. The lunar surface materials are also relatively rich in nickel, copper, gold, and silver.

Changes in the Moon

The Apollo series of moon explorations reveals that the moon is not a cold, unchanging body, but indeed appears to be warm inside and undergoing changes at the surface.

Evidence that the moon may be warm inside is found in the presence of gas clouds detected by the Apollo 11 crew and in bits of glasslike particles mixed in with the lunar soil that was brought back by the Apollo 12 crew. The clouds of gas are believed to be trapped in caverns beneath the surface of the moon. The presence of gas (possibly helium, argon, or krypton) indicates that the moon's core (center) may still be warm. The presence of "glass" indicates that a melting process has taken place. Scientists believe that heat beneath the moon's surface produced masses of molten material which hardened rather quickly and produced glasslike rocks. The presence of glasslike bits on the surface of the moon indicates that a meteorite may have crashed into the moon, shattered the crust, penetrated rather deeply, and scattered the broken particles over the moonscape.

Scientists theorize that the evidence of molten material indicates that the moon's interior may have formed in somewhat the same way as that of the earth, with layers topped by a crust at the surface. The moon may have been molten enough for this material to separate according to its density and composition, with the heaviest materials settling more quickly. From other evidence, some scientists theorize that the moon's core consists of a dense olivine-type rock, rich in iron. Above this rock, they believe there may be a layer composed of olivine and basaltlike rock somewhat similar to the olivine and basalt we find on earth. The top layer, or crust, is described by these scientists as entirely basaltlike, which is confirmed by samples of the crust returned to earth by Apollo crews.

Instruments left by the moon explorers on the lunar surface, followed by 21 days of observation by scientists on earth, revealed an absence of seismic (earthquake) events that we are familiar with in the earth. Scientists account for this observation by assuming that there is much less heat energy in the moon's interior than in the earth's.

Age of Moon Rocks

Some igneous rocks (basaltic) were formed about 3.7 billion years ago. Other fragments have an age of about 4.6 billion years. (Ages of samples were determined by means of radioactive dating, which is explained in the next chapter.) Such observations indicate that, after the moon's formation, igneous activity continued for millions of years. These observations provide important clues to the early years in the formation of the earth.

Life on the Moon?

Before the Apollo moon flights, scientists predicted that the possibility of past or present life on the moon was very unlikely. As predicted, the lunar rock samples returned to earth contain no evidence of life. Actual laboratory studies of moon rocks reveal no concentrations of the types of compounds produced by living things. In addition, there has been no evidence of water in the moon rocks or on the moon. As you know, water is vital to virtually all life forms, even the one-celled organisms found on earth. The absence of water suggests the absence of life on the moon, at least life as we know it.

In the lunar rocks, very small concentrations of carbon—an element vital to living things—are possibly the result of the solar wind (exposure to sun radiation). Graphite, a mineral form of carbon, has been observed. All studies at this time indicate no evidence of life. From data gathered on future flights, scientists will continue to search for the presence of carbon compounds, which—if found—would provide important clues to the origin of life on the earth and on other planets.

A Human Environment on the Moon?

Humans have reached the moon, landed on it, and returned to earth. Someday, people may desire to live on the moon. If they do, they will face several obstacles.

Since the moon is so much smaller than the earth, the moon's gravitational pull is only about one-sixth that of the earth. A person on the moon would have to learn to adjust to this condition of lower gravity. Using the same amount of body energy needed for one walking step of less than a meter on earth, the same person walking on the moon might easily leap ahead 5 meters.

To be able to live on the moon for an extended period of time, people would need to construct some sort of completely enclosed shelter, creating an environment like that on earth, because the moon has no atmosphere that could support human or plant life. Inside this shelter, the people could establish a pressurized artificial atmosphere and a closed environmental system. Except for its larger size, this enclosed system would operate like that described for the spaceship (pages 410–413). In this manner, the people could provide food and oxygen for themselves.

Owing to the absence of a heat-absorbing atmosphere, the sun heats the lighted part of the moon to a temperature of over 100°C. On the other hand, the temperature of the darkened part of the moon falls below −150°C. An air-conditioning system would be necessary to help maintain temperatures more favorable to life.

DETECTING LIFE ON OTHER PLANETS

Before humans attempt to land on a heavenly body other than the moon, spacecraft bearing instruments will be landed there, as they have been on the moon and on Mars. The spacecraft that landed on Mars were the *Viking I* and *Viking II Landers*. Such landers carry instruments able to detect life, should it exist, and radio that information back to earth (Fig. 22–10). The instruments are operated by means of remote controls. In order to avoid accidentally carrying any organisms from earth to a heavenly body, the instruments are thoroughly sterilized before leaving the earth. If this were not done, it would be impossible to tell whether any life discovered on a heavenly body was truly native to it or brought there by our instruments. Furthermore, if there is life on other heavenly bodies, the introduction of living things from our planet could upset the natural balance there.

Some of the life-detecting instruments are *collecting* and *culturing devices, radioactivity detectors*, and *special analyzers*.

Fig. 22–10. Viking Lander bearing instruments.

Collecting and Culturing Devices

Collecting devices operated by signals from the earth scoop up soil and cause valves to open, admitting the materials to a culture medium (food). Living things, such as bacteria, can grow and reproduce in such a medium. Radio signals are sent back to earth to indicate if growth occurs or not.

Radioactivity Detectors

This type of instrument can track a radioactive isotope (pages 8 and 437–438) of carbon as it enters different chemical reactions. The detector instrument collects soil and mixes it with radioactive carbon dioxide. The mixture, in an enclosed chamber, is then exposed to a sun lamp. After a time, with the aid of special analyzers described in the following section, the detector can locate the carbon if it is present in a molecule larger than a carbon dioxide molecule. So far as scientists know, the incorporation of carbon into a large molecule is an indication of photosynthesis or a life process like it. Thus, a soil sample that carries on photosynthesis is evidence of the presence of a simple, plantlike form of life in the soil.

Special Analyzers

With the aid of analyzers, such as certain types of chromatographs (pages 90–91) and special spectroscopes, scientists can determine the chemical composition of very small quantities of gases and other molecules. For example, both amino acids and DNA are characteristic of all living things on earth. If the analyzers disclose the presence of these compounds elsewhere in the universe, we may then have evidence of life there. When the analyses are completed, the information is radioed back to earth. (Thus far, life has not been detected either on the moon or on Mars.)

FUTURE PROBLEMS OF SPACE TRAVEL

Undoubtedly, there are many hazards in space travel that have not yet been encountered. Scientists wonder what effects prolonged space travel will have on a person's physical and mental health. How long can a few people live together in isolation from the world? What new diseases might space travelers bring back to earth? What effect will long space voyages have on the astronauts' ability to control their spacecraft and return to earth? The answers to these and many other questions will have to be found if space exploration is to continue.

Looking Back

Astronauts and scientists traveling by spaceship have reached and explored the environment of the surface of the moon. Numerous survival problems for these space travelers have had to be overcome. These problems include providing adequate air pressure, oxygen, food, water, waste disposal, and protection against harmful radiation.

Modern spaceships, powered by rocket engines, work on the principle that for every action there is an equal and opposite reaction (Newton's third law of motion).

The explorations of the moon by both instruments and men, and of Mars by instruments alone, have added to our knowledge of the structure and composition of the surfaces of the moon and Mars. However, no sign of life has been found on either heavenly body.

Looking Ahead

In the future, explorations of heavenly bodies beyond the moon and Mars will add to our knowledge about these bodies. Should evidence of life be detected elsewhere, it might be at a very different stage of development. Let us now learn more about the life that existed here on earth in prehistoric times. We discuss this subject in Chapter 23.

Multiple-Choice Questions

1. Which process would an unprotected human be unable to carry out in space?
   a. respiration   b. digestion   c. circulation   d. assimilation
2. A rapid decrease in air pressure on the body is dangerous because it can lead to the formation of
   a. poisons in the stomach   c. gas bubbles in the blood
   b. wastes in the cells   d. excess carbon dioxide
3. For a 3-day space flight, the oxygen supply in a spaceship can be maintained by means of
   a. oxygen tanks   c. distillation
   b. chlorella   d. a closed environmental system
4. Compared to the force of gravity on the earth, the force of gravity on the surface of the moon is
   a. the same   b. 6 times less   c. 6 times more   d. 10 times less
5. Rocket engines can be used in outer space because they are
   a. lighter than jet engines
   b. able to carry their own supply of oxygen
   c. more powerful than jet engines
   d. more streamlined than jet engines

6. Before a spacecraft can be placed in orbit around the earth, it must attain a speed of about
   a. 8 kilometers per hour   c. 8 kilometers per second
   b. 11 kilometers per hour   d. 11 kilometers per second
7. The only type of engine that is capable of lifting a spacecraft into orbit at the present time is the
   a. atomic engine   c. turbo-jet engine
   b. ion engine   d. chemical rocket engine
8. A closed environmental system is most like
   a. photosynthesis   c. weightlessness
   b. a balanced aquarium   d. a rocket
9. Although freshly distilled water has a "flat" taste, it is safe to drink because it lacks
   a. oxygen and carbon dioxide
   b. harmful minerals and bacteria
   c. hydrogen and oxygen
   d. dissolved nitrogen and helium
10. If astronauts were to land on the dark side of the moon, they would need to take steps to prevent
   a. burning up   b. using fuel   c. using oxygen   d. freezing
11. If unsterilized equipment should land on some distant planet, there is a possibility that
   a. our astronauts would become diseased
   b. the balance of nature on the planet would be upset
   c. the equipment would stop working
   d. the balance of nature on earth would be upset
12. The instrument that may be able to detect amino acids on a foreign planet is
   a. a TV microscope   c. a type of spectroscope
   b. an electron microscope   d. an electroscope

Modified True-False Questions

1. The Chinese invented rockets almost *100* years ago.
2. The first liquid-fueled rockets were built during the *1940s*.
3. Newton's *third law* states that for every action there is an equal and opposite reaction.
4. If you weigh 60 kilograms on earth, you would weigh about *20 kilograms* on the moon.
5. The fuels used in liquid rockets are kept at extremely cold temperatures to prevent them from *exploding*.
6. A type of rocket that would be most useful for very long voyages through space is the *liquid-fueled* rocket.
7. Exploration of the moon reveals rocks that are composed of elements *absent* on earth.
8. Some craters on the moon are *similar* to those on the earth.

Thought Questions

1. Describe four problems encountered by space explorers that are not usually encountered by explorers traveling on the surface of the earth.
2. Explain how the gases escaping from a rocket engine produce a forward thrust.
3. Explain why jet aircraft cannot go into orbit around the earth.
4. Give three reasons why rocket engines work more efficiently the farther the engines are from the earth.
5. Describe two different ways in which solid-propellant rockets are different from liquid-propellant rockets.
6. By means of a diagram, show how an oxygen-carbon dioxide cycle, a food cycle, and a water cycle would operate in a spaceship.
7. Name the five basic necessities of astronauts traveling in outer space, and explain how a spacecraft might be designed to supply these necessities on a long trip through space.
8. Describe the evidence that seems to indicate that life as we know it does not exist on the moon.

CHAPTER 23

WHAT IS THE HISTORY
OF LIFE ON THE EARTH?

When you have completed this chapter, you should be able to:

1. *Define* strata, half-life, evolution, fossil, index fossil.
2. *Explain* the older and modern methods of estimating the age of the earth and of extinct organisms.
3. *Describe* the ways in which fossils were formed.
4. *Trace* the evolution of living things through the geological eras.

In the laboratory experience that follows, you will imitate the way in which a fossil may be formed.

Laboratory Experience

HOW CAN WE DETERMINE THE APPEARANCE OF AN ANIMAL FROM ITS REMAINS?

A. Press a small shell into a piece of modeling clay to a depth of 5 or 6 millimeters (Fig. 23–1). Either rub a small amount of petroleum jelly on the shell beforehand, or coat the impression with petroleum

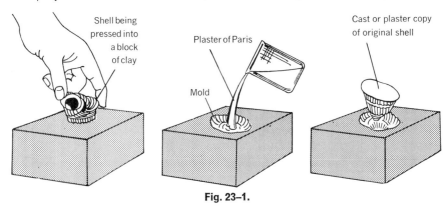

Fig. 23–1.

jelly afterward, using a small, soft brush. Brush the impression gently to avoid destroying the fine lines inside the impression.

B. Mix three tablespoons of plaster of Paris with about two tablespoons of water and add a pinch of table salt. Use just enough water to make the mixture a little thinner than pancake batter.

C. Pour the mixture into the impression in the modeling clay. Tap the sides of the clay with your hand to dislodge any air bubbles that may be trapped in the plaster of Paris.

D. As soon as the plaster of Paris has hardened, remove it from the modeling clay. Examine the cast you have made.
    1. Describe the appearance of the cast.
    2. Explain why the cast resembles the shell so closely.

E. Your teacher will give you a piece of clay containing an impression of an extinct animal that died millions of years ago. Make a plaster cast of the impression.
    3. After the plaster has hardened, carefully remove it from the clay and examine it. Describe what you see.
    4. Does this impression reveal the exact appearance of the extinct animal? Explain.

Introduction

Earthquakes, volcanic eruptions, landslides, and erosional activities occur regularly somewhere on earth. These natural occurrences slowly but constantly change the environment. Changes similar to these have occurred for as long as the earth has existed as a planet. During this long period of time, as the environment changed slowly, so too did the living things on earth. The environment has not remained constant in the past and probably never will.

At the beginning of the nineteenth century, little was known about the past history of the earth. Most people believed that the earth was about 6000 years old and that the earth was much the same at that time as it always had been. By this time, however, a few scientists had come to certain conclusions regarding the origin of different types of rocks. Their theories eventually contributed to our modern understanding of the age of the earth.

THEORIES CONCERNING THE ORIGIN OF ROCKS

A German geologist named *Abraham Werner* (1750–1817) noticed that the rocks in coal mines were arranged in layers, or *strata* (singular, *stratum*) (Fig. 23–2). After examining these rocks carefully, Werner proposed a theory to account for the origin of the strata.

Fig. 23–2. Rock layers in a coal mine.

Werner believed that, originally, the ocean was very muddy. At different times in the past, the mud settled in layers on the bottom of the ocean and then hardened into rock (sedimentary rock). According to Werner's theory, the heaviest particles of rock in the mud, especially particles of granite, settled to the bottom first. Granite, therefore, became the bottom layer. As other particles settled to the bottom of the ocean, new layers of rock gradually formed on top of the layer of granite. Eventually, the entire earth was covered by vast layers of rock. In this way, Werner believed, all the rocks in the earth's crust were formed.

Although some people accepted Werner's theory, others, including *James Hutton* (1726–1797), a Scottish geologist, did not. Hutton, and a few other geologists, believed that granite was related in some way to the lava that flows out of volcanoes. As evidence for their belief, they pointed out that granite is often found in cracks in limestone and other sedimentary rocks (Fig. 23–3). This fact led Hutton to the conclusion that granite had once been a hot, molten liquid (magma), and that the magma had forced its way into cracks in the limestone. The liquid magma then hardened into granite after cooling. Rocks formed in this way are igneous rocks.

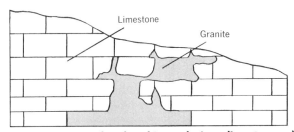

Fig. 23–3. Granite is often found in cracks in sedimentary rocks.

Those who accepted this second theory also believed that rock particles were, in general, the result of the erosion of existing masses of rock. When these particles settled on the bottom of the ocean, they formed sedimentary rocks. If all this is accepted as true, it becomes apparent that the wearing away of existing rocks and the formation of new rocks from deposits of sediments must have taken millions of years.

ESTIMATING THE AGE OF THE EARTH

In the middle of the nineteenth century, most people found it difficult to accept the idea that the rocks of the earth were millions of years old. It took the work of many scientists to convince them. Some of the early methods used by geologists to estimate the age of the earth included estimating the rate at which rocks erode, estimating the rate at which sediments are deposited, and estimating the time it took for the oceans to become as salty as they are today.

Rate of Erosion of Rocks

Since rocks are being eroded continuously, geologists have been able to calculate the age of the rocks in some parts of the earth by observing and measuring the rate at which erosion takes place. Let us assume that geologists estimate that the Colorado River eroded the Grand Canyon at the rate of about 30 centimeters every 1000 years. The Grand Canyon is now about 1800 meters deep. At this rate it might have taken the Colorado River 6 million years to erode the Grand Canyon to its present depth.

Rate of Deposit of Sediments

Since sediments are being deposited continuously in the ocean, geologists can use the same principle in reverse to determine how long it has taken to lay down a deposit of sediment. Geologists estimate that, on the average, it takes between 4000 and 10,000 years to form 30 centimeters of sedimentary rock from deposits of rock particles. A bed of sedimentary rock in New Jersey is about 4 kilometers thick. Calculations indicate that this bed of rock may well be over 50 million years old.

Rate of Accumulation of Salts in the Ocean

Since rivers carry millions of tons of dissolved salts into the ocean every year, it is reasonable to assume that when the ocean was first formed, it must have consisted of fresh water. As time went on, the rivers carried more and more salts into the ocean. As a result, the salinity (saltiness) of the ocean is much greater today than it was in the past.

Today, salts make up about 3.5% of the total weight of the ocean. By comparing the total amount of salts in the ocean today with the amount being carried into the ocean every year, geologists estimate that it has taken about 500 million years for the ocean to become as salty as it is.

Although these methods for estimating the age of the earth are not very accurate, they do indicate that the earth is certainly much older than 6000 years. These methods not only give us some idea of the age of the ocean, they also force us to the conclusion that the earth itself must be much older than the ocean. That is, the earth must be much older than 500 million years.

MODERN METHODS OF ESTIMATING THE AGE OF THE EARTH

Nineteenth-century methods gave only rough estimates of the age of the earth. It has been only since the discovery of *radioactivity*, and the invention of instruments that can measure the amount of radioactivity in rocks, that more accurate estimates of the age of the earth have been made possible.

To date, the best method for unlocking the secret of the earth's age lies in studying the rays, or radiations, given off by the atoms of certain elements. Such elements are called *radioactive elements*.

Radioactive Elements

Radioactive elements consist of atoms that are unstable. These atoms are continuously breaking down, or undergoing *radioactive decay*. In the process of decay, different kinds of rays and particles, called radiations, are emitted.

As a radioactive element decays, it changes into another element. For example, when one type of uranium called *uranium*-238 decays, it emits radiations and changes into the form of lead called *lead*-206. The rate at which a radioactive element decays into another element is not affected by heat, pressure, or any ordinary chemical process.

Rate of Radioactive Decay

The time it takes for one-half of a given quantity of a radioactive element to decay into another element is called the *half-life* of that element. For example, the half-life of uranium-238 is about $4\frac{1}{2}$ billion years. That is, if a block were made of uranium-238, it would take $4\frac{1}{2}$ billion years for half of this block to decay, or change, into lead. It would take another $4\frac{1}{2}$ billion years for half of the remaining half-block to change into lead, and so on (Fig. 23–4).

 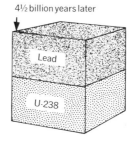 

Fig. 23–4. Half-life of uranium.

Other radioactive elements have half-lives that vary from a fraction of a second to billions of years. Uranium is usually used to date (calculate the age of) rocks that are very old. Another radioactive element, radioactive carbon, is used to determine the age of rocks or other substances that are much younger.

Uranium Dating

Uranium-238 is especially useful in dating rocks that are very old because, as we said, its half-life is about 4½ billion years. By comparing the amount of lead-206 present in a sample of rock to the amount of uranium-238 present, scientists can calculate the age of that rock. Using this method, scientists have calculated that some rocks in South Africa are almost 3½ billion years old. Using the same method, scientists have calculated that rocks in the Black Hills of North Dakota are about 1½ billion years old.

It is obvious that the earth must have been in existence not only before the ocean, but also before the formation of the most ancient rocks in the earth's crust. The earth, therefore, must be older than 3½ billion years. Most geologists believe that the earth is about 5 billion years old.

Carbon Dating

Radioactive carbon, or *carbon-14*, has a half-life that is much shorter than the half-life of uranium-238. The half-life of carbon-14 is about 5700 years. Carbon-14 is used to date materials that range in age from about 1000 years to about 44,000 years.

Carbon dating depends on the fact that both ordinary carbon (carbon-12) and radioactive carbon (carbon-14, also called *radiocarbon*) are found in fixed proportions to each other in the cells of all living plants and animals.

When a plant or animal dies, the radiocarbon present in the cells begins to decay. As a result, the amount of radiocarbon in the cells of the plant or animal decreases at a constant rate. The amount of ordinary carbon-12 in the cells does not change. Consequently, by measuring the proportion of radiocarbon to ordinary carbon in a substance—a piece of wood found in a prehistoric cave, for example—it is possible to estimate how old the wood is (Fig. 23–5). Using this method of dating, scientists have found that the Dead Sea Scrolls, some of which are written on parchment (which is made from animal skins), are about 2000 years old.

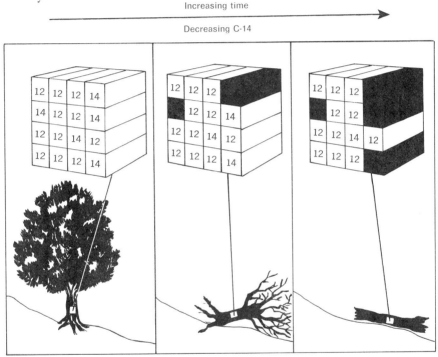

Fig. 23–5. Carbon dating.

DEVELOPMENT OF LIFE ON EARTH

Some scientists believe that the earth originated from a mass of hot gases that gradually cooled and condensed to form the earth. Other scientists believe that the earth originated from clouds of dust particles existing in space that collected together. Whatever the origin of the earth, once the earth had formed, scientists believe that it was much hotter than it is now. It was surrounded by an atmosphere that consisted of a mixture of the gases carbon dioxide, ammonia, methane, and water vapor. The atmosphere lacked the oxygen that is so familiar and important to us.

As the earth cooled, mountain ranges formed, with great depressed areas between the ranges. When the water vapor in the atmosphere became cool enough, it condensed into raindrops and fell to earth, gradually filling the large depressions. The ocean may have been formed in this way.

Life most likely began in the ocean. Since the ocean was formed more than 500 million years ago, it is possible that living things have existed on earth for over 500 million years.

It is believed that the first living things were simple, single cells that lived in the ocean. These organisms fed on chemical compounds already present in ocean water. The organisms did not require free oxygen to release energy for their life activities. Instead, they probably obtained energy from the breakdown of certain compounds present in the food they ate.

In time, more complicated organisms, such as jellyfish and algae, appeared in the ocean. The algae contained *chlorophyl*, a green substance. Chlorophyl, in the presence of light, converts carbon dioxide and water into carbohydrates. During this process (*photosynthesis*), oxygen is released as a by-product. Thus, as the ancient algae carried on photosynthesis, they released oxygen into the water. Some of the oxygen escaped into the air and became part of the atmosphere.

The bodies of the earliest forms of life were probably soft; animals with hard parts, such as shells, appeared later. The hard parts of these animals, preserved in sedimentary rocks, are often found today.

The next form of animal life to develop was fishes. These animals possessed gills, which enabled them to breathe in water. Some fish developed lungs, which made it possible for them to breathe air when they were out of water.

When green (chlorophyl-bearing) plants developed on land, they added much more oxygen to the atmosphere than did the algae. From that time onward, green plants have kept the amount of oxygen in the atmosphere fairly constant.

Eventually, some air-breathing fish probably gave rise to *amphibians*. Examples of amphibians are frogs and newts. Since amphibians have gills when they are born, they must live the early part of their lives in water. As amphibians grow older, they develop lungs and can live on land. The amphibians, however, continue to lay their eggs in water.

Amphibians, it seems, gave rise to *reptiles*, and reptiles in turn gave rise to both *birds* and *mammals*.

During this same period of time, simple plants also developed from simple, one-celled organisms living in water. These early plants eventually gave rise to the trees and other land plants of today.

The study by scientists of a great number of organisms, both living and extinct (no longer in existence), indicates that all forms of life developed from other forms of life that existed before them. This development is called *evolution*. This means that modern forms of life developed gradually from forms that lived before them.

THE EVIDENCE OF FOSSILS

The evidence that extinct forms of life did indeed exist is found in sedimentary rocks in the form of *fossils*. We could say that sedimentary rocks are the earth's "frozen fourth dimension," because locked in sedimentary rocks are the fossils that enable us to decipher the record of past events that have taken place on earth.

Fossils in Rocks

A fossil is the remains of an extinct organism that has been preserved naturally in the crust of the earth. Most fossils are found embedded in sedimentary rocks because, under the conditions in which sedimentary rocks are formed, a dead organism decays slowly enough to leave some trace of its existence in the rocks. Consequently, some evidence of the existence of an organism may be present in sedimentary rocks that are hundreds of millions of years old.

Virtually no fossils are found in igneous rocks. This is because the molten mass from which igneous rocks are formed is so hot that any organism caught in the mass is usually destroyed by heat, leaving no trace of its remains behind.

The study of a fossil can tell us not only what the organism looked like; it can also give us some idea of the habits of the organism and how it became a fossil. In some cases, the entire body of an extinct animal has been preserved. We can see what it looked like and study its parts directly. In other cases, nothing but the footprints of the extinct animal have been preserved, and we must deduce the appearance of the animal from its footprints.

Fossils in Ice

The hard parts of an animal's body, such as its teeth or bones, are more likely to be preserved in rocks than are the soft parts. However, in some situations, even the soft parts may be preserved unchanged.

Would you eat the meat of an animal that died thousands of years ago? A group of Russian explorers did just that! They ate the meat of an elephantlike animal called the *woolly mammoth* that lived during the last ice age (Fig. 23–6). The meat had not decayed because it had been frozen solid, and had thereby been preserved, in the ice of a Siberian glacier.

Fig. 23–6. Woolly mammoth.

Fossils in Tar

Some of the best-preserved remains of animals have been found in natural tar pits. When an animal accidentally stepped on the surface of the tar, it became trapped because of the stickiness of the tar. The trapped animal sank beneath the surface of the tar, where it was isolated from bacteria, animals, the weather, and other agents that might destroy its remains.

When the bones of the animal are removed from the tar pit and cleaned, the bones give us a very good idea of the original appearance of the animal. The *saber-toothed tiger* is an example of a fossil species that has been preserved in tar in this way. A great many remains of the saber-toothed tiger have been removed from the *La Brea Tar Pits*, located in Los Angeles, California.

Fossils in Amber

When the sticky resin produced by some extinct species of pine trees hardened, it turned into *amber* (or *fossil resin*). Millions of years ago, insects that were trapped in the resin before it hardened became embedded in it. Today we can observe not only the form, but also the color, of insects that have been preserved in amber.

Fossil Molds and Casts

Sometimes, the bones and shells embedded in sedimentary rocks are completely dissolved by natural processes. The spaces once occupied by these objects continue to retain the shapes of the original objects. A hollow space such as this in a rock is called a *fossil mold*. When a natural fossil mold fills with a mineral substance that subsequently hardens, a *fossil cast* is formed. You duplicated this process in the laboratory by pressing a shell into clay to form a mold and then filling the mold with plaster of Paris to produce a cast, or plaster copy, of the shell.

Fossil Impressions

When birds or other animals walk over a layer of mud, they leave impressions, or tracks, of their feet in the mud. If the mud then hardens, imprints of their feet remain behind permanently as *fossil impressions*. In a similar way, the trails left by worms, the impressions of animal bodies, and many other impressions of extinct animals and plants have been left in soft sediments that subsequently hardened.

Fossil Replaced Remains

Replaced remains are remains that do not have the composition of the original plant or animal. For example, many of the petrified trees found in Arizona do not consist of wood but of mineral matter. The original wood of these trees has been "changed to stone," or *petrified* (Fig. 23–7).

Fig. 23–7. Petrified wood.

Wood and bone may become petrified when they are buried in a deposit of sand or silt soaked by groundwater containing dissolved minerals. Under these conditions, particles of the decaying object may be replaced gradually by particles of minerals that crystallize out of the groundwater. In time, the original object may be replaced completely by minerals.

The Fossil Record

Running water carries particles of rock—sands and clays—into the ocean. These particles gradually form thick deposits of sediments. In time, these sediments change into sedimentary rocks, such as sandstone and shale.

In addition, the remains of small marine animals sink to the bottom of the ocean. The shells of these animals may also form thick deposits of sediments. In time, these sediments change into sedimentary rocks, such as chalk, which is a form of limestone.

Over a period of time lasting thousands or millions of years, the rate at which a deposit of sediment is being laid down may change, or the materials making up the deposit may change. These changes may be caused by changes in the climate, the gradual wearing down and disappearance of mountain ranges, the aging of young rivers into old rivers, and many other factors. As a result, the appearance and depth of the sedimentary deposit change. Because of these transformations, the rocks that form from these deposits have distinctive-looking strata.

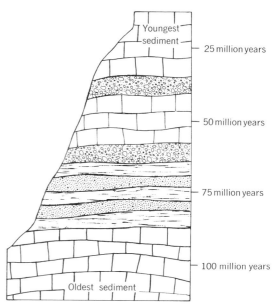

Fig. 23–8. Sedimentary strata.

The strata of sedimentary rocks can be compared to a pile of old newspapers. Every day another newspaper is placed on top of the pile. The oldest newspaper is always on the bottom of the pile, and the most recent newspaper is on the top. When sedimentary strata are not disturbed by natural forces, they are much like the pile of newspapers: the oldest strata are on the bottom, and the more recent strata are on top (Fig. 23–8).

In some parts of the world, the strata are more than 12 kilometers deep. The most magnificent display of strata is in the Grand Canyon, where the Colorado River has carved its way through more than 1800 meters of rocks, exposing strata of different colors.

Fossils as Time-Keepers

In many parts of the world, strata are not piled neatly on top of one another like a pile of old newspapers. Instead, the forces that build mountains and cause earthquakes have twisted, folded, or split the strata. Erosion may even have removed entire strata. Newer sediments may then have been deposited on top of these disturbed strata, changing and confusing the sequence in which they had been deposited. When strata are disturbed in this way, can the strata still be dated accurately?

In the late 1700s, an English civil engineer named *William Smith* (1769–1839) noticed that certain rock strata always contained distinctive kinds of plant and animal fossils, no matter what the positions of the strata might be. Smith found this was true even when the strata occurred in widely separated parts of England. Even though the locations of the strata were different, the similarity of the fossils in similar types of strata led Smith to the conclusion that the rocks were the same age.

Thus, Smith was responsible for the idea that certain easily identified and widely distributed fossils could be used to date periods of geologic time in the earth's history. Fossils used to date strata in this way are called *index fossils*, or *guide fossils*. Such fossils can be used to date strata that are separated from one another by many kilometers (Fig. 23–9). By studying the index fossils both in undisturbed strata and in disturbed strata, as well as by studying the radioactivity of the rocks in nearby igneous rocks, geologists have been able to arrange fossils and strata in the order in which they were deposited originally.

As a result, we have been able to determine the order in which plants and animals have appeared on earth. Scientists have thus confirmed that the simpler forms of life appeared first and that the more advanced and complicated forms of life developed from these simpler organisms.

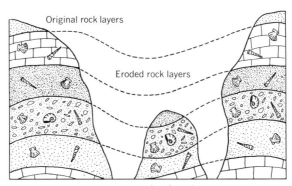

Fig. 23–9. Index fossils.

THE STORY TOLD BY FOSSILS AND ROCKS

The history of the earth extends through the tremendous span of more than five billion years. *Paleontologists*, scientists who study fossils, have divided this span of time into several units called *eras*. Each era, in turn, is divided into several smaller divisions of time called *periods*, and each period is divided into several *epochs*. Each era, period, and epoch represents a major and distinctive chapter in the history of the earth.

Each era covers an interval of time during which particular types of animals and plants existed in great abundance, or were *dominant*. An era usually ended with a general uplifting of the land, the disappearance of the dominant forms of plant and animal life, and the appearance of new types of dominant plants and animals.

Table 23–1 lists the five major eras of geologic history. The name of each era is a Latin or Greek word that describes the relationship of that era to the other eras.

Table 23–1. Major Eras of the Earth's History

Era	Years Ago (began)
Period before appearance of life	?
Archeozoic (primitive, or beginning, life)	4 billion
Proterozoic (former life)	
Paleozoic (old, or ancient, life)	500 million
Mesozoic (middle life)	200 million
Cenozoic (recent life)	75 million

Archeozoic and Proterozoic Eras

The *Archeozoic Era* and the *Proterozoic Era* take up a very large portion of the earth's history; yet we know almost nothing about these eras. Heat, pressure, and chemical action have completely changed the rocks formed during these eras. Fossils are almost entirely absent from these rocks. Heat and chemical action may have destroyed them, or the plants and animals that lived during these eras may have had no hard parts that could be preserved.

Some archeozoic and proterozoic rocks contain carbon. Some paleontologists believe that this carbon originated in the bodies of simple, one-celled, soft-bodied organisms. Any living things that existed during these eras probably were plantlike marine organisms, such as bacteria and algae, and marine animals, such as protozoans, jellyfish, and worms.

Paleozoic Era

The *Paleozoic Era* can be divided into three great *ages*, each age showing marked differences in the dominant forms of life that existed then. These ages are the *Age of Invertebrates*, the *Age of Fishes*, and the *Age of Amphibians*.

1. *Age of Invertebrates. Invertebrates* are soft-bodied animals without backbones, though sometimes the bodies are enclosed in shells. Common examples of invertebrates include worms, lobsters, clams, and insects.

The earliest sedimentary rocks of the Paleozoic Era contain the fossils of a great number of invertebrates that had shells or other hard covering materials. Two outstanding examples of these extinct invertebrates are *trilobites* and *brachiopods* (Fig. 23–10).

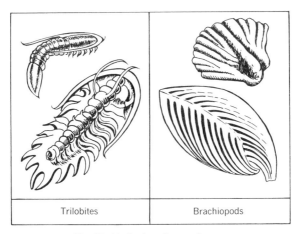

| Trilobites | Brachiopods |

Fig. 23–10. Extinct invertebrates.

In addition to marine invertebrates, large numbers of seaweeds thrived in the Paleozoic oceans.

2. *Age of Fishes.* In the early part of the Paleozoic Era, fish first appeared in the ocean. These fish were the first *vertebrates*, which are animals having backbones. Other common examples of vertebrates include whales, snakes, and humans.

By the middle of the Paleozoic Era, fish were the dominant form of life. At the same time that fish were developing in the ocean, invertebrates such as spiders and scorpions, and plants such as mosses and ferns, first appeared on land.

3. *Age of Amphibians.* All the first forms of life lived originally in the ocean. In time, however, some marine vertebrates developed the ability to crawl on land and to survive while out of the water for relatively long periods of time. Amphibians evolved from these marine animals. Examples of amphibians include frogs, toads, and salamanders. The first amphibians later evolved into the first reptiles.

Insects also developed during the late Paleozoic Era. Large swarms of insects, some with two-foot wingspans, thrived in the swampy fern forests of late Paleozoic times. These swampy forests were later transformed into the fossilized plants that make up beds of coal that are mined today.

The Paleozoic Era ended with the disappearance of some dominant forms of life, including the trilobites, that had lived in the ocean for millions of years. As the Paleozoic Era came to a close, land forms also changed. Large sections of what is now the United States rose above sea level. It was at this time that the Appalachian Mountains rose in what is now the eastern part of the United States.

Mesozoic Era

The *Mesozoic Era* is also known as the *Age of Reptiles. Dinosaurs* were the dominant form of animal life throughout most of this era. Dinosaurs ranged in length from several centimeters to about 25 meters. Some of the more famous types of dinosaurs are the *brontosaurus*, the *tyrannosaurus*, the *diplodocus*, and the *plesiosaurus*. Some modern descendants of the dinosaurs include snakes, turtles, and lizards.

Unlike amphibians, reptiles lay their eggs on land. The leathery shell of the egg contains the food supply for the embryo that is developing within. When the egg hatches, the newborn reptile is ready to live on its own.

The first birds appeared during the Age of Reptiles. These birds had evolved from certain types of reptiles. One of these birds was a strange-looking creature that paleontologists called *archeopteryx* (Fig. 23–11). Archeopteryx had characteristics of both birds and reptiles, including

Fig. 23–11. Archeopteryx.

teeth, claws on the front of its wings, and a feathered tail. Archeopteryx laid its eggs on land.

The Mesozoic Era ended with the appearance of the Rocky Mountains and the disappearance of many dominant forms of life, including the dinosaurs.

Cenozoic Era

The *Cenozoic Era*, the most recent geologic era and the era in which we are living, is also called the *Age of Mammals*. A few mammals appeared during the Mesozoic Era, but it was only after the close of the Mesozoic Era, more than 70 million years ago, that mammals began to increase in numbers. Today, they are the dominant form of animal life.

Mammals have hair, or fur, on their bodies. Their young are fed milk, which is produced by special milk glands in the mother. Examples of mammals include rats, dogs, cats, whales, horses, and humans.

An animal about the size of a fox first appeared at the beginning of the Cenozoic Era; this animal was the ancestor of the modern horse. Primitive monkeys, dogs, mice, squirrels, elephants, and many other ancestors of the mammals living today first appeared during this period. Saber-toothed tigers were also among the new arrivals. Many of these mammals, such as the woolly mammoth and the saber-toothed tiger, became extinct during the ice age that ended about 12,000 years ago.

Highlights of the History of the Earth

Table 23–2 summarizes the highlights of the most important changes that have occurred on the earth, including the development of plants and animals into modern plants and animals.

THE BEGINNINGS OF HUMAN LIFE

No one knows exactly where and when humans first appeared on earth. Archeologists have found human-type bones that are at least 1,300,000 years old. Fossilized bones of our earliest known ancestor, a giant ape man, are even older. These bones have been found in East Africa.

Parts of skeletons found in caves indicate that a primitive type of human, called *Homo erectus* (or *Pithecanthropus*), lived in Europe, Asia, and Africa about 300,000 years ago. The first true human, *Homo sapiens*, lived in Europe over 100,000 years ago, in the form of *Neanderthal man*. Neanderthals lived in caves, used stone tools and fire, and hunted animals for food.

Table 23-2. Highlights of the Earth's History

Era	Years Ago (began)	Animal Forms	Plant Forms	Changes Occurring
Before life appeared	?	No life—only chemical elements and compounds		Formation of the earth and its atmosphere
Archeozoic	?	Unknown simple types of life		—
Proterozoic	4,000,000,000	Invertebrates Protozoans Sponges Worms	Algae	Great volcanic and earthquake activity
Paleozoic	500,000,000	Complex invertebrates Fishes Amphibians	Mosses Ferns	Taconic and Green Mountains appear Great swamps First Appalachians rise
Mesozoic	200,000,000	Reptiles	Cone-bearing plants	Palisades formed Rocky Mountains and Sierra Nevada rise
Cenozoic	75,000,000	Mammals Birds	Flowering plants	Alps and Himalayas rise Appalachians rise again Ice ages

Neanderthals were replaced about 30,000 years ago by *Cro-Magnons,* who looked much as humans do today. Cro-Magnons were proficient at hunting and fishing. They also had remarkable artistic ability, producing magnificent paintings of beasts on the walls of caves located in France and in Spain.

THE HUMAN FUTURE

Throughout the ages, new forms of life have constantly evolved from existing forms of life. A great many different kinds of plants and animals have disappeared from the face of the earth after having existed for millions of years. Other kinds of plants and animals have replaced them.

Considering the amount of time that has passed since life originated on earth, it appears that the *Age of Humans* has just begun. The human brain probably surpasses the brain of any other animal in intelligence. This intelligence has enabled humans to control their environment. Humans even have the capacity to change the environment, and indeed they have done so. What will humans do to the environment in the future?

Looking Back

Evidence from geology and the study of fossils indicates that both the early environment and the organisms present in it were much different from the environment and organisms of today. As the environment changed slowly, the organisms changed gradually along with it. As the changes occurred, many forms of life became extinct. These forms are known to us from their fossils.

The earliest living things were simple, one-celled organisms. They existed as long as the environment suited them. They were followed by other one-celled organisms and more complex many-celled organisms. Today, the dominant form of animal life is the mammal. The most advanced mammals are humans, who often change parts of the environment—sometimes rapidly—to suit their own needs.

Looking Ahead

Now, as in the past history of the earth, organisms survive in the environment only so long as the environment is suitable for them. We will discuss the suitability of the environment—that is, the relationship between organisms and their environment—in Chapter 24.

Multiple-Choice Questions

1. At the beginning of the nineteenth century, most people believed that the age of the earth was about
   a. 6000 years
   b. 6 million years
   c. 100 million years
   d. 5 billion years
2. The salts in the ocean were added to the ocean waters primarily by
   a. landslides   b. salt mines   c. rivers   d. evaporation
3. When uranium decays, it becomes
   a. lead   b. salt   c. tin   d. copper
4. The rate of radioactivity of a sample of uranium is expressed in units of
   a. heat   b. pressure   c. temperature   d. half-life
5. The age of a sample of wood can be determined by carbon dating up to about
   a. 100 years   c. 4.5 million years
   b. 44,000 years   d. 500 million years
6. The first living things were
   a. dinosaurs   c. single-celled organisms
   b. jellyfish   d. bony fish
7. It is believed that amphibians developed from
   a. insects   b. dinosaurs   c. reptiles   d. fish
8. The type of rock in which most fossils are found is
   a. volcanic   b. igneous   c. metamorphic   d. sedimentary
9. The hollowed-out space in a rock that has the original form of the animal that was buried in the rock is called
   a. a cast   b. a mold   c. amber   d. a petrified form
10. A sample of wood that has been changed to stone is said to be
    a. cast   b. molded   c. crystallized   d. petrified
11. Fossils which are useful in dating strata that are not in a normal position are called
    a. datum fossils   b. index fossils   c. easy fossils   d. true fossils
12. A primitive type of human that lived in Europe, Asia, and Africa about 100,000 years ago was
    a. Neanderthal man   c. Java man
    b. Cro-Magnon man   d. Ape man
13. The oldest evidence of life on the earth is found in rocks containing
    a. decayed logs   c. carbon deposits
    b. salt crystals   d. iron deposits
14. In the Age of Amphibians, the dominant life form was an early "cousin" of the
    a. snake   b. spider   c. crab   d. frog
15. Which of the following animals is most closely related to the lizard?
    a. frog   b. fish   c. bat   d. bird

Modified True-False Questions

1. According to estimates based on how rapidly rock erodes, it has taken the Colorado River about 6 *million* years to cut the Grand Canyon.
2. Elements that give off rays when they decay are called *radioactive*.
3. The half-life of a substance is the time it takes for *all* of a given quantity of that substance to change into another substance.
4. Uranium is used in dating *young* rocks.
5. The earth is between 5 and 6 *million* years old.
6. The age of a prehistoric dwelling can be determined by measuring the radioactive *uranium* content of its remains.
7. The first simple forms of life probably appeared on earth *before* the Archeozoic Era.
8. The parts of extinct animals most likely to be preserved in their original form are *muscles*.
9. When sediments are undisturbed, the oldest layers are found at the *top*.
10. Trilobites and brachiopods are invertebrates that lived about 50 million years ago.
11. The first vertebrates were primitive *reptiles*.
12. Present-day "cousins" of the dinosaurs are *elephants*.
13. The remains of large extinct animals have been preserved in ice and in *salt*.
14. *Cro-Magnons* were very capable hunters and artists.

Thought Questions

1. Describe one traditional method and one modern method for determining the age of the earth.
2. Describe how scientists might determine the age of an animal skin found in a cave.
3. It has been said that sedimentary rocks are the earth's frozen fourth dimension. Explain.
4. How do you account for the fact that, although the original remains of worms have never been found in sediments, scientists still know that these worms existed hundreds of millions of years ago?
5. Why can't the trees of the Petrified Forest in Arizona be used as a fuel?
6. Explain what is meant by the following statement: When coal is burned, the energy of sunlight from millions of years ago is released.
7. Explain why there are no fossils present in the oldest rocks on earth.
8. Explain what is meant by the following statement: The human race is in the dawn of its existence; it may never see the sunset.
9. Number the following life forms in the order of their appearance in the earth's history, beginning with 1 for the oldest form: reptiles, fish, worms, amphibians, mammals, one-celled organisms.

CHAPTER 24

WHAT ARE THE
RELATIONSHIPS BETWEEN ORGANISMS
AND THEIR ENVIRONMENT?

When you have completed this chapter, you should be able to:

1. *Define* environmental factor, adaptation, balance of nature, predator, parasite, community.
2. *Discuss* how different organisms are adapted to their ways of life in particular environments.
3. *Appreciate* the value of lichens in forming soil.
4. *Distinguish* between (*a*) a food chain and a food web (*b*) producers, consumers, and decomposers.
5. *Give examples* of the succession of communities.
6. *Describe* each of the following natural cycles: energy, nitrogen, water, carbon dioxide–oxygen.

In the laboratory experience that follows, you will study the role of certain bacteria in the nitrogen cycle.

Laboratory Experience

HOW DO SOME ORGANISMS HELP EACH OTHER?

Some organisms live inside other organisms. In many cases of this type, one organism harms the other. In other cases, there is a partnership in which both organisms benefit. In this laboratory experience, you will become familiar with the relationship between clover plants and certain bacteria, called nitrogen-fixing bacteria.

A. Set the cup containing a growing healthy clover plant on a large sheet of paper. Carefully tear the cup and remove it from the soil. Grasp the plant near the soil line, and immerse the roots and clinging soil in a jar of water. Gently shake the plant to loosen the soil clinging to the roots. Holding the roots in the palm of one hand, allow a gentle stream of water to run over them, and remove any small soil clumps. Set the roots on a paper towel to absorb excess water.

B. Examine the roots carefully. Note some small enlargements on some of them. Each enlargement is called a *nodule.*

  1. How many nodules are present on the roots of your plant?

C. With forceps, remove one small nodule and place it on a microscope slide. Cover the nodule with a drop of water. Cover your specimen with another slide, and crush the nodule by pressing on the upper slide.

  2. Describe the appearance of the crushed specimen.

D. With a medicine dropper, transfer a bit of the specimen to another slide. Add a drop of methylene blue stain to the specimen, and cover it with a cover slip. Examine the stained specimen under the low power and then the high power of the microscope. The tiny objects you see are the nitrogen-fixing bacteria.

  3. Describe the appearance of the bacteria seen under high power.

  4. Draw a few of the different forms of bacteria visible.

  5. What can the bacteria in a nodule receive from the clover plant?

  6. What can the clover plant receive from the bacteria in a nodule?

E. Outline an experiment you can carry out to determine whether similar bacteria are present on bean roots and in corn roots.

Introduction

Studies of the earth's history reveal the natural changes that have taken place in the environment and in the organisms that inhabit it. As a result of these changes, we have come to realize that modern organisms had as distant ancestors some prehistoric organisms which are now extinct. The ancestors became extinct because they were not suited to live in a changed environment. However, before the ancestors died out, they left offspring that were slightly different from themselves. Such offspring, which could have been mutants (individuals bearing new hereditary traits), survived for a while because they were suited to their environment. They lived until the environment changed again and became unsuitable for them. This series of events was repeated until the present time. The organisms on earth now are suited to today's natural environment.

The plants and animals in existence today, like those of the past, depend upon one another and upon the environment. When the environment is suited to the life needs of organisms, the organisms live, reproduce, and carry on their kind, or species. That is, when the species is in harmony with its environment, the species survives. When the harmony is upset, or when the environment and the species are out of balance, many members of the species die. If the harmony is not reestablished, the species will become extinct.

Millions of species of organisms became extinct in ancient times. These organisms are known to us only from their fossils. Some species of organisms have become extinct in modern times. Among such species are the passenger pigeon and the dodo bird. Unless we understand how to keep the environment in balance with the organisms present today, many more species (including the human species) are likely to become extinct in the near future.

In this chapter, we will study the natural balanced relationships that exist between organisms and their environment. These relationships are the subject of study in the science of *ecology*.

NONLIVING AND LIVING FACTORS OF THE ENVIRONMENT

In a natural environment, an organism is influenced by two sets of conditions. One set of conditions consists of the *nonliving* factors of the environment. This part includes air, water, food, heat, and light. The second set of conditions consists of the *living* factors of the environment. This part includes organisms of the same species and organisms of other species.

An organism that survives for any period of time continually struggles with the nonliving and living factors of its environment. When the temperature drops, the organism can survive only if it can escape from the cold or adjust to it. When food becomes scarce, the organism must be able to compete with other organisms for the food. When attacked by an enemy, the organism must have some means of escape.

Every living thing possesses special features or characteristics that enable it to survive in the struggle to exist. For example, a whale, which inhabits cold water, has thick layers of fat that enable the animal to keep its body warm. An ivy vine has roots that enable the plant to climb toward light. Such special characteristics that help the organism fit into its environment and enable the organism to survive are called *adaptations*.

SPECIAL ADAPTATIONS OF ORGANISMS TO THE NONLIVING FACTORS OF THE ENVIRONMENT

Different organisms are adapted, or suited, to survive in different environments. Some organisms are adapted to live in a watery environment. Others are adapted to live in a dry, cold environment. Still others are adapted to live in a dry, warm environment.

Adaptations to Living in Water

Plants such as water lilies have air chambers throughout the plant body. These chambers allow gases to diffuse (spread) inside the plant and enable the leaves to float on the surface of the water. (The stomates, or pores, of such leaves are located only in the upper epidermis, or skin, rather than in the lower epidermis as in most land plants.) Because these leaves float, they are exposed to light and air, which they use in photosynthesis. By this process, green plants make food from carbon dioxide and water in the presence of sunlight.

Animals such as the catfish and the lobster have gills, which are organs that absorb dissolved oxygen from water. The oxygen is used in respiration. By this process, organisms oxidize food, thereby obtaining the energy required for their life activities.

Adaptations to Living on Land

Land plants of temperate regions, such as the oak and the maple, have well-developed root systems that anchor the plants firmly in the ground. The strong supporting tissue (wood) of the trunk enables the leaves and branches to be held up to light and air. Plants of dry regions, such as the cactus, can withstand desert conditions because the stem can store the water that infrequent rains supply. Plantlike organisms, such as lichens, that live in cold regions are low, flat, and leathery. They can survive long periods of cold and of being covered by snow.

Land animals have either lungs or air tubes that absorb oxygen from the air. Lungs are characteristic of such animals as birds and reptiles. Air tubes (*tracheae*) are characteristic of insects. Animals of dry regions, such as the rattlesnake, are able to exist on a limited supply of water because the scaly skin prevents the evaporation of water from the body. Animals of cold regions, such as the polar bear, have thick layers of fat and fur, which enable the bear to withstand cold. Animals, such as monkeys, that live and feed in treetops have fingers and toes—and sometimes a tail—that can grasp a branch.

SPECIAL ADAPTATIONS OF ORGANISMS TO THE LIVING FACTORS OF THE ENVIRONMENT

In the course of obtaining food and other necessities, plants and animals interact in various ways. Some organisms compete with others; some capture others and feed upon them; some are parasites; and some cooperate with others.

Adaptations for Competition

1. *Independent plants*—those that carry on photosynthesis—compete with one another for light. In a forest, the height and spread of trees enable them to receive light, but prevent light from reaching the ground, where grasses might grow. As a result, grasses are not usually found on the floor of a forest. In open regions, however, grasses grow plentifully.

2. *Plant-eating animals*—those that feed on vegetation—compete with one another for food. Grasshoppers, Japanese beetles, and rabbits not only compete with members of their own species for food, but each species also competes with the other species. All plant-eating animals are fitted for eating plants by having teeth or other mouth parts that can cut vegetation.

3. *Flesh-eating animals*—those that feed on other animals (either alive or dead)—like plant-eating animals, compete with their own and other species for food. Flesh-eating animals that feed on other living animals are called *predators*. The animals that are fed upon are called prey. Owls are predators that feed upon field mice, which are the prey. The teeth or other body parts of flesh-eating animals are fitted for grasping, holding, and tearing flesh.

4. *Parasitic animals* — those that spend their lives on the surface or inside the body of another organism, called a *host*—live at the expense of the host. Parasites are fitted for living within or in close contact with the host. The tapeworm, for example, has hooks and suckers by means of which it attaches itself to the intestinal wall of its host (Fig. 24–1). This parasite lacks a digestive system; it absorbs food that has already been digested by its host.

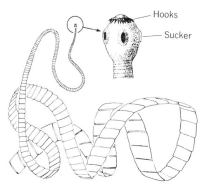

Fig. 24–1. A tapeworm.

Adaptations for Cooperation

1. *Social animals*—those of the same species that live together in colonies—help one another. In a colony of bees (a beehive), the members of the colony—workers and queen (females), and drones (males) —carry out different activities that benefit the colony. The worker bees

gather food for the other members of the hive and care for the young bees that are produced by the queen and a drone.

2. *Mutually helpful organisms*—two different kinds of organisms that live together—cooperate and help each other. The lichen, the plantlike organism that can live in cold regions, is really composed of two organisms—a green alga and a fungus. The fungus provides carbon dioxide, which the alga uses in photosynthesis. As a result of photosynthesis, the alga provides food for the fungus.

The pod-bearing plants, such as soybean, clover, and alfalfa, have beneficial bacteria that grow in their roots (Fig. 24–2). You observed these bacteria in the laboratory experience. The bacteria produce nitrates, which are mineral salts needed by the plants. At the same time, the plants provide the bacteria with food and moisture. We will study how nitrates are produced later in this chapter.

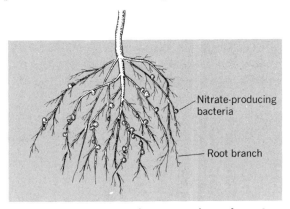

Fig. 24–2. Clover root and nitrate-producing bacteria.

EFFECT OF LIVING THINGS ON THE NONLIVING FACTORS OF THE ENVIRONMENT

As a result of their life activities, living things gradually cause changes in their environment. Important examples involve the formation, mineral content, and organic content of soil.

Soil Formation

Lichens, which can live on bare rock, break down some of the rock into small particles. These particles and dead lichens provide a thin layer of soil in which such plants as moss can grow. Eventually, more rock is broken down and dead moss plants accumulate, forming a thicker layer of soil that can anchor and support other plants. In time, the rock becomes covered with a thick layer of soil in which many types of plants grow.

Changing the Mineral Content of Soil

Most plants require nitrates and other mineral compounds, which they absorb from the soil. Examples are wheat and corn. Other plants, such as the nitrate-producing bacteria, put nitrates into the soil.

Organic Content of Soil

The wastes that animals give off and the plants and animals that die are destroyed in the process called *decay*. This process is carried out by numerous types of bacteria and fungi. These organisms feed upon the complex, organic, dead material and break it down to simple substances. Many of these substances seep down into the soil, become part of it, and fertilize it. We will have more to say about decay later in this chapter.

EFFECT OF LIVING THINGS ON OTHER LIVING FACTORS OF THE ENVIRONMENT

In any particular type of environment, many kinds of plants and animals can be found living in the same area. One kind of animal may feed upon one kind of plant. Another kind of animal may feed upon the first kind of animal. For example, a zebra may eat grass and may, in turn, be eaten by a lion. Such a group of organisms (grass, zebra, lion) in which one organism depends upon another for food is called a *food chain*.

Food chains often meet and cross one another. An animal that is part of one food chain may eat an animal that is part of another food chain. The criss-crossing of many food chains is called a *food web*. For example, plant-eating animals often eat more than one type of plant. Flesh-eating animals usually eat more than one type of plant-eater. Some flesh-eaters may even eat one another. When plants, plant-eaters, and flesh-eaters die, as a result of age or other causes, the dead bodies of all of them are consumed by the organisms that bring about decay. Fig. 24–3, page 460, illustrates a food web.

NATURAL RECYCLING

Every food chain begins with a green (independent) plant. The plant absorbs energy from the sun and makes its own food by photosynthesis. Green plants—grasses, for example—are called *producers*. Animals,

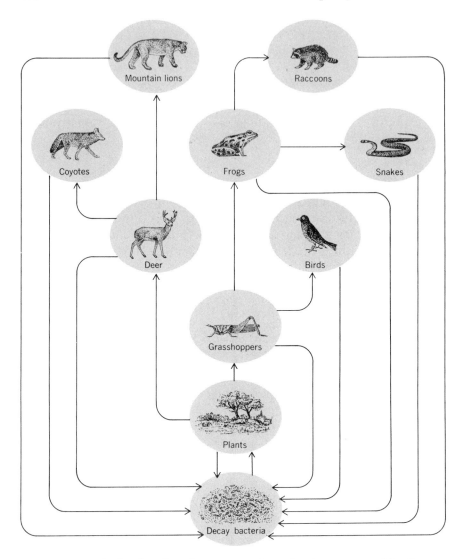

Fig. 24–3. A food web. Follow the arrows to determine the sequence of feeding.

such as grasshoppers, that feed upon green plants are called *first-level consumers*. Animals, such as frogs, that feed upon grasshoppers are called *second-level consumers*. Animals, such as raccoons, that feed upon frogs are called *third-level consumers*, and so on.

When producers and consumers die, organisms such as bacteria feed upon their bodies and decay them. These organisms are called *decomposers*. The decomposers break down the complex organic compounds (such as carbohydrates and proteins) of the dead organisms to simple inorganic compounds (such as carbon dioxide and nitrates). The inorganic compounds become part of the soil and the atmosphere. Eventually, these inorganic compounds are taken in by producers, which use them again as raw materials when they manufacture food. In this way, under natural conditions, the materials of which dead organisms and wastes are composed are *recycled*, or used over and over again.

NATURAL COMMUNITIES

Many species of plants and animals inhabit an area because they can survive in the conditions present there. The entire population of different kinds of organisms in a given area is called a *community*.

Communities are classified according to the type of environment in which they are found. Table 24–1 shows some common communities and the types of organisms that live in them. Each organism mentioned is part of a food web in its community.

Table 24–1. Natural Communities

Community	Common Organisms
Pond	Algae, water lilies, dragonflies, bass
Desert	Barrel cactus, creosote bush, rattlesnake, kangaroo rat
Evergreen forest	Hemlock, birch, moose, squirrel
Seashore	Seaweed, beach grass, snail, crab

Changes in Communities

The organisms in a community are often responsible for an accumulation of soil, wastes, dead branches, and other natural matter. As these materials accumulate, the character of the environment changes. Natural fires, changes in climate, and human activities also change the character of the environment. The plants and animals that are not suited to the changed conditions either die out or go elsewhere. Other plants and animals from other communities may invade the changed community. If these organisms are suited to this environment, they settle there and form a community that is different from the original one. Over a long period of time, the new community may be followed by still another type of community, and so on.

The gradual change of one community into another is called *succession of communities*. For example, a pond community may be replaced by a grassland community. In turn, the grassland community may be succeeded by a forest community. A succession stops with the highest type of organisms that are adapted to the particular environment. Should conditions change for one of the reasons described previously, a new succession of communities would begin again.

Natural Balance in Communities

The *natural balance* (or *balance of nature*) is the tendency for the numbers of organisms in a given community to remain unchanged. Under natural conditions, this balance may be temporarily upset. However, the normal feeding habits of the organisms in the community soon restore the natural balance of numbers.

For example, after a good growing season, when food is plentiful, an increase in the number of rabbits in an area is often followed by an increase in the number of hawks, which eat rabbits. As well-fed hawks reproduce in larger and larger numbers, they devour more and more rabbits. This causes the number of rabbits to dwindle. As a result, there is less food for the numerous hawks, and many of them die of starvation. Soon, as the number of hawks decreases, the number of rabbits begins to increase. Eventually, both the number of rabbits and the number of hawks return to their original level in the area.

NATURAL CYCLES OF ENERGY AND MATTER

We have mentioned before that as all organisms carry on their life activities, they take in certain materials from the environment and give off other materials to it. The repeated shifting of particular materials between organisms and the environment forms *natural cycles* (or *circulations of materials*). Together with food webs, these cycles help maintain the natural balance in each type of community.

Energy Cycle

In all food chains and webs, energy from the sun is transferred to plants, and from them to animals. The transfer of the sun's energy to all organisms is called the *energy cycle* (Fig. 24–4).

Nitrogen Cycle

In making the proteins they need for their own use, green plants require the element *nitrogen*. Although nitrogen makes up four-fifths of the air, plants cannot use nitrogen gas. Only after nitrogen has been combined with other elements, forming *nitrates*, can it be used by plants. The process of combining nitrogen with other elements is called *nitrogen fixation*.

Certain bacteria, such as those you observed in the roots of clover,

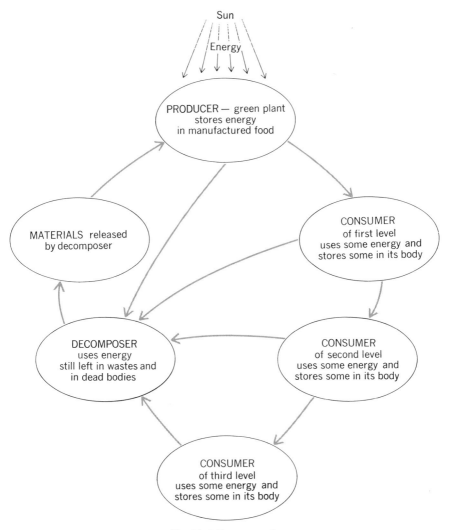

Fig. 24–4. Energy cycle.

carry out the process of nitrogen fixation. After a plant has used the nitrogen of the nitrates in making its own protein, the plant may be eaten by an animal. By digestion, the animal's body changes the plant protein to animal protein. Dead plants and animals are decomposed by *decay bacteria*. The decay bacteria, in soil and elsewhere, break down the proteins of dead plants and animals and liberate the nitrogen present in them.

The complex cycle in which nitrogen circulates from the air to bacteria and plants, from plants to animals, and thence to bacteria and the air once more is called the *nitrogen cycle* (Fig. 24–5, page 464).

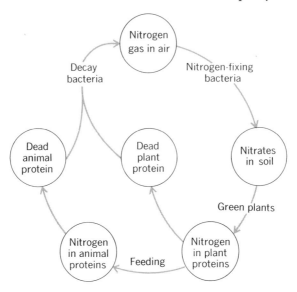

Fig. 24–5. Nitrogen cycle.

Water Cycle

Water vapor enters the atmosphere as a result of evaporation. As a result of condensation, water vapor leaves the atmosphere and enters the soil or bodies of water. Living things absorb water and return it to the atmosphere. The circulation of water in this manner is called the *water cycle* (Fig. 24–6).

Carbon Dioxide–Oxygen Cycle

As a result of the processes of respiration and photosynthesis, carbon dioxide and oxygen circulate between plants and animals. In this cycle, called the *carbon dioxide–oxygen cycle*, plants and animals supply each other with the gases they need for life (Fig. 24–7).

Looking Back

The relationships between organisms and their environment is called ecology. The environment of organisms is made up of both living and nonliving factors. When organisms are in balance with these factors, the organisms survive. Ordinarily the balance is maintained by food chains and food webs in natural communities, and by the natural cycles such as the energy cycle, the nitrogen cycle, the water cycle, and the carbon dioxide–oxygen cycle.

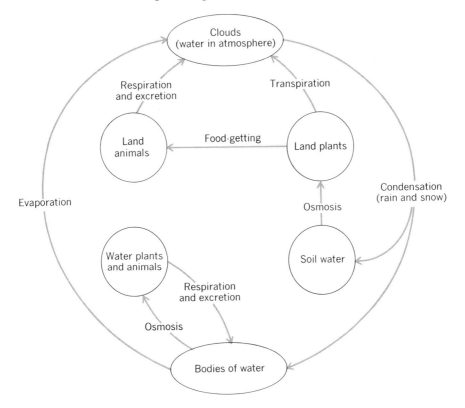

Fig. 24–6. Water cycle.

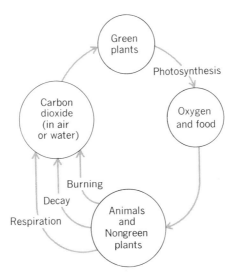

Fig. 24–7. Carbon dioxide–oxygen cycle.

Looking Ahead

The natural balance of communities is upset more often by humans than by any other organism. Such upsets threaten the survival of the communities of plants and animals and even the survival of the human species. In the next chapter, we will discuss what can be done to keep the natural balance in a stable condition.

Multiple-Choice Questions

1. Included in the nonliving environment are
   a. air, soil minerals, water, light   c. bears, oaks, water, minerals
   b. plants, air, food, water   d. minerals, light, snakes, birds
2. Plants that possess floating leaves are suited to life
   a. on land   b. in water   c. on land or in water   d. as parasites
3. When their food is scarce, robins in a community must either starve to death or
   a. make their own food
   b. compete with hawks
   c. change their diet to fish
   d. move to another similar community
4. Plants and animals make up
   a. a succession
   b. the living part of the environment
   c. the decomposer organisms
   d. the producer organisms
5. For breathing, water-dwelling animals usually possess
   a. lungs   b. gills   c. air channels   d. long noses
6. Cactus plants can withstand conditions that are
   a. very moist   b. hot and humid   c. cold   d. very dry
7. Which organism can still live although covered with Arctic snow?
   a. mushroom   b. rose   c. daisy   d. lichen
8. Toads can withstand dry conditions because their skin
   a. prevents the condensation of water
   b. prevents the evaporation of water
   c. allows the entrance of water to the tissues
   d. secretes a poison
9. Grass plants and clover plants growing in the same field or lawn compete with one another for
   a. proteins   b. fat   c. warmth   d. light
10. Two animals that compete with each other for food are the
   a. grasshopper and the bear   c. grasshopper and the rabbit
   b. horse and the mountain lion   d. cat and the mouse
11. Mice are the prey of cats. This means that
   a. cats eat mice   c. dogs chase mice
   b. mice eat cats   d. owls eat mice

12. A lichen consists of two plants; one is a fungus and the other is
    a. a bacterium   b. an alga   c. an apple   d. a water lily
13. The relationship between the tapeworm and human is that of
    a. two independent animals   c. parasite and host
    b. producer and food web   d. producer and parasite
14. The energy cycle on earth begins with the energy of
    a. soil   b. sunlight   c. respiration   d. gasoline
15. A predator-prey relationship normally exists between
    a. humans and wheat   c. deer and mountain lions
    b. sheep and dogs   d. mice and grasshoppers
16. In which cycle do bacteria of decay play an important part?
    a. nitrogen   b. water   c. oxygen   d. energy
17. Certain bacteria put back into the soil substances that many green plants
    take out of the soil. The most important of these substances is
    a. iron sulfide   b. water   c. nitrates   d. carbon dioxide
18. Producer organisms, consumer organisms, and decomposer organisms
    make up
    a. food webs   b. parasites   c. a succession   d. decay
19. Which are the first organisms in a food chain?
    a. fungi   c. independent plants
    b. bacteria   d. dependent plants
20. Bacteria of decay help
    a. form oxygen   b. enrich soil   c. form water   d. deplete soil
21. In a schoolroom aquarium consisting of goldfish and elodea plants,
    a. the fish and plants benefit each other
    b. the fish and plants have no effect on each other
    c. the fish and plants harm each other
    d. the fish harm the plants but the plants help the fish
22. The feature of the polar bear that enables it to withstand Arctic cold is
    a. heavy fur   b. white color   c. sharp teeth   d. sharp claws
23. If some grass seeds started to grow in a forest, we could expect the trees to
    a. help the grass plants to grow
    b. keep the grass plants warm
    c. compete with the grass plants for light
    d. provide the grass plants with carbon dioxide
24. The nitrogen cycle is important to plants because it enables them to get
    a. water from the soil   c. nitrates from the soil
    b. nitrogen gas from the air   d. protein from the insects they eat
25. Plants that can make soil from rock are
    a. bacteria   b. spirogyra   c. mushrooms   d. lichens

Modified True-False Questions

1. Special body features that help an organism fit into its environment are
   called *adaptations*.
2. Ducks breathe by means of *gills*.
3. Bees are animals that *compete* with other members of the hive.

4. Green plants are *consumer* organisms because they make food from inorganic substances.
5. *Decomposer* organisms can feed upon either dead plants or dead animals.
6. The green frog is an example of an animal that is often part of *a pond* community.
7. The creosote bush is usually found in *forest* communities.
8. A *grassland* community can change into a forest community.
9. The gradual replacement of a pond community by a grassland community is called *invasion*.
10. If the plants of a grassland community are replaced by trees, we can also expect that the *animals* of the grassland community will be replaced by other types of animals.
11. By eating field mice, *owls* help keep the number of field mice from increasing.
12. Certain *bacteria* help keep dead bodies from accumulating on the floor of a forest.
13. Evaporation and condensation are two steps in the *nitrogen* cycle.

Thought Questions

1. Show that you understand the following terms by using each in a separate sentence:
   a. producer organism   d. social animal
   b. predator   e. food chain
   c. gills
2. Explain why lichens can become established in regions where it is impossible for other plants to live.
3. A fern plant that grew in a forest was carefully dug up with its complete root system. The fern was then planted in a sunny garden. Although it was carefully tended and regularly watered, the plant died. Explain.
4. Although hawks sometimes carry off chickens, hawks are beneficial to farmers. Explain.
5. An increase in the number of snakes in an area can affect the number of frogs in that area. Explain.
6. Explain why a balanced aquarium containing water plants, goldfish, and catfish requires little attention except for the occasional addition of water.
7. Many plants and animals die every day. Explain why, after a month, the earth is not cluttered with dead bodies.
8. List, in order, five organisms that make up a food chain in a forest community.
9. What reasons can you give for considering the sun as the basic energy source for flesh-eating animals?
10. Explain how both the nitrogen cycle and the carbon dioxide–oxygen cycle are involved in a balanced aquarium.

CHAPTER 25

WHAT CAN WE DO TO KEEP OUR ENVIRONMENT STABLE?

When you have completed this chapter, you should be able to:

1. *Relate* the modern energy crisis to the conservation of renewable and nonrenewable resources.
2. *Discuss* the characteristics of the major types of soil.
3. *Describe* how soil is destroyed and how it may be conserved.
4. *Indicate* how to prevent the pollution of water and air, and how to conserve these resources.
5. *Explain* the relationship between the destruction or conservation of forests and the survival of wildlife.

In the laboratory experience that follows, you will observe how plants can be used as a soil conservation aid.

Laboratory Experience

HOW DO ROOTS AFFECT THE SOIL?

Note: Start this experiment about two weeks before the final laboratory period.

A. Soak 5 radish seeds and 5 oat seeds in water overnight. Fill two paper cups with sand, and moisten the sand in each cup with equal amounts of water. Pour off any excess water. Plant the radish seeds in one cup and the oat seeds in the other. In each cup, plant 1 seed in the center and 4 seeds equally spaced in a circle around the center. All seeds should be planted about 5 millimeters below the surface.

Label each cup. Set the cups in a moderately warm and moderately lighted place. Each day, touch the surface of the sand. If the sand feels dry, water the seeds gently and sparingly. Continue watering in this way daily, and observe the cups for at least two weeks.

1. How many days did it take for each kind of seed to sprout, or *germinate*?

2. Describe the appearance of each young plant (*seedling*) on the first day after sprouting.

B. After one week, measure the height of each seedling.

3. What is the average height of the radish seedlings?

4. What is the average height of the oat seedlings?

C. When the seedlings are at least two weeks old, gently roll each cup back and forth between your palms four times. Then, with one hand, firmly grasp the base of the stems of 3 plants and, with the other hand, hold the cup. Now, with a firm tug, pull the plants out of the cup.

5. Describe what happens. Explain.

6. If these plants were growing in a field, what effect would they have on the soil?

7. What natural process could these plants prevent if they were growing on steeply sloping ground?

Introduction

When America was first discovered by Europeans, its native human population was small. The environment was in its natural state. The populations of wild plants and animals in their natural communities were in balance. When the colonists arrived, the soil of America was fertile. It seemed as though the natural resources of the country could never be used up.

In 1706, the immigrant, or non-native, population of the American colonies was estimated to be one million. By 1800, the population of the new United States had increased to about five million. The population continued to grow to about 75 million by 1900 and to 180 million in 1960. By 1970, the population of the United States exceeded 200 million people.

America's earliest settlers found their new home teeming with natural resources. Rich soil, fresh water, timber, minerals, and game were present in great abundance. But as the population increased, fertile soils became poor, and farmlands were worn out. Great forests were destroyed. Huge scars were left in the earth as the minerals were mined. Beautiful rivers became polluted. Great herds of wild animals were slaughtered, some for food but most for their hides or other parts. Several species of wildlife have become nearly or completely extinct.

Gradually, as a result of this record of carelessness, neglect, and selfishness, Americans have used up a large percentage of the natural resources that had seemed so inexhaustible to the original settlers. In other words, humans have upset the balanced state of the natural environment.

The population of the United States is expected to exceed 300 million by the year 2000. If our generation and future generations are to benefit from what remains of our natural resources, we must practice *conservation*. Conservation means using natural resources wisely in order to restore them, to prevent further waste, and to help keep the natural balance of organisms.

OUR NEED AND USE OF NATURAL RESOURCES

For daily survival, humans must use soil, water, and air. To maintain the present state of civilization, we must also use forests, fuels, certain minerals, and wildlife. In taking care of our needs, however, we humans have often interfered with the natural balance and have upset it.

By cutting down forests, by mining for coal, and by plowing the soil, people make it impossible for wild plants and animals to exist. People also import foreign species of animals that destroy native species of plants. A species that is not harmful in its own country often becomes destructive when it is introduced into a new region. This happens when there are no organisms that feed upon the foreign species and when this species has plenty of food. Examples are the Japanese beetle, which destroys garden and crop plants in the United States, and rabbits, which are responsible for great crop losses in Australia.

RENEWABLE AND NONRENEWABLE RESOURCES

Soil minerals, such as nitrates and phosphates, are absorbed by plants and used in their life activities. The same minerals enter, and become part of, the bodies of animals. When plants and animals give off their wastes or die, the minerals are restored to the soil by natural cycles. Soil minerals that are recycled are examples of *renewable resources*.

Coal, oil, natural gas, and mineral ores, on the other hand, are *nonrenewable resources*. Once these materials have been removed from the earth, they cannot be restored. The heat for our homes, the power for our factories and electric generators, the fuels that propel our automobiles, buses, trucks, ships, trains, and airplanes come from our nonrenewable resources. Natural fuel resources, which took millions of years to form, are rapidly being used up. This is the basis of the modern *energy crisis*—a turning point in our use of fuels. By the end of the twenty-first century, there may be little if any coal, oil, or natural gas left in the earth.

Metals such as iron, copper, lead, zinc, and silver are being consumed at astonishing rates. Enormous amounts of these metals are imported into the United States every year because we use more of these metals than we can mine in the United States. As in the case of the mineral fuels, the ores from which these metals are obtained are not renewable. When all the ores have been exhausted, we shall have no choice but to use plastics, wood, and other substances as substitutes for these metals. We must also keep in mind, however, that plastics are made from crude oil and that wood comes from trees. Both of these resources are being rapidly depleted.

OUR NEED AND USE OF SOIL

Although we do not eat soil, we depend on it for our very existence because it supports the growth of a large variety of plants which we and other organisms need. Soil consists of tiny rock particles mixed with water, air, and *humus* (dead, decaying matter).

Types of Soil

There are three major types of soil:

1. *Clay soil* consists of very fine rock particles (or clay) mixed with some humus and other materials. When water is poured on clay soil, some may seep down very slowly, but most of the water remains on the surface of the soil. This occurs because clay particles pack together so firmly that clay soil can absorb very little water. Most plants are unable to grow in this type of soil.

2. *Sandy soil* consists of rock particles (grains of sand), a little clay, and a little humus. When water is poured on sandy soil, some may remain in the soil, but most of the water seeps through it very rapidly. This occurs because sandy soil is porous. Water moves through it freely and drains out of it rapidly. Some plants can grow in sandy soil.

3. *Loam* is a mixture of some sand, some clay, and a moderate amount of humus. When water is poured on loam, some may drain through it, but most of the water sinks into the soil and remains there. This occurs because, in proper proportions, the mixture of sand, clay, and humus permits this type of soil to absorb water and to hold it without too rapid drainage. Many wild and cultivated plants grow well in loam.

Fertile Soil

The layer of fertile soil that supports plant life is called *topsoil*. Loam makes good topsoil because it provides minerals in addition to admitting air and water to roots. When the layer of topsoil is carried away, or when the minerals in it have been removed, the remaining soil can no longer support desirable plants, especially those that we use as food.

How Fertile Soil Is Lost

The removal of soil by wind or moving water is called *erosion*. From the time of the arrival of America's first colonists until the present, erosion has destroyed more than 30% of the original topsoil. The major agents of soil erosion are wind, water, and people.

In dry regions where vegetation is scarce, the soil is uncovered and unprotected. Such exposed soil is often loose and easily removed by winds.

The water of swiftly flowing streams, runoff rainfall, and floods removes large quantities of soil.

People often assist the process of soil erosion by several unwise practices. Strip-mining of coal and some metals, as well as the piling of the wastes of mining and metallurgy on the surface of the ground (pages 160–161), destroys what could be fertile soil. The removal of trees and other forms of vegetation exposes bare soil. Such unprotected soil can be readily eroded by wind and water. When crops, such as corn, are planted in straight rows with areas of bare soil between them, the soil is exposed and easily eroded.

How Soil Minerals Are Lost

The continuous growing of only one type of crop, such as cotton, in a field year after year removes large amounts of soil minerals. This practice does not allow time for the natural cycles to restore the minerals. In time, this exhausted soil becomes incapable of supporting plant life. The soil then lies bare and is subject to erosion.

OUR NEED AND USE OF WATER

Water is essential for all the life activities of humans and other organisms. Under natural conditions, water is a renewable resource. However, as the amount of farming land increases, and as industry grows more complicated, we use larger and larger quantities of water. We are also wasting larger quantities of water and making water more and more unfit to use.

How We Use Water

We use more than 1700 billion liters of fresh water daily in the United States. Manufacturing industries and farms consume most of this water. The domestic use of water in towns, villages, and cities consumes only a fraction of the total amount available. A comparison of the amounts of water needed for various purposes is shown in Table 25–1, page 474.

Table 25–1. Water Needed for Various Purposes

Activity	Quantity of Water Needed
Flushing a toilet	12 liters
Taking a shower	20 liters
Automatic dishwashing	57 liters
Automatic clothes-washing	80 liters
Producing a ton of steel	230,000 liters
Producing a ton of corn	920,000 liters

At present, our supplies of water are adequate for our needs. However, as the population increases, the requirements of our homes, factories, and farms will also increase, placing an even greater burden on our available supplies of water.

How We Waste Water

Although the total amount of water on earth is constant, we cannot use all of it because water is often wasted by excessive runoff, and because water is made unfit for use by pollution.

A large amount of rainfall is lost and unavailable for the soil because it runs off too quickly into streams, lakes, or the ocean. This excessive runoff may be the result of the removal of vegetation from hillsides, improper plowing, or failure to install dams in streams that are likely to flood.

Other water is made unavailable for use by pollution. Water is often polluted by sewage from homes and wastes from factories. Pollution of our water supply is a serious and growing problem.

America's early settlers found sparkling, clear water wherever they traveled. They could drink safely from almost any river or stream. Then towns were built along the rivers and streams. As the towns grew, they dumped more and more of their sewage into the rivers.

When towns were small, natural decay processes destroyed the organic wastes in the sewage, and the water remained clean. However, as the towns became cities, many rivers were turned into open sewers because all the sewage dumped into the rivers could not be destroyed by natural processes. Today, the water of very few streams is fit to drink in its natural state.

Although the wastes of organisms can be broken down by natural processes of decay, other wastes cannot. Many industries dump large amounts of wastes, such as chemicals, into streams and lakes. Unfortunately, even small amounts of some of these chemicals are deadly to fish and plant life. For example, many of the fish in Lake Erie have been killed as a result of this chemical pollution.

In addition, many industries, especially large power stations, use large amounts of river water as a coolant. The warmed water is then returned to the river. This water is far too warm for most of the plants and fish living in the river. As a result of this heat, or *thermal pollution,* most of the plants and fish in the river die. Some species of algae, on the other hand, may grow and multiply too fast.

In the United States, millions of people obtain the water they use for drinking and cooking from wells rather than from lakes, rivers, or reservoirs. Like the water in rivers and lakes, water in wells can also be polluted by sewage and chemical wastes.

Pollution by sewage is very common in rural areas where groundwater is close to the surface of the land. Where waste water containing detergents has seeped into the groundwater, it is not unusual for a soapy foam to appear in a glass of water drawn from a faucet. Furthermore, many detergents contain phosphates, which are chemicals that stimulate the growth of plants such as algae. This means that lakes, rivers, and other bodies of water may become choked by plants that grow and reproduce at an abnormal rate.

In coastal regions, if groundwater is removed from wells slowly, salt water is kept from moving toward the wells (Fig. 25–1a, page 476). If too many wells are drilled, however, large amounts of groundwater may be withdrawn rapidly (Fig. 25–1b). Under these conditions, salt water may seep into the wells. This type of water pollution has become a problem in Los Angeles, Atlantic City, Miami, and on Long Island.

OUR NEED AND USE OF AIR

Air, like water, is essential for life. Air pollution, like water pollution, is a problem that threatens us all.

Composition of Air

The quantity of air that surrounds the earth is estimated at about five quadrillion (5,000,000,000,000,000) metric tons. The main ingredients of air are the gases nitrogen, oxygen, carbon dioxide, and water vapor. The percentages (by volume) of these gases have remained nearly constant for millions of years.

For example, the percentage of nitrogen, about 78%, remains unchanged as a result of the nitrogen cycle described in Chapter 24. Although breathing, burning, and other types of oxidation constantly use up oxygen and release carbon dioxide, the percentage of oxygen in the atmosphere has remained unchanged at about 21%, and the percentage of carbon dioxide has remained unchanged at about 0.03% to 0.04%.

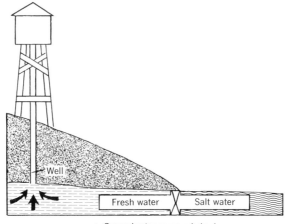

a. Groundwater removed slowly

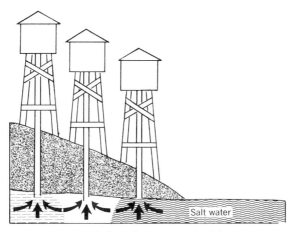

b. Groundwater removed rapidly

Fig. 25–1. Water pollution in coastal regions.

The percentages of these gases in the atmosphere are kept constant by the process of photosynthesis that takes place in green plants (Fig. 25–2). You will recall that in photosynthesis, plants use carbon dioxide and water, in the presence of sunlight and chlorophyl, to manufacture food for themselves. In this process, the plants give off oxygen.

The Growing Problem of Air Pollution

Although the supply of air is plentiful, it has become necessary for us to take steps to preserve its purity. Since the industrial revolution began almost 200 years ago, the number of factories, cities, and homes

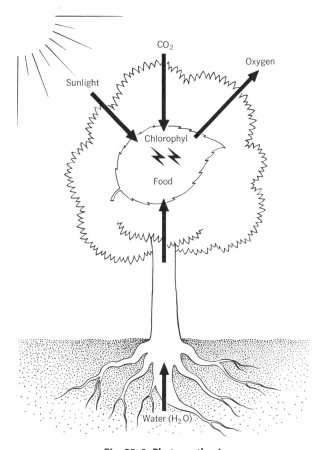

Fig. 25–2. Photosynthesis.

has steadily increased. Larger and larger quantities of fuel are being burned to run these factories and heat these homes. As a result, smoke pours continuously from millions of chimneys. This smoke, laden with harmful gases such as sulfur dioxide, is polluting the air.

In addition, the rapidly growing use of automobiles and other vehicles that pour large quantities of exhaust fumes into the air has added to the pollution problem.

Other sources of air pollution include chemicals given off by factory chimneys, chemical sprays used to control insect pests, and nuclear-bomb explosions.

Until recently, there was little concern about the substances polluting the air. People became aware that a serious health problem existed only following a series of disasters. In October, 1948, twenty people died and about one-third of the population of Donora, Pennsylvania, became ill because of fumes and smoke in the air over their town. In the 1950s, on two separate occasions, polluted air caused about 5000 deaths in London and about 200 deaths in New York City. In London, near the end of 1962, heavy air pollution caused 340 deaths. Even today, in any area of the world where there are periods of excessive air pollution, more people die than are expected to die under normal air conditions.

In addition to the threat to health, polluted air often damages crops seriously, especially leafy crops such as lettuce and spinach. Polluted air also kills wild green plants, such as grasses and trees, which remove excess carbon dioxide from the air and provide us with the oxygen we need.

OUR NEED AND USE OF FORESTS AND WILDLIFE

Forests are valuable for numerous reasons. Since the forest floor is spongy, it absorbs water and thereby prevents soil erosion and floods. Forests provide the wood necessary for producing building materials, furniture, paper, and many chemicals. They also provide places in which wild animals can live and in which people can enjoy camping and other outdoor activities.

Hunting wild animals such as deer is a sport that is enjoyed by many people. Commercial fishing provides employment and food. If uncontrolled, however, activities such as these can upset the natural balance of wildlife.

How Forests Are Destroyed

Forests have been damaged or destroyed by numerous enemies.

1. Parasitic fungi are responsible for the disease and death of many trees. Examples of fungus diseases of trees are white pine blister rust and Dutch elm disease.

2. Many insects damage and often kill trees. Examples are the tent caterpillar, which eats leaves, and the wood-boring beetle, which tunnels into branches and trunks.

3. Once started, naturally or by people, fires destroy or damage forests.

4. The worst enemy of forests is people. They destroy them by carelessly starting forest fires and by improper lumbering practices which do not promote the growth of new trees.

How Wildlife Is Destroyed

The disappearance of many types of wild animals has been the result of human activities. People have overhunted certain birds, such as the moa and the passenger pigeon, to the extent that they have become extinct. Numerous species, such as the elk and the whooping crane, are almost extinct. The salmon and lobster catches are becoming smaller each year.

SAVING OUR ENVIRONMENT

Our understanding of the relationships between organisms and their environment—that is, of ecology—can help us see the way to remedy the damage already done to the environment, to prevent further damage to it, and to conserve our natural resources for ourselves and future generations.

CONSERVATION OF NONRENEWABLE RESOURCES

In order to make our supplies of fuel last as long as possible, fuel companies and the U.S. Government are working together to find additional supplies and to cut down on those practices that waste fuel. In addition, new methods are being used to obtain the maximum amount of oil from the earth. Oil wells are being drilled deeper, and new parts of the earth are being explored for deposits of oil. Research is also being conducted on extracting oil from *oil shales*, rocks that have large amounts of oil trapped in them. At present, however, the extraction of oil from oil shales is very expensive.

Radioactivity (*nuclear energy*), the sun's rays (*solar energy*) and the heat in the depths of the earth (*geothermal energy*) are possible sources of energy. Devices that make the energy from these sources usable are now employed only to a limited extent. Among such devices are nuclear power plants, solar furnaces, solar batteries, and geothermal power plants. None of these devices burns fuel. Consequently, they not only can help conserve natural fuels, but they can also help reduce air pollution.

Some answers to the problem of using up our mineral resources and, at the same time, keeping the environment uncluttered are:

1. Avoid wasteful uses of metals.

2. Reuse, or recycle, the metals that make up old automobiles, old pipes, and discarded beverage cans.

CONSERVATION OF SOIL

You will recall that poor farming, mining, and metallurgical practices have resulted in the loss of soil through destruction and erosion, as well as the loss of essential minerals from the soil. With proper care, these losses can be reduced greatly.

Preventing Soil Destruction

The major ways of preventing the destruction of soil by poor mining and metallurgical practices are the following:

1. When an area is being prepared for strip-mining, remove the top-soil and store it. After the strip-mine is exhausted, fill the excavated depression with rocks or similar unwanted material, replace the topsoil, and plant crops that tend to enrich the soil.

2. Do not allow mining and metallurgical wastes to accumulate. Rather, use them as landfills where roads are built in low-lying areas.

3. In places where mining and other wastes have accumulated on the soil surface, remove the wastes. Transport them to landfill areas and cover them with soil. Plant cover crops, as explained in the next section, until the soil is fertile once more.

Preventing Erosion

The major ways in which the erosion of soil can be reduced are the following:

1. After harvesting a crop, a farmer should not leave the soil uncovered. Instead, a *cover crop*, such as alfalfa, should be planted. Alfalfa plants spread and grow close together, thus covering the soil. The roots of these plants also bind the soil, as the plants in your laboratory experience did. In addition to covering and binding soil, alfalfa is beneficial because its roots have nitrogen-fixing bacteria in them. These bacteria restore nitrates to the soil.

2. *Strip cropping* is the planting of one crop in every other strip in a field and a second crop in the strips in between. Strips of corn are planted between strips of clover, for example (Fig. 25–3). The corn provides no ground cover, but the clover does. The cover crop—clover in this case—protects the soil and absorbs runoff from the corn strip. Like alfalfa, clover also restores soil nitrates.

Fig. 25–3. Crops planted in strips.

3. The outline of a rounded body (such as a hill) when viewed from above is called a contour. In *contour plowing* (Fig. 25–4), furrows (grooves) are made across slopes instead of up and down. Such furrows prevent runoff rainfall from washing topsoil down the slope.

Fig. 25–4. Contour plowing on a slope.

4. *Terraces* are steplike, flat areas that are dug on steeply sloping farmland (Fig. 25–5). The terraces slow the runoff of rainfall that would otherwise carry away topsoil.

Fig. 25–5. Crops planted on terraces.

5. Belts of trees and rows of hedges reduce the force of strong winds. Such plantings around fields are called *windbreaks*. When the force of the wind is broken, loose soil is less likely to be blown away.

Reducing Loss of Soil Minerals

The permanent removal of essential minerals from the soil can also be reduced by sound farming practices.

1. Repeatedly changing one crop with another in the same field is called *rotation of crops*. In a rotation scheme, cotton may be planted first. After gathering the cotton, the farmer cultivates a pod-bearing plant in the same field. Peanuts, peas, beans, clover, and alfalfa are

examples of pod-bearing plants. Plants of this family have nitrogen-fixing bacteria in their roots. Any one of these plants can be used in a crop-rotation scheme. After harvesting the pod-bearing crop, the farmer again plants cotton, and so on. The nitrogen-fixing bacteria that live in the roots of the pod-bearing plant restore the soil nitrates that the cotton has absorbed.

2. *Fertilizers*, which are materials that enrich soil, are added to soil to restore its mineral content. These materials include chemicals, such as sodium nitrate, and organic materials, such as manure or decaying plant and animal bodies.

CONSERVATION OF WATER

If we are to have a clean, adequate supply of water in the future, we must collect and store larger amounts of unpolluted water than we are collecting and storing now. We must also check excessive runoff of rainfall and melted snow by planting grass or evergreen trees on hills adjoining fields, and by contour plowing, terracing, and building dams. These practices not only conserve water but also conserve soil.

The federal and state governments and private industry have begun to make greater efforts to reduce the pollution of our water. Many sewage-treatment plants have already been built and others are being planned. Sewage treatment kills harmful bacteria and removes the solid wastes from the sewage. These solid wastes are disposed of in various ways. Some wastes are burned in incinerators. Other wastes are used to enrich soil. The purified sewer water can then be returned safely into the stream from which it came originally.

Chemicals such as DDT and ordinary household detergents continue to be a pollution problem because they usually pass through sewage-treatment plants unchanged. Many communities have passed laws prohibiting the use of DDT and other chemical sprays and the use of certain chemicals in detergents. Research is also being carried out to find detergents that will decompose by natural processes to form substances that will not pollute water. Such detergents are said to be *biodegradable*.

Every one of us can contribute to the water conservation program by using water carefully in our homes. For example, we can keep a bottle of water in the refrigerator during hot weather instead of wastefully allowing the water to run from the faucet in order to have a cold drink. Fixing a dripping faucet can save many liters of water a day. We could save billions of liters of water each year if we all followed these and similar common-sense practices.

CONSERVATION OF AIR

Like water, air is a renewable resource. That is, up to a point, natural processes can usually eliminate pollutants from the air or reduce the quantity of pollutants to a safe level. If we are to keep the air safe for breathing, however, we must greatly reduce the quantity of pollutants that we add to the air. Among the steps we can take are reducing the exhaust of pollutants from chimneys and engines, controlling nuclear explosions, and controlling the use of pesticides.

Reduction of Exhausts

Many factory smokestacks and automobile exhausts have already been equipped with devices that, to some extent, remove potentially poisonous chemicals. Some factories have replaced their oil-burning or coal-burning furnaces with electrically heated boilers. Engineers are trying to design new types of automobile engines that could considerably reduce air pollution.

In many communities, electricity is generated by burning coal or oil. As atomic energy replaces these fuels, the amount of smoke pollutants in the air will decrease. Solar and geothermal energy are being studied as nonpolluting energy sources for the future.

Control of Nuclear Explosions

Since the invention of the atomic bomb in 1945, nuclear explosions have added radioactive substances to the atmosphere. Some of these radioactive substances may get into our food supplies and, eventually, into our bodies. The radiations given off by radioactive substances damage the cells of the body and may even result in death. To decrease the dangers of radioactivity, our government and the governments of other countries are taking steps to reduce the number of nuclear explosions and to confine the explosions deep underground.

Control of Pesticides

Chemical sprays that kill insects and other pests help increase our supply of food. However, some of these chemicals are harmful to humans if they enter the body. Research is being carried out to develop sprays that will kill the pests but, at the same time, will be harmless to humans. Scientists are also working on methods of controlling the number of insects without using poisonous sprays. For example, X rays might be used to prevent insects from reproducing.

Personal Responsibility

All of us can help prevent the pollution of the atmosphere. We can refrain from burning leaves, garbage, and trash in the open air. We can make sure that the furnaces and incinerators in our homes are adjusted properly for complete combustion. We can write our legislators and ask them to support bills intended to prevent air pollution.

CONSERVATION OF FORESTS

In order to maintain our valuable forests, several steps can be taken.

1. As with other crops, only mature trees should be harvested. These should be replaced with plantings of young trees.

2. Several practices are necessary for good forest management. Dead or diseased trees should be removed. All imported trees and other plants should be inspected to prevent the introduction of new fungus and insect pests. Harmful insects should be controlled by introducing birds or other organisms that feed upon the insects.

3. Lookout towers, organized firefighters, and the use of modern firefighting equipment can help limit forest fires as soon as they are detected. Educating the public in using care when discarding matches and when tending campfires can help prevent forest fires.

4. More forest preserves should be established by federal and state governments. Such preserves could prevent forest destruction by indiscriminate mining and building of hotels and factories.

CONSERVATION OF WILDLIFE

We now realize that wild animals of all kinds, whether directly useful to us or not, are essential in maintaining the balance of nature. Whenever one species becomes extinct, other species that are part of the same food web are also affected.

In order to maintain animals in their natural state, the following steps have already been taken.

1. Government agencies build fish hatcheries where young fish, such as trout, are raised and protected. When old enough, the trout are added to lakes and streams.

2. Providing feeding stations during the winter months helps many birds survive. Special parks, called bird sanctuaries, provide undisturbed breeding places for the birds. In many states, laws limit or even prohibit the killing of certain birds.

3. Game laws, which are laws controlling hunting, are designed to

insure that there will be enough animals left alive to breed. Among such laws are those that forbid hunting during the breeding season and that limit the number of animals that may be taken by one person.

4. In national and state parks, wildlife is protected and provided with natural homes.

Looking Back

To help us survive, we use the renewable and nonrenewable resources provided by the environment. In doing so, we often upset the environment. To keep the environment stable, we must take into account the needs of every kind of plant and animal. We must also take steps to conserve all the available natural resources. Thus, we must treat the environment in ways that do the least damage to the natural balance. In addition, we must conserve fuel, metals, soil, soil minerals, water, forests, and wildlife.

Looking Ahead

Most of the steps we have discussed concerning how to keep the environment stable cannot be carried out by every individual. Rather, these steps are workable if carried out by large organizations, such as national government, a local government, or an entire industry. In Chapter 26, we will discuss what you as an individual can do to prevent the worsening of our environment and to improve it for yourself and for your future family.

Multiple-Choice Questions

1. The following plants are all grown to add nitrogen to the soil *except*
   a. alfalfa   b. soybeans   c. clover   d. wheat
2. After an entire forest has been cut down for lumber, we can expect the soil to
   a. improve   b. form layers   c. remain the same   d. be eroded
3. Of the following, the largest consumers of fresh water are
   a. private homes and apartment houses   c. commercial fisheries
   b. livestock on farms   d. industries
4. Nitrate-producing bacteria naturally grow on the roots of the
   a. geranium plant   c. clover plant
   b. celery plant   d. potato plant
5. A special type of pollutant that may affect groundwater supplies of coastal cities is
   a. raw sewage   b. heated water   c. detergents   d. salt

6. Which animal has most often upset the balance of nature?
  a. the Dutch beetle   c. the English sparrow
  b. the Japanese beetle   d. civilized humans
7. Most plants grow best in soil made of
  a. only sand   c. only humus
  b. only clay   d. a mixture of sand, clay, and humus
8. Forests, grasses, and farm plants are supported by the soil layer called
  a. sand   b. topsoil   c. subsoil   d. eroded soil
9. The destructive process that removes topsoil is called
  a. erosion   c. terracing
  b. the natural water cycle   d. contour plowing
10. Two natural agents of soil erosion are
  a. wind and running water   c. farming and irrigation
  b. wind and lightning   d. running water and bacteria
11. Plowing across a hill instead of up and down is called
  a. strip plowing   c. contour plowing
  b. terrace plowing   d. cover plowing
12. Peanuts are a good crop to use in a scheme of crop rotation because their roots bear
  a. humus   c. nitrate-producing bacteria
  b. root hairs   d. decay bacteria
13. How can soil erosion on very hilly farmland best be reduced?
  a. frequent plowing   c. removing dead trees
  b. growing cotton   d. terracing
14. A belt of trees growing all around a field of corn is an example of
  a. a cover crop   c. strip cropping
  b. a forest succession   d. a windbreak
15. Contour plowing is most likely to help in the
  a. evaporation of water   c. runoff of water
  b. absorption of water   d. making of nitrates
16. The humus content of soil can be restored by adding to the soil
  a. manure   b. potash   c. saltpeter   d. phosphate
17. The reforestation of a burned-over area eventually results in increased
  a. soil water   b. floods   c. aridity   d. runoff
18. The extinction of the moa bird was caused by
  a. a poultry disease   c. drought
  b. overhunting   d. increases in the hawk population
19. Special parks in which birds can breed without human interference are called
  a. bird hatcheries   c. licensed hunting grounds
  b. bird sanctuaries   d. game preserves
20. Robins often eat earthworms which live in moist soil. If the soil should become dry, we could expect the number of
  a. robins to increase   c. robins to remain the same
  b. robins to decrease   d. earthworms to remain the same
21. The air pollutant sulfur dioxide gas, which is harmful to the lungs and respiratory tract, is largely produced by burning coal and
  a. oil   b. charcoal   c. natural gas   d. sewage

22. Pollutants that may alter reproductive cells are pesticides and
   a. radioactive dust
   b. carbon monoxide
   c. coal fumes
   d. sulfuric acid

Modified True-False Questions

1. Soil consists of particles of rock, air, *humus*, and water.
2. Clay soil can hold more water than can *sandy* soil.
3. The planting of a row of wheat, a row of alfalfa, a row of wheat, and so on, is an example of *hillside terracing*.
4. Wheat that is planted in soil having plenty of water but no *nitrates* can be expected to produce a poor crop of grain.
5. Factories near streams often contribute to the *conservation* of water.
6. A disease responsible for the death of thousands of elm trees is caused by a type of *rabbit*.
7. A species of bird that is nearly extinct in the United States is the *whooping crane*.
8. In the United States and other countries, the loss of natural resources is most often the result of the action of *lightning*.
9. The seepage of salt water into wells is threatening to pollute the water supplies of many *inland* communities.
10. The process by which green plants produce their food is very important in maintaining the *oxygen* content of the atmosphere.
11. A field in which *corn* is grown becomes richer in nitrate minerals.
12. Proper sewage disposal helps control *air* pollution.

Thought Questions

1. Give a similarity and a difference between the terms in the following pairs:
   a. clay soil and loam
   b. terracing and contour plowing
   c. strip cropping and crop rotation
2. If you live in a large city, such as Chicago or New York, why should you be interested in a proposal that Congress establish a national park in Oklahoma?
3. If you live in the country, why should you be concerned about the water or air pollution problems of a large city 1000 kilometers away from your home?
4. If you have a small vegetable garden, why is it a good idea to grow different crops in different parts of the garden each year?
5. Explain the difference between a renewable resource and a nonrenewable resource. Give two examples of each.
6. A container held under a dripping faucet shows the accumulation of 12 liters of water at the end of 24 hours. If the dripping faucet is not repaired, how many liters of water will drip through this faucet in one year?

CHAPTER 26
WHAT CAN WE DO TO IMPROVE
THE ENVIRONMENT?

When you have completed this chapter, you should be able to:

1. *Describe* at least ten things you can do yourself to improve the quality of the air.
2. *Indicate* at least six things you can do yourself to conserve water and prevent polluting water.
3. *Discuss* some of the things you can do personally to help conserve mineral resources and wildlife.
4. *Give examples* of what you can do to make your community more pleasant.
5. *List* the activities you can carry out with other people to improve the environment.

Note: A laboratory experience is not provided for this chapter because it deals with activities you can experience outside a laboratory in the environment as it is.

Introduction

When humans first appeared on earth, they needed few resources to keep themselves alive except some plants and animals. Humans obtained these directly from the environment. As humans progressed, however, they used their intelligence to build civilizations. In doing so, they used more and more natural resources from the environment. They made human life safer and more comfortable. Then the human population grew. Today the human population is so large that satisfying all its needs raises major problems. Among these problems are supplying increasing amounts of food, depleting our natural resources, polluting the air and water, disposing of increasing amounts of wastes, and destroying forests and the wildlife in them.

These problems threaten the continued existence of the human race. Before many generations pass, the earth may become too small for its human population. Food may become so scarce that people will starve. The environment may become so poor that it will not support life.

What should we do before we find we cannot live on our planet? Should we abandon the earth and try to establish life elsewhere in the universe? (Current information indicates that the environments of the moon, Venus, Mars, and other bodies are so different from ours that life would be impossible for us and our familiar organisms.) Does it not make sense for us to do what we can to restore our environment, improve it, and prevent it from becoming worse? By doing these things, we can hope to have an environment that will support us for the rest of our lives and be satisfactory for those who will come after us. If this is what we want, each of us must take some action with regard to our air, water, wastes, resources, and wildlife.

By itself, our government cannot take all the necessary steps to insure a satisfactory environment. Each of us can participate in environmental improvement as individuals and as members of a community. In other words, some of the things we can do are "do-it-yourself" activities. Others are activities we can carry on with the help of other people.

DO-IT-YOURSELF AIR CONSERVATION

1. If your family owns its home, keep the furnace clean and properly adjusted. Such care will insure complete burning of fuel and will reduce the amount of polluting exhausts released to the atmosphere.

2. Do not add polluting smoke to the atmosphere by burning paper, leaves, trash, and garbage.

3. Do not smoke. In addition to being a personal health hazard, the smoke produced by burning tobacco pollutes the air around you.

4. Do not allow garbage to accumulate. Garbage smells and fouls the air. Garbage should be stored properly and be ready for removal according to the schedule set in your community.

5. If you live in an apartment, obey the house rules for garbage disposal.

6. When having a cook-out, make a fire that will burn without excessive smoking. When done, collect all refuse, but do not burn it in the fire.

7. Urge your family to have the family car tuned and inspected at regular intervals. Adjustments of the carburetor, fuel pump, antipollution devices, and spark plugs will result in the formation of fewer air pollutants. Such adjustments will also save gasoline and help to relieve the energy crisis.

8. Urge your family driver to avoid racing the engine, starting quickly, and stopping suddenly. Engine-racing and quick starts increase engine exhausts and waste gasoline. Quick starts and sudden stops cause particles of rubber and brake linings to be thrown into the atmosphere.

9. Empty vacuum-cleaner bags and dust mops into containers that will prevent dust from reaching the air.

10. Conserve electricity. Every use of electric power usually requires the burning of more fuel at the power plant. Burning fuel, especially incomplete combustion, produces air pollutants.

11. Report to your Air Pollution Control Center whenever you see a chimney smoking excessively (Figs. 26–1 and 26–2).

Fig. 26–1. Report such smoking chimneys.

Fig. 26–2. Effect of air pollution in Los Angeles.

12. Plant green vegetation wherever you can. Remember that green plants absorb carbon dioxide from the air and release oxygen.

DO-IT-YOURSELF WATER CONSERVATION

1. Do not let water in your home run unnecessarily.

2. Learn how to fix dripping faucets.

3. Do not flush toilets unnecessarily.

4. Use shower baths rather than tub baths. Shower baths consume less water than do tub baths.

5. Run dishwashers when full. Do not waste water on a few dishes.

6. Avoid using fertilizers, weed killers, and insect killers on your lawn. Runoff rainwater and seepage can carry these substances into your drinking water supply.

7. When washing clothes, use soaps and other detergents that are low in phosphates. These compounds promote the growth of water plants that choke out water-dwelling animals.

8. To keep bodies of water and shorelines near you clean, do not flush plastics, heavy paper, cloth, grease, and solvents into your sewage system. Dispose of such items with garbage.

DO-IT-YOURSELF CONSERVATION OF NONRENEWABLE RESOURCES

1. Collect and save aluminum cans, lawn chairs, and other metal objects, and contribute them to recycling drives.

2. Collect all unused coat hangers that accumulate in your home. Return them to the cleaner, or contribute them to recycling drives.

3. Buy sodas and other beverages that come in returnable bottles. Nonreturnable bottles are wasteful.

4. Report the presence of abandoned or junked cars to your Sanitation Department or other city agency that removes them and disposes of them as scrap metal.

DO-IT-YOURSELF WILDLIFE CONSERVATION

1. If you go hunting or fishing, do not kill or capture any animals you do not need.

2. If your family must use weed and insect killers, point out to them that these substances last a long time and are poisonous to many kinds of helpful animals. Among these substances are weed killers, such as 2,4D and insect killers, such as DDT. Persuade your family to use substitute products such as pyrethrum (a natural substance) for killing insects, and offer to help pull up weeds by hand.

3. Ladybugs, praying mantises, and dragonflies should not be killed because they eat many insect pests.

4. Set up bird feeders, bird houses, and squirrel feeding-boxes in your backyard or garden.

5. When camping or picnicking, be sure to extinguish all fires thoroughly (Fig. 26–3).

Fig. 26–3. Preventing forest fires helps protect wildlife.

DO-IT-YOURSELF FOR A PLEASANT COMMUNITY

1. Do not litter your street, home, or school with gum wrappers, gum, candy wrappers, and other rubbish. Use litter baskets.

2. If you see other people littering, tell them politely that they are spoiling their own environment (and yours).

3. Throw empty bottles and other nonreturnable containers into garbage containers.

4. After a day at the beach or a park, be sure you leave nothing behind. Put the wastes of your good time in a wastebasket.

DO-IT-WITH-OTHERS ACTIVITIES FOR ENVIRONMENTAL IMPROVEMENT

1. Read and discuss with friends and family books such as *Silent Spring* and magazines such as *Natural History*.

2. In school, register in a course dealing with ecology and environmental problems.

3. Prepare an environment exhibit for your school or local Science Fair.

4. Teach younger children what you know about improving the environment.

5. Join groups in your school and community that engage in activities such as those in the following list.

- Organizing local clean-up activities (Fig. 26–4)
- Cleaning littered vacant land
- Cleaning local parks
- Planting trees and shrubs

Fig. 26–4. What is wrong in this community?

- Removing junk from the banks of streams

- Preparing Earth Day and Arbor Day programs

- Inspecting streams for signs of pollution

- Collecting for recycling materials such as waste paper, used bottles, and scrap metals

- Writing to government agencies to pass and enforce laws dealing with the reduction of pollution and the preservation of forests and wildlife

6. Attend community meetings that deal with environmental problems.

Looking Back and Looking Ahead

Your study of science has helped you understand how important our environment is in providing us and all other living things with the necessities for survival. Now it is your turn to do something for the environment. What will you do to make sure that the environment will continue to support life on earth?

APPENDIX

The following tables show you simple ways to convert (change) units from the customary system of measurement to the metric system, and the reverse.

Table A–1. Weight Conversions

When You Know	Multiply By	To Find
Ounces (oz)	28.3	Grams (g)
Pounds (lb)	0.45	Kilograms (kg)
Tons (T)	0.91	Metric tons (MT)
Grams (g)	0.035	Ounces (oz)
Kilograms (kg)	2.2	Pounds (lb)
Metric tons (MT)	1.1	Tons (T)

Table A–2. Length Conversions

When You Know	Multiply By	To Find
Inches (in)	2.54	Centimeters (cm)
Feet (ft)	30.5	Centimeters (cm)
Feet (ft)	0.3	Meters (m)
Yards (yd)	0.91	Meters (m)
Miles (mi)	1.6	Kilometers (km)
Centimeters (cm)	0.4	Inches (in)
Centimeters (cm)	0.033	Feet (ft)
Meters (m)	3.3	Feet (ft)
Meters (m)	1.1	Yards (yd)
Kilometers (km)	0.62	Miles (mi)

Table A–3. Volume Conversions

When You Know	Multiply By	To Find
Ounces, fluid (fl oz)	29.6	*Cubic centimeters (cc)
Pints (pt)	0.47	Liters (l)
Quarts (qt)	0.95	Liters (l)
*Milliliters (ml)	0.034	Ounces, fluid (fl oz)
Liters (l)	2.1	Pints (pt)
Liters (l)	1.06	Quarts (qt)

* *Note:* A milliliter (ml) and a cubic centimeter (cc) are approximately equal in volume. They are often used interchangeably.

Table A–4. Temperature Conversions

When You Know	Do This	To Find
Degrees Fahrenheit (F)	1. Subtract 32 2. Multiply by 5 3. Divide by 9	Degrees Celsius (C)
Degrees Celsius (C)	1. Multiply by 9 2. Divide by 5 3. Add 32	Degrees Fahrenheit (F)

USING SIGNIFICANT FIGURES

Uncertainty in Measurement

A student weighs a block of metal on three different balances and obtains the following weights: 14.61 grams, 14.62 grams, and 14.63 grams. What is the weight of the block? In each of the weighings, only the first three digits have been reproduced. This is the same as saying that in each weighing the last digit is doubtful. The weight of the block can therefore be described as lying between 14.61 grams and 14.63 grams. The block could be weighed on any number of balances and the weights would agree only in the first three digits. This experiment and many similar ones that could be performed suggest that it is impossible to reproduce a series of measurements without error.

The limitation of measurement caused by errors is called *uncertainty*. It results from shortcomings of the experimenter or of the equipment used. Consequently, our experimental observations, which we call facts, are uncertain to some degree. The experimenter, by developing his powers of observation and by refining his equipment, cannot eliminate uncertainty but can only reduce it. Thus scientists continue to refine the values of such important quantities as the velocity of light.

Expressing Uncertainty With Significant Figures

The weight of the metal block in the above example was described as lying between 14.61 grams and 14.63 grams. To express the proper uncertainty, we can describe the weight as 14.62 grams $\pm$ 0.01 gram. The symbol $\pm$ (plus or minus) expresses the uncertainty range.

The measurement 14.62 grams contains three certain digits (1, 4, and 6) and one doubtful digit (2). We can summarize this information by stating that 14.62 grams contains four significant figures. The numbers that express a measurement (including the last digit, which is doubtful) are called *significant figures*.

The number of significant figures obtained in a measurement is determined by the calibration (scale marking) of the measuring instrument. Some balances are calibrated to the nearest 0.01 gram. Hence, measurements obtained from such balances are expressed to at least two decimal places—indicating that the doubtful digit is in the hundredths place, the second figure to the right of the decimal point. In expressing the result of a measurement, use the proper number of significant figures. Where possible, also indicate the $\pm$ range.

Rules for Working With Significant Figures

The interpretation and use of significant figures require the understanding of some fundamental rules:

1. Zeros that appear before other digits or zeros that show only the position of a decimal point are not considered significant figures. The measurement 0.0043 gram has two significant figures, 4 and 3.

2. Zeros that appear between other digits are significant figures. The measurement 4.003 grams has four significant figures, 4, 0, 0, and 3.

3. Zeros that appear after other digits may or may not be significant, depending on the precision of the measuring instrument. Consider the measurement 14.2 grams. Can it also be expressed as 14.20 grams? If a balance that measures weight to the nearest centigram is used, the measurement must be expressed as 14.20 grams. If a decigram balance is used, the measurement must be expressed as 14.2 grams.

4. In an arithmetic operation involving addition or subtraction, the result of the operation should contain only the number of decimal places of the quantity with the fewest decimal places. Suppose we are required to add 1.46 centimeters and 2.1 centimeters. If we write the sum as 3.56 centimeters, we are assuming that 2.1 centimeters has three significant figures, that it is really 2.10 centimeters. However, 2.1 centimeters has only two significant figures. The correct sum is 3.6 centimeters, obtained by rounding off 3.56 centimeters to two significant figures. Subtraction is performed in a similar manner.

Rounding off a number means decreasing the number of significant figures. If the new number is to have one less significant figure, follow these rules for rounding off:

  a. If the digit to be discarded is greater than 5, increase the last certain digit by 1. Thus 15.66 becomes 15.7.
  b. If the digit to be discarded is less than 5, retain all the certain digits. Thus 15.63 becomes 15.6.
  c. If the digit to be discarded is 5, the number preceding this digit becomes the nearest *even* number. Thus 15.25 becomes 15.2, and 15.35 becomes 15.4.

5. Multiplying or dividing a measurement by a *number* does not alter the number of significant figures. For example, 2 times the weight of an object weighing 4.131 grams is 8.262 grams.

If 4.130 grams (four significant figures) is multiplied by 200,000, the answer (826,000) appears to have six significant figures but actually has four. This is the same as saying 8.260 × 100,000.

6. In multiplication and division of *measurements*, the result can contain no more significant figures than are contained in the least certain measurement.

The product obtained from multiplying 4.12 inches by 2.1 inches can contain only two significant figures. The product (8.652) must be rounded off to contain the proper number of significant figures. Thus 4.12 inches × 2.1 inches equals 8.7 square inches.

PERIODIC TABLE

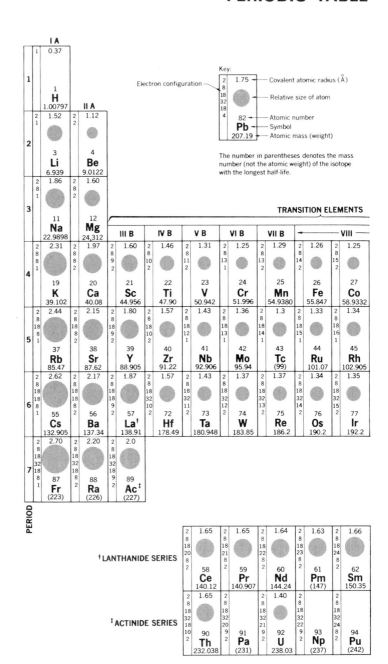

OF THE ELEMENTS

							0
							2 0.93
							2 **He** 4.0026

III A	IV A	V A	VI A	VII A	
2 3 0.88	2 4 0.77	2 5 0.70	2 6 0.66	2 7 0.64	2 8 1.12
5 **B** 10.811	6 **C** 12.01115	7 **N** 14.0067	8 **O** 15.9994	9 **F** 18.9984	10 **Ne** 20.183
2 8 3 1.43	2 8 4 1.17	2 8 5 1.10	2 8 6 1.04	2 8 7 0.99	2 8 8 1.54
13 **Al** 26.9815	14 **Si** 28.086	15 **P** 30.9738	16 **S** 32.064	17 **Cl** 35.453	18 **Ar** 39.948

I B	II B						
2 8 16 2 1.24	2 8 18 1 1.28	2 8 18 2 1.33	2 8 18 3 1.22	2 8 18 4 1.22	2 8 18 5 1.21	2 8 18 6 1.17	2 8 18 7 1.14	2 8 18 8 1.69
28 **Ni** 58.71	29 **Cu** 63.54	30 **Zn** 65.37	31 **Ga** 69.72	32 **Ge** 72.59	33 **As** 74.9216	34 **Se** 78.96	35 **Br** 79.909	36 **Kr** 83.80
2 8 18 18 1.38	2 8 18 18 1 1.44	2 8 18 18 2 1.49	2 8 18 18 3 1.62	2 8 18 18 4 1.40	2 8 18 18 5 1.41	2 8 18 18 6 1.37	2 8 18 18 7 1.33	2 8 18 18 8 1.90
46 **Pd** 106.4	47 **Ag** 107.870	48 **Cd** 112.40	49 **In** 114.82	50 **Sn** 118.69	51 **Sb** 121.75	52 **Te** 127.60	53 **I** 126.9044	54 **Xe** 131.30
2 8 18 32 17 1 1.38	2 8 18 32 18 1 1.44	2 8 18 32 18 2 1.55	2 8 18 32 18 3 1.71	2 8 18 32 18 4 1.75	2 8 18 32 18 5 1.46	2 8 18 32 18 6 1.4	2 8 18 32 18 7 1.40	2 8 18 32 18 8 2.2
78 **Pt** 195.09	79 **Au** 196.967	80 **Hg** 200.59	81 **Tl** 204.37	82 **Pb** 207.19	83 **Bi** 208.980	84 **Po** (210)	85 **At** (210)	86 **Rn** (222)

2 8 18 25 8 2 1.65	2 8 18 25 9 2 1.61	2 8 18 27 8 2 1.59	2 8 18 28 8 2 1.59	2 8 18 29 8 2 1.58	2 8 18 30 8 2 1.57	2 8 18 31 8 2 1.56	2 8 18 32 8 2 1.70	2 8 18 32 9 2 1.56
63 **Eu** 151.96	64 **Gd** 157.25	65 **Tb** 158.924	66 **Dy** 162.50	67 **Ho** 164.930	68 **Er** 167.26	69 **Tm** 168.934	70 **Yb** 173.04	71 **Lu** 174.97
2 8 18 32 25 8 2 95 **Am** (243)	2 8 18 32 25 9 2 96 **Cm** (247)	2 8 18 32 26 9 2 97 **Bk** (247)	2 8 18 32 28 8 2 98 **Cf** (251)	2 8 18 32 29 8 2 99 **Es** (254)	2 8 18 32 30 8 2 100 **Fm** (253)	2 8 18 32 31 8 2 101 **Md** (256)	2 8 18 32 32 8 2 102 **No** (253)	2 8 18 32 32 9 2 103 **Lw** (257)

INDEX